To
Matt, Will, and Andrew
Love Dad

LAKE SIDNEY LANIER

"A Storybook Site"

The Early History and Construction of Buford Dam

By
Robert David Coughlin

©Robert David Coughlin 1998
Published by
RDC Productions
Atlanta, Georgia

Library of Congress Catalog Card Number: 97-77681
No part of this publication may be reproduced without
the permission of the author

ISBN 0-9662245-0-7

Book Design
by Nancy Pesile

Printed in Costa Rica
by Litografía e Imprenta LIL, S.A.
www.lilinternational.com

www.lakelanierhistory.com
david@lakelanierhistory.com

Table of Contents

In Appreciation	*Page* ii
Preface	iii
Special Thanks	v
Introduction: Apalachicola, Chattahoochee, Flint River System Development	1
Chapter One: Why Build a Dam?	19
Chapter Two: Early Proponents	35
Chapter Three: Appropriations	47
Chapter Four: Land Acquisitions	57
Chapter Five: Ground Breaking Ceremony, Wednesday, March 1, 1950	69
Chapter Six: Construction Begins, Saddle Dikes and Spillway	81
Chapter Seven: Forebay Excavation and Intake Construction	91
Chapter Eight: Tailrace Excavation and Powerhouse Construction	117
Chapter Nine: Main Earth Dam Construction	139
Chapter Ten: Bridge and Highway Relocation and Construction	171
Chapter Eleven: Contribution of a Georgia Poet	213
Chapter Twelve: Lake Sidney Lanier	225
Chapter Thirteen: Dedication, Wednesday, October 9, 1957	239
Chapter Fourteen: Biography	249
Appendix I: Appropriations and Contractorial Statistics	261
Appendix II: Impoundment Statistics	266
Appendix III: Land Acquisitions Information	269
Appendix IV: Pertinent Statistical Data	380
Index	383

IN APPRECIATION

Trying to thank all those individuals who contributed to or had some role in the creation of this publication is no easy task but it is one that should be noted. I would like to thank my family, Debby, Matt, Will, and Andrew for sharing afternoons and weekends for research. To my wife Debby, mother Roxie Coughlin, and niece Lisa Elsenheimer for spending a great deal of time on the editing of both the first and second printings. To my mother, father Robert Coughlin, and brother Bill Coughlin who provided financial assistance in seeing this project through to its end. To all my other family members for listening to my stories over the years and wondering if they would ever see anything in print.

To the Department of the Army, U.S. Army Corps of Engineers; the staff, both present and past, of the U.S. Army Corps of Engineers, Project Manager's Office at Lake Sidney Lanier; Mobile District, Office of Public Affairs; Office of History, U.S. Army Corps of Engineers, Fort Belvoir, Virginia and the Office of the Chief of Engineers, U.S. Army Corps of Engineers, Washington, D.C. for their invaluable assistance in providing access to or information about historical resources available.

The Atlanta Journal and the Atlanta Constitution; Chestatee Regional Library; Emory University, Robert W. Woodruff Library, Special Collections Department; Forsyth County News; Gainesville Daily Times; Georgia Department of Archives; Georgia Freight Bureau; Georgia Power Company; KSL Corporation; Library of Congress; Tri-Rivers Association; University of Georgia, Main Library, Georgia Room, Press, and the Richard B. Russell Memorial Library; University of North Carolina Press; U.S. Government Printing Office; and West Point Military Academy were all organizations that were helpful in seeing the research completed.

There were also a few individuals who provided historical research materials that added a great deal to the publication. Mrs. Weldon Gardner, Buford, Georgia; Mrs. Jo Ann Weathers, Norcross, Georgia provided a vast collection of photographs, newspaper articles, documents, and other historical data on the project's history.

PREFACE

Lake Sidney Lanier, named after the 19th Century Georgia poet Sidney Clopton Lanier, is located in a five county area of North Georgia about 35 miles northeast of Atlanta. The reservoir flooded land in Gwinnett, Forsyth, Hall, Dawson, and Lumpkin Counties. At normal pool of elevation 1071.0 the lake has 540 miles of shoreline with a surface area of 38,000 acres. It was constructed in the 1950's by the Mobile District, U. S. Army Corps of Engineers and today is one of their most popular recreational areas in the United States drawing over 20 million people annually to enjoy its many attractions.

Buford Dam was built in post-war America during what is considered by many historians as its golden age. The United States came out of the second World War as the only industrial and military power not crippled by this global conflict. Construction on the dam began in the first few months of 1950 and would continue through most of the decade. The tremendous change this country experienced historically during this period is still being felt even today. Many of the economic, political, and social upheavals we experienced during the decades of the 60's got their start here. The two unofficial wars this country fought without winning began during this period. Ike was in the White House during most of this decade and a young politician known as JFK began honing his political skills. Rock and Roll was born as the "King" changed the way we listened to music while a group of Liverpool musicians would listen and learn eventually following in his footsteps. The "Red" scare and a young brash Senator from Wisconsin threatened many of the everyday freedoms we take for granted today. Separate but equal was no longer the status quo and bigger than life personalities such as Albert Einstein, Henry Ford, and James Dean would die. The U.S.S.R. would shock the world with Sputnik beginning the space race while the cold war was picking up momentum. Polio, having long been a terrifying disease, would finally be conquered by Jonas Salk and cancer was still a puzzle. The French would begin and end a campaign in Indochina leaving the United States to continue the conflict. Although the 50's bring to mind an era of fun, change, and innovation we all know they were scary times as well. It is in the mists of all that was the 50's that Buford Dam had its beginning and chronicling the project's early history would not begin for decades after its completion.

As is the case with most worthwhile endeavors the final product usually goes through many changes and transitions in its development. This publication was no different, having evolved in the early 1980's from a visual instructional aid intended for use in the classroom. It took the form of a slide presentation and told the story of the lake's early development using hundreds of old Army photographs taken during the project's construction. While compiling research for the slide presentation it became apparent that little if any historical work had been completed on the subject. The majority of information was still in private hands which usually meant it was stuffed away in a box or trunk in someone's attic or basement along with hundreds of other pieces of family memorabilia. Many of the project's historical resources were just beginning to move into the public domain where a number of libraries and historical societies had created special collections that were part of some notable dignitaries papers willed to these institutions. For the most part the bulk of this information was still fragmented and splattered about, still waiting to be collected and categorized into a single body of work.

In the lengthy and tedious process of completing research for a book it is inevitable that some people, places, times, and stories will be left untold. Views of historical perspectives will sometimes take directions not popular or perceived as incorrect. Much of history, after all, is interpretive. Sometimes the facts presented do not provide enough information to be an exact truth and historians have to make judgments on the information present. What is one man's fact is another man's fiction. This statement is never more true than when dealing with the study of history. More often than not we are not given the luxury to be present when history is in the making. We have to rely on what little information is left behind by those few persons that take the time to record events while they are actually taking place. In

Preface

many cases recorded history is happen stance or by accident rather than something produced for posterity's sake. Spur of the moment letters or memos, photographs taken when a camera was handy, bureaucratic red tape, newspaper stories, notes scribbled on a pad or piece of paper, even recollections that have long since been forgotten can act as a window to the past. Many times we simply do not recognize history when it is taking place or we do not think that anyone in the future will be interested. That was just as true then as it is now.

In trying to describe singular events that make up the fabric of the project's history there was never any overt intent to determine right or wrong, good or bad, even for or against what was taking place. That is best left up to the reader in the hope that you will regard this work as an historical log that shows the evolution of a lake and its effect on the people and places it evolved from. Errors in describing facts can be made, even with the most diligent research they can be askewed or mistakenly reported. Recording history is often like putting a jigsaw puzzle together, sometimes the pieces do not fit or they are missing all together. There is a certain amount of subjectivity present when describing events especially when research information is absent or contradictory. You try to supply the missing pieces of the puzzle or fill in the gaps of the story but sometimes you can not and you make an assumption based on the information you do have.

Many of the people and places described here have long since gone or have changed in appearance considerably. Hopefully these pages will afford you an opportunity to turn back the clock, to look at a section of North Georgia in the foothills of the Appalachians, as its land and people once were. It is history and our history defines what we are, where we were, and where we are going. It is also a story of time, once upon a time, before the Chattahoochee and Chestatee Rivers gave way to a 38,000 acre lake. A time we can never return to except in our memories and our history.

David Coughlin

A Special Thanks

A great deal of the information used in this book was obtained from the first hand knowledge of a number of people. These individuals all worked on the project in various capacities and it was my good fortune to have the opportunity to work with and know each one of them. I would indeed be remiss in my duty as a historian if I did not note the special contribution to this publication that they provided. Cecil Patterson, Charlie Singleton, and Art Bagwell all retired after many years of service with the United States Army Corps of Engineers. It was through their experiences on the project during the early years that I was able to put together a small piece of the puzzle of what this project was like and its impact on this area of North Georgia now and for generations to come.

Most of the technical information about the construction of the project was provided by Cecil Patterson. He was an engineer on the project as well as several other projects including Allatoona and Hartwell. He returned to Lake Lanier in the early 1960's as the project resource manager, *Fig 1* and **Fig. 2**, and remained in this post until his retirement in 1983. I first met

Fig. 1 (L-R) Charlie Singleton and Cecil Patterson (Courtesy U.S. Army Corps of Engineers, Mobile District)

Fig. 2 Cecil Patterson inspecting damage at one of Lake Lanier's marinas. (Courtesy U.S. Army Corps of Engineers, Mobile District)

Cecil when I worked as a park ranger on Lake Lanier. It was not until years later when I began research for this publication that I got to know him personally. His contribution to this publication was invaluable. He spent an untold number of hours carefully explaining to me the terribly complicated and at times simple process that was involved in building Buford Dam. Pouring over the hundreds of photographs and text he provided special insight from personal experience as an engineer on the project. He remained in Cumming, Georgia after his retirement until his death in January, 2004.

Charlie Singleton, **Fig. 1**, provided me with a great deal of information about the acquisition of land for the reservoir. Charlie outlined the method by which the

Fig. 3 (L-R) Charlie Singleton and Art Bagwell at Art's retirement party. (Courtesy U.S. Army Corps of Engineers, Mobile District)

government acquired land for the reservoir. On several occasions I had the opportunity to just sit with him on his porch in Forsyth County while he explained the workings of the appraisal section he was assigned to. He went to work for the government in the early 1950's assigned to the Real Estate Project Office in Gainesville, Georgia. Eventually he became a park ranger and retired from government service in 1985. By the time I came to work with the Corps of Engineers Charlie was the project's Chief Ranger. *Fig. 3* Many times I sat and listened as he talked of the early years on the project and the many jobs he had. He spoke of how land was appraised, of being stationed near or on bridges all over the proposed reservoir for hours on end conducting traffic surveys, and his work with trying to keep the rising mosquito population in check while the reservoir was filling up. He lived out his retirement years at his home in Forsyth County where he passed away in April, 1992.

Art Bagwell, like Charlie Singleton, was a ranger on the project for nearly 25 years, *Fig. 4* and *Fig. 5*,. He too began his

A Special Thanks

career with the Corps of Engineers working out of the same Real Estate Project Office in

*Fig. 4
Art Bagwell on citation training. (Courtesy U.S. Army Corps of Engineers, Mobile District)*

*Fig. 5
Art Bagwell (Courtesy U.S. Army Corps of Engineers, Mobile District)*

Gainesville. He also saw his job description change from time to time as the infant project began to develop. Appraising the value of timber on reservoir land, building boat ramps, working as a construction foreman, and on reservoir clearing crews were a few of the many jobs he held. I had the pleasure of working with Art for many summers and enjoyed sitting on his front porch and listening to his memories about the goings on around the project all those years ago. He spent his retirement days on his farm in Forsyth County where he remained fairly active until his death in August, 1994.

It is unlikely that the quality of information found in these pages would have been possible had it not been for the contributions of these individuals as well as others who shared with me bits and pieces of what they knew. Over the many years that I spent researching this book I was always able to use them as a priceless well of historical knowledge. Their often times humorous remembrances and stories brought realism to an event that many times seemed very far removed from contemporary life. They constantly reminded me of what a valuable resource human experience is and how too often it is taken for granted, until it is gone.

Lake Sidney Lanier "A Storybook Site"

*Buford Dam,
built in the 1950's would become the key link in
a series of dams constructed on the
Apalachicola, Chattahoochee,
Flint River System*

INTRODUCTION

APALACHICOLA, CHATTAHOOCHEE, FLINT RIVER SYSTEM

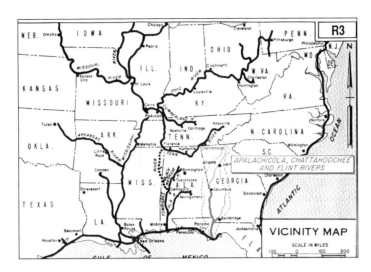

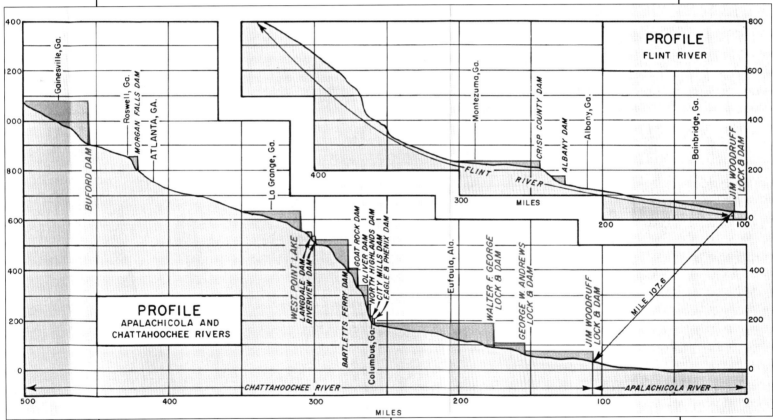

Maps showing the geographic location and profile of the Chattahoochee and Flint Rivers.(Courtesy U.S. Army Corps of Engineers, Mobile District. 1989 Project Maps)

Buford Dam is one of five major public works dams, *Fig. I-1*, constructed on the Chattahoochee and Flint Rivers to develop the Apalachicola, Chattahoochee, and Flint Rivers for flood control, navigation, hydro power, water regulation and supply, and recreation.[1] There are nine small privately owned dams located on the Chattahoochee River and two on the Flint River but they were constructed primarily for power production and the majority were in operation years before the larger public works projects were built. The present system of dams, locks, and reservoirs on the ACF Rivers represent years of planning and development on the federal level and history has shown that it was a slow often times uphill battle in seeing visions become reality.

Prior to any congressional river and harbor legislation early development on the Apalachicola, Chattahoochee, and

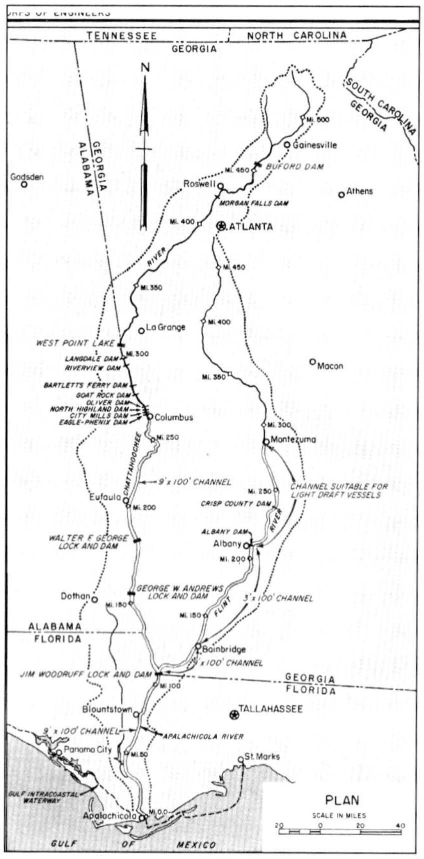

Fig. I-1 Map of ACF River System development. (Courtesy U.S. Army Corps of Engineers, Mobile District, 1989 Project Maps)

Flint Rivers was primarily limited to small scale dredging and clearing operations. Historically, expenditures on the federal level for many years were small and slow in coming. Between 1828 and 1831 some 13,000.00 was spent removing trees and other snags from the Apalachicola and Lower Chipola Rivers. In 1853 an engineering survey on the Chattahoochee River was completed, the primary focus were points on the river below Columbus, Georgia. Twenty years later, in 1874, another survey was completed on the Apalachicola River and the Flint River below Albany, Georgia. As was the case in the earlier surveys navigation was the primary concern.[2]

Shortly after the Civil War ended Congress passed the River and Harbor Act of 1874. Future sessions of Congress would pass river and harbor legislation with each session augmenting the scope and nature of laws enacted in previous years. The 1874 legislation provided for widening and dredging of the Apalachicola River providing a 6x100 foot navigation channel at an estimated cost of $80,333.00. The Chattahoochee River was beginning to see navigation work completed from its mouth in the North Georgia foothills to Columbus some 161 miles away.[3] The Flint River was provided a 3x100 foot channel 102 miles from its mouth to Albany, Georgia at an estimated cost of $184,862.00. The same legislation authorized a survey of the Chattahoochee River from Columbus to Chattahoochee. It was recommended that a channel four feet deep and 100 feet wide be provided by removing snags, wrecks, and loose rocks.[4] Six years later in 1880 another Congress added to the river and harbor legislation and the Flint River saw a vast improvement in river navigation of some 79 miles from Albany to Montezuma at an estimated cost of $15,100.00.[5]

The River and Harbor Act of 1888 authorized an examination and survey of the Chipola River, Florida from its mouth to Wewahitchka and the cut-off, and Lee's Slough running from the Apalachicola River to the Chipola River. Recommendations were that a channel five feet deep and 60 feet wide be provided. Funds were provided by the River and Harbor Acts of 1890 and 1902.[6]

The turn of the century saw more legislation aimed at improving navigation. The River and Harbor Act of 1902 included an extensive modification of the Apalachicola and Lower Chipola Rivers. The River and Harbor Act of 1915 authorized a preliminary examination and survey of the Chattahoochee River in Georgia and Alabama. The resulting report submitted three plans of improvements. The first plan called for a radical improvement of the Chattahoochee River from its mouth all the way to Atlanta by construction of several locks and dams between Columbus and Atlanta. It suggested implementation of both navigation and power above Columbus with a constant six foot low-water depth at all times below Columbus. The total estimated cost was put at $32,790,000.00. It is here that you see the first serious consideration of navigation all the way to Atlanta. The second plan called for the construction of a regulating dam, with locks, 19 miles below Columbus with a four foot low-water depth at all times at an estimated cost of $1,000,000.00. The third plan called for the construction of a system of locks and dams between Columbus and

INTRODUCTION

the confluence of the Chattahoochee and Flint Rivers. This would, upon improvements below that point, provide for a six foot depth throughout this system of rivers below Columbus. Estimated costs were put at $8,400,000.00 and no power development was considered with this plan. In the end recommendations were made that no improvements be undertaken other than as authorized by the existing projects at that time.[7]

ACF River development was first authorized by Congress under Section 8 of The River and Harbor Act of 1925.[8] Although the legislation gave the green light for more ambitious attempts at developing the ACF River System it was just authorization not appropriation of funds to begin construction. The River and Harbor Act of 1934 provided snagging and dredging operations to clear some 2,500 feet of the lower Styx River. The first true construction on the Apalachicola, Chattahoochee, Flint River System appeared in 1935 when Congress passed the Emergency Relief Appropriations Act. Until this time the majority of the work completed on the ACF River System had been in private hands or limited to tree and snag removal, dredging, and shoreline protection efforts. Now for the first time you began to see the funding of a flood control project near West Point, Georgia which provided an increased river channel, clearing of floodway areas, construction of a 1,500 foot levee, and bridge construction. It was an image of things to come.[9]

Initial investigations for a dam near Atlanta* were conducted in the 1930's when the U.S. House of Representatives authorized preparation of a report on the Apalachicola River basin as part of House Document no.308, 1st Session, 69th Congress.[10] The report authorized the Corps of Engineers to complete surveys on those navigable streams and their tributaries where power development, navigation, flood control, and irrigation seemed feasible and practical.[11] The House of Representatives Committee on Rivers and Harbors requested the Army Corps of Engineers to re-examine the Apalachicola, Chattahoochee and Flint Rivers in Georgia and Florida. In 1939 The Secretary of War submitted a letter, transmitting an 86 page report by the Chief of Engineers, dated April 20, 1939, to the Committee on Rivers and Harbors detailing plans for ACF River development.[12] The report along with an accompanying map examined the existing as well as proposed projects on the Apalachicola, Chattahoochee, and Flint Rivers, **Fig. I-2**,.[13] At last it appeared as

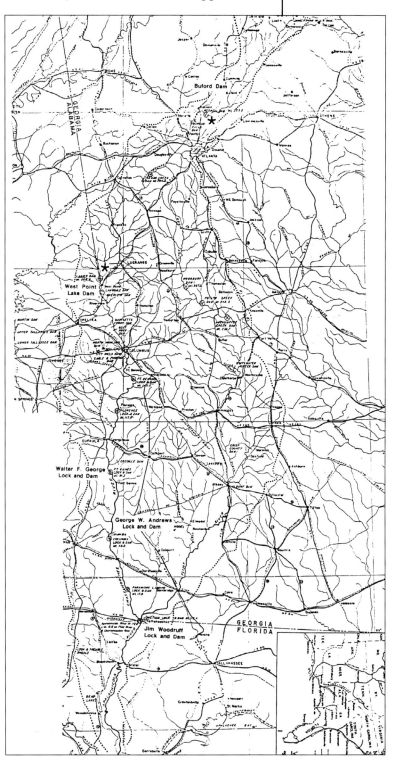

Fig. I-2 Map of proposed ACF River System development submitted as part of U.S. House Document no.342, 1st Session, 76th Congress. (U.S. Congressional Record)

---

*In the 1930's when plans were being formulated for a dam north of Atlanta a site near Roswell, Georgia was chosen for the proposed dam. In the 1940's that site lost out to the Buford site. A further explanation of the reasoning for choosing Buford over Roswell for a dam is found on page 13.

though Congress was beginning to seriously examine these underdeveloped waterways.

The advent of World War II played an important role in slowing down further development of the ACF River System for most of the remainder of the first half of the twentieth century. Prior to the end of the war Section 4 of the Flood Control Act of 1944 authorized the Chief of Engineers ".... to construct, maintain, and operate public parks and recreational facilities in reservoir areas under the control of the Secretary of Army, and to permit the construction, maintenance, and operation of such facilities".[14] With the end of World War II Congress turned to new river and harbor legislation that would far exceed any legislation attempted to date. The River and Harbor Act of 1945 provided major construction on the ACF River System. In this legislation you began to see flood control, navigation, and power production aspects of river development being implemented through a series of locks and dams that were being planned up and down the ACF River System. The same legislation was developing rivers and waterways all over the United States.[15]

Buford Dam was first recommended for construction in a report issued by the Mobile District on November 20, 1945. This report outlined modifications to a plan that called for basin wide development of the area. The report called for a dam at the Buford site with a conservation pool elevation of 1065 but without flood control protection. The plan was returned to the district by the Chief of Engineers for revisions to provide for flood control and augmented navigation to Atlanta, Georgia. Here you see a serious effort on the part of the Army, even this far back, to make the river navigable all the way to Atlanta.

On March 20, 1946 the South Atlantic Division Engineer submitted a report to the Army Chief of Engineers which was based on information from the November, 1945 report. A flood storage prism between elevations 1065.0 and 1085.0 had been provided. The design of the dam was proposed as a concrete gravity-type 1,626 feet long with a top elevation of 1090.0 and a 616 foot gated spillway.[16]

Ten days later on March 30, 1946 a public notice, ***Fig. I-3***, was issued by the War Department, Office of the Division Engineer, South Atlantic Division. This notice mapped out the development of this section of the intracoastal waterway

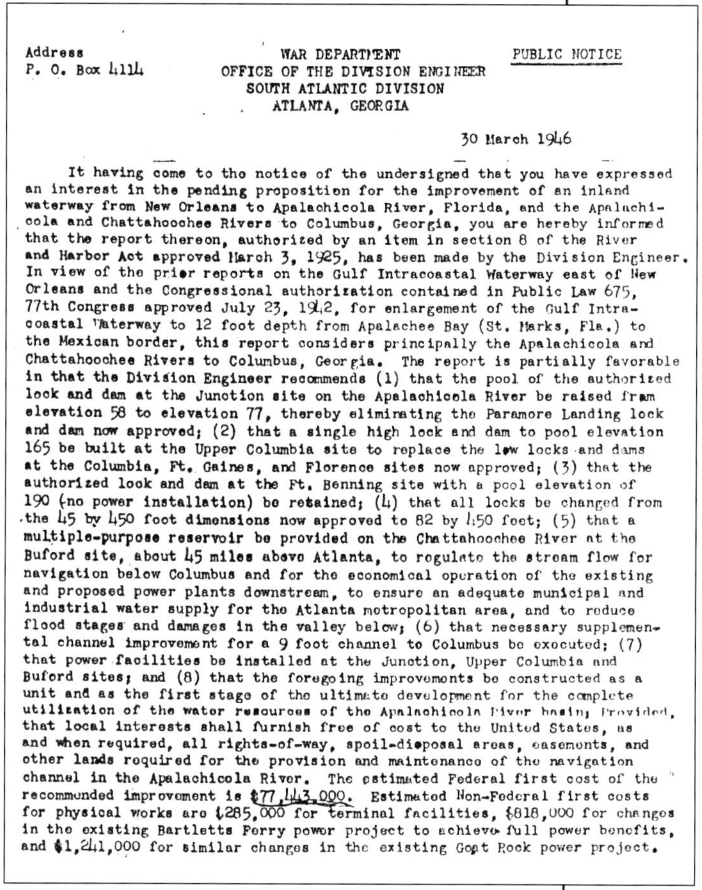

Address
P. O. Box 4114

WAR DEPARTMENT
OFFICE OF THE DIVISION ENGINEER
SOUTH ATLANTIC DIVISION
ATLANTA, GEORGIA

PUBLIC NOTICE

30 March 1946

It having come to the notice of the undersigned that you have expressed an interest in the pending proposition for the improvement of an inland waterway from New Orleans to Apalachicola River, Florida, and the Apalachicola and Chattahoochee Rivers to Columbus, Georgia, you are hereby informed that the report thereon, authorized by an item in section 8 of the River and Harbor Act approved March 3, 1925, has been made by the Division Engineer. In view of the prior reports on the Gulf Intracoastal Waterway east of New Orleans and the Congressional authorization contained in Public Law 675, 77th Congress approved July 23, 1942, for enlargement of the Gulf Intracoastal Waterway to 12 foot depth from Apalachee Bay (St. Marks, Fla.) to the Mexican border, this report considers principally the Apalachicola and Chattahoochee Rivers to Columbus, Georgia. The report is partially favorable in that the Division Engineer recommends (1) that the pool of the authorized lock and dam at the Junction site on the Apalachicola River be raised from elevation 58 to elevation 77, thereby eliminating the Paramore Landing lock and dam now approved; (2) that a single high lock and dam to pool elevation 165 be built at the Upper Columbia site to replace the low locks and dams at the Columbia, Ft. Gaines, and Florence sites now approved; (3) that the authorized lock and dam at the Ft. Benning site with a pool elevation of 190 (no power installation) be retained; (4) that all locks be changed from the 45 by 450 foot dimensions now approved to 82 by 450 feet; (5) that a multiple-purpose reservoir be provided on the Chattahoochee River at the Buford site, about 45 miles above Atlanta, to regulate the stream flow for navigation below Columbus and for the economical operation of the existing and proposed power plants downstream, to ensure an adequate municipal and industrial water supply for the Atlanta metropolitan area, and to reduce flood stages and damages in the valley below; (6) that necessary supplemental channel improvement for a 9 foot channel to Columbus be executed; (7) that power facilities be installed at the Junction, Upper Columbia and Buford sites; and (8) that the foregoing improvements be constructed as a unit and as the first stage of the ultimate development for the complete utilization of the water resources of the Apalachicola River basin; Provided, that local interests shall furnish free of cost to the United States, as and when required, all rights-of-way, spoil-disposal areas, easements, and other lands required for the provision and maintenance of the navigation channel in the Apalachicola River. The estimated Federal first cost of the recommended improvement is $77,443,000. Estimated Non-Federal first costs for physical works are $285,000 for terminal facilities, $818,000 for changes in the existing Bartletts Ferry power project to achieve full power benefits, and $1,241,000 for similar changes in the existing Goat Rock power project.

Fig. I-3 ***Public notice issued by the War Department. (Courtesy U.S. Army Corps of Engineers, Mobile District)***

including Buford Dam.[17] A report from the Board of Engineers for Rivers and Harbors dated April 29, 1946 looked to augment the 1945 ACF River development legislation. This report was part of a larger report on the Apalachicola, Chattahoochee, and Flint Rivers, submitted to the Secretary of War by the Chief of Engineers on May 13, 1946, that looked to revise the report issued to Congress on the ACF River System in 1939. The 40 page report and accompanying map, ***Fig. I-4***, updated the Army's plans for developing the ACF River System. Specifically it noted that the overall plan should be revised to include a multi-purpose reservoir at the Buford site rather than the Roswell site, as proposed in the 1939 report. It also called for the construction of the Fort Benning Lock and Dam, multiple purpose improvements on the Upper Columbia Lock and Dam (George W. Andrews Lock and Dam) and Junction Lock and Dam (Jim Woodruff Lock and Dam) projects, and a

INTRODUCTION

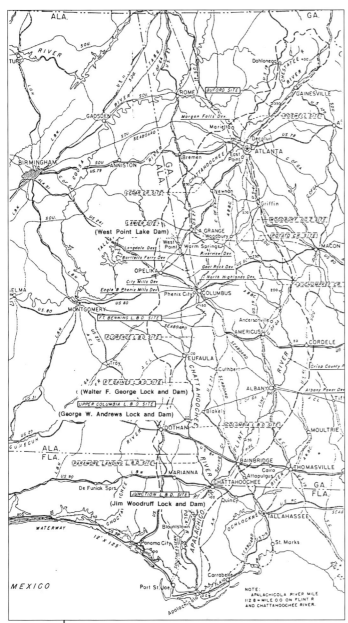

Fig. I-4 Map of proposed ACF River System development submitted as part of U.S. House Document no.300, 1st Session, 80th Congress. (U.S. Congressional Record)

9x100 foot channel depth from the Apalachicola River north to Columbus, Georgia on the Chattahoochee River and Bainbridge, Georgia on the Flint River.[18]

During the second session of the 79th Congress a House of Representatives Bill H.R. 6407, authorizing the construction, repair and preservation of certain public works on rivers and harbors and for other purposes, was introduced. The bill intended to augment the legislation and scope of similar laws concerning rivers and harbors that had passed previous sessions of Congress this included the Rivers and Harbors Act of 1945, that had passed the year before during the first session of the same Congress.[19]

House Bill H.R. 6407 began its long journey through Congress when it was referred to the House Committee on Rivers and Harbors.[20] The 20th region listed in the record for development, *Fig. I-5*, was the Apalachicola, Chattahoochee, and Flint

> H. R. 6407
> A bill authorizing the construction, repair, and preservation of certain public works on rivers and harbors, and for other purposes
> Be it enacted, etc. That the following works of improvement of rivers, harbors, and other waterways are hereby adopted and authorized to be prosecuted under the direction of the Secretary of War and supervision of the Chief of Engineers, in accordance with the plans and subject to the conditions recommended by the Chief of Engineers in the respective reports hereinafter designated: *Provided,* That penstocks or other similar facilities adapted to possible future use in the development of hydroelectric power shall be installed in any dam herein authorized when approved by the Secretary of War upon the recommendation of the Chief of Engineers and of the Federal Power Commission, and such recommendations shall be based upon consideration of the proper utilization and conservation in the public interest of the resources of the region:
> Portland Harbor, Maine; House Document No. 510, Seventy-ninth Congress;
> Fall River Harbor, Mass.; in accordance with the report of the Chief of Engineers dated April 15, 1946;
> Wickford Harbor, R. I.; Senate Document No. 141, Seventy-ninth Congress;
> New Haven Harbor, Conn.; House Document No. 517, Seventy-ninth Congress;
> Bridgeport Harbor, Conn; in accordance with the report of the Chief of Engineers dated April 26, 1946;
> Stamford Harbor, Conn; in accordance with the report of the Chief of Engineers dated May 3, 1946;
> Barnegat Inlet, N. J.; House Document No. 358, Seventy-ninth Congress;
> Absecon Inlet, N. J.; House Document No. 504, Seventy-ninth Congress;
> Delaware River, vicinity of Biles Creek, Pa.; in accordance with the report of the Chief of Engineers dated April 8, 1946;
> Schuylkill River, Pa.; House Document No. 529, Seventy-ninth Congress; and in accordance with the report of the Chief of Engineers dated May 7, 1946;
> New Jersey Intracoastal Waterway; pending fulfillment of the conditions of local cooperation for this project as authorized by the River and Harbor Act of March 2, 1945, appropriations heretofore or hereafter made for maintenance and improvement of rivers and harbors may be used for a period of not to exceed 5 years for maintenance of the canal from Cape May Harbor to Delaware Bay constructed as an emergency wartime project with Navy Department funds, including the cost of maintaining the temporary railroad and seashore highway bridges over said canal;
> Middle River and Dark Head Creek, Md.; maintenance work in accordance with the report on file in the Office, Chief of Engineers;
> Mattaponi River, Va.; House Document No. 766, Seventy-eighth Congress;
> Newport News Creek, Va.; House Document No. 559, Seventy-ninth Congress;
> Norfolk Harbor, Va.; House Document No. 563, Seventy-ninth Congress;
> Savannah Harbor, Ga.; in accordance with the report of the Chief of Engineers dated April 1, 1946;
> St. Johns River, Fla., Jacksonville to Lake Harney; in accordance with the report of the Chief of Engineers dated April 10, 1946;
> Hollywood Harbor (Port Everglades), Fla.; House Document No. 768, Seventy-eighth Congress;
> Withlacoochee River, Fla.; House Document No. 293, Seventy-ninth Congress;
> Apalachicola, Chattahoochee, and Flint Rivers, Ga. and Fla.; in accordance with the report of the Board of Engineers for Rivers and Harbors dated April 29, 1946, on file in the Office, Chief of Engineers;
> Tombigbee and Tennessee Rivers, Ala. and Miss.; House Document No. 486, Seventy-ninth Congress;
> Mississippi River, Baton Rouge to the Gulf of Mexico; barge channel through Devils Swamp, La.; in accordance with the report of the Chief of Engineers dated May 7, 1946;
> Plaquemine-Morgan City Route, Intracoastal Waterway, La.; in accordance with the report of the Chief of Engineers dated April 25, 1946;
> Franklin Canal, La.; in accordance with the report of the Chief of Engineers dated April 8, 1946;
> Mermentau River and tributaries, and Gulf Intracoastal Waterway and connecting waters, Louisiana; in accordance with the report of the Chief of Engineers dated April 16, 1946;
> Lake Charles Deep Water Channel and Calcasieu River and Pass, La.; in accordance with the report of the Chief of Engineers dated March 18, 1946;
> Red River below Fulton, Ark.; in accordance with the report of the Chief of Engineers dated April 19, 1946: *Provided,* That the improvement herein authorized between Shreveport and the mouth, shall when completed be named the Overton-Red River waterway in honor of Senator JOHN H. OVERTON, of Louisiana;

Rivers in Georgia, Alabama and Florida.[21] The legislation was monumental in concept and design. It covered over 40 pages of the congressional record and affected projects all over the United States. The total cost was estimated at $600,000,000.00 and would take eight to ten years to see full development.[22] On July 24, 1946 after several months of discussion and debate President Truman signed into law H.R. 6407 making it Public Law 525. The second session of the 79th Congress had started the ball rolling and given the green light for development of the ACF River System to

Fig. I-5 Congressional Record for H.R. 6407. (U.S. Congressional Record)

Fig. I-6 Congressional Record for H.R.6407. (U.S. Congressional Record)

> **RIVER AND HARBOR BILL**
>
> Mr. MANSFIELD of Texas. Mr. Speaker, I move that the House resolve itself into the Committee of the Whole House on the State of the Union for the consideration of the bill (H. R. 6407) authorizing the construction, repair, and preservation of certain public works on rivers and harbors, and for other purposes.
>
> The motion was agreed to.
>
> Accordingly the House resolved itself into the Committee of the Whole House on the State of the Union for the consideration of the bill H. R. 6407, with Mr. LUTHER A. JOHNSON in the chair.
>
> The Clerk read the title of the bill.
>
> By unanimous consent, the first reading of the bill was dispensed with.
>
> Mr. MANSFIELD of Texas. Mr. Chairman, as is generally known, we have refrained from reporting rivers and harbors bills during the time of the war. One bill was put through early last year which was reported in 1944 and passed in 1944, but went dead in conference on account of a certain provision in it pertaining to a reclamation project in California which the Senate would not agree to. That same bill was revived and brought up and passed in March of last year.
>
> The bill before us now is for some 56 projects that have been reported by the engineers since that time. Four of them authorize maintenance work only. Some of them are on surveys ordered a number of years ago. Some of them have been under consideration by the engineers for several years, all of them, in fact, for a considerable length of time, for thorough investigation.
>
> The bill carries a total of approximately $600,000,000. The larger projects are in the main works to extend over a long period of time, probably 8 or 10 years or more, depending on what future Congresses may want to do in making appropriations.

begin. It would be up to future sessions of Congress to provide the necessary funds for actual construction to commence.

National defense, augmentation of the South and its resources, and agricultural benefits were but a few of the potential windfalls that were expected as a result of the intracoastal waterway development of this region. The readiness of the United States economically and militarily prior to World War II was a hot topic in post-war America. The development of inland waterways was seen as an important investment in the United States military preparedness. Multi-purpose projects such as Buford Dam would provide limitless power on demand as well as other benefits like navigation, which was seen as an extremely important resource for the nation in times of peace and war.

In late 1947 Colonel Joseph J. Twitty, then the incoming Mobile District Chief, stressed these points. He explained that post-war policy had the United States stockpiling scarce and strategic metals as well as other commodities for future needs, should military conflicts arise. He echoed a familiar sentiment, many in both the government and military felt, that large public works projects could and would provide multi-benefits for a nation to bolster its defensive posture. This was seen as an extremely important benefit considering the nation was just beginning its trek through the cold war.[23]

Prior to the ACF River System development programs of the River and Harbor Act of 1946 large scale development of the Chattahoochee River was nonexistent. The south was viewed as a wasted region. The potential natural resources that this region of the United States was presupposed to have, and which over the years has proven to be factual, seemed to be limitless. For the most part the watershed region of the South stretching eastward from the Pearl River in Mississippi to the Ochlocknee River in Georgia was described as virgin territory. This untamed area had some of the greatest resource potential of any place in the United States.[24] Many government and military leaders at the time had their roots in the South. They saw its development as essential, not just in the area of navigation augmentation, which today has provided argumentative benefits, but in other areas such as flood control, power production, soil conservation, reforestation, protection of wildlife, and recreation. The Deep South was compared to the Ruhr Valley in Germany in its resource potential for not only the South but for the United States as well.[25] This region was viewed as having the natural and human resources as well as the geographical location to finally make use of this seemingly limitless potential.[26]

Eventual river development would see a chain of dams and reservoirs constructed along the entire length of the Chattahoochee River from its head waters in the North Georgia mountains to the Gulf of Mexico further south. At the convergence of the Chattahoochee and Flint Rivers, where these two bodies of water form the Apalachicola River, is the Jim Woodruff Lock and Dam originally proposed as Junction Lock and Dam and Reservoir, *Fig. I-1, Fig. I-7, Fig. I-8.* This project was named after Jim Woodruff Sr. who was considered

Fig. I-7 Jim Woodruff Lock and Dam (Courtesy U.S. Army Corps of Engineers, Mobile District)

by many as the father of resource and water development on the lower Chattahoochee. The 37,500 acre Lake Seminole, *Fig. I-9*, formed by the dam extends a 9x100 foot navigation channel 46.8 miles up the Chattahoochee River and 27.7 miles up the Flint River to Bainbridge, Georgia. The

Fig. I-8 Jim Woodruff Lock and Dam diagram (Courtesy U.S. Army Corps of Engineers, Mobile District, 1989 Project Maps)

Fig. I-9 Lake Seminole (Courtesy U.S. Army Corps of Engineers, Mobile District, 1989 Project Maps)

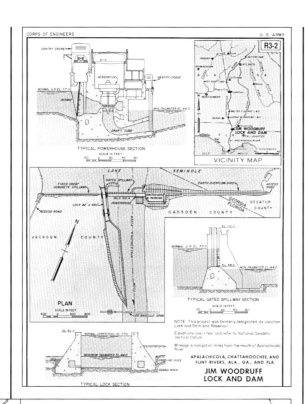

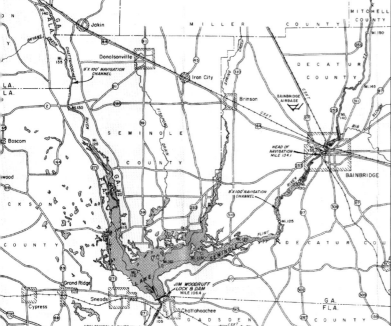

Fig. I-10 George W. Andrews Lock and Dam (Courtesy U.S. Army Corps of Engineers, Mobile District)

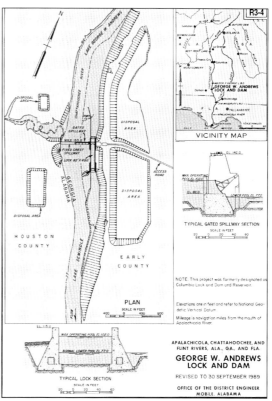

Fig. I-11 George W. Andrews Lock and Dam diagram (Courtesy U.S. Army Corps of Engineers, Mobile District, 1989 Project Maps)

Fig. I-12 George W. Andrews Lake (Courtesy U.S. Army Corps of Engineers, Mobile District, 1989 Project Maps)

project provides no flood protection but does provide hydroelectric service with three 10,000 kilowatt power units. Work on this first link in the river development began in 1947 and was completed in 1957 with cost totaling $46,467,522.00. [27]

The next project traveling north up the Chattahoochee River is the George W. Andrews Lock and Dam, *Fig. I-1*, *Fig. I-10*, and *Fig. I-11*. The dam is located about 50 miles northwest of the Jim Woodruff Lock and Dam and was originally proposed as the Upper Columbia Lock and Dam project. It created the 1,540 acre Lake George W. Andrews, *Fig. I-12*, which provides a 9x100

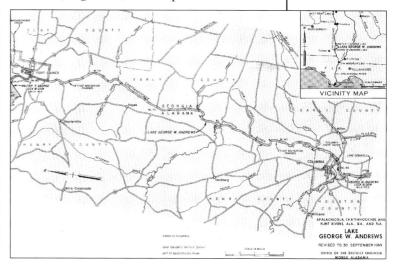

8

foot navigation channel extending the full length of the reservoir. This is a single-purpose project providing navigation but no flood protection or power production. Work on the project began in 1959 and was completed in November, 1963 at a total cost of $12,954,413.00.[28]

Continuing north the third project

Fig. I-13 Walter F. George Lock and Dam (Courtesy U.S. Army Corps of Engineers, Mobile District)

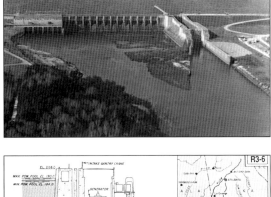

Fig. I-14 Walter F. George Lock and Dam diagram (Courtesy U.S. Army Corps of Engineers, Mobile District, 1989 Project Maps)

on the Chattahoochee River is the Walter F. George Lock and Dam, F*ig. I-1*, *Fig. I-13* and *Fig. I-14*, which is located 140 miles from the Jim Woodruff Lock and Dam. This project was originally proposed as the Fort Gaines Lock and Dam. The 45,181 acre Walter F. George Lake, *Fig. I-15*, named in honor of Georgia's long time Senator Walter F. George, provides a 9x100 foot navigation channel extending the full length of the reservoir 80.0 miles to Columbus were the development of a constant navigation

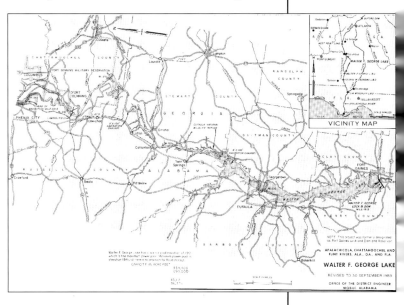

Fig. I-15 Walter F. George Lake (Courtesy U.S. Army Corps of Engineers, Mobile District, 1989 Project Maps)

channel stops. Four power units produce a combined total of 130,000 kilowatts of electricity but no flood protection is provided. Work on the project began in 1963 and was completed in 1972 at a cost of $96,312,436.00.[29]

A series of eight private dams, *Fig. I-1*, are located upstream from Walter F. George Lake. The majority of these dams and power facilities are owned by the Georgia Power Company and although they may have minor recreational and other benefits their primary function is to produce electrical power.

The first two, the Eagle-Phenix Dam and the City Mills Dam, *Fig. I-1*, are the only two not owned by Georgia Power and are no longer in operation. The Eagle-Phenix Dam was a pioneer textile plant in Columbus but was originally called Eagle Mill. It was constructed to manufacture cotton and woolen goods. Grey uniform tweed, cotton ducks for tents, cotton stripes for army shirts, cotton jeans, osnaburgs, sheeting, rope and India rubber cloth were produced for the Confederacy and the State of Georgia during the Civil War. The mill was burned down by Union forces on April 17, 1865. It was rebuilt literally from ashes a year later in 1866, hence the addition of the added name Phenix to indicate a rebirth.[30] The City Mills Dam, *Fig. I-1*, went into operation in 1828 when Governor Gilmer gave a land grant to Seaborn Jones who built a grist mill to manufacture corn meal. The original dam was made of wood and remained until 1906 when a stone dam

Fig. I-16 North Highlands Dam (Courtesy Georgia Power Company, Corporate Communications)

was constructed.³¹

The North Highlands Dam, **Fig. I-1** and **Fig. I-16**, is the oldest plant in a series of private dams owned and operated by Georgia Power. It was constructed in 1898-99 by the Columbus Electric and Power Company which was eventually purchased by the Georgia Power Company. In 1959 the old powerhouse was replaced with a 7.6 million dollar structure with four power units having a total capacity of 29,600 kilowatts. The stone masonry dam constructed in 1903 is 33 feet high and 728 feet across. The reservoir created by the dam has a surface area of 131 acres, a shoreline of

Fig. I-17 Oliver Dam (Courtesy Georgia Power Company, Corporate Communications)

3 miles and a crest elevation of 269 feet.³²

The Oliver Dam, **Fig. I-1** and **Fig.I-17**, was constructed in 1959 and named after James M. Oliver, a Georgia Power executive at the time the plant was constructed. The reservoir, Lake Oliver, has a surface area of 2,150 acres, a shoreline of 40 miles and a crest elevation of 337 feet. The concrete dam is 70 feet high and 2,021

Fig. I-18 Goat Rock Dam (Courtesy Georgia Power Company, Corporate Communications)

feet in length. The powerhouse has four units with a total capacity of 60,000 kilowatts.³³

The Goat Rock Dam, **Fig. I-1** and **Fig. I-18**, was constructed by the Columbus Electric and Power Company and later

Fig. I-19 Goat Rock Dam under construction in 1912 (Courtesy University of Georgia Press)

purchased by Georgia Power. The dam acquired its name because a goat served as mascot during construction, **Fig. I-19**. The facility went into commercial operation in 1912 with 2 power units. Today there are six power units with a capacity of 26,000 kilowatts. Goat Rock Lake has 1,050 acres of surface water, 25 miles of shoreline, and a crest elevation of 404 feet. The concrete dam is 68 feet high and 1,320 feet long.³⁴

Fig. I-20 Bartletts Ferry Dam (Courtesy Georgia Power Company, Corporate Communications)

The Bartletts Ferry Dam, *Fig. I-1* and *Fig. I-20*, is located about 20 miles above Columbus and is the largest of the Chattahoochee Hydro Group dams. It was constructed in the early 1920's by the Columbus Electric and Power Company and acquired by Georgia Power Company in 1930. In 1985 a 104.6 million dollar addition to the dam brought the number of power units to six with a total capacity of 173,000 kilowatts. Lake Harding has 5,850 acres of surface water, 156 miles of shoreline and a crest elevation of 521 feet. The concrete dam is 120 feet high and 1,900 feet in length.[35]

Fig. I-21 Riverview Dam (Courtesy Georgia Power Company, Corporate Communications)

The Riverview Dam, *Fig. I-1* and *Fig. I-21*, was originally constructed to supply power to a number of West Point Manufacturing Company textile mills. The dam was sold to Georgia Power Company in 1930. The powerhouse has two power units with a total capacity of 480 kilowatts. The

Fig. I-22 Langdale Dam (Courtesy Georgia Power Company, Corporate Communications)

reservoir has 75 acres of surface water, five miles of shoreline and a crest elevation of 532 feet. The dam is a stone masonry type 15 feet high and 1,194 feet long.[36]

The Langdale Dam, *Fig. I-1* and *Fig. I-22*, was constructed in 1904 by the West Point Manufacturing Company. It was purchased by Georgia Power, along with the Riverview Dam, in 1930. The two power units have a total capacity of 1,040 kilowatts. The reservoir has 152 acres of surface water, four miles of shoreline and a crest elevation of 548 feet.[37]

West Point Lake Dam, *Fig. I-1*, *Fig. I-23* and *Fig. I-24* is located about 220 miles upstream from Jim Woodruff Lock and Dam. The 25,864 acre West Point Lake, *Fig. I-25*, provides flood protection and along with three power units produces

Fig. I-23 West Point Lake Dam (Courtesy U.S. Army Corps of Engineers, Mobile District)

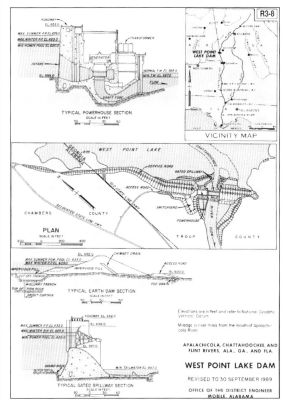

Fig. I-24 West Point Lake Dam diagram (Courtesy U.S. Army Corps of Engineers, Mobile District, 1989 Project Maps)

Introduction

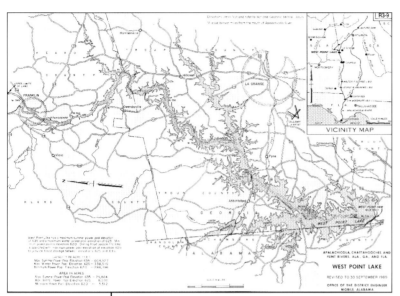

Fig. I-25 West Point Lake (Courtesy U.S. Army Corps of Engineers, Mobile District, 1989 Project Maps)

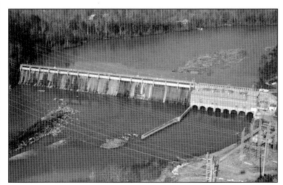

Fig. I-26 Morgan Falls Dam (Courtesy Georgia Power Company, Corporate Communications)

73,375 kilowatts of power. Construction began in June, 1966 and was completed in 1984 at a cost of $131,565,287.00.[38]

Morgan Falls, *Fig.I-1* and *Fig. I-26* originally known as the Bull Sluice Project was Atlanta's first source of hydroelectric power. The plant was designed and constructed near Bull Sluice Shoals by Westinghouse Church, Kerr & Company in 1904. Shortly after the death of S. Morgan Smith, the principal developer of the project, the Atlanta Water and Electric Power Company, which eventually became Georgia Power Company, renamed the plant Morgan Falls. Apparently this was the maiden name of S. Morgan Smith's mother. The dam was a cyclopean masonry type and the power plant began delivering electricity in October, 1904. There have been a number of renovations completed on the project since its construction at the turn of the century and is the last project moving north on the Chattahoochee before reaching Buford Dam.[39]

The Buford Dam Project, *Fig. I-1*, *Fig.I-27* and *Fig. I-28* was the second public works project constructed in the series of dams and locks located on the ACF River System. The dam is located 350 miles upstream from the Jim Woodruff Lock and Dam. The reservoir created by the dam,

Fig. I-27 Buford Dam (Courtesy U.S. Army Corps of Engineers, Mobile District)

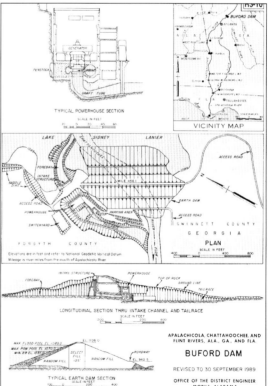

Fig. I-28 Buford Dam diagram (Courtesy U.S. Army Corps of Engineers, Mobile District, 1989 Project Maps)

Lake Sidney Lanier, *Fig. I-29*, has 38,000 acres of surface water at normal pool of 1071.00 with the main arm of the reservoir working its way up the Chattahoochee River 44 miles and the Chestatee River 19 miles.[40] It is considered a multi-purpose project because it provides flood control protection, power production, navigation, water regulation and supply, recreation, and other benefits. The reasons for Buford Dam's importance to the river development are

Fig. I-29 Lake Sidney Lanier (Courtesy U.S. Army Corps of Engineers, Mobile District, 1989 Project Maps)

directly linked to the project and what it provides. Buford Dam is located geographically in an area of North Georgia where a great deal of rainfall accumulates. This allows for the reservoir to catch winter and spring rains that provide both flood protection downstream, a uniform river flow for municipal water use, and navigation all the way to the Gulf of Mexico.[41] The reservoir as part of a system of reservoirs and dams provides 65 percent of the total federal system storage for the ACF inland waterway and low river system.[42] The project also helps "firm " the power production for other projects south of Buford Dam.[43] Work on the project began in 1950 and continued until 1960 with a price tag of $44,795,093.00.

The Buford location was considered an ideal site for a dam as noted by Colonel Mason J. Young, then the South Atlantic Division Chief for the U.S. Army Corps of Engineers. "This is a storybook site for a dam. I've seen similar sites in the Northeast but there is always a city a few miles away. Here we have the site with no such complications. I don't think I've ever seen a better site for a dam."[44] It was as if the natural terrain had been created for just such a purpose. The site was not located near any large city, but was in a rural area that should prove to not present too many relocation problems, steep escarpments were on either side of the Chattahoochee River Valley, and a solid foundation of granite was underneath. For these reasons and others, this site was chosen for one of the most heavily used and visited lakes operated by the United States Army Corps of Engineers.

This was not to say that other sites were not considered in fact there were many sites studied but they were found to be less economical than Buford. Early on a dam near Roswell, Georgia seemed the odds on favorite. A report issued by the Chief of Engineers in 1939 outlining details for developing the ACF River System had the Roswell site listed as the proposed site for a dam north of the city of Atlanta. It was suppose to be located 16 miles north of the city. Estimates were submitted to construct a concrete gravity dam and spillway but even at this site the Corps was looking at changing the construction material to earth.[45] Although a similar report issued in 1946 opted for the Buford site, the Roswell site was still listed on the ACF River development map as a proposed project, *Fig. I-4*.[46] In a letter from the South Atlantic Division summarizing proposed improvements for the Apalachicola, Chattahoochee, Flint River System, dated April 5, 1946, there was continued reference to a reservoir at a site near Buford, Georgia and its favorable status over a site some 29 miles downstream. Paragraph 10 describes the reasons for choosing the Buford site."Buford was compared with the Roswell, Georgia site, some 29.6 miles downstream from the Buford site, with a maximum power pool at elevation 982.0. With the Roswell site at this level extensive highway and railroad relocation would be necessary. The resultant high cost coupled with less regulated flow downstream renders this site less attractive than the Buford development."[47]

In late 1947 Cannon and Jeffries a company based in Compton, California was contracted to begin test drilling at the Buford site. Hundreds of borings were made in the hills and valleys surrounding the area in order to determine if it was as good as presupposed. In December of that year a number of federal, state, and local officials,

Introduction

among them the South Atlantic Division Chief, Colonel Mason J. Young and 5th District Representative James C. Davis, visited the test sites, *Fig. I-30* and *Fig. I-31*. They were there to watch as government geologists for the Army Corps of Engineers collected samples of the granite for careful examination. Subsequent visits to the proposed dam site were made over the years, before construction on the project actually began, by some of those same officials, *Fig. I-32* and *Fig. I-33*. These visits were made as much for the Army Corps of Engineers as they were for the local gentry and their representatives for it was here that

they were painted a picture of just what it was the government had in mind for their "neck of the woods."

In 1950 geologists began boring a deep shaft into the granite at the approximate site that the intake structure rests today, *Fig. I-34*,. The geologic substrate of this region was formed during the Precambrian Era some 2.5 billion years ago and is part of the same geological formation of rock that protrudes out of the ground in several places in this region of Georgia, one of them being Stone Mountain.[48] A rotary

diamond drill was used to create a calyx hole which was 36 inches in diameter and 120 feet in depth. A small section of the granite plug that was pulled from that hole,

Fig. I-30 Visitors at test drillings (L-R) Young; Linder; Weir; Davis; Coogan and Shaw. (Courtesy U.S. Army Corps of Engineers, Mobile District)

Fig. I-31 Visitors at test drillings (L-R) Weir; Linder; Shaw; Davis; Coogan; Shea and Young. (Courtesy U.S. Army Corps of Engineers, Mobile District)

Fig. I-32 Visitors at the dam site. (Courtesy U.S. Army Corps of Engineers, Mobile District)

Fig. I-33 Visitors at the dam site. (Courtesy Mrs. Weldon Gardner)

Fig. I-34 Drilling of calyx hole. (Courtesy U.S. Army Corps of Engineers, Mobile District)

Fig. I-35 Core plug pulled from calyx hole placed in Buford City Park. (Courtesy U.S. Army Corps of Engineers, Mobile District)

Fig. I-36 Inside the calyx hole. (Courtesy U.S. Army Corps of Engineers, Mobile District)

Fig. I-37 Core plug placed at West Bank Overlook. (RDC)

Fig. I-38 Core plug located behind old operations building. (RDC)

Fig. I-35, was placed at Buford City Park and is still located there today. Using a narrow metal cage geologists were lowered deep into the narrow shaft to examine its geologic composition, ***Fig. I-36***.[49] Other small portions of the drilling can be seen today at the West Bank Overlook, ***Fig. I-37***, and the Upper Overlook, ***Fig. I-38***, behind the old Resource Manager's Office.

As the decade of the 1950's began, the long years of planning were over and the project moved from the drawing board to the construction phase. Politics would continue to play an important role in the project's success as there was still much to do. Aside from the actual construction of the dam, appropriation battles on Capitol Hill for continued funding as well as acquiring over 50,000 acres of private land for the reservoir were still events reserved for the future.

Fig. I-39 Forsyth County side of dam site. (Courtesy U.S. Army Corps of Engineers, Mobile District)

Fig. I-40 Gwinnett County side of dam site. (Courtesy U.S. Army Corps of Engineers, Mobile District)

Fig. I-41 Extended section of the core drilling on the ground. (Courtesy U.S. Army Corps of Engineers, Mobile District)

NOTES

1. 1989 Project Maps. Produced by the United States Army Corps of Engineers, R3

2. ACF Inland Waterway and River System Development History. Produced by the TRI Rivers Waterway Development Association.

3. Letter from the Secretary of War transmitting a report from the Chief of Engineers to the U.S. House of Representatives Committee on Rivers and Harbors, House Document no.342, 1st Session, 76th Congress, pp. 25-26.

4. Ibid.

5. ACF Inland Waterway and River System Development History. Produced by the TRI Rivers Waterway Development Association.

6. Letter from the Secretary of War transmitting a report from the Chief of Engineers to the U.S. House of Representatives Committee on Rivers and Harbors, House Document no.342, 1st Session, 76th Congress, pp. 25-26.

7. Ibid.

8. Congressional Record

9. ACF Inland Waterway and River System Development History. Produced by the TRI Rivers Waterway Development Association.

10. Apalachicola Basin Reservoir Regulation Manual, Appendix B, Buford Dam (Lake Sidney Lanier), Chattahoochee River, Georgia, February, 1991.

11. Letter from The Secretary of War transmitting a report from the Chief of Engineers to the U.S. House of Representatives Committee on Rivers and Harbors, House Document no.308, 1st Session, 69th Congress, pp.1-6.

12. Congressional Record, 76th Congress, 1st Session.

13. Letter from The Secretary of War transmitting a report from the Chief of Engineers to the U.S. House of Representatives Committee on Rivers and Harbors, House Document no.342, 1st Session, 76th Congress, pp.64-67.

14. Updating of the Master Plan, Lake Sidney Lanier, Chattahoochee River, GA, Volume 1, Produced by the United States Army Corps of Engineers, Mobile District, Mobile, Alabama, June, 1987, p.1-01.

15. ACF Inland Waterway and River System Development History. Produced by the TRI Rivers Waterway Development Association.

16. Apalachicola Basin Reservoir Regulation Manual, Appendix B, Buford Dam (Lake Sidney Lanier), Chattahoochee River, Georgia, February, 1991, pp. B1-5

17. Public notice issued by the War Department, Office of the Division Engineer, South Atlantic Division, Atlanta, Georgia, March 30, 1946. Courtesy the United States Army Corps of Engineers.

18. Letter from the Secretary of War transmitting a report from the Chief of Engineers to the U.S. House of Representatives Committee on Rivers and Harbors, House Document no. 300, 1st Session, 80th Congress, pp. 1-40.

19. ACF Inland Waterway and River System Development History. Produced by the TRI Rivers Waterway Development Association.

20. Congressional Record, 79th Congress, 2nd Session, Volume 92, Part 4, p. 4966, May 13, 1946.

21. Ibid., Part 5, p. 6251, June 4, 1946.

22. Ibid., p. 6260, June 4, 1946.

23. Atlanta Journal Constitution, Sunday, September 14, 1947.

24. Atlanta Constitution, Tuesday, September 16, 1947.

25. Atlanta Journal Constitution, September 21, 1947.

26. Ibid., September 18, 1947.

27. 1989 Project Maps. Produced by the United States Army Corps of Engineers, R3-2.

28. Ibid., R3-4

29. Ibid., R3-6

30. Georgia Power Company

31. Ibid.

32. Ibid.

33. Ibid.

34. Ibid.

35. Ibid.

36. Ibid.

37. Ibid.

38. 1989 Project Maps, The United States Army Corps of Engineers, R3-8

39. Georgia Power Company

40. Updating of the Master Plan, Lake Sidney Lanier, Chattahoochee River, GA, Volume 1, Produced by the United States Army Corps of Engineers, Mobile District, Mobile, Alabama, June, 1987, p.2-01.

41. Ibid., R3

42. ACF Inland Waterway and River System Development History. Produced by the TRI Rivers Waterway Development Association.

43. United State House of Representatives Appropriation Hearings, 1953, in testimony by General Chorpening, p. 76.

44. Colonel Mason J. Young, South Atlantic Division Chief, United States Army Corps of Engineers as reported in the Atlanta Constitution, December 30, 1947.

45. Letter from The Secretary of War transmitting a report from the Chief of Engineers to the U.S. House of Representatives Committee on Rivers and Harbors, House Document no.342, 1st Session, 76th Congress, p.66.

46. Letter from the Secretary of War transmitting a report from the Chief of Engineers to the U.S. House of Representatives Committee on Rivers and Harbors, House Document no.300, 1st Session, 80th Congress, pp. 1-40.

47. Letter from the South Atlantic Division on April 15, 1946 concerning alternate sites for Buford Dam.

48. Updating of the Master Plan, Lake Sidney Lanier, Chattahoochee River, GA, Volume 1, Produced by the United States Army Corps of Engineers, Mobile District, Mobile, Alabama, June, 1987, p.5-02.

49. Cecil Patterson, United States Army Corps of Engineers, retired.

Flooding in front of the main earth dam site. Seasonal flooding of this type was one of the main reasons the dam was constructed.

CHAPTER ONE

Why Build a Dam?

The Chattahoochee River as it appeared in 1909 near Riverside Military Academy. (Courtesy Chestatee Regional Library from The Pictorial History of Hall County to 1950 by Sybil McRay)

The dam at Buford was not built for a singular reason. It was designed as a multi-purpose reservoir in that it would provide more than one benefit to the eventual development of the Apalachicola, Chattahoochee, Flint River System. Although it is a single public works project you must look at it from a broader perspective. Aside from being multi-purpose in nature it is one of a series of projects that allows the ACF River System to function effectively. Flood control, navigation, power production, water supply and regulation, pollution abatement, industrial and residential growth, and recreation were all the multiple benefits that construction of the dam would provide. It is generally conceded that flood control, navigation, and power production were considered primary reasons for the project's construction. Many may argue their order of importance or the fact that recreation, such a large part of the project's popularity, is given such a low priority. When viewing the project from an historical perspective you are not afforded the luxury of contemporary thinking. Regardless of what present generations believe is important the fact remains that social, economic, and political conditions were different in the late 1940's. The order of reasons for building Buford Dam reflect what was considered as paramount concerns for the era in which it was constructed. This doesn't mean the future was not considered.

Flood Control

Until the Chattahoochee and Flint Rivers were developed, with the creation of dams and large reservoirs, very little flood control work had ever been completed on these rivers. The Chattahoochee, the name coming from the Creek Indian language meaning pictured rocks, has its source in a mountain spring some 4,000 feet above sea level four miles south of Brasstown Bald in the Chattahoochee National Forest, 71 miles northeast of Buford Dam and nearly 500 miles from the Gulf of Mexico.[1]

The problem with the Chattahoochee is that it is given to extremes. For many years it could be the source of great destruction when its flood waters wreaked havoc on surrounding communities. Nearly 39 percent of the annual rainfall this area experiences occurs from December through March with 20 percent occurring from September through November.[2] During other times dry spells would reverse the conditions. This seemingly back and forth condition of the river for many years kept many large industries out of this area as they needed a more stable flow of water than the Chattahoochee could provide.

In March, 1956 a Forsyth County grocery store owner, Mr. Sorghum Crow described in vivid detail what he saw during flooding on the river several years earlier. "I'm the only man living who ever saw Brown's Bridge washed away by the Chattahoochee.... That was January 7, 1947 during the worst flood I ever saw. Somebody told me a chicken house was floating down the river and I got down there just in time to see the bridge go out. It broke right in two. Half of it floated downstream and the other half swung back this way toward the bank".[3]

Although flood control seems of little importance today, mainly because the largest portion of it has been eradicated by dams, it was of major importance in the years proceeding the dam's construction, **Fig.1-1**. As citizens of this region today, we tend to view the lakes importance based on what we view as important to our lives and the lives of those around us. We sometimes forget what life was like in years gone by. There are still areas below the dam that experience flooding but not as often or to the severity that they once did. Seasonal flooding along the Chattahoochee River as far south as the Gulf of Mexico came to be expected and was of paramount importance to the people who lived and worked the land along the flood plains of the Chattahoochee, Chestatee and Flint Rivers as per Mr. Crow's recollection, **Fig. 1-2**,. Although today it is impossible to view these areas above the dam they are highly visible below it, **Fig. 1-3** and **Fig. 1-4**, and have allowed for an abundance of commercial and residential development in areas that would still be wooded fields had

Fig. 1-1 Gainesville Daily Times article. (Courtesy Gainesville Daily Times)

Fig. 1-2 Flooding on the Chattahoochee River in front of the main earth dam. (Courtesy U.S. Army Corps of Engineers, Mobile District)

Fig. 1-3 Flood plain at McGinnis Ferry Road Bridge. (R.D.C.)

Fig. 1-4 Flood plain near Duluth. (R.D.C.)

Flood Waters Reach 20.3 Feet at Dawsonville Bridge; Crops Damaged

High water swept through the bottom lands around Gainesville last week causing considerable crop damage on the Chattahoochee river.

At the Dawsonville road bridge, water rose to 20.3 feet overnight. At 11 o'clock Thursday night the water was nearing the flood stage but still within the regular run of the river. By 2 o'clock Friday morning, the water had swept out of the banks and into bottom lands of freshly planted oats, knee high corn, and other crops.

According to persons who have lived alongside the Chattahoochee for a number of years, the water reached 26 feet two years ago. It was at that time that several bridges were destroyed near here.

Further up the Chattanoochee the waters rose to endanger residential sections around Helen. The hard rains in this section, plus the water sweeping down the mountains from other sections caused the river to rise so rapidly, authorities stated.

Small creeks in this section swelled to the overflow stage and at the local golf course, several bridges spanning the creek were swept away.

Pictures of the Chattahoochee at the Dawsonville and Cleveland bridges are found elsewhere in this issue.

the dam not been constructed all those years ago. Before construction of Buford Dam development of any kind along the river corridor below the proposed dam was very limited. Since its construction large numbers of businesses and industries not to mention housing has sprung up from what was basically rural agricultural land along the river corridor. Commercial, industrial, and residential development not only brings of Mexico witnessed the same scene. Whole fields of crops knee high and higher in water were completely lost or had to be harvested prematurely because of the rising waters. Crops were not the only things affected. Homes and other property would sometimes find it hard to escape the cresting waters. The many tributaries that fed the main channels would also overflow spreading out over land not located next to the river but

business but people and an increased tax revenue to the area. Whether this development was then or is today viewed as beneficial is probably up for debate. There are certainly enough ardent supporters on both sides but the fact that the dam opened up thousands of acres for not only business but increased agricultural use is pretty much a moot point.

At the time the project's plans were being formulated studies were made to determine just what effect floods were having and the cost involved. Nearly $200,000.00 a year was being spent on flood control damage and these were 1940 dollars.[4] By today's standards these figures would be in the millions. If you add the lost revenue generated by development that would not have been possible then the figures become even more astonishing. A 1973 study completed by the United States Army Corps of Engineers on the river's flood plain indicated that nearly $10,000,000.00 had been saved in flood control damage since the dam had been completed in 1957.[5] Today that figure is considerably higher as it has been estimated that over $33,000,000.00 worth of flood control damage has been prevented by the dam since its completion.[6]

Before the development of the Chattahoochee and Flint Rivers rural and urban areas from North Georgia to the Gulf

still becoming its victims because the swollen river could no longer take anymore water. There were even newspaper reports of the great flood of 1886 in which two steam boats moved up the city streets of West Point.[7] The recent flooding South Georgia experienced provides an excellent example of what the general populous along the river corridors experienced in some degree in years past., *Fig. 1-5*

With the dam's completion flooding to a large degree downstream has been kept in check. The reservoir provides an extremely effective tool in controlling floods along the river to areas 10 miles downstream.[8] Along the 45 miles of the river from Buford Dam to Atlanta, where most of the commercial and residential development has occurred and the 104 miles between Atlanta and the West Point Reservoir there is over 32,700 acres of land that receives limited flood protection.[9]

The flood control plan for the Buford Dam Project calls for the reservoir to be lowered from 1071.0 to 1070.0 in the fall. It is to remain as close to this elevation as possible from December through mid-April, which is considered the critical flood season, but sometimes temporary variations may occur during floods or droughts. The flood storage between elevations 1070.0 and 1085 is 38,200 acre feet.[10]

Lake Sidney Lanier has 637,000 acre

Fig. 1-5 Streets of West Point underwater during a flood in 1929. (Courtesy Gainesville Daily Times)

feet of flood storage between elevations 1,071.0 and 1,085.0. It was provided solely for the purpose of controlling floods downstream.[11] Engineers determined these elevations by calculating the record flooding over the Chattahoochee River basin above the dam's present site and adding a comfortable safety margin to that. If the storms are centered over the river above the dam, where the nearly 1,040 sq. miles of drainage can be utilized, then there is an effective retarding of floods downstream. The problem arises when storms are centered below the dam where the flood storage of the reservoir can not be utilized. It is in this uncontrolled drainage area below the dam that severe flooding still occurs. Even here though the degree to which the river causes damage has been minimized by the dam's presence. There are nearly 400 square miles of uncontrolled drainage between Buford Dam and Atlanta and there has been numerous and severe flooding there many times over the years since the dam was completed.[12]

In 1973 a Flood Plain Information booklet, prepared for the Atlanta Regional Commission by the Department of the Army, Mobile District, Corps of Engineers, Mobile, Alabama, discussed the likelihood of future flooding downstream. Since flooding in the uncontrolled drainage area below the dam is the problem, studies were made to determine the flood potential in the area. By studying flooding that had occurred in areas of similar topography and physical terrain they were able to classify flooding into three types, (1) a 50-year Flood, (2) an Intermediate Regional Flood or 100-year Flood, and (3) a Standard Project Flood.[13]

A 50-year Flood could occur on the average once every 50 years although it is possible to occur at any time. An Intermediate Regional Flood on an average can occur every 100 years. This type of flood is also possible to occur at any time.[14] The Standard Project Flood is defined as "a major flood that can be expected to occur from a severe combination of meteorological and hydrological conditions that is considered reasonably characteristic of the geographical area in which the study area is located excluding extremely rare combinations."[15]

50-year and Intermediate Regional Floods are expected to occur more often but are usually not as severe as a Standard Project Flood. The frequency for these floods are based on averages and other factors. On any given year there is a one percent chance of an Intermediate Regional Flood occurring and a two percent chance of a 50-year flood. Because of the rarity of a Standard Project Flood occurring any year it is impractical to equate an average frequency.[16] The study by the Corps of Engineers showed that if an Intermediate Regional Flood occurred approximately 14,400 acres below the dam would be flooded. A Standard Project Flood would inundate over 47,182 acres. These figures did not take into account the acreage affected by flooding of tributaries.[17]

Fig. 1-6 and *Fig. 1-7* are maps of the Chattahoochee River basin below the dam. They show the areas that would be affected by an Intermediate Regional Flood and a Standard Project Flood. *Fig. 1-6* shows the

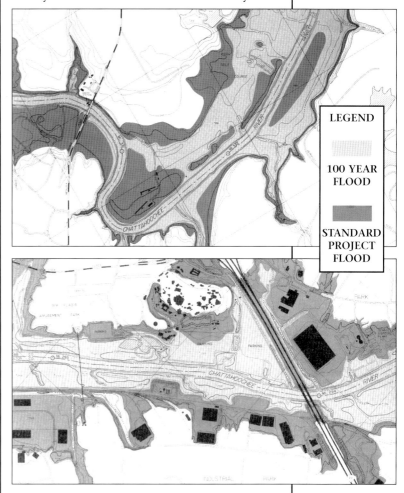

Fig. 1-6 Project map showing Medlock Bridge. (Courtesy U.S. Army Corps of Engineers, Mobile District, Flood Plain Information Book)

Fig. 1-7 Project map showing Six Flags area. (Courtesy U.S. Army Corps of Engineers, Mobile District, Flood Plain Information Book)

area where Medlock Bridge on highway 141 crosses over the Chattahoochee River near Duluth, Georgia. *Fig. 1-7* shows the area near Six Flags Amusement Park. Flood information shown on these maps as well as other information from the Flood Plain Information book put together by the United States Army Corps of Engineers is based on the 1973 study and supplemental information from a revised 1982 study. Although some figures may have changed due to commercial and residential development as well as other factors, it is still the most recent and best information to date on the potential for flooding on the Upper Chattahoochee River corridor from Whitesburg, Georgia to Buford Dam.

The flooding that occurred in early July, 1994 in Central and Southern Georgia was generally considered a Standard Project Flood and was the worst ever recorded in Georgia. The human toll was high as over 30 people lost their lives not to mention the thousands of survivors left homeless. It had a crippling effect on the state's infrastructure as a number of highways, roads, bridges, rail lines, dams, levees, and water and sewage treatment plants were destroyed or put out of commission. Had the storm been centered a little further north then some 22,000 acres of land below Buford Dam could have experienced record flooding.

Navigation

Navigation was another priority high on the "reasons" list for construction of the dam. Although today it may take a back seat to power production, water resources, and recreation, it nevertheless still plays an important role in how the river is used. The problem with navigation on the ACF River System is that it never really attracted the traffic that was presupposed when considering it as a key factor in the Buford Project as well as other projects on the ACF River System. Even with this short coming and high operating cost per ton of commodities shipped, transportation by water is still cheaper than by rail or truck. It also uses less fuel and eases the pollution burden.[18] Water from Lake Lanier as well as other reservoirs further south of Buford Dam would insure a nine foot navigation channel from Columbus south to the Gulf of Mexico.

Without Buford Dam releasing water downstream, water it has obtained during the rainy season, navigation from Columbus south to the Gulf of Mexico would only be possible with the use of heavy and expensive dredging of the river channel, which in fact is used even with an adequate water supply.[19] Prior to the dams construction the river was not navigable on a reliable basis for most of the year. For three months during the year, from late summer to early fall, when the river was usually dry, navigation was nearly impossible. Most freight was moved between December and June when sand bars posed little threat. Even then when the rainy season was excessive, in the winter and spring, there would sometimes be too much water.[20]

Commercial and recreational navigation all along the ACF River System would benefit from the creation of a constant and reliable navigation channel. Industries specializing in paper products, fertilizers, rock, gravel, and sand production as well as the military transporting troops and supplies make up the bulk of the commercial use of the river south of Columbus.[21] Seasonal highs and lows were not the only barriers to navigation. Many parts of the river were simply too shallow to allow safe passage up or down the stream. Prior to development of the ACF River System river depth near Columbus, Georgia was recorded between 2.5 and 3.0 feet.[22]

When viewing navigation today you see an ever increasing population making more and more demands on what was once seen as a seemingly endless supply of water. Recent federal lawsuits concerning the use of the Chattahoochee River has seen navigation and other benefits such as flood control, power production and even recreation on the defensive. But navigation in the 1950's was seen as a very high priority in the overall scheme of the river development. An example of its importance can be seen in the extended plan engineers and many government officials had concerning navigation on the Chattahoochee and Flint Rivers. In the late 1930's the government was considering a channel extension on the Chattahoochee

River as far north as Atlanta. Today this may seem to have no merit but in years gone by it was a very real possibility and surveying the upper Chattahoochee for possible navigation was not a new topic. Making Atlanta a port city had been discussed as far back as 1874 when the Army surveyed the Chattahoochee River and found that the river posed no significant problems in developing navigation as far north as Atlanta. A drop of ten feet per mile between West Point and Columbus, where there was a series of rapids and broken rocks, posed the only rough section of the river. Promoters of the project pointed out that locks could be built around those rough waters.[23] The fact of the matter was that making Atlanta a port city was not so much an engineering problem as an economic one. A series of private dams and power plants located above Walter F. George Lock and Dam was just one example of the type of economic roadblocks that would remain in the path of developing the Chattahoochee River above Columbus.[24] For Congress to allocate any money for such a project the Army would have to prove that the project would be self-supporting or show that the benefits would out weigh the cost. It had always run into money problems and unfortunately for the planners of this mammoth undertaking it never got off the drawing board.

In the late 1930's the government was again considering a channel extension on the Chattahoochee River as far north as Atlanta. This would have provided a nine foot navigation channel for commercial use of the river from Atlanta south to the Gulf of Mexico.[25] An Army survey done in 1936 showed that although it was economically doubtful, building locks and dams would not pose much of an engineering problem. Another survey paid for by Atlanta and Fulton County indicated that such a development of the Chattahoochee River above Columbus was a sound economic venture. They predicted that there would be a significant increase in the commercial tonnage on the river if the project was ever fully developed. The Atlanta Freight Bureau and the Chamber of Commerce pushed hard for further studies and the United States Army Corps of Engineers granted $20,000.00 of federal funds to investigate further.[26] Although the commercial use of the river never developed as was anticipated who knows what effect adding Atlanta to the navigable chain would have had on the ultimate success of the river as a major transportation resource in Georgia.

Whether the government will ever extend the navigation channel further north to Atlanta is up for debate. Economically the project would carry a hefty dollar price tag, one which may be to great to overcome. Even in the face of all this according to a 1991 government report on the Apalachicola Basin a navigation review study of survey scope was authorized to examine the economic and engineering feasibility of just such a channel extension.

Water Source

The reservoir at Lake Lanier accounts for about 65 percent of the total usable water stored in the ACF River System and plays a primary role in the regulation of water within the basin. Hydropower, navigation, recreation, stable, and constant stream flow for adequate quality and supply of water, and protection of fish and wildlife are all areas that benefit from the waters of Lake Lanier.

Having a much needed water supply for drinking, cooking, bathing, etc. and being able to regulate the flow of the Chattahoochee River was a much needed benefit that would be provided with the construction of Buford Dam. Atlanta Mayor William B. Hartsfield once responded to questions about the creation of the lake for the purpose of providing Atlanta with a vast water reservoir. "Atlanta's water supply is not an issue. It's not water we need but the regulation of that water."[27] Hartsfield was an outspoken advocate for the dam's construction because he believed that future growth of Atlanta and all of North Georgia depended on finding a method of controlling the Chattahoochee. Industrial and residential growth for this area would be directly linked to the creation of the dam. It was estimated that for an 800,000 population of Atlanta, in 1960, some 200 cubic feet per second of water flow would be needed.[28]

Commercial, industrial and residential

demands of today have far exceeded even the minimum 1960 figures. The minimum river flow that must be maintained by Buford Dam is 450 cubic feet per second (cfs). Depending on certain conditions such as water elevation, electrical production, seasonal conditions, etc., that number can be increased to a maximum flow of over 10,000 cfs. Generally with one power unit supplying water downstream the river flow can be maintained between 450 to 700 cfs.[29] Tributaries that feed the Chattahoochee River below the dam, where a number of cities and counties draw their water supplies, can increase the cfs flow of the river providing an even greater supply of water. A number of counties like Forsyth, Gwinnett, Hall, and others draw their water supplies directly out of the lake. Regulations provide a cap on the amount of water that can be taken from the reservoir daily. These counties are licensed by the state and have a contract with the government to withdraw certain amounts of water depending on their needs. Like the cfs flow of the river, amounts of rain fall, outside water use, commercial and residential use, seasonal conditions, government water restrictions, and reservoir elevation are all things that affect the amount of water taken by city and county water agencies. Gwinnett County, for example, records a yearly average of about 100,000,000 gallons a day.[30] This amount could be higher or lower depending on the conditions affecting that days use. Without the dam's construction regulation of the river's water flow would not have been possible. The dam does not provide additional water, it simply regulates the flow and provides a more uniform rate, releasing more water in times of drought and holding back water during excess periods. This type of controlled flow provides the uniformity that commercial, industrial and residential use needs. Droughts this area experienced in the 1980's would have been devastating had the dam not been constructed. As bad as things got they could have been a great deal worse. An unregulated flow of the Chattahoochee would invite conditions to develop similar to the early 1920's when the river flow dropped below 140 cfs.[31] Regulation of the Chattahoochee River also provides a method by which pollution of the streams can be minimized during dry periods, this resource being particularly beneficial in light of today's concerns for the environment.

When Buford Dam was constructed in the 1950's engineers made studies and developed plans for a reregulation dam below the present site of Buford Dam. The project would provide an added water supply during severe drought conditions as well as off-set the heavy demands placed on Lake Lanier because of commercial and residential development of the area. In those early years the benefit to cost ratio studies made could not justify the funding for the project. Over the years since Buford Dam was completed the concern that developed with the problems of having an adequate water supply coupled with the severe water restrictions the area experienced during the better part of the 1980's caused renewed interest in the reservoir. In 1981 the Metropolitan Atlanta Waters Resources Management Study recommended the dam's construction.[32] Although alternative plans to the dam such as raising the present elevation of the lake were developed, Congress authorized construction of the reregulation dam under Section 601 of the Water Resources Act of 1986. It was approved as Public Law 99-662 on November 17, 1986. As was the case with Buford Dam, authorization for construction is not the same thing as appropriating money for construction. As of today Congress has not appropriated the money for any construction on the dam. This does not mean it is a moot point because Congress, to date, has not deregulated the proposed project as it did for three dams on the Flint River in 1986. Sprewrell Bluff Lake Dam, Lazer Creek Lake Dam, and the Lower Auchumphee Creek Lake Dam were all projects on the Flint River that had been given prior approval by Congress for

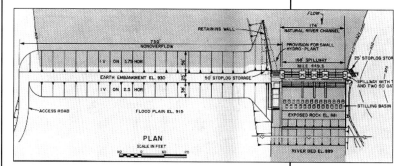

Fig. 1-8 Reregulation dam diagram (Courtesy U.S. Army Corps of Engineers, Mobile District, 1989 Project Maps)

Lake Sidney Lanier "A Storybook Site"

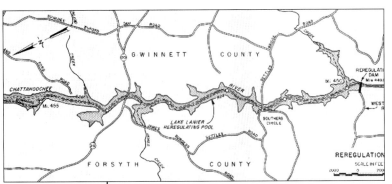

Fig. 1-9 Project map showing reregulation dam site. (Courtesy U.S. Army Corps of Engineers, Mobile District, 1989 Project Maps)

construction. They were all three deauthorized by Congress as part of the same Public Law 99-662 that authorized construction of the reregulation dam at Buford.

The reregulation dam, *Fig. 1-8*, was designed to provide an added water supply as well as hydro power production. It would be located 6.3 miles downstream from Buford Dam, *Fig. 1-9*, and would exhibit a 150 foot gravity type dam with a spillway and stilling basin as well as a 750 foot long earth embankment on the west side of the river. The lake created behind the dam would widen the present river channel at a depth of 35 feet with a surface area of 819 acres.[33]

Power Production

Fig. 1-10 Powerhouse photograph showing generators. (R.D.C.)

Power production was a key facet of the multi-purpose reservoir. In fact 80% of the benefit for the construction of Buford Dam was based on power production.[34] The project has two generating units of 40,000 kilowatts and one 6,000 kilowatts, *Fig. 1-10*,. They have a combined output of 150,000 kilowatts per year or 200,000,000 kilowatt hours per year. The dam's electrical generation produces added power for commercial, industrial, and residential use. The power produced is sold to public bodies, municipalities, and public co-operatives. The Southeastern Power Administration (SEPA) is responsible for negotiating contracts for the sale of power from the Buford Project under guidelines of the Flood Control Act of 1944. Power is transmitted to the Georgia Power Company for delivery to public power suppliers.[35] In 1957 it was reported that the government would gain $1,524,600.00 worth or revenue from the sale of electrical power in just the first year alone.[36] Estimates have put the revenue created by electrical generation at over $47,000,000.00 which has more than paid for the project's original construction cost.[37]

Buford Dam not only provides power for those in the immediate area of the dam it also helps "firm" or guarantee power for other projects south of the dam. These include the many private dams and power plants not built or operated by the United States Army Corps of Engineers that are located on the Chattahoochee River.[38] It was estimated at the time of construction that the project would be able to add a dependable capacity of some 16,000 kilowatts of power to these other projects alone. This would mean an additional 38 million kilowatts of power annually just for building Buford Dam and having it operate at full capacity.[39]

Recreation

Although recreation may not have been a major reason for the dam's construction it plays a primary role in the project's popularity as being one of the most heavily visited lakes operated by Army Corps of Engineers in the United States. In the late 1940's and early 1950's when the Army and officials in Georgia were trying to get congressional approval for the project recreation was viewed more as an incidental benefit than a reason for the construction of the dam. In view of the lake's popularity today that may not seem the case. One would have a very strong argument for listing recreation on Lake Lanier as a primary resource, mainly due to its enormous popularity. In fact today recreation is considered by the Corps as one of the primary resources for the project. The problem historically is you must view the project from the perspective of the era in which it was constructed. On many occasions Georgia officials were more than willing to note the recreational potential the project would have, after all they were trying to sell the government on the idea and it helped to have as many aces in the hole as possible. In fact it is probably safe to say that they underestimated the potential that recreation would eventually prove to have. The lake's shores are literally dotted with summer homes and cottages as well as year round residents that look to the seemingly endless potential the lake has for recreation and fun. These homeowners have acquired over 7,500 docks and other

Fig. 1-11 Boat docks on Lake Lanier. (Courtesy U.S. Army Corps of Engineers, Mobile District)

facilities, **Fig. 1-11**, that provide a more private use of its waters. This mixture of residential development and recreation has created a popularity not found at other lakes and reservoirs.

As noted, Lake Lanier is one of the most heavily visited lakes built and operated by the United States Army Corps of Engineers. It is estimated that over 20 million people visit the lake annually.[40] They come to enjoy the lake's many parks and day use areas as well as the 38,000 acres of surface water. The numerous businesses that are in direct proximity to the lake cater to the special needs of the many diverse and varied visitors from all over the United States. They provide a host of products and services for a number of water related activities such as boating, fishing, skiing, swimming, and other recreational activities, **Fig. 1-12** and **Fig. 1-13**. The government

leases certain areas of the lake to private businesses as well as state and local governments, (marinas, parks, etc.).

For many years the State of Georgia leased from the federal government a large number of islands located at the southern end of the lake known as Lake Lanier

Islands. **Fig. 1-14** The idea for a large state park was first given serious consideration in 1955 when then State Senator Howard Overby introduced a resolution in the Georgia General Assembly urging the development of such a facility on the project.[41] It would eventually become the largest state park in Georgia. These islands developed in the early 1970's became an enormous recreational complex, today offering a variety of recreational activities

Fig. 1-12 Sailing on Lake Lanier. (Courtesy U.S. Army Corps of Engineers, Mobile District)

Fig. 1-13 Boating on Lake Lanier. (Courtesy U.S. Army Corps of Engineers, Mobile District)

Fig. 1-14 Lake Lanier Islands (Courtesy KSL Corporation)

Lake Sidney Lanier "A Storybook Site"

Fig. 1-15

Fig. 1-15 and Fig. 1-16 Construction of Lanier Islands Bridge in the late 1960's. (Courtesy U.S. Army Corps of Engineers, Mobile District)

Fig. 1-16

Fig. 1-17 Swimming at Lanier Islands Beach. (Courtesy KSL Corporation)

Fig. 1-18 Main recreational complex at Lanier Islands. (Courtesy KSL) Corporation)

Fig. 1-19 One of two golf courses located at Lanier Islands. (Courtesy KSL Corporation)

Fig. 1-20 Rental boating at Lanier Islands. (Courtesy KSL Corporation)

Fig. 1-21 Renaissance PineIsle Hotel (Courtesy Renaissance PineIsle Hotel)

for the nearly 20 million people that visit the lake annually, *Fig. 1-17*, *Fig. 1-18*, *Fig. 1-19*, *Fig. 1-20*, *Fig. 1-21*, and *Fig. 1-22*. In May, 1996 under a privatization effort sponsored by Georgia Governor Zell Miller the KSL Recreation Corporation contracted with the state to manage the

Fig. 1-22 Hilton Resort (Courtesy KSL Corporation)

Fig. 1-23 Lazy Days Marina (Courtesy Lazy Days Marina)

Fig. 1-24 Bald Ridge Marina (Courtesy Bald Ridge Marina)

Fig. 1-25 Lanier Harbor Marina (Courtesy Lanier Harbor Marina)

Fig. 1-26 Holiday Marina (Courtesy Holiday Marina)

Fig. 1-27 Starboard Marina (Courtesy Starboard Marina)

Fig. 1-28 Aqualand Marina (Courtesy Aqualand Marina)

Fig. 1-29 Sunrise Cove Marina (Courtesy Sunrise Cove Marina)

Fig. 1-30 Gainesville Marina (Courtesy Gainesville Marina)

Fig. 1-31 Lan-Mar Marina (Courtesy Lan-Mar Marina)

Fig. 1-32 Habersham Marina (Courtesy Habersham Marina)

Fig. 1-33 One of many public boat ramps located on the lake. (Courtesy U.S. Army Corps of Engineers, Mobile District)

Fig. 1-34 Balus Creek boat ramp (RDC)

Fig. 1-35 Camping on Lake Lanier. (Courtesy U.S. Army Corps of Engineers, Mobile District)

Fig. 1-36 Visitors enjoying one of many day use facilities on the lake. (Courtesy U.S. Army Corps of Engineers, Mobile District)

sprawling 1,100 acre complex.[42] Lake Lanier has become a mecca for boat enthusiasts and outdoor recreationalists of all kinds. Privately owned marinas, **Fig. 1-23** through **Fig. 1-32**, serve thousands of boaters and boat related activities that are a big part of the lake's popularity. There are over 70 boat ramps, **Fig. 1-33** and **Fig. 1-34**, located in day-use parks, campgrounds, marinas, and leased areas all over the lake. These ramps launch hundreds of boats daily for fishing, skiing, and pleasure cruises to mention just a few. The Corps of Engineers also operates over 50 campgrounds and day-use sites on the lake, **Fig. 1-35** and **Fig. 1-36**. These areas range from very primitive sites to modern fully stationed ones with gate attendants and all the comforts of home. The 25 beaches located on the lake provide thousands of visitors daily a chance to enjoy the sand and sun in a more natural setting.

It is easy to see that Buford Dam and Lake Sidney Lanier provide a host of benefits to the people of North Georgia as well as visitors from all over the United States and the world. It does not represent one particular interest but is truly a multi-purpose reservoir. Its designers saw that because of its geographic location it was possible to construct a dam that would provide a multitude of benefits and the importance of these benefits are directly linked to the overall development of the ACF River System.

Why Build A Dam?

NOTES

1. Atlanta Journal, March 29, 1953

2. Apalachicola Basin Reservoir Regulation Manual, Appendix B, Buford Dam (Lake Sidney Lanier), Chattahoochee River, Georgia, February, 1991, p. B2-3

3. Atlanta Journal and Constitution Magazine, March 4, 1956

4. Atlanta Constitution, October 9, 1947

5. Flood Plain Information book on the Chattahoochee River from Buford, Georgia to Whitesburg, Georgia. Produced from a survey made in 1973 and revised in 1982 by the Department of the Army, Mobile District Corps of Engineers, Mobile Alabama, p. 3.

6. Gwinnett Daily News, August 23, 1990

7. Atlanta Journal, March 29, 1953.

8. Gainesville Daily Times, November 13, 1949

9. Flood Plain Information book on the Chattahoochee River from Buford Dam to Whitesburg, Georgia. Produced from a survey made in 1973 and revised in 1982 by the Department of the Army, Mobile District Corps of Engineers, Mobile, Alabama, p. 2.

10. Apalachicola Basin Reservoir Regulation Manual, Appendix B, Buford Dam (Lake Sidney Lanier), Chattahoochee River, Georgia, February, 1991, p. B4-2

11. Flood Plain Information book on the Chattahoochee River from Buford Dam to Whitesburg, Georgia. Produced from a survey made in 1973 and revised in 1982 by the Department of the Army, Mobile District Corps of Engineers, Mobile, Alabama, p.2

12. Ibid., p. 6

13. Ibid., pp. 9-10

14. Ibid., p. 9

15. Ibid., pp. 9-10

16. Ibid., p. 11

17. Ibid., p. 11

18. South, Sunday, August 11, 1991

19. Atlanta Journal, March 29, 1953

20. United States House of Representatives Civil Functions Appropriation Hearings, Tuesday, March 1, 1949, pp. 479-480. Congressman James C. Davis in reference to comments made by G.U. Parker of Blountstown, Florida at a House Appropriation hearing in 1948 concerning the operation of a barge on the Chattahoochee River as a young man.

21. U.S. Army Corps of Engineers, Mobile District

22. United States House of Representatives Civil Functions Appropriation Hearings, Monday, January 25, 1954, p. 426, as reported by General Chorpening.

23. Atlanta Journal, March 29, 1953

24. Cecil Patterson, United States Army Corps of Engineers, Retired

25. Atlanta Journal, February 28, 1948

26. Ibid., March 29, 1953

27. Gainesville Daily Times, November 13, 1949

28. Atlanta Journal, June 1, 1947

29. United States Army Corps of Engineers, Buford Dam Powerhouse

30. Gwinnett Water Authority, March 4, 1991

31. Atlanta Journal, June 1, 1947

32. Apalachicola Basin Reservoir Regulation Manual, Appendix B, Buford Dam (Lake Sidney Lanier), Chattahoochee River, Georgia, February, 1991, p. B7-1.

33. 1989 Project Maps. Produced by the United States Army Corps of Engineers, R24

34. United States House of Representatives Civil Functions Appropriation Hearings, Friday, January 18, 1952, p.79 as reported by Congressman Gerald R. Ford in reference to testimony the year before about Buford Dam concerning power output of the project.

35. Apalachicola Basin Reservoir Regulation Manual, Appendix B, Buford Dam (Lake Sidney Lanier), Chattahoochee River, Georgia, February, 1991, p. B4-1

36. Gainesville Daily Times, June 18, 1957

37. Gwinnett Home Weekly, August 23, 1990

38. United States House of Representatives Civil Functions Appropriation Hearings, Friday, January 18, 1952, p.76, as reported by General Chorpening.

39. Ibid., Tuesday, April 28, 1953, p.504, as reported by Colonel Paules.

40. Estimated annual visitation records provided by the Project Management Office, Buford Dam Project, Lake Sidney Lanier, Buford, Georgia.

41. Gainesville Daily Times, January 19, 1955

42. Lakeside Magazine, September, 1996

Colonel Harding, Congressman Davis, and Mayor Hartsfield examine a model of the dam that today is exhibited in the lower lobby of the Buford Dam Powerhouse. (Courtesy William B. Hartsfield Papers, Special Collections, Robert W. Woodruff Library, Emory University)

CHAPTER TWO

EARLY PROPONENTS

Although many people and officials of almost every township, city, and county in the surrounding area of the proposed dam had dreamed, discussed, and planned for many years, for the dam and the reservoir it would create, it would take something more. To win approval the project would need the concerted effort of the U.S. Army Corps of Engineers along with federal, state, and local officials representing Georgia. Public works projects of this type and magnitude often require years of behind the scene political maneuvering before they are approved and the same amount of work or more to see any money appropriated before actual construction begins. The Buford Dam Project would experience its share of political battles both on an off Capitol Hill. For the Army's part further studies and planning would be needed as they prepared for the long ardent process of first getting the dam approved then seeing money appropriated for construction.

To list all the people directly or indirectly involved in the long slow process of getting congressional approval for the project would be impossible. Many of the more prominent state and local officials in North Georgia moved to the forefront of the fight, using both their positions and celebrated status as public officials to carry their message to their constituents. Those both in and out of the public limelight came together at backyard barbecues, luncheons, and formal dinners to discuss and many times argue for and against the development of the Chattahoochee and Chestatee Rivers. Churches, schools, front porches, city streets, local businesses to mention just a few were all favorite spots for discussions of just about every kind and number of participants, *Fig. 2-1*. It was the grass roots politics of these places that local, state and federal officials would use to first formulate a strategy then implement and promote the idea of just such a tremendous undertaking. In many instances these informal meetings would probably have as much to do with the final outcome of the project as the formal meetings held in Washington years later. Flood control, power production, water regulation and supply, pollution abatement, industrial and residential growth, and recreation were topics often times analyzed over and over. Countless numbers of barber shop chit chats, church socials, and just about anywhere two or more people could stop and talk helped solidify the one aspect of winning approval for the project that was a must, public support. This is not to say that everyone approved but without public support it is doubtful the first shovel of dirt would have ever broken the ground. It would be a tough enough fight on Capitol Hill as it was, even with the army of people who showed up year after year at the many sub-committee hearings held in both houses. Had this public support not surfaced it would have shed a serious cloud of doubt over whether Congress would have seen the project as being beneficial or worthwhile. Certainly Georgia's congressional leaders in both the House and Senate would not have gone to bat over an issue that they knew their constituents simply did not want.

The person probably involved longest in both the early struggle to win approval for the project, then laboring through many long hard years of wrestling with Capitol Hill over money, was Atlanta Mayor William Berry Hartsfield. *Fig. 2-2*. Hartsfield's influence on the project was felt at nearly every level. He was a long time Georgia politician serving first as a city alderman and then in the General Assembly before being elected mayor in 1937.[1] Even though the dam would not be located in Atlanta much of the metropolitan area would benefit enormously from the dam and reservoir it would create.

Hartsfield was a strong willed, quick witted politician who dreamed of one day making Atlanta the showcase of the South

Fig. 2-1 Starting second from left, William B. Hartsfield, Charles A. Jackson, and Colonel Mason J. Young at a dinner for the Buford Dam Project. (Courtesy Gainesville Daily Times)

Fig. 2-2 William Berry Hartsfield (Courtesy Georgia Department of Archives and History)

and beyond. One of his long term goals, that he never saw realized, was to make Atlanta a port city by making the Chattahoochee River navigable from the Gulf of Mexico to Atlanta.[2] Although he never lived to see the realization of that dream he nevertheless saw Buford Dam constructed and the effect it would ultimately have on North Georgia as well as the rest of the state. On numerous occasions, beginning in the mid 1940's and continuing until the late 1950's he made the trek to Washington, D. C. with other Georgia citizens to gain approval, then funding for construction. He had the Frederick R. Harris organization, under a commission from the City of Atlanta and Fulton County, survey the Chattahoochee River.[3] This survey would provide the mayor with the necessary information about the river and its ability to provide water and the regulation of that water for industrial and residential use. It would be one of many items used by the mayor in order to get the appropriations the project desperately needed. He would talk to anyone who would listen about the project and would do so in the form of personal visits, letters, memos, anything and everything that would get his point across.

He often times would enlist the aid of many other city and county officials in the area surrounding the proposed reservoir. In 1947 he left Atlanta with a delegation of officials for Washington, D.C. to testify before Congress about the importance of the dam. He took representatives of Fulton, DeKalb, Gwinnett, Forsyth and Hall Counties, the Atlanta Chamber of Commerce, the Atlanta Freight Bureau (now called the Georgia Freight Bureau) as well as representatives from the cities of Cumming, Lawrenceville, Norcross, Duluth, Buford, Flowery Branch and Gainesville.[4] Hartsfield would show up at these sub-committee meetings with an army of supporters to bolster the project's position. Many times there would not be enough time for the entire delegation to speak but Hartsfield would make sure that they were recognized and would request any statements they wished to make too be entered into the official record.

In 1947 he was informed by Georgia congressional leaders that trouble might develop in the House of Representatives concerning appropriations for the 1948 fiscal year. He quickly contacted Congressman Davis and Wood as well as several other city and county organizations. He personally contacted Republican leaders in Congress and received pledges of support wherever possible.[5] He asked the help of the United States Army Corps of Engineers to hold public interest information meetings in order to obtain favorable public opinion and support for the project. His efforts would often times go unrewarded as was the case when Congress failed to appropriate any money for the project that year. Nevertheless he would continue his campaign to get the necessary appropriations for construction to begin.

Hartsfield often times drew criticism from those who saw the project as simply a source of water for the City of Atlanta, which it was. A regulated water supply was a benefit of the dam and in answering such questions he once commented that "Atlanta's water supply is not an issue here. It is not water that we need but regulation of that water."[6] He was never shy about the potential benefits that would befall the city of Atlanta from the construction of Buford Dam. At the same time though he was not above pointing out the other varied benefits the project would provide to other regions both north and south of Atlanta. In testimony before the Senate in March, 1948

Hartsfield stressed this same point. He spoke of the House's elimination of the funds for the project because it was viewed as an important water benefit for the City of Atlanta and that they (Atlanta) should share the cost of its construction. The mayor was quick to show the project's other advantages such as flood control, navigation, and power production. "The most intelligent thing Congress can do for the South is to put us in a position to help ourselves."[7]

In January of that same year in testimony before the House Sub-Committee on Appropriations he spoke of his city and its contribution to the South offering a bit of historical irony. "General Sherman recognized it (Atlanta) as [the great distribution center of the South] 75 years ago when he fought so hard to get it and was so full of jubilation when he burned it. He said he had done something which would break the whole backbone of the Confederacy when he took Atlanta and he was right. And the thing General Sherman wanted then is the thing that made us the great city we are today......We are dependent on the river today. With the villages in suburban areas, we need it for our water supply. Let me give you one little statement to impress you with the desperate necessity of this thing..... In 1925, we had a great drought in the South. That river (Chattahoochee) fell to 132 cubic feet per second by Atlanta. Gentlemen, we are taking out of that river, in our peak loads now, more water than went by it in that 1925 drought."[8]

In April, 1949 he again led a large contingent to Washington, D.C. in order to obtain $3,000,000.00 in federal appropriations for the project. Once again he did not come to Capitol Hill alone. Hartsfield and a delegation of North Georgians appeared before a Senate sub-committee on appropriations to testify on behalf of the project receiving allocations for start of construction. H. Paul Hover, Weldon Archer, H. Jack Turner, and Stanley Allen, all from Buford; Roy P. Otwell, of Cumming; Lester W. Hosch, of Gainesville; Jess Baggett, of Lawrenceville; and John M. Cooper, representing the Atlanta Freight Bureau and the Atlanta Chamber of Commerce, accompanied the mayor.[9] He spoke in length that day about the benefits the project would provide. He informed the committee that the Buford Dam Project would be the key to flood control and navigation on the Chattahoochee River. He had done his homework well as the Jim Woodruff Project was already under construction and it would depend on Buford Dam to provide the necessary regulate water flow to operate at maximum efficiency. He presented the committee

Fig. 2-3 Copy of a November 29, 1948 issue of the Atlanta Journal. (Reprinted with permission from The Atlanta Journal and The Atlanta Constitution. Reproduction does not imply endorsement.)

with a folder of newspaper articles, one of which was a copy of a November 29th issue of the Atlanta Journal. *Fig. 2-3*. It displayed a picture of flooding along the river. The headlines read "Flood Damages to Hit High Figures".[10] "Gentlemen, I should like to show you the present interest of Atlanta from the standpoint of flood control. Here is the Chattahoochee River the last of November. Here at the bottom are pictures of the Chattahoochee River immediately outside of Atlanta..... As a result of this uncontrolled flow on the river, we have not a single water using industry along the river except a steam plant of the Georgia Power

Fig. 2-4 Hartsfield visiting construction work at Buford Dam. (Courtesy U.S. Army Corps of Engineers, Mobile District)

Fig. 2-5 Letter from Hartsfield to Burton Bell concerning a meeting on Buford Dam. (Courtesy U.S. Army Corps of Engineers, Mobile District)

Company which furnished current to metropolitan Atlanta. Gentlemen, last year that power plant was nearly put out of commission. There it sits on the flooded Chattahoochee River. The water in that power plant is so undependable that before this plant was built the power company came to the city of Atlanta to buy from us purified water on account of the changing characteristics of the water in the unregulated river".[11]

Mayor Hartsfield used political savvy and tireless efforts in promoting the construction of Buford Dam. He was the unofficial orchestrator of the behind the scenes events that eventually led to the successful start and completion of the project.

The project would also need the support of Georgia's congressional leaders in both houses. In the United States House of Representatives James C. Davis, the 5th District Congressman from Stone Mountain, *Fig. 2-6*, took the point in his own chamber as early as 1947 trying to get that body to appropriate money for the project. Davis who was a member of the House Post Office, Civil Service, and District of Columbia Committees represented the people of Atlanta and the surrounding area. The site eventually chosen by the United States Army Corps of Engineers for the dam was not even in his district and had it been, he might have had more than just a water interest in the project. Even though, the Buford site was still of great interest to his constituents and gained his undying support and efforts. Davis could see the effects the dam would have on the future water supply and growth of metropolitan Atlanta. "This project is needed urgently; the rapid growth of the Atlanta region will not permit postponement."[12]

Once congressional approval was given Davis moved quickly to use early appropriations for planning as a wedge to open wide the door for further allocations. He knew that initial fights over funding would not only benefit the Buford Project but other Georgia projects as well. Davis was also keenly aware that early monies were often times the most important. Funding for the project would be much easier once initial construction began. Keeping local Georgia officials well informed as to when appropriation sub-committee meetings would be held was an important part of the process that would eventually lead to construction of the dam. As a member of the United States House of Representatives he had a unique point of perspective from which to view the congressional process testifying on many different occasions before both houses in support of the project. He came to Washington, D.C. with other Georgians to

Fig. 2-6 James C. Davis, 5th District Representative. (Courtesy James C. Davis Papers, Special Collection, Robert W. Woodruff Library, Emory University)

lobby for both approval and construction appropriations. In 1947 Davis spearheaded an effort to obtain congressional allocations of $250,000.00 for advanced planning being completed by the United States Army Corps of Engineers.[13] In December of that same year he asked the President's Budget Commission for $1,000,000.00 to complete planning for the dam.[14] His requests for proposed appropriations were not always greeted enthusiastically, even in his own House where it would seem the biggest obstacle to the entire process lay. In early 1948 the House of Representatives passed an appropriations bill for fiscal year 1949 that had severely cut appropriations for other Georgia public works projects while knifing out the Buford Dam Project altogether. The Truman administration had recommended only $67,000.00 and that was for planning and not much else. The Senate on the other hand had allocated $1,000,000.00 for the

Fig. 2-7 Davis, second from left, with other visitors at the construction site. (Courtesy U.S. Army Corps of Engineers, Mobile District)

project and Davis had initiated a strategy that would soon become a pattern.[15] Realizing that his own House was not going to provide the money the project needed to begin construction he turned to the Senate and enlisted the help of Georgia's two long standing Senators, Walter F. George and Richard B. Russell Jr. Davis appeared before the Senate Appropriations Sub-Committee and requested that body to allocate $3,000,000.00 to start construction. It was his hope that the Senate could reverse both the House and Administration's stance and allocate the funds needed. Davis knew as with most appropriations this would involve a Senate-House Conference Committee. Here the two Houses would have to iron out the differences in funds allocated, which in the House's case was zero. It is important to note that here you see the emergence of Georgia's Junior Senator, Richard B. Russell Jr. who was a

Fig. 2-8 John S. Wood, 9th District Representative. (Courtesy of the Library of Congress)

member of the conference committee.[16]

John S. Wood, **Fig. 2-8**, who was the 9th District Representative would have limited influence in the early approval rounds on Capitol Hill but would testify, in person and through letters of support, on several occasions during the appropriations hearings. Wood represented the people where the proposed project was located and in early 1949 he caught considerable flack for not even being present at the Buford Dam Appropriation Hearings held by the Senate that same year. He was present at similar hearings held in the Senate in January, 1948 and testified before both House and Senate sub-committees on several occasions after initial appropriations were made during the 1950 fiscal year. An explanation for this contradiction may be found in part in that major early opposition for the approval of the project came from the Gainesville-Hall County area which represented a large portion of his constituents.

Senators Richard B. Russell Jr., **Fig. 2-9** and Walter F. George, **Fig. 2-10**, were important figures in the project's early congressional struggles. Senator Russell, Georgia's Junior Senator, was an immensely popular politician who would obtain national prominence when running for the Democratic nomination for President of the United States in the mid 1950's, was a

Fig. 2-9 Richard B. Russell Jr. (Courtesy Congressional Research Service, Library of Congress)

Fig. 2-10 Walter F. George (Courtesy Congressional Research Service, Library of Congress)

member of the Senate Sub-Committee which would recommend the funds for proceeding with the development of the project. He was also a member of the conference committee that would work out the differences between the House and Senate appropriation figures that would provide initial funding for the start of construction. He would shoulder more of the responsibility for seeing the project through the political process because it was located in the northern region of Georgia. Senator George's influence in the process was probably collegial in nature in that there had been a long standing tradition in Georgia politics that the state have a senator representing South Georgia and one representing North Georgia. Like his colleague in the House, Senator Russell was in the forefront of the congressional battles for the project. He was able to use his political influence, knowledge of rules in the Senate, and many years of service to his advantage when it came to guiding bills through the complicated process of committee work and then on to the floor of the Senate for approval. But it was his behind the scenes work that was a plus for the project.

When the Army Civil Functions Bill, of which Senator Russell was a member, came to the sub-committee he was able to gain committee approval of $2,000,000.00 for the dam. As mentioned earlier the House of Representatives had failed to allocate any money for the project and at the same time had cut millions of dollars from other Georgia projects. Russell found himself on the conference committee that would hammer out the differences between the two house versions of basically the same bill. This joint conference committee began holding meetings in the early summer months of 1949. Representative Clarence Cannon, a Democrat from Missouri who was Chairman of the House Appropriations Committee that had slashed money for the Buford Dam Project to begin with, didn't want to change the House version of the bill. He wanted to hold a tough line on increasing expenditures above present levels even though realistically he probably felt he would have to eventually relinquish the reins just a bit. There were a number of different projects located all over the United States that were up for debate and the focus of the committee's work for most of the summer. The Buford Dam Project just happened to be one of them and with Senator Russell serving on the committee it appeared as if it was going to be a long hot and very taxing session. At one point in the proceedings it was reported that the committee had run into an impasse. Over the long summer months it looked as if very little was going to come out of the committee. Cannon was holding firm to his guns and refusing to increase a penny above what had already been approved. He wanted funding for all projects, not just Buford, to be kept to a minimum and for most of the remaining months of the summer it appeared he was going to get his way. Senator Russell would later recall that toward the end of the process very few of the conference members were even on speaking terms with Congressman Cannon. However, one member, Albert J. Engels, was and Senator Russell knew it. Russell had on occasions the opportunity to talk to Engels. It was his hope that he could get Engels to speak to Cannon and perhaps soften his position. In all likelihood Russell knew there was no way he was going to get anywhere close to the $2,000,000.00 that the Senate had appropriated for Buford Dam but it is just as likely that he knew this from the beginning. The Senate's version of the bill was so high because the House had cut funding altogether. It is here that you begin to see just a glimpse of the type of political maneuvering that was a Russell trademark. Russell with Engel's help was able to get Cannon to agree to allocate $750,000.00 for the Buford Dam Project as part of an overall $30,000,000.00 package for Georgia's public works projects.[17]

Acquiring funds for the project was never an easy task for Senator Russell, not even in his beloved Senate. At one time in the appropriations process the junior senator charged the Republican majority of the Senate of throwing out the appropriations for "political reasons". He even threatened to offer an amendment on the floor of the Senate, in order that the proposal be restored.[18] It is doubtful that this was truly a serious consideration but rather a ploy on the Senator's part to bring home his point on the matter. At the dedication years later he would again echo similar sentiments concerning the general view held by many in Congress concerning domestic versus international public works projects.

There were many other people involved in the work that eventually culminated in the approval and then construction of Buford Dam. The vast majority of those involved were local city and county officials, businessmen and women and just average citizens of the many communities that lived and worked in the area. In these cities and counties a few would move to the forefront and take on more active roles. In Gwinnett County

Fig. 2-11 Weldon Gardner (Courtesy Mrs. Weldon Gardner)

there was Weldon Gardner, a Buford Insurance Agent; L.D. Ewing, of Norcross and Secretary of the Gwinnett County Chamber of Commerce; County Commissioners Weldon Archer; Paul Dover and Stanley Allen; Jess Baggett of Lawrenceville; Jack Turner, Buford City Manager. Atlanta and Fulton County had their representatives John Cooper and Eugene Hart, of the Atlanta Freight Bureau (now called the Georgia Freight Bureau); Elbert Tuttle; Harry Sommer; Frank Shaw of the Atlanta Chamber of Commerce and Paul Weir, Manager of the Atlanta Water Works. Forsyth County saw Roy P. Otwell, Mayor of Cumming lend his communities support. J. Larry Kleckley and Lester W. Hosch represented Gainesville-Hall County.

The list of local individuals who

Fig. 2-12 Weldon Gardner, Charles Jackson, and Paul Weir at the construction site. (Courtesy William B. Hartsfield Papers, Special Collections, Robert W. Woodruff Library, Emory University)

Fig. 2-13 L.D. Ewing (Courtesy Mrs. Jo Ann Weathers)

Fig. 2-14 Jess Baggett (Courtesy Joe Baggett)

Fig. 2-15 Eugene Hart (Courtesy Georgia Freight Bureau Inc.)

traveled to Washington, D.C. over the years to testify before the House of Representatives and Senate acknowledged the concerted effort put forth by a large number of people. Frank Shaw, Atlanta Chamber of Commerce; Bob Underwood, Pine Mountain Granite Company; Wiley Moore, Wolford Oil Company; English Clark, Atlanta Hardwood Company; Lester W. Hosch, Hall County Citizens Committee on Buford Dam; J. Larry Kleckley, Gainesville; Roy P. Otwell, Mayor of Cumming; F.P. Dover, Gwinnett County Commissioner; Weldon Archer, Gwinnett County Commissioner; Stanley Allen, Gwinnett County Commissioner; John M. Cooper, Atlanta Freight Bureau and Chamber of Commerce; Douglas Wood, Atlanta; Paul Weir, Manager Atlanta Water Works; Jimmy Vickers, Atlanta; T.O. Galloway, Upper Chattahoochee Development Association; Representative E.L. Forrester, Georgia; Weldon Gardner, Upper Chattahoochee Development Association; Jess Baggett, Lawrenceville; Julius McGurdy, DeKalb County; A.L. Clark, Buford City School Superintendent; C.B. Culpepper, Atlanta Freight Bureau; Fred Moore, Atlanta Chamber of Commerce; H. Jack Turner, Buford City Manager; Lionel Drake; Drew Hamilton; Winfield Rowe; Representative J.L. Picher, Georgia; Arthur L. Harris, Atlanta Freight Bureau; R.S. Lynch, Chattahoochee Valley Development Committee; Edmond F. Jared, Gainesville Chamber of Commerce; Robert M. Holder, Atlanta; Sylvan Meyer, Gainesville Daily Times; Joe Cheeley, Buford.[19]

Many of the same people who helped see the realization of the project were also part of a movement that saw the creation of the Upper Chattahoochee Development Association or UCDA for short. Although this organization was not directly linked to

Fig. 2-16 Roy P. Otwell (Courtesy Jack Baggett Jr.)

Fig. 2-17 J. Larry Kleckley (Courtesy U.S. Army Corps of Engineers, Mobile District)

Fig. 2-18 Lester W. Hosch (Courtesy Chestatee Regional Library)

Fig. 2-19 (L-R) L.Y. Irvin of Cornelia; Weldon Gardner of Buford and President of the Upper Chattahoochee Development Association; W.P. Lee, Vice President of the DeKalb County Chamber of Commerce; L.D. Ewing, Secretary and a future President of the UCDA and Clark Harrison of the DeKalb County Chamber of Commerce look over a drawing of the proposed Peachtree Industrial Boulevard extension. This photograph was taken at the General Motors Assembly Plant in Doraville, Georgia where representatives of the 10 counties northeast of Atlanta that made up the UCDA met. (Courtesy Mrs. Weldon Gardner)

the project itself it was no coincidence that its formation came into being as construction on the project began. The UCDA developed out of the concern for the transformation this area of North Georgia was soon to experience. The organization held its first meeting at Buford High School on Thursday, April 27, 1950 representing Stephens, Habersham, Hall, Gwinnett, White, Lumpkin, Dawson, Forsyth, and DeKalb Counties.[20] Fulton County would later join the organization making it ten counties strong. It was officially incorporated in Hall county on Wednesday, July 1, 1953.[21] Weldon Gardner of Buford would serve as the first president. He had been a long time proponent of the Buford Dam Project and wanted to see the UCDA as having an active role in development of the North Georgia region. L.D. Ewing of Norcross was the organizations first secretary-treasurer and would later serve as the president. At first there were nine vice presidents representing each of the counties that made up the UCDA (ten when Fulton County became a member).[22]

The goals of the UCDA were varied but primarily they wanted to see the resources of

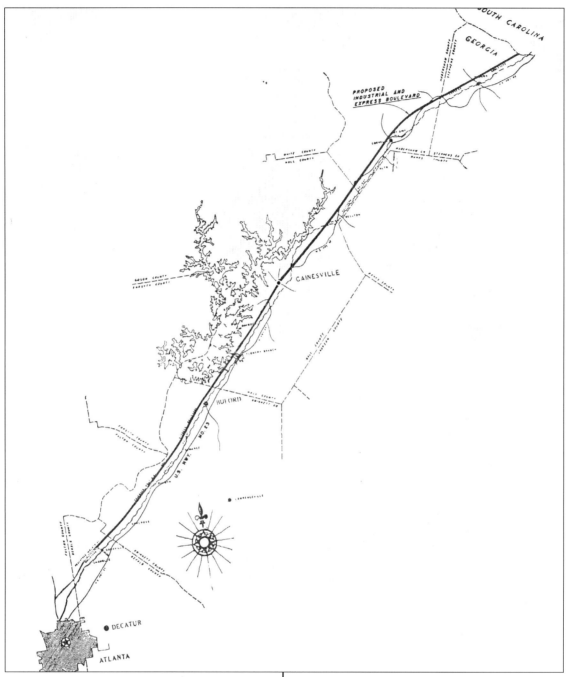

Fig. 2-20 Proposed highway extension running east of Lake Lanier that would someday become Peachtree Industrial Boulevard and McEver Road. (Courtesy U.S. Army Corps of Engineers, Mobile District)

the area, that would increase in years to come as a direct result of the Buford Dam Project, developed for future generations to enjoy. Developing the natural resources of the Buford Dam Project and the lake it would create was a high priority but the organization also wanted to see the surrounding areas, that would benefit from the reservoirs existence, developed. One of the first areas of concern was the extension of the four lane highway from Doraville to Gainesville, *Fig. 2-20,*. The association eventually wanted this extension to reach all the way to South Carolina which gives you some indication as to the long range goals and planning they wished to accomplish for the area in the years to come.[23] During the construction years the UCDA would hold its annual meetings on the project in order to heighten support and interest in the organization's activities and goals. It would continue to function for nearly forty years until it was administratively dissolved on Friday, April 29, 1988.[24]

NOTES

1. Coleman, K., & Gurr, C. S. (1983). Dictionary of Georgia Biography. Athens: The University of Georgia Press.

2. Atlanta Journal, March 29, 1953

3. Atlanta Constitution, 1947

4. Atlanta Journal, June 2, 1947

5. Ibid, July 23, 1947

6. Ibid.

7. Atlanta Journal, March 17, 1948

8. United States House of Representatives Civil Functions Subcommittee Appropriation Hearings, January, 1948

9. Atlanta Constitution, April 20, 1949

10. Atlanta Journal, April 20, 1949

11. United States House of Representatives Civil Functions Sub-Committee Appropriation Hearings, April, 1949

12. Atlanta Constitution, 1947

13. Ibid., August 4, 1947

14. Ibid., December 11, 1947

15. Atlanta Journal, April 7, 1948

16. Ibid., April 20, 1949

17. Gainesville Daily Time, 1957

18. Ibid.

19. Witnesses appearing before House and Senate Appropriation Sub-Committee Hearings between 1948-1957.

20. Untitled newspaper article circa 1950

21. Secretary of State's Office

22. Untitled newspaper article circa 1950

23. Ibid.

24. Secretary of State's Office

Early appropriations were for advanced planning and construction including 400,000.00 just for the design of the powerhouse.

CHAPTER THREE

APPROPRIATIONS

The U.S. Capitol Building where approval, then funding for the project was obtained in the late 1940's. (Courtesy Library of Congress)

When the United States Army Corps of Engineers looked to the job of building Buford Dam they had become more than familiar with such public works projects. It was not the first, nor would it be the last dam they would build. In 1948 it was estimated that along with the 71 dams and other water projects that they were already involved in they had drawn up plans for 130 more.[1] The fact was they were very busy developing rivers and waterways all over the United States. This experience with public works projects also gave them a special insight into the world of congressional appropriations.

Funding for Buford Dam would have to come from Congress and getting them to authorize something is not the same thing as getting them to pay for it. Often times appropriations lagged many years behind approval and the legislation being proposed here, of which Buford Dam was a part, was no different. River and harbor legislation passed over the years, as well as post war legislation such as the River and Harbor Acts of 1945 and 1946, would be the tools used to push the necessary appropriations through Capitol Hill. It would be a long, hard fought battle for many years before Congress approved the River and Harbor and Flood Control Appropriations Bill of 1949. This bill would allocate $30,000,000.00 to projects in Georgia with Buford Dam receiving $750,000.00 of the money appropriated to begin construction.[2]

Original estimates for the dam's cost were put at $17,000,000.00. In early 1947 the cost escalated to $22,000,000.00. That same year plans for constructing a concrete gravity dam were scraped in favor of an earth dam.[3] The rationale for the change was that the materials needed to construct an earth dam were in great abundance and in close proximity to the dam site. The switch in design along with other changes pushed the cost to $42,000,000.00.* The United States Army Corps of Engineers explained that the increased cost was not solely due to changes in design. Apparently, inflationary factors played a heavy hand in driving the cost of the project up. When original plans were put together the estimates were based on the belief that construction costs for materials and labor would slide back to or somewhat higher than pre-war costs. Unfortunately, this never happened and when designs were altered to add better safety features and higher outputs of power production along with the aforementioned factors the price tag for the project had jumped considerably.[4]

In 1947 $250,000.00 was advanced by Congress for planning only, not construction. This money was used for core drilling samples and engineering surveys. A year later another $400,000.00 was provided for advanced planning.[5] Even though the project received money for advanced planning in 1947 and 1948 there were no specific allocations for the project during those years. Advanced monies had to be obtained for early planning by using funds from projects that had already been approved and financed by Congress. This procedure was explained in part by Colonel Bernard L. Robinson, **Fig. 3-1**, then the South Atlantic Division Chief at the time the United States Army was asking Congress for construction money. The following excerpt appeared in the Gainesville (GA) Daily Times in November, 1949.

Fig. 3-1 Colonel Bernard L. Robinson (Courtesy Office of History, U.S. Army Corps of Engineers)

"Obtaining money for construction is a terribly complicated procedure. Request for funds often overlap in the Budget Bureau with appropriation bills often in preparation before earlier requests are approved. Civil function appropriations are drawn up with a ceiling limitation forcing money for new projects under construction under the ceiling and money for new projects (like Buford Dam) over the ceiling. Until 1949 Buford Dam was considered an over-ceiling project as it was sent to Congress without the approval of the Bureau of Budget which is in effect the President of the United States since it serves as an adjunct of the executive branch..... Money for over-ceiling projects must come from funds allotted for projects underway, which are correspondingly delayed."[6]

Fig. 3-2 General Raymond Wheeler (Courtesy Office of History, U.S. Army Corps of Engineers)

---

* Even with the inflated cost there was still an estimated 2 million dollar savings in building an earth dam over a concrete structure.

Fig. 3-3 Colonel Walter K. Wilson (Courtesy U.S. Army Corps of Engineers, Mobile District)

In 1949 when Congress appropriated $750,000.00 to the Buford Dam Project as part of the Rivers and Harbors and Flood Control Appropriations Bill this money was for the fiscal year ending June 30, 1950. It was for advanced planning and start of construction.[7] Half of the $750,000.00 appropriation was used for planning the other half for construction of saddle dike no.3 and the spillway, *Fig. 3-4* and *Fig. 3-5*,

Fig. 3-4 Saddle dike no.3 (Courtesy U.S. Army Corps of Engineers, Mobile District)

Fig. 3-5 Spillway (Courtesy U.S. Army Corps of Engineers, Mobile District)

both located southeast of the main earth dam site.[8]

This is how the project acquired money for advanced planning which was needed to gather enough intelligent information and statistics together to get Congress to allocate money for its construction.

Congressional appropriations are based on fiscal, not calender years. A fiscal year is any twelve month period at the end of which business accounts are balanced. The project was not given a blanket amount of money to cover the entire construction cost. Each year the Department of the Army had to present its request for money to carry the cost of construction on this project, as well as other projects, to the next fiscal year. Each house would have a sub-committee of its Appropriations Committee hear requests for money. These sub-committees would report their findings back to the committee for the whole, with recommendations, if any. This is basically the method used in initiating funding although the actual process is somewhat more lengthy. Hearings, in which members of Congress, state and local officials, interested parties, and citizens could attend, were held by these sub-committees. As with most sub-committee meetings on the project congressional leaders in Georgia would organize interested officials and individuals to appear before the sub-committee armed with statistics, studies, and other information in order to promote their cause.

It was estimated at the time that approximately four percent of the total cost of the project, which equated to roughly $1,667,000.00, would be spent on planning; $141,000.00 for surveys; $188,000.00 for geological borings, test pits, soil analysis, and rock test; $118,000.00 for consultants for power investigation, electrical studies, and special studies on powerhouse; $45,000.00 for plans and drawings; $400,000.00 for powerhouse design; and $775,000.00 for detailed specifications.[9]

In 1949 the fight was still ongoing in Congress for appropriations to begin construction. The 1950 appropriations bill for the United States Senate was requesting $2,261,000.00 for the start of construction on the project. The Truman Administration had only placed $67,000.00 in its budget and that was for planning while the United

States House of Representatives appropriated no money at all.[10] In all likelihood the only reason the Senate appropriated such a large amount of money was to force the House of Representatives into a compromise. Early on they set a pattern of appropriating large sums of money for the project even when the House of Representatives' appropriations were little, if any. It would take the Senate-House Conference Committee, as mentioned in Chapter Two, to allocate the $750,000.00 needed to begin work.

In 1950 when Congress held its hearings on Buford Dam, work on the project had not started. The ground breaking, *Fig. 3-6*, work on the first saddle

Fig. 3-6 Ground Breaking Ceremony, March 1, 1950. (Courtesy U.S. Army Corps of Engineers)

dike, *Fig. 3-4*, and spillway, *Fig. 3-5* were several months away.

The 1951 appropriations again saw the United States Senate allocate $900,000.00. The Truman Administration placed $1,000,000.00 in its budget for the project while the United States House of Representatives allocated $400,000.00.[11] The fact that the two houses and administration were appropriating such vastly different amounts of money was not unusual. Even today appropriations are rarely, if ever, the same. It is generally conceded that bills of this nature, involving financing, will have to go through a conference committee in order to arrive at a figure both houses and even the administration can agree on. The congressional appropriation for the 1951 fiscal year was $900,000.00.[12]

In 1951 work on the project's saddle dikes, *Fig. 3-7*, were underway while excavation of the forebay, *Fig. 3-8*, and the tailrace, *Fig. 3-9*, would begin. The 1952 appropriation for Buford Dam was

Fig. 3-7 Saddle dike no. 2A in Forsyth County. (Courtesy U.S. Army Corps of Engineers, Mobile District)

Fig. 3-8 Forebay excavation begins. (Courtesy U.S. Army Corps of Engineers, Mobile District)

Fig. 3-9 Tailrace excavation begins. (Courtesy U.S. Army Corps of Engineers, Mobile District)

$500,000.00 but Congress had to provide for a stop-gap emergency allocation of $900,000.00 in October, 1951. Even this measure looked as if it would be too little too late. Charles Jackson, *Fig. 3-10*, the

Fig. 3-10 Charles Jackson, (far left), the resident engineer for the project is explaining a model of the forebay and tailrace cuts to visitors. (Courtesy U.S. Army Corps of Engineers, Mobile District)

project's resident engineer could not see work continuing much pass early 1952.

Laborers were working two ten hour shifts with the aid of flood light towers and would continue until the funds ran out.[13] By January 25, 1952 Congress had still failed to allocate enough money to continue work on the project until July Ist when fiscal appropriations for 1953 would be made. It was estimated at the time that about thirty days of work, if construction remained at its present rate, was left before construction would have to halt. An article appearing in the Atlanta Constitution on Friday

TLANTA CONSTITUTION

For 84 Years the South's Standard Newspaper

ATLANTA (2), GA., FRIDAY MORNING, JANUARY 25, 1952

Buford Dam Work Halt Imminent

Work on Buford Dam must be stopped within 30 days due to depletion of funds, U. S. Army Engineers spokesman said Friday.

Notice came from Col. W. K. Wilson Jr., district engineer in Mobile, Ala., as Georgia leaders attempted to prevent threatened stoppage of construction on the $42,000,000 Chattahoochee River dam.

Col. Wilson said contractors had been notified work will cease.

Only about one-third of the contractors' $2,832,767.75 worth of work is completed, the engineer said.

COMING TOO LATE

A new budget submitted Monday to Congress by President Truman carried a $3,000,000 item for the Buford work, but even if it is appropriated, this money will not become available until July 1.

Sen. Richard B. Russell, Rep. James C. Davis, Mayor Hartsfield, and Weldon Gardner of Buford, president of the Upper Chattahoochee River Development Association, Thursday were reportedly throwing their influence into an effort to make it possible for U. S. Army Engineers to authorize contractors to proceed until Congress can act.

RUSSELL AT WORK

Hartsfield said Russell had promised he would seek sanction from chairmen of the House and Senate appropriations committees for continuance of the work pend-

Continued on Page 14, Column 4

BUFORD

Continued From Page 1

ing action on the President's recommendation.

The mayor said Russell is attempting to get committee chairmen to advise Army engineers to transfer funds from other projects to insure that work on Buford Dam will go on.

Col. C. K. Harding, division engineer for the South Atlantic states, with Atlanta headquarters, warned Thursday that cancellation of the present contract might prove costly.

"I would like to see work carried through without interruption," he said. "We have a good contract at a favorable price now; if it was canceled I believe it would cost more to get a new contract because the work is now being done in rock."

Colonel Harding explained that if funds stop the contractor can void the contract. He added that officials of Groves, Lundin & Cox, the contractors, indicated they could not proceed with the work without pay as the construction progresses.

Fig. 3-11 Article appearing in the Atlanta Constitution, January 25, 1952. (Reprinted with permission from The Atlanta Journal and The Atlanta Constitution. Reproduction does not imply endorsement.)

morning, January 25, 1952, ***Fig. 3-11***, explained the problem the project was having over funding. Contractors were informed of the possibility that funding might run short before Congress would give an emergency allocation. They (contractors) voluntarily agreed to continue work. In actuality though, it would be safe to assume that the contractors realized that money would continue to be provided. They were not taking much of a risk by continuing on with their work. From this point on, and until 1957 when heavy construction on the project began to wind down, the amount of money the United States Army requested and received each year would increase in proportion to the work being completed.

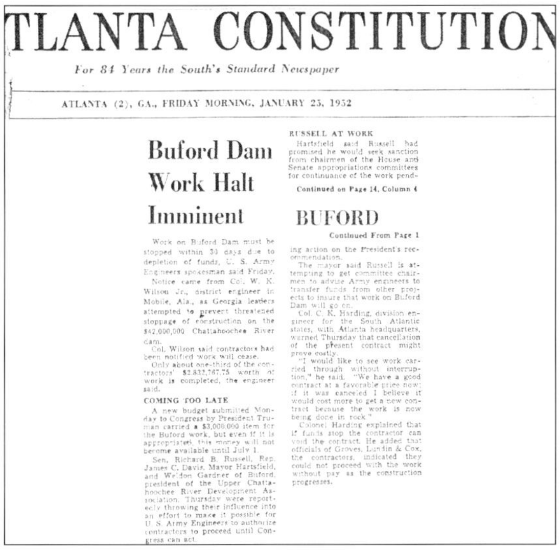

The 1953 appropriation jumped to $3,000,000.00 as construction on the project began to swing into full gear.[14] As in previous years the United States Army Corps of Engineers went before each house to lobby for the money they would need to continue work. 1952 saw the completion of the saddle dikes, ***Fig. 3-12***, while the

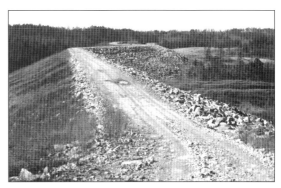

Fig. 3-12 Saddle dike no.3 (Courtesy U.S. Army Corps of Engineers, Mobile District)

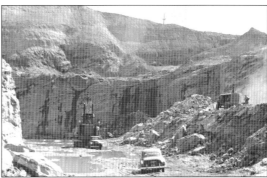

Fig. 3-13 Forebay excavation continues. (Courtesy U.S. Army Corps of Engineers, Mobile District)

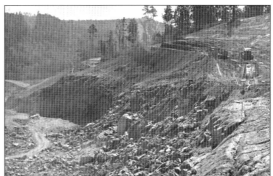

Fig. 3-14 Tailrace excavation continues. (Courtesy U.S. Army Corps of Engineers, Mobile District)

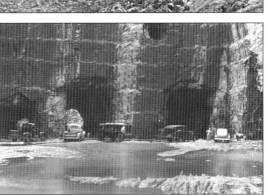

Fig. 3-15 Tunneling of penstocks and sluice has been completed. (Courtesy U.S. Army Corps of Engineers, Mobile District)

forebay and tailrace cuts, ***Fig. 3-13*** and ***Fig. 3-14***, were beginning to take on their distinctive outlines in the rock. By early 1953 excavation for the forebay and tailrace were completed as tunneling of the penstocks and sluice began, ***Fig. 3-15***. On June 24, 1953 the United States Senate approved $8,000,000.00 for the continuation of the project. Earlier, on May

22nd, the United States House of Representatives had approved an appropriation that was $3,000,000.00 less. President Eisenhower's budget request was $500,000.00 over the Senate's appropriation.[15] House and Senate conferees hammered out the differences and on Monday, July 27, 1953 President Eisenhower signed a $440,093,600.00 appropriation bill for the United States Army Corps of Engineers for fiscal year 1954.[16] The Buford Dam Project was allocated $7,500,000.00 of the total appropriation.[17]

In late 1953 budgetary reductions in expenditures during the 1954 fiscal year were ordered. Brigadier General Holle who was the South Atlantic Division Chief explained that the ordered reductions would force the postponement, for at least several months, of awarding contracts. This threatened the delay of the earth dam's construction. It was estimated by the United States Army that a 38 percent cut in money actually allocated might delay construction of the dam for a year, until 1955.[18] By October 1953, Brigadier General Holle had been given the go ahead to continue with construction as had originally been scheduled. The apparent change of heart by the United States Army was due to a new allotment of $2,000,000.00 for the present fiscal year. This came after an apparent restudy of the Chattahoochee project by Congress which probably involved some last minute political maneuvering.[19]

Work on the earth dam begin in 1954, *Fig. 3-16*, as the old river channel was altered to build the mammoth earth

Fig. 3-16 Earth dam construction begins. (Courtesy U.S. Army Corps of Engineers, Mobile District)

Fig. 3-17 Intake construction begins. (Courtesy U.S. Army Corps of Engineers, Mobile District)

Fig. 3-18 Stilling basin construction. (Courtesy U.S. Army Corps of Engineers, Mobile District)

structure. Early in the year intake construction in the forebay, *Fig. 3-17*, and stilling basin framing in the tailrace, *Fig. 3-18*, were well underway.

On February 9, 1954 it was reported in the Atlanta Constitution that the United States Senate appropriations sub-committee had directed the United States Army to determine how much money could be saved by slowing down work on the project. They (United States Army) had gone before Congress to ask for an $11,000,000.00 appropriation for the 1955 fiscal year. They certainly did not want to hear about any work slow down and to add insult to injury the Budget Bureau had only asked for $5,800,000.00 for the same fiscal year. Atlanta Mayor William Hartsfield felt this type of hand to mouth funding would not do. As he had done before he again enlisted the help of Georgia's congressional leaders as well as a delegation of citizens and local officials to go to Washington, D.C. to fight for the $11,000,000.00. Making the trip to Washington with Hartsfield was Frank Shaw, of the Atlanta Freight Bureau and Chamber of Commerce; C.B. Culpepper, of the Atlanta Freight Bureau; Arthur L. Harris of the Atlanta Paper Company; Robert Holder, an Atlanta industrial real estate developer; Robert S. Lynch, President of the Atlanta Steel Corporation; Fred Moore, of the Atlanta Chamber of Commerce; Sylvan Meyer, of Gainesville; T.O. Galloway, President of the Upper Chattahoochee Development Association; Weldon Gardner, of Buford and Weldon Archer, Chairman of the Gwinnett County Board of Commissioners. This delegation went before both houses to lobby for their cause and for construction to continue on schedule.[20]

The United States House of Representatives appropriated $5,000,000.00 while the United States Senate approved $9,500,000.00.[21] On June 21, 1954 House and Senate conferees appropriated $9,300,000.00 which was not the original $11,000,000.00 requested but was considerably more than the $5,800,000.00 proposed by the United States House of Representatives and Budget Bureau. On June 30, 1954 President Eisenhower removed any road blocks on the slow down of construction when he signed the multi-million dollar United States Army Appropriations Bill which included $9,300,000.00 for Buford Dam for the 1955 fiscal year.[22]

In 1955 work on the main earth dam was nearing completion, *Fig. 3-19*. The

Fig. 3-19 Main earth dam nears completion. (Courtesy U.S. Army Corps of Engineers, Mobile District)

Fig. 3-20 Intake structure is just about finished. (Courtesy U.S. Army Corps of Engineers, Mobile District)

Fig. 3-21 Powerhouse construction begins. (Courtesy U.S. Army Corps of Engineers, Mobile District)

Fig. 3-22 Bridge and highway relocation and construction is underway. (Courtesy U.S. Army Corps of Engineers, Mobile District)

intake structure was completed, *Fig. 3-20* and construction of the powerhouse would begin, *Fig. 3-21*. Bridge and highway relocation and construction was also beginning, *Fig. 3-22*.

The 1956 appropriation of $11,830,000.00 was the largest single appropriation to date and no appropriation afterwards would be as large.[23] In January, 1955 the President's budget submitted to Congress recommended $11,830,000.00 for the 1956 fiscal year.[24] On June 17, 1955 the United States House of Representatives Appropriations Committee recommended only $10,000,000.00 for the project but reversed its decision and voted back the $1,830,000.00 that had been cut from the President's budget proposal. On Thursday, June 30, 1955 the United States Senate Appropriations Committee went along with the House and Administration and allocated $11,830,000.00.[25] At the time the 1956 fiscal year appropriations were being considered heavy construction on the project was coming to a close.

The majority of the work on the project was coming to an end in 1956. The main earth dam was completed, *Fig. 3-23* and the gates of the intake structure would

Fig. 3-23 Main earth dam is completed. (Courtesy U.S. Army Corps of Engineers, Mobile District)

Fig. 3-25 Bridge and highway relocation and construction draws to a close. (Courtesy U.S. Army Corps of Engineers, Mobile District)

Fig. 3-24 Powerhouse nears completion. (Courtesy U.S. Army Corps of Engineers, Mobile District)

be closed on February 1st beginning the slow process of creating Lake Lanier. The powerhouse, **Fig. 3-24**, as well as bridge and highway relocation and construction, **Fig. 3-25**, were nearing completion.

The 1957 appropriation was for $4,553,000.00, 1958 for $572,000.00, and 1959 for $2,560,613.00.[26] The 1960 appropriation was $1,524,613.00 and that same year the Annual Report of the Chief of Engineers noted on the Buford Dam Project the following statistics. As of the end of the 1960 fiscal year, June 30, 1960, the total appropriations for the project were $44,009,182.00. Total cost as of this date was $44,765,095.00 with $44,009,182.00 being spent on new work and $755,913.00 on operation and maintenance. Fifty-six percent of the project's total cost or $25,068,453.00 was spent on design and construction while 44 percent or $19,472,068.00 was for purchasing lands, damages, and relocation costs.[27]

NOTES

1. Atlanta Journal, February 27, 1948

2. Gainesville Daily Times, November, 1949

3. bid., November 11, 1949

4. Ibid.

5. Ibid., November 10, 1949

6. Ibid., November 11, 1949

7. Congressional Record, United States Army Civil Function Appropriations, 1950, p.24

8. Gainesville Daily Times, November 10, 1949

9. Ibid., November 11,1949

10. Congressional Record, United States Army Civil Function Appropriations, 1950, p.24

11. Congressional Record, River and Harbors Program Appropriations, Fiscal Year 1951, p.235

12. Buford Dam Project Allocations, Fiscal Year 1951, General File, Series XI, Sub-Series C, Richard B. Russell Collection, Richard B. Russell Library, University of Georgia Libraries, Athens, Georgia

13. Atlanta Constitution, October 29, 1951

14. Congressional Record, United States Army Civil Function Appropriations, Fiscal Year 1953, p.5

15. Ibid., Fiscal Year 1954, p.5

16. Atlanta Journal, July 27, 1953

17. Congressional Record, United States Army Civil Function Appropriations, Fiscal Year 1954, p.5

18. Atlanta Journal, September 2, 1953

19. Atlanta Constitution, October 2, 1953

20. Atlanta Constitution, February 17, 1954

21. Congressional Record, United States Army Civil Function Appropriations, Fiscal Year 1955, p.4

22. Atlanta Journal, July 1, 1954

23. Congressional Record, United States Army Public Works Appropriations, Fiscal Year 1956, p.7

24 Atlanta Constitution, January 18, 1955

25. Untitled newspaper, June, 1955

26. Annual Report of the Chief of Engineers, 1960, Vol.2, p.492

27. Ibid., pp.492-493

The Real Estate Property Office for the U.S. Army Corps of Engineers was located on the second floor of the Hosch Building in downtown Gainesville. (top) This is the way the building appeared in the early 1950's when land was being acquired for the reservoir. (Courtesy Chestatee Regional Library from the Pictorial History of Hall County to 1950 by Sybil McRay) (bottom) The building was remodeled in the late 1980's but it still very much resembles the older photograph taken nearly 40 years earlier. The faint words Hosch Bros. Co. advertising the business can barely be seen at top right in the contemporary photograph. (RDC)

CHAPTER FOUR

LAND ACQUISITIONS

Probably one of the most difficult tasks undertaken by the government was acquisition of land where the reservoir would be located. The government did not purchase all the land at once. Tracts were acquired where construction was taking place first, such as the main earth dam site, bridges, highways, etc. Land that would simply be inundated by rising water was purchased a little at a time over several years. Although the project officially began in March, 1950 the first tract of land for what would become the reservoir was not purchased until April, 1954, **Fig. 4-1**,. A Forsyth County farmer, Henry Shadburn 81, was paid $4,100.00 for his home place and 100 acres near the Young Deer area of the county.[1]

It would be impossible for such a large public works project, affecting such a tremendous amount of land not to mention people and families, to not be perceived by some people as adverse. At the same time it would be wishful thinking to believe that the government would be able to purchase over 56,000 acres of land and not have many of these cases end up in court for final disposition. Many factors determined how people felt about the creation of a 38,000 acre lake with 56,000 acres of government property in their own backyard. Whether or not the lake would flood your land was a major factor influencing the side of the fence you sat on. A person's age, economic status before and after the reservoir's creation, friends or relatives affected and those not, affects on businesses, schools, churches, highways, communities, in short anything and everything that could change a persons lifestyle or his/her perception of a change was a determining factor for or against. The particular slant one had when viewing the proposed lake was not restricted to just these things and more often than not was a combination of those mentioned and many more. There were just too many people and families, involving too much land to think otherwise.

Sometimes families who had occupied the land for generations simply did not want to move. It was a question of their belief that the government did not have the right to ask them to pull up stakes and start all over again. Many felt it was impossible

Fig. 4-1 Photograph showing Henry Shadburn signing over land to government. The date is April 14, 1954. (Courtesy Gainesville Daily Times)

to put a price tag on years of work, memories, and everyday living and dying that had taken place on their land. This is a particularly touchy issue, especially when you consider the image the American home and family had in the 1950's. Families then were more extended than nuclear, as they are today. It was not unusual for parents, grandparents, children even aunts or uncles to be living under the same roof, or for the land and property to have been in the family for generations. Early rumors of the dam seemingly threatened the lifestyles of nearly everyone living on or near the proposed reservoir. The early planners who studied the feasibility of such a body of water met anger, apprehension, bewilderment, resentment, and a host of other emotions. It is sometimes hard to foresee the public good of something when it is happening to you and not the other person. This is a fairly common human reaction and one that was probably expected. It would be as true today as it was forty years ago. As time passed many people began to view the project in a different light, they began to view it more favorably. As would be the case today, some did not, some never would. Even today there are still those who hold resentment at being required to leave their land.

Buford Dam was not the first public works project that the United States Army Corps of Engineers had overseen. They had experience in building dams and acquiring private land for public use before. They knew in advance that there would be some problems, it was inevitable. Today the lake seems a natural part of this area, a foregone conclusion but that was not always the case. When the United States Army Corps of Engineers first began formulating plans for the dam's construction the problem of opposition, coming mostly from Hall County and Gainesville, stemmed from the lack of time and information. The necessary studies, planning, and acquisitions of money had not been given time to develop. Engineers simply could not talk accurately about land, bridges, roads, etc. They would need the years of study they would eventually have to speak intelligently about specifics concerning the project. In the infant states of planning they could only rely on knowledge and experience they had developed while working on other projects similar to the one they were proposing. People, families, and even whole communities around the proposed project wanted concrete answers to their questions, questions about everyday situations that might be affected by the lake. How will the land be purchased, and at what price? What about our schools, our churches, our businesses, what will happen to them? What about the loss of tax revenues for counties and towns surrounding inundated areas? What happens if we can not find other lands suitable to our needs? What then? Where do we go from here? How long do we have before we must vacate our land? All these questions and many more were asked. In all likelihood these examples of questions asked only represented the tip of the iceberg.

A question and answer series concerning the construction of a dam in the Buford area appeared in the Gainesville Daily Times in 1954. The questions were compiled by the Times over several years and reflected the common concerns people

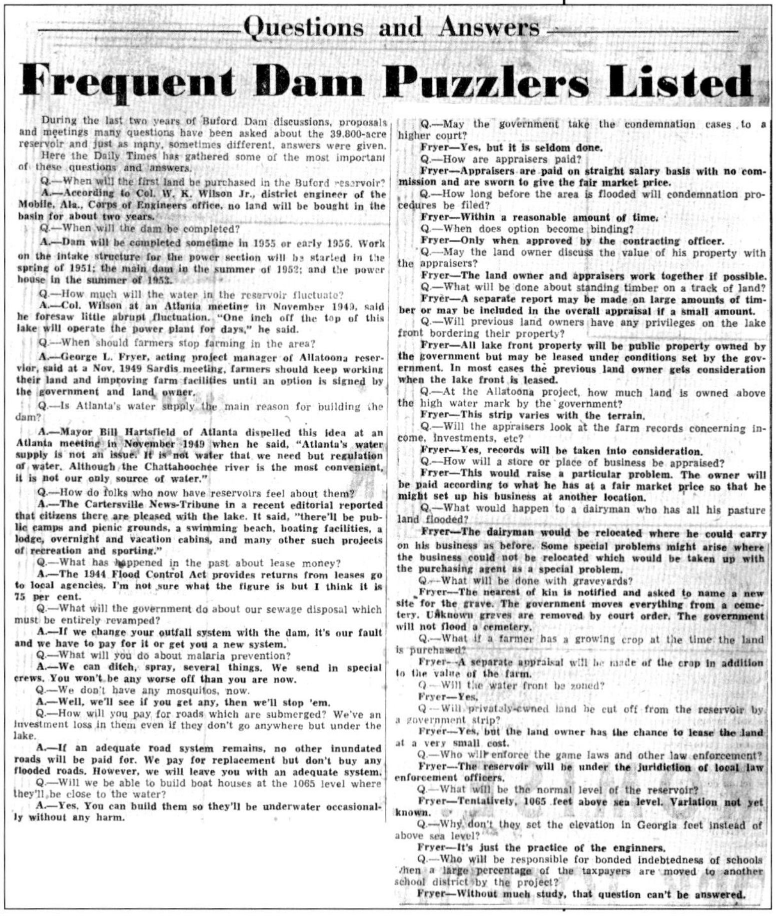

Questions and Answers

Frequent Dam Puzzlers Listed

During the last two years of Buford Dam discussions, proposals and meetings many questions have been asked about the 39,800-acre reservoir and just as many, sometimes different, answers were given.

Here the Daily Times has gathered some of the most important of these questions and answers.

Q.—When will the first land be purchased in the Buford reservoir?

A.—According to Col. W. K. Wilson Jr., district engineer of the Mobile, Ala., Corps of Engineers office, no land will be bought in the basin for about two years.

Q.—When will the dam be completed?

A.—Dam will be completed sometime in 1955 or early 1956. Work on the intake structure for the power section will be started in the spring of 1951; the main dam in the summer of 1952; and the power house in the summer of 1953.

Q.—How much will the water in the reservoir fluctuate?

A.—Col. Wilson at an Atlanta meeting in November 1949, said he foresaw little abrupt fluctuation. "One inch off the top of this lake will operate the power plant for days," he said.

Q.—When should farmers stop farming in the area?

A.—George L. Fryer, acting project manager of Allatoona reservior, said at a Nov. 1949 Sardis meeting, farmers should keep working their land and improving farm facilities until an option is signed by the government and land owner.

Q.—Is Atlanta's water supply the main reason for building the dam?

A.—Mayor Bill Hartsfield of Atlanta dispelled this idea at an Atlanta meeting in November 1949 when he said, "Atlanta's water supply is not an issue. It is not water that we need but regulation of water. Although the Chattahoochee river is the most convenient, it is not our only source of water."

Q.—How do folks who now have reservoirs feel about them?

A.—The Cartersville News-Tribune in a recent editorial reported that citizens there are pleased with the lake. It said, "there'll be public camps and picnic grounds, a swimming beach, boating facilities, a lodge, overnight and vacation cabins, and many other such projects of recreation and sporting."

Q.—What has happened in the past about lease money?

A.—The 1944 Flood Control Act provides returns from leases go to local agencies. I'm not sure what the figure is but I think it is 75 per cent.

Q.—What will the government do about our sewage disposal which must be entirely revamped?

A.—If we change your outfall system with the dam, it's our fault and we have to pay for it or get you a new system.

Q.—What will you do about malaria prevention?

A.—We can ditch, spray, several things. We send in special crews. You won't be any worse off than you are now.

Q.—We don't have any mosquitos, now.

A.—Well, we'll see if you get any, then we'll stop 'em.

Q.—How will you pay for roads which are submerged? We've an investment loss in them even if they don't go anywhere but under the lake.

A.—If an adequate road system remains, no other inundated roads will be paid for. We pay for replacement but don't buy any flooded roads. However, we will leave you with an adequate system.

Q.—Will we be able to build boat houses at the 1065 level where they'll be close to the water?

A.—Yes. You can build them so they'll be underwater occasionally without any harm.

Q.—May the government take the condemnation cases to a higher court?

Fryer—Yes, but it is seldom done.

Q.—How are appraisers paid?

Fryer—Appraisers are paid on straight salary basis with no commission and are sworn to give the fair market price.

Q.—How long before the area is flooded will condemnation procedures be filed?

Fryer—Within a reasonable amount of time.

Q.—When does option become binding?

Fryer—Only when approved by the contracting officer.

Q.—May the land owner discuss the value of his property with the appraisers?

Fryer—The land owner and appraisers work together if possible.

Q.—What will be done about standing timber on a track of land?

Fryer—A separate report may be made on large amounts of timber or may be included in the overall appraisal if a small amount.

Q.—Will previous land owners have any privileges on the lake front bordering their property?

Fryer—All lake front property will be public property owned by the government but may be leased under conditions set by the government. In most cases the previous land owner gets consideration when the lake front is leased.

Q.—At the Allatoona project, how much land is owned above the high water mark by the government?

Fryer—This strip varies with the terrain.

Q.—Will the appraisers look at the farm records concerning income, investments, etc?

Fryer—Yes, records will be taken into consideration.

Q.—How will a store or place of business be appraised?

Fryer—This would raise a particular problem. The owner will be paid according to what he has at a fair market price so that he might set up his business at another location.

Q.—What would happen to a dairyman who has all his pasture land flooded?

Fryer—The dairyman would be relocated where he could carry on his business as before. Some special problems might arise where the business could not be relocated which would be taken up with the purchasing agent as a special problem.

Q.—What will be done with graveyards?

Fryer—The nearest of kin is notified and asked to name a new site for the grave. The government moves everything from a cemetery. Unknown graves are removed by court order. The government will not flood a cemetery.

Q.—What if a farmer has a growing crop at the time the land is purchased?

Fryer—A separate appraisal will be made of the crop in addition to the value of the farm.

Q.—Will the water front be zoned?

Fryer—Yes.

Q.—Will privately-owned land be cut off from the reservoir by a government strip?

Fryer—Yes, but the land owner has the chance to lease the land at a very small cost.

Q.—Who will enforce the game laws and other law enforcement?

Fryer—The reservoir will be under the juridiction of local law enforcement officers.

Q.—What will be the normal level of the reservoir?

Fryer—Tentatively, 1065 feet above sea level. Variation not yet known.

Q.—Why don't they set the elevation in Georgia feet instead of above sea level?

Fryer—It's just the practice of the enginners.

Q.—Who will be responsible for bonded indebtedness of schools when a large percentage of the taxpayers are moved to another school district by the project?

Fryer—Without much study, that question can't be answered.

Fig. 4-2 Article appearing in the Gainesville Daily Times issue listing questions and answers of most interest concerning the project. (Courtesy Gainesville Daily Times)

had over the proposed project, *Fig. 4-2*. Another article written in the Gainesville Daily Times, *Fig. 4-3*, paints a conflicting picture concerning residents in the area that would soon become Lake Sidney Lanier. Land up to elevation 1085.0 would eventually be subject to flooding so land below this elevation was purchased by the government although in some cases land above this level was purchased. The policy that affected the acquisition of land on the Buford Project had recently been changed and would change many times over the years depending on the policy makers in Washington. Prior to beginning the Buford Dam Project the policy for purchasing property involved buying large tracts of land around a reservoir as was the case with Lake Allatoona. If only a small section of a property owner's land was needed for the project the government would purchased the entire tract of land. This policy provided wide belts of federal land around a reservoir which provided more control of lake side development and public facilities.[2] Purchasing land for the reservoir on the Buford Dam Project was basically controlled by the elevation of the land which caused the irregular pattern of land acquisitions around the proposed reservoir. To be economically practical and follow accepted surveying methods engineers often tried to follow straight lines whenever possible rather than curving, erratic, and many times hard to describe contour lines. Over 50,000 acres of land had to be purchased from land owners in order to create the reservoir. There were some

Fig. 4-3 Article appearing in the Gainesville Daily Times concerning families having to move because of the lake. (Reprinted with permission from The Atlanta Journal and The Atlanta Constitution. Reproduction does not imply endorsement)

2-C The Atlanta Journal AND CONSTITUTION SUNDAY, JULY 10, 1955

Buford Dam Area Families Set to Give Way to Reservoir

Final Crops Now Growing on Familiar Land

By AUBREY MORRIS
Journal-Constitution Staff Writer

FLOWERY BRANCH, Ga., July 9—Mrs. A. B. Reeves put on her cloth bonnet and began hoeing the garden peas in a plot beside the white house she and her husband have called home since the fall of 1936.

It will be the last crop on this land for the Reeves family. The entire 395-acre farm will soon be covered by waters of Buford Reservoir.

Pointing to a huge oak tree spreading its branches over the front yard, Mrs. Reeves commented:

"They say the water will be five feet deeper than the top of that tree."

* * *

THE ARMY ENGINEERS have awarded a $1,611,560 contract to the Wade Lahar Construction Co. of Mountain Home, Ark., for clearing the Buford Dam reservoir area.

Workmen and machinery have already moved in to start the gigantic task, and hundreds of families like the Reeves have begun final arrangements for moving. Some have already found new homes. Others will be permitted to gather this season's crops before pulling up stakes.

The Corps of Engineers land purchase division, located in Gainesville, is in charge of relocation of families. A spokesman said negotiations are under way with many of the rural settlers for moving them to new homes. It will take many more months to finish the task, he said.

Mr. and Mrs. Reeves, their son George and his wife and twin daughters, Joyce and Janice (born May 11) will move to a new 19-acre plot adjacent to the reservoir area. "It's just a place to go to," Mrs. Reeves, 66, said. They must be out by Christmas.

* * *

THE REEVES FARM, in Forsyth County, is situated on the west bank of the Chattahoochee River near the ramshackle, one-lane Flowery Branch bridge and includes many acres of bottom land, planted for the last time in corn.

Staff Photo—Aubrey Morris
WATER TO SUBMERGE THIS FARM
Mrs. A. B. Reeves, Children, Flora Reeves, Lucy Benton

Up the river, near Brown's Bridge, on State Highway 141 (Gainesville-Cumming), 16-year-old Donald Waldrip was using a tractor and cable to yank down some of the timbers in the two story frame house that until recently was the home of his aunt, Mrs. Claudie Mathis, and her husband.

The lumber will be used to build a new chicken house at the Mathis couple's new home a few miles away, Donald said. This is chicken-raising country.

Just a quarter of a mile further up the river, Mark Hargrove of Nashville, Tenn., work-hardened erection superintendent for the Bristol Steel Co., Bristol, Va., nonchalantly walked along the beams of the new cantilever-type Brown's Bridge 208 feet above the present water level.

* * *

"ITS A FINE bridge," Mr. Hargrove said. "We're using 1,460 tons of prefabricated steel . . . started the steel job on May 17 . . . due to finish Nov. 1."

One of several bridges to be built as highways are rerouted in the reservoir area, Brown's Bridge was begun last August. The giant concrete piers now jut grotesquely up from the river bottoms between two wooded hillsides.

As the Buford Dam project gradually nears completion, the resettlement brought about by clearing of 14,156 acres of land and partial clearing of 9,390 other acres means considerable trading in home sites.

* * *

AT THE COUNTRY stores the talk is all about what the sprawling lake will mean to this section of the state. The area covers about 37 square miles, or 23,000 acres.

Appraisals, titles, purchase prices, condemnations, court cases, dismantling or moving of buildings, cemetery relocations—all afford plenty of conversation material for the local folks.

Ed Barter, chief of the government's land purchase division office in Gainesville, says the government by Aug. 1 will have acquired most of the Forsyth County section of the reservoir. By Jan. 1, he added, a large portion of the Hall County section will have been acquired.

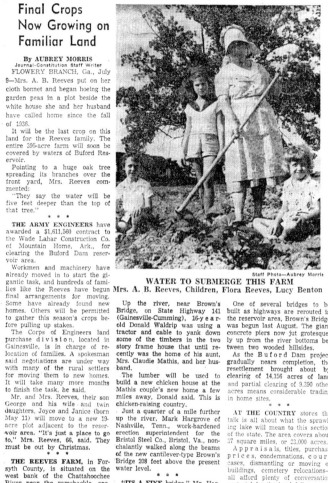

Fig. 4-4 Article dealing with families and farming in the proposed reservoir area. (Reprinted with permission from The Atlanta Journal and The Atlanta Constitution. Reproduction does not imply endorsement)

instances where land owners paid for surveys of their property which eventually allowed for use up to the waters edge. In 1957 Congressman Landrum even proposd legislation in Congress to allow for returning land to owners that had no definite explicit public use. Apparently the legislation was aimed at land the government purchased for the lake that was not used.[3]

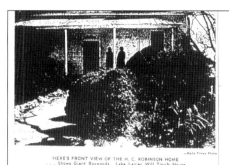

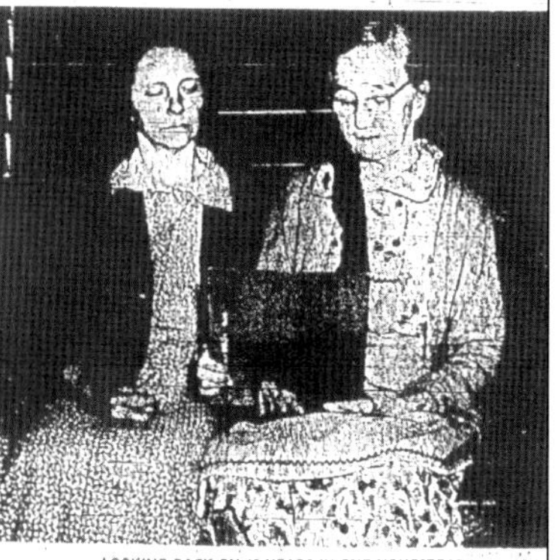

There were a number of newspaper articles over the years that chronicled the process of acquiring land for the reservoir. One article dated July 10, 1955, looked at families and farming, ***Fig. 4-4***. Another one looked at a family who lived in a house built

—Daily Times Photo
HERE'S FRONT VIEW OF THE H. C. ROBINSON HOME
. . . Shows Giant Boxwoods. Lake Lanier Will Touch House

Lake To Reach Home, Robinsons Moving Out

By HOWARD GORHAM
Daily Times Staff Writer

By the time the water has begun to back up from the Buford Dam early next year, people of the inundated areas will have sold their homes and lands and moved on to other sections.

This pulling up of roots established by a lifetime in one home or farm or community, will call for many changes for the affected people. It will mean working new fields, moving into new homes, and making new friends.

There are many, however, who feel that the change, despite the disruption, will be for the better.

ONE SUCH family is the H. C. Robinsons, who have lived the better part of 48 years on their farm just north of the Thompson Bridge on the Dahlonega highway.

"We hate to tear up after so many years on this land," Mrs. Robinson said. "But we have bought a new place on the Atlanta Highway and we are willing to make a change."

The thing that will hurt the Robinsons most about leaving is losing the twin line of boxwood hedges which line the sides of the front walk. Mrs. Robinson estimates the boxwoods to be about 100 years old. They were set out when the house was first built, which was just before the Civil War, she said.

The house is a history in itself, having been built just before the War Between the States, in the last great Golden Age in Georgia history, with the large plantations and southern hospitality.

THE HOUSE was built by Ode Thompson, famous earlier settler of Hall County, for his bride, sometime just before the Civil War. The house itself is solidly constructed with seven rooms and twin hallways which make it one of the coolest houses in the area, Mrs. Robinson explains, with the wind blowing in from both directions.

Mrs. Thompson, who was the grandmother of Mrs. Charles Martin Sr., set out the first strands of boxwood which line the walk today, with the aid of Lee Dan, a slave.

Mrs. A. L. Robinson moved into the house with her husband in 1907 from a spot about three miles down on the Chattahoochee River, which runs nearby. Here, they raised their children and spent most of their lives wresting a living from the land. They raised corn, cotton, vegetable and other crops on the 200 odd acres they owned until the engineers came and told them they would have to sell their land to provide for the Buford Dam.

THEY QUIT crop-farming in 1947 to devote their time to dairying, selling their milk to a wholesale buyer.

"Then they told us we would have to sell our land because the water backing up from the Buford Dam would cover most of it," Mrs. Robinson said. "They told us that the water when it backed up to the point it will finally reach, would be above the top of our door." And she pointed out the place.

"We'd like to sell the boxwood if we could," Mrs. Robinson said. "I hate to see 100 years of growth killed by the water. Maybe someone will want to buy it."

The Robinsons, by September, will move to their new home on the Atlanta highway, and set up their dairy on their new 55 acres of land.

LOOKING BACK ON 48 YEARS IN ONE HOMESTEAD
. . . Mrs. H. C. Robinson and Mrs. A. L. Robinson In Swing

Fig. 4-5 Article, dated March 27,1955, dealing with a family having to move because of Lake Lanier. (Courtesy Gainesville Daily Times)

Keith's Bridge To Be 96 Feet Under Water If Buford Dam is Built

The News is delighted at the growing number of people who are becoming interested in the social and economic conditions that will affect Gainesville and Hall county if the Buford Dam is constructed and are willing to take a part in demanding that the promoters of the project take into consideration the wishes of the people of this county. However, not enough people have come forward yet and entirely too many are indifferent.

Again we stress, that construction of the dam at Buford is a tremendous thing and will affect the social and economic conditions of everyone in the county. It is not a thing to be taken lightly. We've got to stand up and demand our rights, else 25,000 acres of farm land will be inundated and a great proportion of business from the west of Gainesville will be diverted elsewhere. Anyone can see what a serious blow that would be.

Some additional light on how Hall county will be affected is contained in a letter received this week by the Gainesville Chamber of Commerce. According to the letter, Brown's bridge will be 85 feet under water. Keith's bridge will be 96 feet under water. Kelley bridge will be 88 feet under and the Shallow Ford bridge leading out the Dawsonville paved highway will be 70 feet under water.

That means that all roads west of Gainesville will have to be relocated and that in some places the lake will be so wide that it will not be spanned by a bridge thus causing businessmen to the west of Gainesville to detour far to the south, or to the north to reach Gainesville. This they may do for a time, but will be much easier and quicker for them to transact their business with firms closer home and more accessible.

Continuing the letter, the Sidney Lanier bridge will be 65 feet underwater, Thompson's bridge will be 65 feet under water and Longstreet bridge on the Clermont highway north of Gainesville will be 29 feet under water and the lake will extend far out on both sides.

Fortunately for the citizens of Hall county Congress only appropriated $400,000 for planning purposes for the dam, which will give us time to consult with engineers and make our wishes known on various matters that will come up during the planning stages.

We've got to have some assurance that people to the west of us will not be inconvenienced by lack of bridges. We've got to be assured that something will be done to keep down mosquitoes. We want to know where the county will receive money to offset that which it will lose from the 25,000 acres being taken from the tax books. And there are innumerable other questions that we should raise and know the answers to before we approve construction of the dam. Of course the people from Buford south approve the construction, for they stand to benefit, but Hall county will be the heaviest hit of all counties.

We do not wish to keep exhorting, but the Buford dam poses some mighty big questions that the citizens of Hall county should know before construction is started and the only way to get the answers is by aroused public opinion demanding satisfaction.

Fig. 4-6 Article concerning loss of bridges. (Courtesy Gainesville Daily Times)

LAND ACQUISITIONS

Fig. 4-7 Article, dated Nov. 11, 1949, concerning remaining land use. (Courtesy Gainesville Daily Times)

Two-Year Period Of Land Use

Farmers who hold land in the Chattahoochee valley in Hall county, land destined to be on the bottom of the reservoir projected to back up behind the Buford Dam, have at least two more years of productivity on their land.

Col. W. K. Wilson Jr., Army engineer in charge of detailed planning and construction on the proposed dam revealed this information, repeated it under a direct question, and re-emphasized it once again. It will be at least two years before the Army begins buying land except at the actual location of the dam.

Engineers don't expect to begin work on the main dam structure until the summer of 1952. Actually, that is almost three years away although it is only two summer growing seasons away.

Even this schedule depends on whether or not congressional appropriations come through as rapidly as hoped to fit the Army's construction program. Any hold-up in funds or delay in building may push the purchase of reservoir area land off another year, until 1953.

Dam building is a long-run job. It takes years to build a dam. Land purchasing is one of the last steps and will not begin until the water is almost ready to back up over the valley.

Land further upstream, say five to 35 miles from the dam itself, may well be immune to purchase by the government until 1954. So, don't become panicky about land and try to get rid of it in a hurry. Uncle Sam doesn't want it for a long time yet. He doesn't want it until you've had a chance to get two or three money-making crops off of it, anyway.

Fig. 4-8 Article, dated Nov. 14, 1949 concerning destroyed property. (Courtesy Gainesville Daily Times)

Anything Destroyed by Buford Project Will Be Replaced--Army

6—GAINESVILLE, (GA.) DAILY TIMES, MONDAY, NOV. 14, 1949

(Ed. Note: Effects of the construction of Buford Dam and its reservoir on Hall county are discussed in this fourth article in an exclusive Daily Times series.)
by Sylvan Meyer

"We will replace anything we must destroy," the Army reiterated in assuring Hall county against severe losses incident with construction of the Buford dam and its 60,000,000 acre reservoir.

Col. W. K. Wilson Jr., head of the district engineers Mobile, Ala. office, recently played host to a delegation from Gainesville and Hall county and made that promise.

"But," he added, "I repeat that until detailed specifications are prepared, our promises can be only may ones and we can make no definite predictions. A good deal depends on appropriations, also."

Gainesville's water works, which represents a tremendous local investment, will be replaced when waters backed by the dam submerges everything, including pump house and settling basins. That promise was definite.

"If Gainesville wants a larger water works, then we'll pay for the old one but local money will have to finance anything above that," Colonel Wilson said.

Concerning county and state roads and bridges, Colonel Wilson again fell back on lack of details. Although the state highway planners have mapped their tentative reconstruction schedule, full federal approval to their schemes has not been granted. However, in keeping with their policy, the Army will relocate through highways, construct what bridges are necessary and prevent large areas of population from becoming isolated.

Loss of county revenue resulting from abandoned schools and flooded lands which now return taxes may be alleviated by a bill pending in congress to provide for such exigencies. That, too, is definite.

To ease damaging effects of fluctuation and hold certain areas level for recreation purposes, it has long been a dream of the Hall county Buford dam planning committee and the Chamber of Commerce committee headed by W. H. Slack Jr. to construct impoundment dams. There would hold large coves to a steady water level and would center recreation in controlled areas.

The Army, however, doesn't see how such coffer-dams can be written into their appropriation nor constructed by them. One answer to their reluctance, of course, is to have the appropriation bill so written through pressure on local congressmen.

At Altoona, said Colonel Wilson, West Georgians were promised three new bridges and approaches. They turned down the bridges, asked that an equivalent amount of money be put into an impoundment dam topped by a highway. This was done and a large area of the Allatoona project will be retained at a steady level.

Colonel Wilson viewed this as a most unusual procedure and would not forecast that a similar strategy would work at Buford.

In short, the Army's not talking promises but continues to indicate in every conversation on the possible future, that whatever Hall county obtains in connection with the dam, it will obtain for itself through its own best offices.

just before the Civil War, F*ig. 4-5.* Concerns over bridge construction and relocation, *Fig. 4-6*, remaining land use, *Fig. 4-7*, replacing destroyed property, *Fig. 4-8*, and land acquisition talks, *Fig. 4-9*, were all aspects of the project that sparked public interest in the early years when approval for the project was a bitter debate.

GAINESVILLE, (GA.) DAILY TIMES, SUN., NOV. 20, 1949

Army Land Agent Talk Seen Airing Dam Buys

Hall county land owners will get their first chance Tuesday night to hear first-hand answers to questions about land acquisition under the Buford Dam development.

County agent L. C. Rew has arranged through the Army engineer office in Atlanta to have George L. Fryer, acting project manager of the Allatoona dam reservoir, speak before the Tuesday meeting of the Sardis farm bureau.

The meeting will be held at the Sardis school at 7:30 pm.

Fryer is now engaged in land acquisitions at the Allatoona project and will discuss that phase of the Buford Dam project, according to Rew.

Rew said that members of the Hall county farm bureau, citizens of Sardis community, and those who have filled out survey blanks for the Buford project, have been sent written invitations to attend the meeting. But, he said, everyone having particular interest in the dam is invited to come and hear the discussion.

"This will give the farmer a first-hand chance to obtain information for planning his future farm program and how it will be affected by the reservoir," Rew said.

Plans for the meeting are being worked out by G. S. Cash, president of the Sardis farm bureau.

Fig. 4-9 Article, dated Nov. 20, 1949 concerning land acquisition meeting. (Courtesy Gainesville Daily Times)

Eminent Domain gives the government the right to acquire private land for public use and guidelines spelled out under the River and Harbor Acts were followed in the acquisition of such land.[4] In July, 1954 the government was granted permission to take possession of over 444 acres of land in the Buford reservoir area. It was the first "take possession" case reviewed in Georgia involving Buford Dam. Years before similiar cases in the state had been reviewed but they involved TVA construction. Six seperate tracts of land involving almost 100 individuals who were heirs and relatives of the owners were part of the litigation. The government sought permission to take the land and Secretary of the Army, Robert T. Stevens petitioned the court to exercise eminent domain on the property. Federal Judge Boyd Sloan granted the Corps of Engineers possession of the land and said compensation for the property would have to be determined by a jury.[5] The United States Army Corps of Engineers realized that many sales would be challenged and subject to legal interpretation. For this reason land acquisitions were made trying to cover every detail. It would serve the government's best interest to insure that all sales were as equitable as possible. As in most cases, even with the best of intentions, problems would develop.

The Real Estate Project office for the government was set up in Gainesville, Georgia. Its function was to handle mapping, appraisal, and negotiation of land sales for the government. Edward J. Barter was chief of the real estate office which was located on the second floor of the old Hosch Building in downtown Gainesville, ***Fig. 4-10***,. In July, 1955 he estimated that

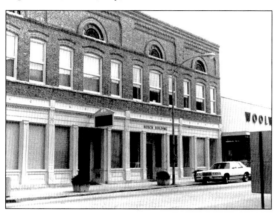

Fig. 4-10 Photograph of the old Hosch Building in Gainesville. (RDC)

most of the land in Forsyth County would be acquired by August with the largest portion of the land for the reservoir, located in Hall County, being acquired by January 1, 1955. All totaled about 700 families would be affected in the purchasing of property for the reservoir.[6] The Extension Service working with the U.S. Army Corps of Engineers established a special office to give assistance and advice in helping families find new homes. An office was set up in the Federal Building in Gainesville where families being affected by the relocation could get information about Northeast Georgia farms and homes for sale or rent.[7]

Topographic maps made by using aerial photographs would provide the government with necessary information regarding the land that would need to be purchased. The government would use recent land sales in determining a fair market or comparable sale value of the land. The acquisition of private land could not be handled with a blanket sell policy. Appraisers from the Real Estate Project Office would check court records of recent sales of various types of land in and around the proposed reservoir. The estimated value of the property would depend on the type as well as the use of the land in question. Good bottom land used for pasture or farm land and woodland, depending on the type of timber present, could appraise between $25.00 and $50.00 an acre. These estimates were just that, estimates. Sometimes they were higher or lower and represented what the market value of land was in the mid 1950's. By checking court records before land acquisitions took place appraisers were able to affix a price free of land speculation, that could drive the prices up. An article appearing in the Gainesville (Ga.) News on May 12, 1949, ***Fig. 4-11***, addressed just such speculation.

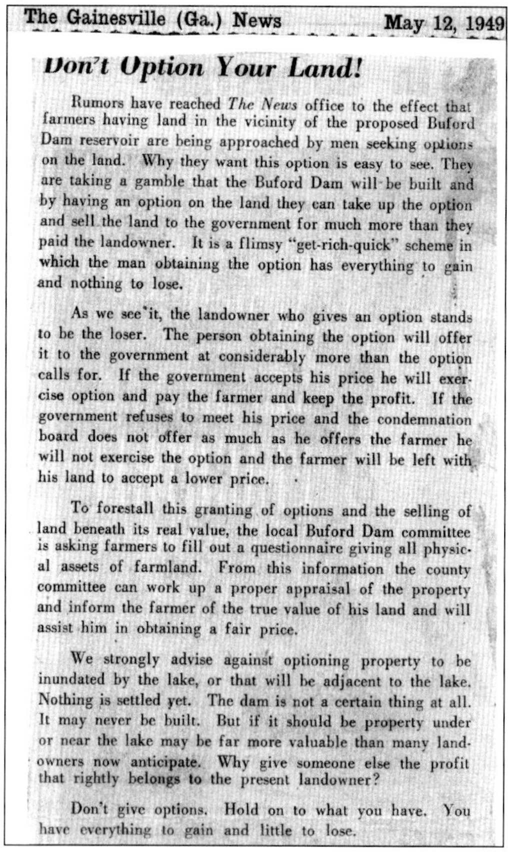

The Gainesville (Ga.) News **May 12, 1949**

Don't Option Your Land!

Rumors have reached *The News* office to the effect that farmers having land in the vicinity of the proposed Buford Dam reservoir are being approached by men seeking options on the land. Why they want this option is easy to see. They are taking a gamble that the Buford Dam will be built and by having an option on the land they can take up the option and sell the land to the government for much more than they paid the landowner. It is a flimsy "get-rich-quick" scheme in which the man obtaining the option has everything to gain and nothing to lose.

As we see it, the landowner who gives an option stands to be the loser. The person obtaining the option will offer it to the government at considerably more than the option calls for. If the government accepts his price he will exercise option and pay the farmer and keep the profit. If the government refuses to meet his price and the condemnation board does not offer as much as he offers the farmer he will not exercise the option and the farmer will be left with his land to accept a lower price.

To forestall this granting of options and the selling of land beneath its real value, the local Buford Dam committee is asking farmers to fill out a questionnaire giving all physical assets of farmland. From this information the county committee can work up a proper appraisal of the property and inform the farmer of the true value of his land and will assist him in obtaining a fair price.

We strongly advise against optioning property to be inundated by the lake, or that will be adjacent to the lake. Nothing is settled yet. The dam is not a certain thing at all. It may never be built. But if it should be property under or near the lake may be far more valuable than many landowners now anticipate. Why give someone else the profit that rightly belongs to the present landowner?

Don't give options. Hold on to what you have. You have everything to gain and little to lose.

Fig. 4-11 Article, dated May 12, 1949, concerning land speculation for profit. (Courtesy Gainesville (Ga.) News)

Extensive research had to be made in order to assure that landholders had ownership of property and that a deed could be acquired by the government. Draftsmen would draw individual plot maps of the property.[8] The Real Estate Project Office would send officials, working out of the appraisers section, to make an on-site inventory of the property. They would take pictures of the property and every dwelling, building, personal items, etc. attached to the property. A complete description of the property and contents were drawn up and along with the pictures would provide ample information for appraisal. Nothing was left to chance. The value of the land was established by using the recent court records of sales of land similar in size and use to the land in question. From this point the value of the property would have to be adjusted in order to affix a value on things like the persons home, barns, utility buildings, wells, fences, and other buildings on the property. All these things would be appraised and could readjust the dollar value of the sale. The owner could reserve property, to be removed at a later date, which was considered salvage and would be subtracted from the appraisal price. Reserved property could be anything the owner wished to move from the property before the government took control of the land. This reserve property had to be removed by a certain date and would appear on the deed which transferred ownership to the government. ***Fig. 4-12*** and ***Fig. 4-13***. Appraisers, many of which were chosen from the local community, were paid on straight salary receiving no commissions but they were human and the manner in which they approached the property owner often times determined how smooth the appraisal process went.[9] At the same time using local folks to deal with local folks would usually have a settling effect and there would be less chance of problems developing from what could be a very difficult and sensitive task at best.

There were other things that affected the final appraisal of the property. Improvements made to the property, its location to schools, churches, stores and other public facilities, and conditions of highways and roads, such as whether they were paved or not, were all items that could adjust the dollar value of the sale. If by impounding the water a person had to drive many miles out of the way, at great added expense, to get to schools, stores, churches, etc. then this could adjust the dollar value of the land. If acquisition of partial tracts of land left a person's land that was not purchased without private access, then the government could offer to purchase such land, even if it was above the 1085.0 elevation mark. In short everything of value on the land or attached to the land was taken into consideration when making an appraisal on the property.

Removal of reserve property had its own kind of problems. Many property owners were able to establish farms or homes on higher ground up out of the water's reach. Dismantling property for removal to another location was not much

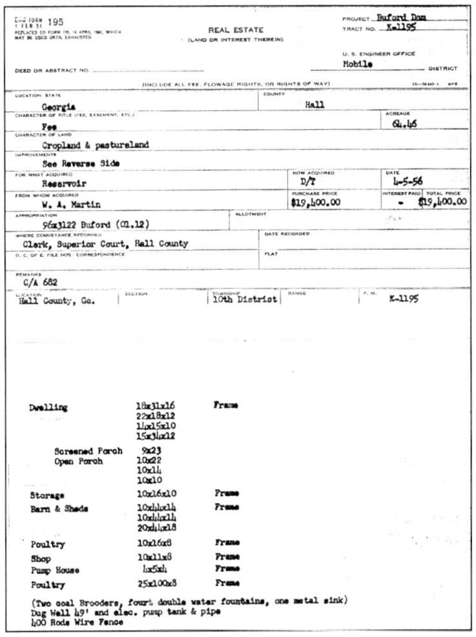
ENG FORM 195
1 FEB 51
REPLACES ED FORM 195, 14 APRIL 1945, WHICH MAY BE USED UNTIL EXHAUSTED.
REAL ESTATE
(LAND OR INTEREST THEREIN)
PROJECT Buford Dam
TRACT NO. K-1195
U. S. ENGINEER OFFICE
Mobile DISTRICT
DEED OR ABSTRACT NO.
(INCLUDE ALL FEE, FLOWAGE RIGHTS, OR RIGHTS OF WAY)
LOCATION: STATE Georgia
COUNTY Hall
CHARACTER OF TITLE (FEE, EASEMENT, ETC.) Fee
ACREAGE 64.46
CHARACTER OF LAND Cropland & pastureland
IMPROVEMENTS See Reverse Side
FOR WHAT ACQUIRED Reservoir
HOW ACQUIRED D/T
DATE 4-5-56
FROM WHOM ACQUIRED W. A. Martin
PURCHASE PRICE $19,400.00
INTEREST PAID -
TOTAL PRICE $19,400.00
APPROPRIATION 96x3122 Buford (01.12)
ALLOTMENT
WHERE CONVEYANCE RECORDED Clerk, Superior Court, Hall County
DATE RECORDED
O. C. OF E. FILE NOS. CORRESPONDENCE
PLAT
REMARKS C/A 682
LOCATION Hall County, Ga.
SECTION
TOWNSHIP 10th District
RANGE
P. M. K-1195

Dwelling	18x31x16	Frame
	22x18x12	
	14x15x10	
	15x34x12	
Screened Porch	9x23	
Open Porch	10x22	
	10x14	
	10x10	
Storage	10x16x10	Frame
Barn & Sheds	10x44x14	Frame
	10x44x14	
	20x44x18	
Poultry	10x16x8	Frame
Shop	10x11x8	Frame
Pump House	4x5x4	Frame
Poultry	25x100x8	Frame

(Two coal Brooders, fourt double water fountains, one metal sink)
Dug Well 49' and elec. pump tank & pipe
400 Rods Wire Fence

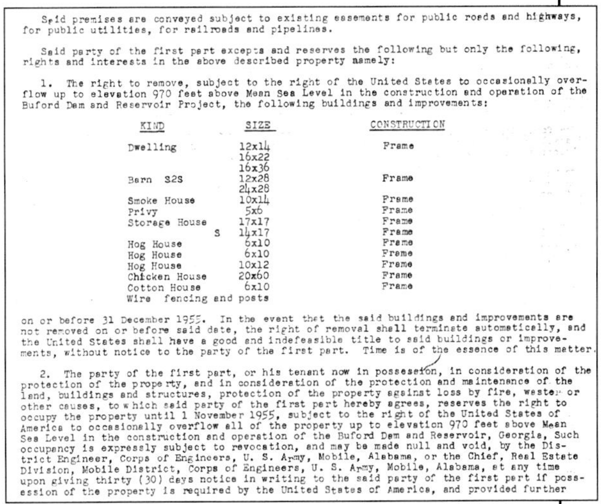
Said premises are conveyed subject to existing easements for public roads and highways, for public utilities, for railroads and pipelines.

Said party of the first part excepts and reserves the following but only the following, rights and interests in the above described property namely:

1. The right to remove, subject to the right of the United States to occasionally overflow up to elevation 970 feet above Mean Sea Level in the construction and operation of the Buford Dam and Reservoir Project, the following buildings and improvements:

KIND	SIZE	CONSTRUCTION
Dwelling	12x14	Frame
	16x22	
	16x36	
Barn S2S	12x28	Frame
	24x28	
Smoke House	10x14	Frame
Privy	5x6	Frame
Storage House	17x17	Frame
S	14x17	Frame
Hog House	6x10	Frame
Hog House	6x10	Frame
Hog House	10x12	Frame
Chicken House	20x60	Frame
Cotton House	6x10	Frame
Wire fencing and posts		

on or before 31 December 1955. In the event that the said buildings and improvements are not removed on or before said date, the right of removal shall terminate automatically, and the United States shall have a good and indefeasible title to said buildings or improvements, without notice to the party of the first part. Time is of the essence of this matter.

2. The party of the first part, or his tenant now in possession, in consideration of the protection of the property, and in consideration of the protection and maintenance of the land, buildings and structures, protection of the property against loss by fire, water or other causes, to which said party of the first part hereby agrees, reserves the right to occupy the property until 1 November 1955, subject to the right of the United States of America to occasionally overflow all of the property up to elevation 970 feet above Mean Sea Level in the construction and operation of the Buford Dam and Reservoir, Georgia, Such occupancy is expressly subject to revocation, and may be made null and void, by the District Engineer, Corps of Engineers, U. S. Army, Mobile, Alabama, or the Chief, Real Estate Division, Mobile District, Corps of Engineers, U. S. Army, Mobile, Alabama, at any time upon giving thirty (30) days notice in writing to the said party of the first part if possession of the property is required by the United States of America, and provided further

Fig. 4-12 Deed Records, Forsyth County Courthouse. (Courtesy Forsyth County Courthouse)

Fig. 4-13 Deed Records, Forsyth County Courthouse. (Courtesy Forsyth County Courthouse)

of a problem but trying to move whole structures intact was. This property was often times isolated without a system of roads which made it difficult to transport from one location to another.[10] Property not removed by the owner as part of reserve property was either removed by the government by a contractor as part of modified reservoir clearing or was sold to the public under sealed bids. Some 130 buildings were sold by the government in 1954 as part of the bidding process to remove structures from land that would eventually become Lake Lanier. An article appearing in the Gainesville Daily Times, dated November 17, 1954, *Fig. 4-14*, discusses the sale. Farm homes, smoke houses, barns, chicken houses, garages, cribs, well shelters, privies, and even a grist mill were all examples of the property being sold by the government.

Fig. 4-14 Article, dated Nov. 17, 1954, concerning sale of property by government auction. (Courtesy Gainesville Daily Times)

'HAINTS, HOOT-OWLS'
Lake Lanier Reservoir Section Now Barren, Quiet Ghost-Land
By George Porter

There is a desolate land in the heart of Hall County.

It is a land where the weeds choke the fields and have crept up to the very doorsteps of the empty farmhouses. The red clay roads are rutted and in disrepair.

The only sounds are the metallic banging of a loose piece of tin roofing in the wind; the thud of a door swinging in an empty house; the twitter of small birds seeking weed seeds in the yard or spilled grain in the abandoned barn. No dog barks. No mule hee-haws. No pig grunts. No tractor chugs. Only when the wind dies for a moment can the far-distant sounds of motor vehicles be heard.

SOON EVEN the houses, their windows like big blank eyes, will be gone, leaving the land to the weeds and wild things.

This desolate land ("Ain't nothin' in thar but haints' and hoot-owls," one old-timer said.) is located on what will be the bottom of the Buford Dam reservoir when the waters start backing up early in 1956.

The buildings are to be sold next Tuesday by sealed bids by the Real Estate Project Office of the Corps of Engineers in Gainesville.

There are some 130 structures up for sale. They range from farm homes, smoke houses, barns, chicken houses, garages, cribs, well shelters to privies. There is one grist mill on the list issued by the Engineers for prospective buyers.

MANY OF THE buildings are described as being of log construction, testifying to their age and the number of human generations they have served in the bottomlands of the Chattahoochee River.

For prospective privy buyers, the list gives no further description than the dimensions, type construction of door cut-out decorations.

The buildings are listed as items, and each item contains the building found on individual farms. There are 28 items on the list, containing the total of 130 buildings.

THE CORPS of Engineers invite prospective buyers to inspect the buildings by making arrangements with Edward J. Harter, Real Estate Project Office manager, 108 Maple Street, Gainesville, Ga.

Concerning the condition of the buildings offered for sale, the Corps of Engineers has this to say under "Terms and Conditions of the Sale:"

"The property offered for sale will be sold 'as is' and 'where is,' without warranty or guaranty as to quantity, quality, character, condition, size or kind, or that the same is in condition or fit to be used for the purpose for which intended; and no claim for any allowance or deduction upon such ground will be considered after the bids have been opened."

Severance damage would add to the price of the overall appraisal. This could be the difference in the appraisal of the land that was used by the government and the value of the land that was not taken. An example would be a farm valued at $8000.00. If the government purchased a tract of land for let's say $4,000.00 but the remaining acreage left was only valued at $2,500.00 then the severance damage in this case would be $1,500.00.[11] The reasoning here was that in certain cases the land not affected by the sale would be devalued because of the loss of acreage or property attached to it that the government had purchased and could no longer be used. As mentioned earlier the policy that governed the acquisition of land for this project had not been used on earlier projects. Previously the entire tract of land would probably have been purchased.

Moving expenses could also be reimbursed by the government which was a new policy affecting property owners ceding land over to the Corps. For moving household goods, farm equipment, animals, etc. to a new location up to 25 percent of the total appraisal price would be allowed for each property owner. The Mobile District Chief, Colonel Fox, advised anyone moving to a new place to keep accurate records, save bills, and invoices connected with moving expenses so that reimbursement could be handled in an expedient manner. This money was separate from any funds connected with the appraisal price.[12]

Appraisers would take their findings to the chief appraiser of the Real Estate Project Office. Negotiators working out of this office would then contact the owners. Options signed by the landowner and the government had to be examined by the land buying agent.[13] If the land owner did not agree with the appraiser's price, and many did not, then the land would be acquired by condemnation procedures. The land owner would get the full amount the appraiser set at this time with a chance to get more through the courts. Often times the landowners who were seeking larger appraisal values from the government would petition the court for acquisitions of all or portions of the money already being held in escrow by the court in their names. This was a common practice especially since several years would pass before final disposition of many of the cases were resolved.[14] The cases would be tried using state procedures and with a regular twelve man jury.[15] The jury would determine if the government had given a fair appraisal of the land. In these cases the government would use the early appraisal information such as the pictures, property inventories, and recent land sales records of similar property to justify its offer. If the court ruled in favor of the government then the landowner would have to settle at the price appraised. If the court ruled against the government then the difference between what was appraised and what was determined as the fair market value, by the court, would have to be paid. Both sides could appeal to a higher court. There were many property owners that challenged the government's appraisal. They took the matter to court with the outcomes varying considerably. A number of the cases, where litigation was initated, were settled out of court before they actually went to trial.

Each case tried in court was unique in acreage and property involved as well as compensation requested and no two seemed the same. One case involved 25 acres owned by Olen Stephens living in Hall County. The government appraised the land at $4,500.00 The owner filed suit in The United States District Court on March 29, 1955 asking for $9,000.00. Two years later the jury awarded the property owner and additional $1,500.00 for his land. As was true in almost every case of this type the property owner had petitioned the court for $4,300.00 of the original appraisal several years before the case was decided. When final disposition of the case was completed he received the remaining $200.00 plus the additional $1,500.00 awarded to him by the jury hearing the case.[16]

Another case involved 342.81 acres of land on the Chattahoochee River owned by Toy Minor and parties. The government appraised the property at $20,250.00. This case was interesting because of the owners claim to the property's fertile agricultural land and its potential as a rock quarry and gold deposits. He was also seeking just compensation for 28 acres of land the government was not purchasing that was part of the original 300 plus acres. The land owner was asking for a reappraisal of some $250,000.00. On September 28, 1957 a jury awarded an additional $28,285.13 to the appraisal.[17]

There was a case involving 3,035.49 acres of land in Forsyth County owned by Gus H. Ashcraft and parties in which several different juries awarded additional monies for multiple tracts of land that belonged to the entire acreage in question. In June, 1955 the government appraised a large part of the acreage at $33,000.00. The jury in this case awarded an additional $10,765.00.[15] Another tract received a government appraisal at $4,500.00 with the jury only adding another $200.00. For 176 acres the government appraisal was set at $4,000.00. The jury awarded only an additional $400.00.[18]

In August, 1955 a number of cases were finalized in court. They all involved land and property in Forsyth County. Case number 627 involved tracts E-500 and E-502. The owner A.B. Rieves (et.al) was asking the court for $118,000.00 for 1,764 acres. The government appraised the property at $31,000.00. On August 3rd the jury award Mr. Rieves $42,397.00. A tract of land owned by the Scales estate received a government appraisal of $11,500.00 for 184 acres. The owners were seeking $75,000.00 but the jury felt that $18,500.00 was appropriate. On August 4th the final award in this case amounted to about $97.00 an acre. Tracts G-710 and G-711 owned by Hoke Parks involved 78.75 acres located on Keith's Bridge Road. The government appraised tract G-710 at $2,700.00 and tract G-711 at $7,500.00. Mr. Parks felt that G-710 was worth $5,750.00 and tract G-711 worth $12,000.00. On August 8th the jury awarded $10,000.00 for both tracts.

That same year J.C. Hamner had several tracts of land in Forsyth and Hall Counties involved in litigation. The government appraised 627.07 acres of his land in Hall County near Shoal Creek Church for $20,000.00. He was asking for $65,000.00. On August 16th the jury awarded him $24,000.00. A tract of land, C-304, involving 316 acres he owned near Light's Bridge in Forsyth County, received a government appraisal of $8,000.00. He requested $31,000.00. On August 16th the jury awarded him $9,000.00. Three hundred and twenty five acres, tract D-402, located off of the same Light's Bridge but in Hall County received a government appraisal of $14,500.00. Mr. Hamner felt that $64,000.00 was more appropriate. On August 16th the jury awarded him $24,219.00.[19]

In 1956 a Jackson County resident, James Frank Boyd, was awarded $22,950.00 for 97 acres of farm land that was originally appraised at $13,000.00. The property was once the site of the historic Vanns Tavern.[20] That same year Mrs. Vera M. Dollar received $22,000.00 for 97 acres of land originally appraised at $17,000.00.[21] Buford Lumberman J.C. Hamner received $13,500.00 for a 325 acre tract originally appraised at $12,500.00 and $4,700.00 for a 101.90 acre tract originally appraised at $4,500.00. Hamner was asking $24,375.00

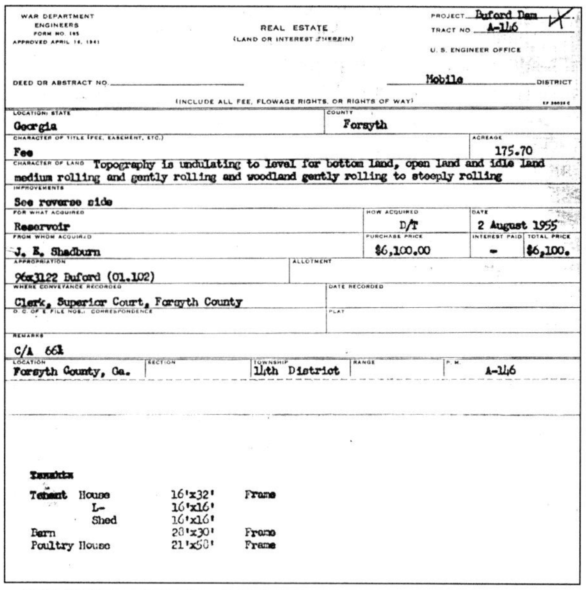

WAR DEPARTMENT ENGINEERS FORM NO. 195 APPROVED APRIL 14, 1941

REAL ESTATE (LAND OR INTEREST THEREIN)

PROJECT Buford Dam
TRACT NO. A-146
U. S. ENGINEER OFFICE
Mobile DISTRICT
DEED OR ABSTRACT NO.
(INCLUDE ALL FEE, FLOWAGE RIGHTS, OR RIGHTS OF WAY)

LOCATION: STATE Georgia — COUNTY Forsyth
CHARACTER OF TITLE (FEE, EASEMENT, ETC.) Fee — ACREAGE 175.70
CHARACTER OF LAND Topography is undulating to level for bottom land, open land and idle land medium rolling and gently rolling and woodland gently rolling to steeply rolling
IMPROVEMENTS See reverse side
FOR WHAT ACQUIRED Reservoir — HOW ACQUIRED D/T — DATE 2 August 1955
FROM WHOM ACQUIRED J. E. Shadburn — PURCHASE PRICE $6,100.00 — INTEREST PAID - — TOTAL PRICE $6,100.
APPROPRIATION 96x3122 Buford (01.102) — ALLOTMENT
WHERE CONVEYANCE RECORDED Clerk, Superior Court, Forsyth County — DATE RECORDED
O. C. OF E. FILE NOS.; CORRESPONDENCE — PLAT
REMARKS C/A 661
LOCATION Forsyth County, Ga. — SECTION — TOWNSHIP 14th District — RANGE — P. M. A-146

Tenant House	16'x32'	Frame
L-	16'x16'	
Shed	16'x16'	
Barn	28'x30'	Frame
Poultry House	21'x50'	Frame

Fig. 4-15 Promissory Real Estate Card, A-146. (Courtesy U.S. Army Corps of Engineers, Mobile District)

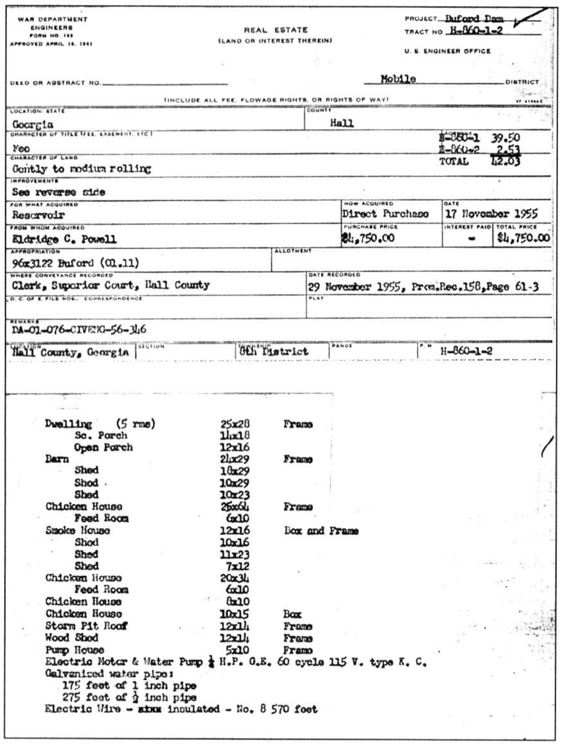

WAR DEPARTMENT ENGINEERS FORM NO. 195 APPROVED APRIL 14, 1941

REAL ESTATE (LAND OR INTEREST THEREIN)

PROJECT Buford Dam
TRACT NO. H-860-1-2
U. S. ENGINEER OFFICE
Mobile DISTRICT
DEED OR ABSTRACT NO.
(INCLUDE ALL FEE, FLOWAGE RIGHTS, OR RIGHTS OF WAY)

LOCATION: STATE Georgia — COUNTY Hall
CHARACTER OF TITLE (FEE, EASEMENT, ETC.) Fee — H-860-1 39.50; H-860-2 2.53; TOTAL 42.03
CHARACTER OF LAND Gently to medium rolling
IMPROVEMENTS See reverse side
FOR WHAT ACQUIRED Reservoir — HOW ACQUIRED Direct Purchase — DATE 17 November 1955
FROM WHOM ACQUIRED Eldridge C. Powell — PURCHASE PRICE $4,750.00 — INTEREST PAID - — TOTAL PRICE $4,750.00
APPROPRIATION 96x3122 Buford (01.11) — ALLOTMENT
WHERE CONVEYANCE RECORDED Clerk, Superior Court, Hall County — DATE RECORDED 29 November 1955, Prom.Rec.158,Page 61-3
O. C. OF E. FILE NOS.; CORRESPONDENCE — PLAT
REMARKS DA-01-076-CIVENG-56-346
LOCATION Hall County, Georgia — SECTION — TOWNSHIP 8th District — RANGE — P. M. H-860-1-2

Dwelling (5 rms)	25x28	Frame
Sc. Porch	14x18	
Open Porch	12x16	
Barn	24x29	Frame
Shed	18x29	
Shed	10x29	
Shed	10x23	
Chicken House	25x64	Frame
Feed Room	6x10	
Smoke House	12x16	Box and Frame
Shed	10x16	
Shed	11x23	
Shed	7x12	
Chicken House	20x34	
Feed Room	6x10	
Chicken House	8x10	
Chicken House	10x15	Box
Storm Pit Roof	12x14	Frame
Wood Shed	12x14	Frame
Pump House	5x10	Frame

Electric Motor & Water Pump ¼ H.P. G.E. 60 cycle 115 V. type K. C.
Galvanized water pipe:
175 feet of 1 inch pipe
275 feet of ½ inch pipe
Electric Wire - insulated - No. 8 570 feet

Fig. 4-16 Promissory Real Estate Card, H-860-1-2. (Courtesy U.S. Army Corps of Engineers, Mobile District)

for the 325 acre tract and $7,642.00 for the 101.90 acre tract.[22] H.W. Summerour received $22,410.00 for 111.60 acres of land that had been appraised at $14,000.00.[23] A jury awarded Clyde W. Lawson of Atlanta $20,000.00 for 85.70 acres of land located in Forsyth County that was appraised at $14,950.00.[24] On April 3, 1957 a jury awarded Roy P. Otwell an additional $750.00 for 116.37 acres of land in Forsyth County.[25]

These are but a few of the many cases heard in federal court concerning land appraisals. Information concerning disposition of these cases does not include appeals by either side that may have been heard at a later date. In some cases the jury awarded large sums of money to property owners. In others they felt the appraisal price, if not completely accurate, was close enough. Many of the rulings were not finalized for years, the cases moving well into the 1960's and beyond before final disposition.

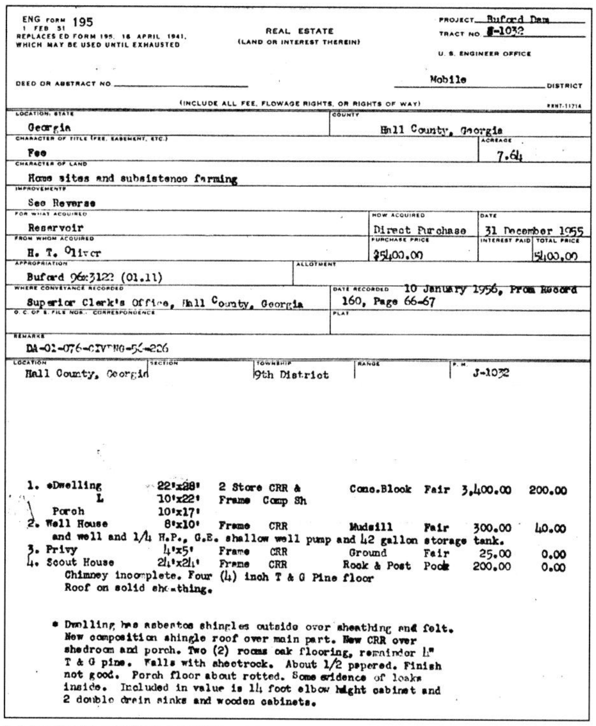

ENG FORM 195 1 FEB 51 REPLACES ED FORM 195, 14 APRIL 1941, WHICH MAY BE USED UNTIL EXHAUSTED

REAL ESTATE (LAND OR INTEREST THEREIN)

PROJECT Buford Dam
TRACT NO. J-1032
U. S. ENGINEER OFFICE
Mobile DISTRICT
DEED OR ABSTRACT NO.
(INCLUDE ALL FEE, FLOWAGE RIGHTS, OR RIGHTS OF WAY)

LOCATION: STATE Georgia — COUNTY Hall County, Georgia
CHARACTER OF TITLE (FEE, EASEMENT, ETC.) Fee — ACREAGE 7.64
CHARACTER OF LAND Home sites and subsistence farming
IMPROVEMENTS See Reverse
FOR WHAT ACQUIRED Reservoir — HOW ACQUIRED Direct Purchase — DATE 31 December 1955
FROM WHOM ACQUIRED H. T. Oliver — PURCHASE PRICE $5400.00 — INTEREST PAID — TOTAL PRICE 5400.00
APPROPRIATION Buford 96x3122 (01.11) — ALLOTMENT
WHERE CONVEYANCE RECORDED Superior Clerk's Office, Hall County, Georgia — DATE RECORDED 10 January 1956, Prom Record 160, Page 66-67
O. C. OF E. FILE NOS.; CORRESPONDENCE — PLAT
REMARKS DA-01-076-CIVENG-56-206
LOCATION Hall County, Georgia — SECTION — TOWNSHIP 9th District — RANGE — P. M. J-1032

1. *Dwelling	22'x28'	2 Store CRR &	Conc.Block	Fair	3,400.00	200.00
L	10'x22'	Frame Comp Sh				
Porch	10'x17'					
2. Well House	8'x10'	Frame CRR	Mudsill	Fair	300.00	40.00
and well and 1/4 H.P., G.E. shallow well pump and 42 gallon storage tank.						
3. Privy	4'x5'	Frame CRR	Ground	Fair	25.00	0.00
4. Scout House	24'x24'	Frame CRR	Rock & Post	Poor	200.00	0.00

Chimney incomplete. Four (4) inch T & G Pine floor
Roof on solid sheathing.

* Dwelling has asbestos shingles outside over sheathing and felt. New composition shingle roof over main part. New CRR over shedroom and porch. Two (2) rooms oak flooring, remainder 4" T & G pine. Walls with sheetrock. About 1/2 papered. Finish not good. Porch floor about rotted. Some evidence of leaks inside. Included in value is 14 foot elbow hight cabinet and 2 double drain sinks and wooden cabinets.

Fig. 4-17 Promissory Real Estate Card, J-1032. (Courtesy U.S. Army Corps of Engineers, Mobile District)

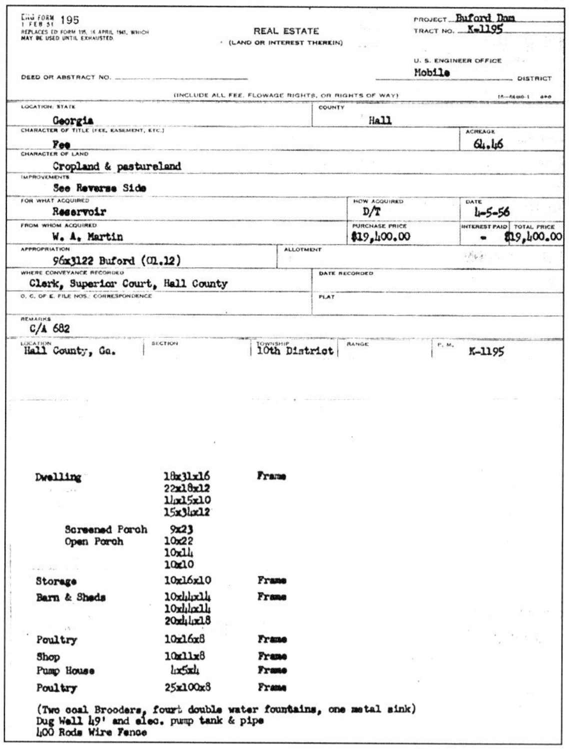

ENG FORM 195 1 FEB 51 REPLACES ED FORM 195, 14 APRIL 1941, WHICH MAY BE USED UNTIL EXHAUSTED

REAL ESTATE (LAND OR INTEREST THEREIN)

PROJECT Buford Dam
TRACT NO. K-1195
U. S. ENGINEER OFFICE
Mobile DISTRICT
DEED OR ABSTRACT NO.
(INCLUDE ALL FEE, FLOWAGE RIGHTS, OR RIGHTS OF WAY)

LOCATION: STATE Georgia — COUNTY Hall
CHARACTER OF TITLE (FEE, EASEMENT, ETC.) Fee — ACREAGE 64.46
CHARACTER OF LAND Cropland & pastureland
IMPROVEMENTS See Reverse Side
FOR WHAT ACQUIRED Reservoir — HOW ACQUIRED D/T — DATE 4-5-56
FROM WHOM ACQUIRED W. A. Martin — PURCHASE PRICE $19,400.00 — INTEREST PAID - — TOTAL PRICE $19,400.00
APPROPRIATION 96x3122 Buford (01.12) — ALLOTMENT
WHERE CONVEYANCE RECORDED Clerk, Superior Court, Hall County — DATE RECORDED
O. C. OF E. FILE NOS.; CORRESPONDENCE — PLAT
REMARKS C/A 682
LOCATION Hall County, Ga. — SECTION — TOWNSHIP 10th District — RANGE — P. M. K-1195

Dwelling	18x31x16	Frame
	22x18x12	
	14x15x10	
	15x34x12	
Screened Porch	9x23	
Open Porch	10x22	
	10x14	
	10x10	
Storage	10x16x10	Frame
Barn & Sheds	10x44x14	Frame
	10x44x14	
	20x44x18	
Poultry	10x16x8	Frame
Shop	10x11x8	Frame
Pump House	4x5x4	Frame
Poultry	25x100x8	Frame

(Two coal Brooders, four double water fountains, one metal sink)
Dug Well 49' and elec. pump tank & pipe
400 Rods Wire Fence

Fig. 4-18 Promissory Real Estate Card, K-1195. (Courtesy U.S. Army Corps of Engineers, Mobile District)

Notes

1. Gainesville Daily Times, April 4, 1954

2. Ibid., February 11, 1957

3. Ibid.

4. Ibid., circa 1950

5. Ibid., July 18, 1954

6. Ibid., circa 1950

7. Ibid., May 14, 1954

8. Ibid., circa 1950

9. Ibid.

10. Ibid., May 14, 1954

11. Ibid., circa 1950

12. Ibid., April 1, 1954

13. Ibid., circa 1950

14. Land appraisal cases tried in United States District Court, Federal Courthouse, Gainesville, Georgia.

15. Gainesville Daily Times, circa 1950

16. Land appraisal cases tried in United States District Court, Federal Courthouse, Gainesville, Georgia, Case no. 637.

17. Ibid., Case no. 644

18. Ibid., Case no. 651

19. Gainesville Daily Times, August, 1955

20. Ibid., April 11, 1956

21. Ibid, April 12, 1956

22. Ibid., April 14, 1956

23. Ibid., April 12, 1956

24. Ibid., June 28, 1956

25. Land appraisal cases tried in United States District Court, Federal Courthouse Gainesville, Georgia Case no.661.

Hartsfield heads a long list of dignitaries present at the ground breaking.

CHAPTER FIVE

GROUND BREAKING CEREMONY,
WEDNESDAY, MARCH 1, 1950

Throngs of people make their way along a dirt road that will someday become Buford Dam Road. The small ridge in the background is where the ground breaking ceremony will be held. (Courtesy U.S. Army Corps of Engineers, Mobile District)

Nearly five years had passed since Congress had approved the Buford Dam Project as part of the Apalachicola, Chattahoochee, Flint River System development but it was not until late 1949 that the green light for construction was given. Work was scheduled to begin in early 1950 and a fitting ceremony had been planned to mark the occasion. A tremendous change was about to befall this region of North Georgia, the rippling effects being felt even today. A multi-million dollar public works project was about to begin and the influence it would have on the land as well as the people of this area has yet to be equaled. This region of North Georgia, mostly rural, had never experienced anything like the Buford Dam Project and in years to come that same rural setting would be transposed into a sprawling 38,000 acre reservoir unmatched in popularity anywhere in the United States.

The ceremony chosen to commemorate this event was scheduled to be held on Wednesday, March 1, 1950. The ground breaking, marking the start of this massive public works project, would take place on the left bank of the Chattahoochee River in Gwinnett County on a high peak overlooking the site chosen for the earth dam that would hold back the waters of Lake Lanier. The planners of the ceremony chose this date as it was the 59th birthday of one of the most ardent supporters of the project, Atlanta Mayor William Berry Hartsfield, *Fig. 2-2*,.[1] Early on Hartsfield had been appointed as the acting chairman of the committee set up to plan the

Fig. 5-1 Memo concerning luncheon held on Buford Dam ground breaking ceremony. (Courtesy U.S. Army Corps of Engineers, Mobile District)

Fig. 5-2 Program for ground breaking, March 1, 1950. (Courtesy U.S. Army Corps of Engineers, Mobile District)

Georgia. Buford Dam represented the means to an end in seeing Georgia and the South's economic and industrial muscles flexed.

In January, 1950 he held a luncheon in the President's Room of the Capital City Club in Atlanta to work out and finalize details for the upcoming ground breaking ceremony with the committee. The committee was made up of local people many of whom had been involved in earlier approval then funding battles with Harfsfield on Capitol Hill. Weldon Archer, Gwinnett County Commission Chairman; Weldon Gardner, President of the Buford Kiwanis Club; L.D. Ewing, Executive Secretary of the Gwinnett County Chamber of Commerce; Roy P. Otwell, Mayor of Cumming, Georgia; Sylvan Meyer, Gainesville Daily Times and J. Larry Kleckley, President of the Gainesville Chamber of Commerce all were invited to attend the luncheon.[2]

Several well known dignitaries were originally slated to speak at the ceremony among them Senators Richard B. Russell Jr., *Fig. 2-9*, and Walter F. George; *Fig. 2-10*, Representatives James C. Davis, *Fig. 2-6*, and

Fig. 5-3 Governor Herman Talmadge. (Courtesy U.S. Army Corps of Engineers, Mobile District)

John S. Wood; *Fig. 2-8*, Governor Herman Talmadge; *Fig. 5-3*, General Lewis A. Pick, Chief of Army Engineers; *Fig. 5-4*, Colonel Bernard L. Robinson the South Atlantic Division Chief; *Fig. 3-1*, and Colonel Walter K. Wilson, Mobile District Chief, F*ig. 3-3*.[3] On February 22, 1950 the names of eight men who would officially break ground at the ceremony appeared in the Gainesville Daily Times. Those chosen to break ground represented a cross section of federal, state, and local officials from this area. Representatives James C. Davis, 5th District and John S. Wood, 9th District; Atlanta Mayor William B. Hartsfield; Governor Herman Talmadge; Colonel Bernard L.

ceremonial program. This would be right up his alley as his tenure as Mayor of Atlanta had prepared him well for just such a task. Also, being seen in the forefront of such a well publicized event could only enhance his image as a mover and a shaker. This is not to say that anyone else deserved the honor. He had long been an advocate of the project looking to the multiple benefits it would provide in ushering in a new industrial age for not only Atlanta but all of

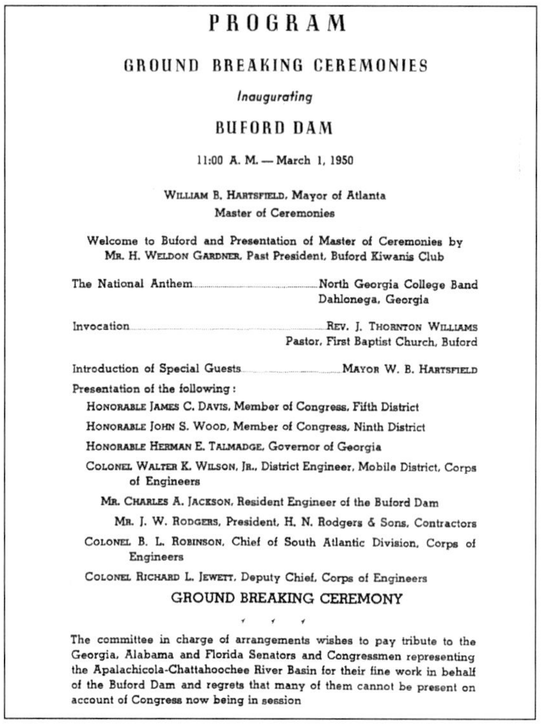

Ground Breaking Ceremony

Fig. 5-4 General Lewis Peck, Chief of Army Engineers at the time of the ground breaking. (Courtesy Office of History, U.S. Army Corps of Engineers)

Robinson; Cumming Mayor Roy P. Otwell; Weldon Gardner of Buford and Gwinnett County and J. Larry Kleckley of Gainesville and Hall County were scheduled to break earth that day.[4] Eugene Hart from the Atlanta Freight Bureau; Colonel J.R. Jewett, Deputy Chief of Engineers; and Colonel Walter K. Wilson, Mobile District Chief also broke ground that day although not originally slated to do so.

Fig. 5-5 The Atlanta delegation of the motorcade pulls of the road at Carroll's Texaco filling station on Highway 23 just south of Buford to link up with the Buford Motorcade. (Courtesy Mrs. Weldon Gardner)

Fig. 5-6 Contemporary photograph of the same area. (RDC)

The ground breaking committee wanted to make the event memorable but perhaps the one aspect of the ceremony that would forever remain in the minds of those who attended was not part of the plan, the

Fig. 5-7 Governor Herman Talmadge is among the group waiting for the motorcade to proceed on into Buford. (Courtesy Mrs. Weldon Gardner)

weather. It had rained the night before and to say the conditions at the ground breaking site were less than desirable would be an understatement. The fact that there were clear skies and it was not raining was the only plus for holding the ceremony that day. Couple the bad weather from the night before with the conditions of the dirt roads and it would not be hard to imagine what travel in and out of the area was like. Since the ground breaking ceremony was being held at the construction site, in a rural area, the roads, especially those close to where the ceremony would be held, were no more than access roads cut for construction. You have to remember that this was a rural area of North Georgia in the early 1950's. The system of roads was not as extensive or in as good a shape as it is today.

This was a well publicized event and it seemed everybody and his brother wanted to come and perhaps catch a glimpse of one of the many dignitaries that were scheduled to speak. It was a big and important event taking place in an area that had never seen such excitement. It was reported that a motorcade of some 200 vehicles from several cities and counties south of the project near Atlanta were going to make their way to the ceremony. They linked up with another motorcade about two miles south of Buford at Carroll's Texaco Filling Station on Highway 23 where they proceeded through the town that was decked out in full regalia. There were flags and streamers draped all over the streets in honor of the occasion. The motorcade made its way through the streets of town, horns blasting and sirens, from the many local law enforcement agencies participating in the event, ringing loudly. The influx of cars and trucks was not limited to the Buford area. Droves of vehicles bringing thousands of people were coming to the site from seemingly every direction.[5] The motorcade in Buford traveled through Sugar Hill and several miles outside of town rolled onto a dirt road where the casualty list of stranded vehicles began to mount up. Eventually all routes to the ceremony ended up on an access road which would become Buford Dam Road in the future. Even though it was not raining at the time the miserable conditions from the night before, creating damp and muddy roads, were taking their toll. Just about everywhere along the ceremony route cars and trucks were mired in the muck. They were sliding off in the ditches or being left abandoned, unable to get traction. Thousands of people, many of them school children given the day off to witness history, made their way to the ceremony site in spite of the miserable conditions, *Fig. 5-8* and *Fig. 5-9*. A seemingly endless line of cars and trucks carrying thousands of people eventually ended up lining the ceremony route. It was estimated that nearly 5000 people attended the ground breaking that day. Thousands of others were turned away because of the traffic and crowds that quickly flooded into the area.[6]

Fig. 5-8 Visitors at the ground breaking. (Courtesy James C. Davis Papers, Special Collections, Robert W. Woodruff Library, Emory University)

Fig. 5-9 Ground breaking area on the Gwinnett County side of the dam site. (Courtesy U.S. Army Corps of Engineers, Mobile District)

Fig. 5-10 Visitors at the ground breaking. (Courtesy U.S. Army Corps of Engineers, Mobile District)

GROUND BREAKING CEREMONY

Fig. 5-11 Grandstand where the ceremony would take place. (Courtesy U.S. Army Corps of Engineers, Mobile District)

Fig. 5-13 William B. Hartsfield at the podium. (Courtesy U.S. Army Corps of Engineers, Mobile District)

Fig. 5-14 William B. Hartsfield stands above the shovels that will be used to break ground for the project to begin. (Courtesy U.S. Army Corps of Engineers, Mobile District)

At 11:00 A.M. the ceremony began. A small grandstand draped with an American flag was set up on a high hill overlooking the Chattahoochee River. The platform was located about where the Upper Overlook is today. This high bluff overlooking the river would be the site of the Operations Building constructed a year or so after the ground breaking and served as the Resident Engineer's Office, *Fig. 5-10* and *Fig. 5-11*. Prior to construction of this building the Resident Engineer's Office was located in an old building in Buford, Georgia. *Fig. 5-12*

Fig. 5-12 Resident Engineer's Office in the early 1950's prior to construction of a building on the project site. (Courtesy U.S. Army Corps of Engineers, Mobile District)

Although the ground breaking ceremony would be held here actual construction would begin northeast of this site where the first of three saddle dikes (saddle dike no.3) and the spillway would be constructed. The North Georgia College Band was on hand to present the National Anthem to the crowds, then Mayor Hartsfield, *Fig. 5-13* and *Fig. 5-14*, welcomed the many visitors who had braved the cold, damp, and windy day to give the project a proper sending off. As the wind blew up over the hillside and across the high open bluff where the grandstand was sitting Hartsfield spoke of seeing the project become a reality. "The project will revolutionize life in the basin of the Chattahoochee River......and will be another long step in the multi-purpose development of the Chattahoochee-Flint-Apalachicola River System of waterways with navigation first to Columbus and eventually Atlanta."[7] It is in this statement that you see Hartsfield's dream of Atlanta becoming a port city. It would be a familiar theme that he would echo seven years later at the dedication. Unfortunately for the mayor it would be a dream that would never become a reality. In fact, when the mayor retired from public life it was one of the few areas of public service that he felt he was a failure. Not seeing the Chattahoochee River navigable all the way to Atlanta was a bitter pill to swallow.

After Hartsfield had presented his opening remarks he turned the podium over to his friend Weldon Gardner, an insurance agent from Buford who was a vigorous proponent at the local level. Gardner had worked closely with the mayor for many years and like the mayor was slated to break ground and begin the massive $42,000,000.00 dam. He looked to the people who had joined him on the hillside and talked of the river below them. "It will be made to serve mankind instead of being an angry red river that is carrying away the wealth of North Georgia at the rate of thousands of tons of top soil per year."[8]

The keynote speaker of the day was

Governor Herman Talmadge, *Fig. 5-15*, who would become the states junior senator in 1956 when he defeated Walter F. George for

Fig. 5-15 Governor Herman Talmadge. (Courtesy U.S. Army Corps of Engineers, Mobile District)

reelection. Talmadge was a very popular politician in Georgia who like his father Eugene Talmadge had his own eloquent way with words. Although Senators Russell and George as well as Representatives Davis and Wood were originally slated to speak at the ground breaking they were unable to attend the ceremony. Talmadge emphasized the importance the project would have to the Georgia economy. "Georgia and the South have been "passed up" in several of the big industrial revolutions that have taken place since the turn of the century. The automobile makers centered in Detroit. The tire makers concentrated at Akron. The airplane companies chose New England, Baltimore, the Middle West, and the Pacific Coast. We did not get a slice of any of the big expansions in radio and television, nearly all of them being manufactured north of the Mason-Dixon Line. We only got a fragmentary part of the steel development.....Perhaps some of you have noticed the trend which, in the last few years, has brought to the South branch factories of great national manufacturing interests. In the last few years we have witnessed the establishment of big automobile assembly plants, farm machinery factories, electrical supply companies, and other factories which found it necessary to get closer to our rapidly expanding Southern markets."[9]

Talmadge in an ironic twist of history spoke of the plight of the Southern economy and its inequity of trade. "According to the last estimate of the U.S. Census Department, made in 1947, we manufactured a million and a half dollars worth of agricultural implements and bought thirteen million worth from other states. We made four and a half million dollars worth of shoes and bought seventeen and a half million dollars worth. We bought three times as much feed for farm animals as we produced ourselves.....We must make good use of our own advantages. We must build the plants and manufacture the goods that our people are buying in vast quantities in other states.....As we have said before, Georgia and the South are no longer the nation's number one economic problem. This section is now the number one economic opportunity in this country."[10]

The United States Army Corps of Engineers, who would oversee the construction and operation of the project, was represented at the ceremony by Colonel B.L. Robinson, *Fig. 5-16*, the South Atlantic Division Chief and Colonel Walter K. Wilson, *Fig. 5-17*, the Mobile District Chief. Wilson as District Engineer would supervise

Fig. 5-16 Colonel B.L. Robinson, South Atlantic Chief. (Courtesy U.S. Army Corps of Engineers, Mobile District)

Fig. 5-17 Colonel Walter K. Wilson, Mobile District Chief. (Courtesy U.S. Army Corps of Engineers, Mobile District)

construction of the dam. Colonel Robinson spoke of the good this project and others like it would have on America as a whole, "the Buford Dam Project was one which the federal government can not afford not to build.....the factors of water and soil conservation are pressing upon the industrial and agricultural life of the American people and the Buford Project is an ideal method for the advancement of both factors."[11]

The man who would be the resident engineer for the project, Charles A. Jackson, **Fig. 5-18**, was introduced to the crowd.

Fig. 5-18 Charles A. Jackson, Resident Engineer at Buford Dam. (Courtesy U.S. Army Corps of Engineers, Mobile District)

Jackson would be coming from the Allatoona Project and when the Buford Dam Project was completed he became the resident engineer for the Hartwell Dam Project. Also introduced was H.N. Rodgers representing the firm that had been contracted to construct the 1600 foot earth dam as well as the spillway and saddle dike no.3.[12]

With the preliminaries out of the way the focus of the day's events moved to the ceremonial breaking of ground. The dignitaries lined up next to the grandstand and positioning the bright silver shovels in front of them posed for several photographs before driving the spades into the red Georgia clay, **Fig. 5-19**. Governor Herman Talmadge, who was reported to have sank his shovel deeper than anyone; Weldon Gardner, representing Buford and a Buford member of the Buford Dam Planning Committee; E.L. Hart, Manager of the Atlanta Freight Bureau (now the Georgia Freight Bureau); William B. Hartsfield, Mayor of Atlanta; J. Larry Kleckley, President of the Gainesville Chamber of Commerce; Colonel B.L. Robinson, South Atlantic Division Chief; Roy P. Otwell, Mayor of

Fig. 5-19 Breaking earth to begin the project. (Courtesy James C. Davis Papers, Special Collections, Robert W. Woodruff Library, Emory University)

Cumming; Colonel Walter K. Wilson Jr., Mobile District Chief; and Lt. Colonel J.R. Jewett, Deputy Chief of Engineers, Washington, D.C. all turned the red earth to officially begin the project.[13]

Prior to the ground breaking the ceremonial shovels and picks that would be used to break earth were put on display in

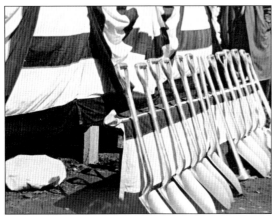

Fig. 5-20 Twelve ceremonial shovels and two picks that will be used to break ground are seen positioned in front of the grandstand. (Courtesy U.S. Army Corps of Engineers, Mobile District)

front of the grandstand. *(Fig.5-20)* There were 12 shovels and two picks on display. The ground breaking photographs show only nine men breaking ground. In completing research for this publication it has been discovered that several individuals not pictured breaking ground that day have souvenir shovels with their names inscribed on them commemorating the event.

At the conclusion of the ceremony out of town visitors were invited to a luncheon sponsored by the Buford Kiwanis Club. This event was held at a new school building recently constructed just off of Highway 23 in Buford, Georgia which today is an

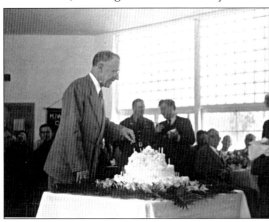

Fig. 5-21 Cutting the birthday cake at the luncheon after the ground breaking. (Courtesy William B. Hartsfield Papers, Special Collections, Robert W. Woodruff Library, Emory University)

administrative building for the Buford City School System. At this luncheon Mayor Hartsfield was presented with a cake in honor of his 59th birthday, Fig. 5-21.[14]

Several hours after the ceremony the crowds had thinned considerably but there were still lines of people making their way back to their vehicles, many of which were still stranded in the mud and had to be towed out with cars, trucks, and tractors. For those who attended the event it would be something they would never forget.

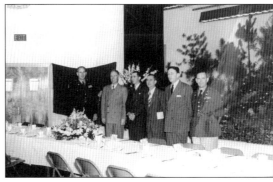

Fig. 5-22 Colonel Wilson; Mayor Hartsfield; H. Jack Turner; Weldon Gardner; ______ ; and Colonel Robinson waiting for the ground breaking luncheon to begin. (Courtesy Mrs. Weldon Gardner)

GWINNETT COUNTY CHAMBER OF COMMERCE
P. O. BOX 123
LAWRENCEVILLE, GEORGIA
February 23, 1950

The Daily Times
303 West Washington Street
Gainesville, Georgia

Gentlemen:

The people of Gwinnett County rejoice with the citizens of Buford and surrounding territory in the realization of the construction of the Buford Dam, which is to be celebrated in the ground breaking ceremonies to be held Wednesday, March 1.

As President of the Gwinnett County Chamber of Commerce, and on behalf of the members of this fine organization who have worked so earnestly for the approval of this project, I wish to extend good wishes and hearty congratulations to all who had a part in this accomplishment.

Sincerely,
J. Floyd Brannan
J. Floyd Brannan
President, Gwinnett County
Chamber of Commerce

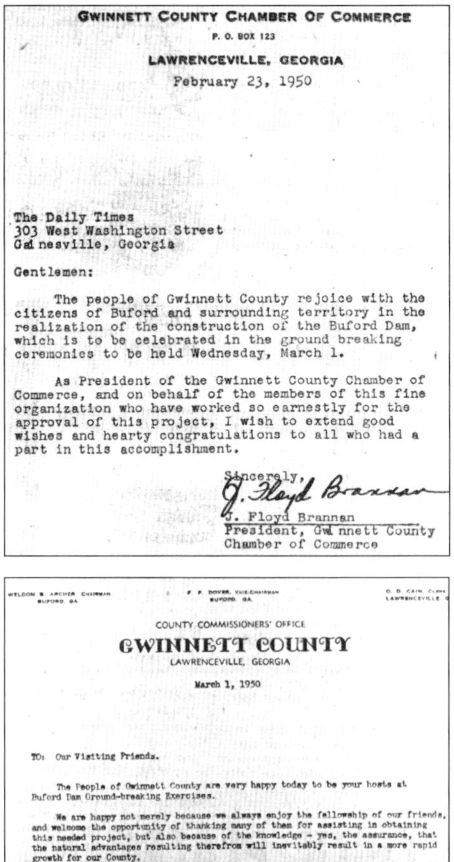

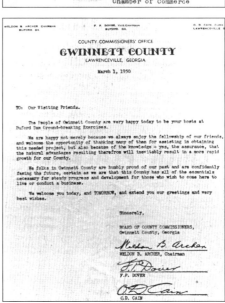

Fig. 5-23 Letter concerning ground breaking-Gwinnett County Chamber of Commerce. (Courtesy Gainesville Daily Times)

WELDON B. ARCHER, CHAIRMAN, BUFORD, GA — F. P. DOVER, VICE-CHAIRMAN, BUFORD, GA — O. D. CAIN, CLERK, LAWRENCEVILLE, G

COUNTY COMMISSIONERS' OFFICE
GWINNETT COUNTY
LAWRENCEVILLE, GEORGIA
March 1, 1950

TO: Our Visiting Friends.

The People of Gwinnett County are very happy today to be your hosts at Buford Dam Ground-breaking Exercises.

We are happy not merely because we always enjoy the fellowship of our friends, and welcome the opportunity of thanking many of them for assisting in obtaining this needed project, but also because of the knowledge - yes, the assurance, that the natural advantages resulting therefrom will inevitably result in a more rapid growth for our County.

We folks in Gwinnett County are humbly proud of our past and are confidently facing the future, certain as we are that this County has all of the essentials necessary for steady progress and development for those who wish to come here to live or conduct a business.

We welcome you today, and TOMORROW, and extend you our greetings and very best wishes.

Sincerely,

BOARD OF COUNTY COMMISSIONERS,
Gwinnett County, Georgia

Weldon B. Archer
WELDON B. ARCHER, Chairman
F.P. Dover
F.P. DOVER
O.D. Cain
O.D. CAIN

Fig. 5-24 Letter concerning ground breaking-Gwinnett County Commissioners Office. (Courtesy Gainesville Daily Times)

Fig. 5-25 Letter concerning ground breaking- City of Atlanta. (Courtesy Gainesville Daily Times)

WILLIAM B. HARTSFIELD
MAYOR

ERNEST J. BREWER
EXECUTIVE SECRETARY

CITY OF ATLANTA
OFFICE OF THE MAYOR
ATLANTA 3, GEORGIA

February 8, 1950

Editor
The Daily Times
Gainesville, Georgia

Dear Sir:

Wednesday, March 1, will be a great day for all of North Georgia and, indeed, all of that part of Georgia drained by the Chattahoochee River.

The beginning of construction of the Buford Dam means, first, the expenditure of some forty million dollars in the North Georgia area and, second, the creation of a large body of water for recreational purposes, the prevention of floods, a program of increased prevention of soil erosion, and the production of badly needed electric power.

The people of Atlanta and Fulton County join with their sister cities and counties of North Georgia in hailing the start of the Buford Dam as the beginning of a new era in the industrial development of North Georgia.

Yours very truly,

Wm B Hartsfield

Mayor

Fig. 5-26 Letter concerning ground breaking- John S. Wood. (Courtesy Gainesville Daily Times)

COMMITTEE ON
AMERICAN ACTIVITIES

MEMBER
COMMITTEE ON
EDUCATION AND LABOR

Congress of the United States
House of Representatives
Washington, D. C.
February 8, 1950

OFFICE ADD
319 HOUSE OFFICE
WASHINGTON,

Mr. Sylvan Meyer,
Managing Editor,
THE DAILY TIMES,
Gainesville, Georgia.

Dear Mr. Meyer:

On the first day of March, the ground will be broken for the great Buford Dam, a giant and encompassing project which will mean many things to many people in northern Georgia.

The beginning of work on this vast project, the first of its character in all the history of this Congressional District, will bring into our communities, and into our lives, the Corps of Army Engineers, a diligent body of men who work constantly for the improvement of the physical condition of our country in time of peace.

I am sure that hospitable Georgians will welcome these newcomers; I am equally certain that they will deserve that welcome and, when they leave, will forever be welcome to return.

The Buford Dam itself, one of the largest in the Nation, will mean an immediate economic gain to the people of our area, and its future benefits to our section of the state promise to be large. I am aware that its building will cause inconvenience, and even more, to some of the people, particularly in Hall County, and will mean to them, and to several governmental subdivisions certain losses. But the history of the world shows that all progress is attained at some cost to certain individuals, and I am hopeful that the benefits to be derived now and in the future from the Buford Dam will be so great that those individuals who suffer by reason of its construction will be adequately compensated by the knowledge that they have made what is, afterall, the greatest contribution to the common good.

I want to congratulate the DAILY TIMES on its plans for publication of a commemorative edition marking the breaking of ground for the dam. I am certain that in the years to come, this issue will be a document of historical importance.

Sincerely yours,

Jno S. Wood

JSW:rac

Jno. S. Wood, M. C.

CHAMBER OF COMMERCE

127 E. WASHINGTON ST.
TELEPHONE 467

Gainesville Georgia

March 1, 1950

Daily Times
Gainesville, Georgia

Sirs:

The Gainesville Chamber of Commerce recognizes the events of today as having historical importance in the industrial reconstruction to fall on this entire area.

We join in welcoming the distinquished guests and Army Corp of Engineering Officials to the Ground Breaking Ceremonies. We are priviledged to be one of their hosts at the luncheon following the ceremonies.

Once again we declare our willingness to cooperate fully with cities, counties, and other chambers of commerce in planning and developing the entire Buford Dam Area so that it will serve the best purposes of this region and perform all the important functions for which it is destined.

Sincerely yours,

J. Larry Kleckley

J. Larry Kleckley
President

JLK:sm

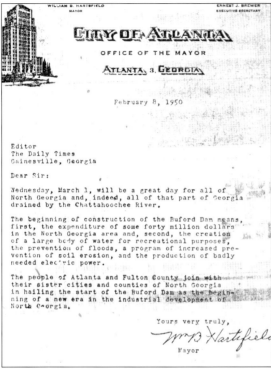

Fig. 5-27 Letter concerning ground breaking- Gainesville Chamber of Commerce. (Courtesy Gainesville Daily Times)

CITY OF GAINESVILLE
GAINESVILLE, GEORGIA

March 1, 1950

Editor
The Daily Times
Gainesville

Sir:

On behalf of the people of the City of Gainesville, the Commissioners join today in dedicating the beginning of the Buford Dam, a structure destined to have a great effect on this region.

Gainesville appreciates the cooperative spirit shown throughout this section on planning for the great project and in preparing for the changes it will bring about.

On this day, the Commissioners salute their neighbors throughout Georgia, the Army engineers, and all those responsible for the dam and its planning.

By working together, with mutual considerations and constant attention to the public good, the people of Northeast Georgia can make the Buford project a signal event in the industrial and recreational development of our region.

The Commissioners

C. O. Sorley
A. Wright
Geo. H. Oxford

Fig. 5-28 Letter concerning ground breaking- City of Gainesville. (Courtesy Gainesville Daily Times)

Fig. 5-29 The dignitaries are given the go to break ground and the project officially begins. (Courtesy U.S. Army Corps of Engineers, Mobile District)

Notes

1. Atlanta Journal, March 1, 1950

2. Memo from Mayor Hartsfield's Office, January 10, 1950, Courtesy U.S. Army Corps of Engineers, Mobile District

3. Untitled and undated newspaper article, circa February, 1950

4. Gainesville Daily Times, February 22, 1950

5. Atlanta Journal, March 1, 1950

6. Ibid.

7. Atlanta Constitution, March 2, 1950

8. Speech given by Weldon Gardner at the ground breaking ceremony on March 1, 1950. Courtesy Mrs. Weldon Gardner, Buford, Georgia.

9. Speech given by Herman Talmadge and released to the United States Army Corps of Engineers for the ground breaking. Released 12:00 noon, March 1, 1950. Courtesy U. S. Army Corps of Engineers, Mobile District

10. Ibid.

11. Atlanta Constitution, March 2, 1950

12. Gainesville Daily Times, March 1, 1950

13. Atlanta Constitution, March 2, 1950

14. Ibid.

Looking north up the length of the spillway toward what will someday be Lake Lanier. The date is October 3, 1950.

CHAPTER SIX

CONSTRUCTION BEGINS - SADDLE DIKES AND A SPILLWAY

A 1950 era station wagon is parked atop the construction of Saddle Dike no.3. This saddle dike and the spillway further north were the first areas of construction on the project. (Courtesy U.S. Army Corps of Engineers, Mobile District)

The first areas of construction on the project are barely visible today unless you know where to look for them. Saddle dike no.3 and the spillway, both located a mile or so from the main earth dam site, are where construction on the project got its start. A saddle dike is a concrete, earth or rock structure that is positioned on a low lying saddle or swale in the topography of the land. Simply put, it keeps water out of the "saddle" or low lying dips in the ground.[1] In this case the three saddle dikes built for Buford Dam are made of the same material as the main dam, earth, and for the same reason, the plentiful supply of this resource. Without the saddle dikes many of the low valleys that intersect hills near the dam would have been breached by the rising water as they were not high enough to prevent the flow of water over them. The elevations of these dikes were matched with that of the main earth dam. Saddle dike no.1, *Fig. 6-1*, is located between Sawnee Campground and West Bank Park. Saddle dike no.2, *Fig. 6-1*, is located between West Bank Park and the main earth dam. This saddle dike is divided into two sections, the first, 2-A is positioned between West Bank Park and the West Bank Overlook. The second, 2-B, is located between the West Bank Overlook and the main earth dam. A natural geological formation something similar to a ridge or hill divides 2-A and 2-B on the lake side. Only the downstream sides of the dike appear as one long section without division. The third saddle dike, *Fig. 6-1*, which was the first one built, is adjacent to the spillway to its east between

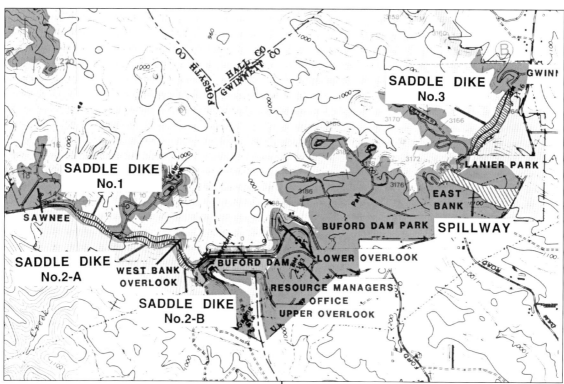

Fig. 6-1 Location of saddle dikes and the spillway for Buford Dam. (RDC)

Lanier Park and Gwinnett Park. It remains today as the only saddle dike not serving as a highway as both entrances are barricaded off to prevent travel over the dike.

The spillway is adjacent to saddle dike no.3 to its west. Had Buford Dam exhibited a concrete dam as originally planned then the spillway would probably have been constructed at the dam site but being an earth structure prevented this. The spillway on this project was constructed a mile and a half from the main earth dam and is designed to allow for an unrestricted and uncontrolled flow of water to escape the reservoir should the lake level reach flood stage. It is not a concrete structure with gates to control the flow of water but rather a flat level area adjacent to the lake with a base elevation of 1085.0. The elevation of the spillway was determined by taking the highest known level that water from the Chattahoochee River had ever obtained during a flood and then adding a comfortable safety margin to that. Engineers designed the spillway with the belief that it would never be used and to date it has served that purpose, as water has never moved from the lake into the huge

Fig. 6-2 Saddle dike no.1 simply appears as a large land clearing. It has yet to take on its distinctive triangular serpentine shape. Although originally it was not intended for use as a highway today Buford Dam Road runs over the top of this saddle dike, saddle dike no.2, and the main earth dam. Your view is east toward what will become West Bank Park. It is Wednesday, August 15, 1951. Saddle dike no.1 and no.2 were both contracted by the same company that cut the forebay, penstocks, sluice, and the access road, Groves, Lundin and Cox, Incorporated of Minneapolis, Minnesota for $2,836,712.00.[3] (Courtesy U.S. Army Corps of Engineers, Mobile District)

Construction Begins - Saddle Dikes and a Spillway

Fig. 6-3 Looking west toward Cumming, Georgia and it is beginning to take shape. (Courtesy U.S. Army Corps of Engineers, Mobile District)

Fig. 6-4 Same saddle dike but two months later from the opposite direction looking east toward West Bank Park. The rock strewn top of the structure here will be replaced with a hard black top in the future. (Courtesy U.S. Army Corps of Engineers, Mobile District)

Fig. 6-5 On Friday, December 26, 1952 it appears as it does today. This photograph was taken from the entrance to what will become West Bank Park. Your view is west and if you were to continue on in this direction you would pass the entrance to what will someday be Sawnee Campground which is one of the most popular camping facilities located on Lake Lanier. The snake like design of the saddle dike is one of form following function and purely economic in its conception. Engineers followed the highest ground in the area linking the crest of ridges together whenever possible.[4] (Courtesy U.S. Army Corps of Engineers, Mobile District)

chute.[2] About the only time you can see the spillway, other than viewing it from the water, is during the winter months when the trees, that line its sides and end, have lost their thick coating of foliage and reveal what is hidden during most of the year. Both saddle dike no.3 and the spillway were completed many years before the project was finished.

Fig. 6-4

Fig. 6-5

Fig. 6-6

Fig. 6-7

Fig. 6-6 Today the black top and time have changed the surrounding area immensely. (RDC)

Fig. 6-7 Surveyors work on the outline of the infant saddle dike no.2-A. Your view is east. You are moving in the direction of the main earth dam. It is Tuesday, July 17, 1951. (Courtesy U.S. Army Corps of Engineers, Mobile District)

Fig. 6-8 Four months later and the valleys have been filled in with earth and rock. Lakeside will be on the left. West Bank Overlook will be located at the end of this road in the background. (Courtesy U.S. Army Corps of Engineers, Mobile District)

Fig. 6-10 Saddle dike no. 2-A looking northwest to what will become the West Bank entrance. It is Tuesday, July 17, 1951. (Courtesy U.S. Army Corps of Engineers, Mobile District)

Fig. 6-9 Four decades in the blink of an eye. (RDC)

Fig. 6-11 Two months worth of earth work and it takes on its snake like design. (Courtesy U.S. Army Corps of Engineers, Mobile District)

Construction Begins - Saddle Dikes and a Spillway

Fig. 6-12 Same direction and place one month and a day later on Monday, November 5, 1951. The lake side is to the right. The future entrance to West Bank Park is at the end of the road in the background. (Courtesy U.S. Army Corps of Engineers, Mobile District)

Fig. 6-13 Today only the saddle dike remains the same. (RDC)

Fig. 6-14 Saddle dike no. 2-B looking south. If you take a left at the end of the road in the background you would come to the forebay excavation. Construction there has only recently started. The wood framing being constructed to the right is a vehicle maintenance and repair building. Today this area serves as the headquarters for a private contractor that provides general maintenance for the government. It is Tuesday, July 17, 1951. (Courtesy U.S. Army Corps of Engineers, Mobile District)

Fig. 6-14

Fig. 6-15 Two months later and the saddle dike is nearly finished. You can see the various heavy equipment vehicles, tires, and other items lying about the repair yard at right background. (Courtesy U.S. Army Corps of Engineers, Mobile District)

Fig. 6-16 A contemporary photograph of saddle dike no. 2-B looking south. (RDC)

Fig. 6-17 You are looking at the first contracted work started on the project, saddle dike no.3. It was awarded to H.M. Rodgers and Son of Memphis, Tennessee. They also built the spillway for a contract price of $297,627.00.⁵ Here heavy machines level and pack the saddle dike fill. Water will appear to the right in about six years. (Courtesy U.S. Army Corps of Engineers, Mobile District)

Fig. 6-18 Thursday, November 30, 1950 and your view is toward the western edge of Gwinnett Park looking toward Lanier Park. (Courtesy U.S. Army Corps of Engineers, Mobile District)

Fig. 6-19 On Friday, December 26, 1952 saddle dike no. 3 has been completed for nearly 19 months and it looks as if it has been here for a thousand years. Your view is west and another five years will pass before the Chattahoochee River will rise up and put this structure to good use. (Courtesy U.S. Army Corps of Engineers, Mobile District)

Fig. 6-20 Now the lake, dense undergrowth, and the march of time project a very different image. (RDC)

Construction Begins - Saddle Dikes and a Spillway

Fig. 6-21 Saddle dike no. 3 on Thursday, October 3, 1950. (Courtesy U.S. Army Corps of Engineers, Mobile District)

Fig. 6-22 Circa 1953 and the saddle dike has been completed for several years. The trees shown growing on the slope will have to be removed as their root systems could compromise the structural stability of the dike. (Courtesy U.S. Army Corps of Engineers, Mobile District)

Fig. 6-24 Excavation is well underway here to bring the base elevation of the spillway to 1,085 feet above sea level. If the lake elevation ever rises above 1085.0 then water will rush toward you, in this photograph, and continue to do so until the elevation of the lake falls below that level. The highest elevation ever obtained since the dam's construction was recorded at 1077.19 on April 14, 1964 which was still eight feet below flood stage. (Courtesy U.S. Army Corps of Engineers, Mobile District)

Fig. 6-23 Today the grass slope is manicured and smooth. (RDC)

Fig. 6-25 The completed spillway on April 20, 1951. (Courtesy U.S. Army Corps of Engineers, Mobile District)

Fig. 6-26 A contemporary photograph from about the same location. (RDC)

Fig. 6-27 A granite seam that ran across the width of the spillway near the southern end had to be removed. This rock had to be blasted and cut away in order to bring the base of the spillway to elevation 1085.0, which is flood stage for the reservoir. (Courtesy James C. Davis Papers. Special Collections, Robert W. Woodruff Library, Emory University)

Fig. 6-28 A rip-rap of granite layers the northern end of the spillway near what is today the lake. The granite seam mentioned in the previous photograph abuts the rip-rap in the upper right of this photograph. (Courtesy James C. Davis Papers. Special Collections, Robert W. Woodruff Library, Emory University)

Fig. 6-29 This scene today would be very difficult to view because of the thick undergrowth of trees and other foliage that has developed over the years. You are standing on the access road, which will become Buford Dam Road in the near future, looking north down the completed spillway. Evidence of the rock excavation is easily visible here. It is November 26, 1952 and the lake will form in the background in about 5 years. (Courtesy U.S. Army Corps of Engineers, Mobile District)

Fig. 6-30 It is easy to see why viewing the spillway today is so difficult. (RDC)

Notes

1. United States Senate Civil Functions Sub-Committee Appropriation Hearings, Tuesday, April 19, 1949, p.1244, as reported by Colonel Jewett in testimony before the sub-committee concerning the reason for the added cost of saddle dikes on the project.

2. Gainesville Daily Times

3. Ibid., 1957

4. Cecil Patterson, U.S. Army Corps of Engineers, Retired

5. Gainesville Daily Times, 1957

A downstream view of the forebay excavation.

CHAPTER SEVEN

Forebay Excavation and Intake Construction

The forebay is a channel cut of solid granite that allows water to flow through the intake structure. It is located on the lake side of the dam and is hidden from view by Lake Lanier. It very much resembles, in shape and size, the tailrace cut on the river side of the dam. Most of the granite removed from the forebay, as well as the tailrace, cuts were stored in the two stockpile areas, *Fig. 9-8*, that were located in the borrow area adjacent to the main earth dam construction. These granite chunks would eventually be used to layer the lake side of the main earth dam, saddle dikes, and bridge abutments. Excavation of the forebay was contracted by Groves, Lundin and Cox Inc. of Minneapolis, Minnesota on May 25, 1951 for $2,836,712.00.[1]

The intake structure, *Fig. 7-1*, rests against the face cut of the forebay and is comprised of three mammoth one hundred and ninety five foot concrete towers called monoliths. The base of the intake is at elevation 911.0 and the top at elevation 1106.0 but because the intake is located on the lake side of the dam only a very small portion of this structure is visible. It was built by J.A. Jones Construction Company of Charlotte, North Carolina for $2,011,402.00.

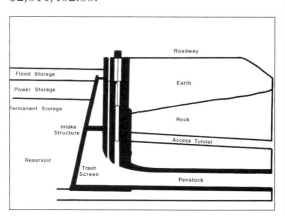

Fig. 7-1 (RDC)

Fig. 7-2 This is what the forebay area of the dam looked like on Friday, April 20, 1951. It is hard to imagine that this serene rural wooded area of Forsyth County would soon become the heart of a 38,000 acre reservoir. Your view is west and the hillside in the background is where the forebay cut and intake structure will be located in about four years. (Courtesy U.S. Army Corps of Engineers, Mobile District)

Fig. 7-3 The overburden has been removed and the process of chipping away at the granite has begun. In the center of this photograph fractured rock is being scooped up for removal. The construction site here was a very busy place as heavy vehicles carrying earth and rock were constantly moving about in all directions. It is Thursday, October 4, 1951.(Courtesy U.S. Army Corps of Engineers, Mobile District)

Fig. 7-4 A close up view of a wagon drill, a device attached to air hoses that drilled holes in the granite for placement of dynamite. The machine acted like a huge jack hammer cutting slender holes in the granite. The holes were cleaned out with compressed air and capped to prevent debris from falling down inside. After a prescribed pattern of holes had been cut they were filled with dynamite and set off breaking up the granite. (Courtesy U.S. Army Corps of Engineers, Mobile District)

Forebay Excavation and Intake Construction

Fig. 7-5 Another truck load is readied for removal. Cables and pulleys are doing the work here that hydraulics do today. (Courtesy U.S. Army Corps of Engineers, Mobile District)

Fig. 7-6 November 5, 1951 (Courtesy U.S. Army Corps of Engineers, Mobile District)

Fig. 7-7 The faint outline of the forebay has begun to appear. The eye shaped rock in the center of the dig is a natural geological formation created when the rock was formed eons ago. Using this rock you can gauge the progress of the work completed. (Courtesy U.S. Army Corps of Engineers, Mobile District)

Fig. 7-8 Broken pieces of granite lie beneath the face cut of the forebay. There is still some one hundred feet of solid rock left to be cut down. It is Friday, February 1, 1952. (Courtesy U.S. Army Corps of Engineers, Mobile District)

Fig. 7-9 The forebay is becoming deeper and more pronounced with each passing day. It is Thursday, February 21, 1952. (Courtesy U.S. Army Corps of Engineers, Mobile District)

Fig. 7-10 Wednesday, May 7, 1952. (Courtesy U.S. Army Corps of Engineers, Mobile District)

Forebay Excavation and Intake Construction

Fig. 7-11 You are looking downstream on June 5, 1952. (Courtesy U.S. Army Corps of Engineers, Mobile District)

Fig. 7-12 Today this machine would be a collector's item but in 1952 it was probably state of the art. (Courtesy U.S. Army Corps of Engineers, Mobile District)

Fig. 7-13 The Chattahoochee River can be seen in the background as the curved shape of the forebay is etched out of the rock. In about two years water will be diverted into this cut and head for the intake towers. It is Tuesday, July 10, 1952. (Courtesy U.S. Army Corps of Engineers, Mobile District)

Fig. 7-14 Another view of the forebay cut looking up stream. (Courtesy U.S. Army Corps of Engineers, Mobile District)

Fig. 7-15 This is a downstream view of the deepened forebay cut. It is Monday, October 6, 1952. (Courtesy U.S. Army Corps of Engineers, Mobile District)

Fig. 7-17 Drilling for penstock no.2 is in progress. Before they are finished more than 240 feet of solid granite will have to be cut away. It is Tuesday, November 25, 1952. Although Groves, Lundin and Cox Inc. contracted with the government to cut the penstocks the actual work was carried out as a sub-contract by Gates and Fox Inc. from Grants Pass, Oregon. This company specialized in this type of excavation and was given the mammoth task of cutting the penstock and sluice tunnels.[2] (Courtesy U.S. Army Corps of Engineers, Mobile District)

Fig. 7-16 The different layers etched out of the rock are easily visible here. It is Wednesday, November 5, 1952.(Courtesy U.S. Army Corps of Engineers, Mobile District)

Forebay Excavation and Intake Construction

Fig. 7-18 The same drilling operation as in the previous photograph only you are looking at the forebay face cut. The narrow vertical lines in the rock are a result of line drilling with the wagon drill six or seven inches apart. This method of drilling allowed for a more precise vertical cut in the rock. (Courtesy U.S. Army Corps of Engineers, Mobile District)

Fig. 7-19

Fig. 7-20

Fig. 7-19 An Eimco rockershovel mucking machine used to scoop up rock and transport it up, over, and directly behind the machine to a dumptor, Fig. 7-20, for transporting to the stockpiles. These machines were designed to operate inside the penstocks and sluice excavations. The rockershovel's design allowed the machine to transport the rock debris to the waiting dumptor without turning around inside the tunnel. Notice that the operator's seat on the dumptor appears to be backward. The driver would move the machine in the tunnel then back it out. Although the machines used diesel fuel and blowers pumped fresh air into the tunnels they were equipped with air scrubbers which ran the emissions through special filters so as not to asphyxiate the operators while inside the close quarters of the tunnel. (Courtesy U.S. Army Corps of Engineers, Mobile District)

Fig. 7-21 Penstock no.2 mucking operation is in progress. You can see a rockershovel depositing its load to a waiting dumptor that has positioned itself directly behind the rockershovel. As the cutting continues the portal is cleared of debris. It is Monday, December 8, 1952. (Courtesy U.S. Army Corps of Engineers, Mobile District)

Fig. 7-22 Portal of penstock no.1.(Courtesy U.S. Army Corps of Engineers, Mobile District)

Fig. 7-23 Forebay, penstock, and sluice excavation continues. (Courtesy U.S. Army Corps of Engineers, Mobile District)

FOREBAY EXCAVATION AND INTAKE CONSTRUCTION

Fig. 7-24 An upstream view of the forebay cut on Friday, December 26, 1952. (Courtesy U.S. Army Corps of Engineers, Mobile District)

Fig. 7-27 Mucking operation inside penstock no. 2 on January 21, 1953. (Courtesy U.S. Army Corps of Engineers, Mobile District)

Fig. 7-25 The access tunnel that will allow for easy access between the powerhouse and intake structure can be seen at upper left. The mass of rocks in the foreground was caused by a large section of the right forebay wall that broke away and came crashing down. (Courtesy U.S. Army Corps of Engineers, Mobile District)

Fig. 7-28 Excavation with a diamond tipped drill inside penstock no.2 on January 21, 1953. (Courtesy U.S. Army Corps of Engineers, Mobile District)

Fig. 7-26 Entrance to one of the penstock excavations. (Courtesy U.S. Army Corps of Engineers, Mobile District)

Fig. 7-29 Deep inside one of the penstocks. (Courtesy U.S. Army Corps of Engineers, Mobile District)

Fig. 7-30 Looks like a dark, dirty, and isolated place to work. (Courtesy U.S. Army Corps of Engineers, Mobile District)

Fig. 7-31 This is the base level of the forebay cut on Monday, August 10, 1953 and the intake structure will rest snugly against the face cut in the background. If you look closely you can see through penstock no.1 to the tailrace cut over 246 feet away. The sluice is on the far left, penstock no.2 on the far right. The access tunnel is above penstock no.2. If you were standing at this spot today you would be nearly 150 feet underwater. It is one of the deepest areas of the lake with the exception of the river channel areas near the dam. (Courtesy U.S. Army Corps of Engineers, Mobile District)

FOREBAY EXCAVATION AND INTAKE CONSTRUCTION

Fig. 7-32 Inside looking out. (Courtesy William B. Hartsfield Papers, Special Collections, Robert W. Woodruff Library, Emory University)

Fig. 7-33 This is the steel reinforcing framing for the transition section of penstock no.1 which allowed the rectangular opening here to match the circular penstock. (Courtesy U.S. Army Corps of Engineers, Mobile District)

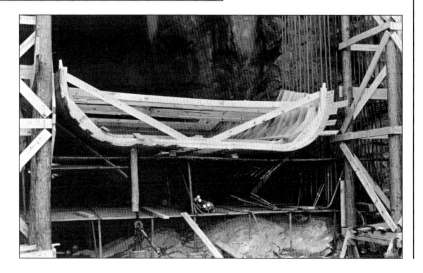

Fig. 7-34 Wood framing and steel reinforcing for penstock no.2. The penstock here will be framed for a huge rectangular gate that will be raised and lowered in front of this opening. (Courtesy U.S. Army Corps of Engineers, Mobile District)

Fig. 7-35 Concrete work is in progress on the sluice invert. The sluice will be used to release water from the dam without generating electrical power. (Courtesy U.S. Army Corps of Engineers, Mobile District)

Fig. 7-36 On January 12, 1954 you are looking at the intersecting point of penstocks no.2 and no.3. These two penstocks share a common opening on the intake side but halfway between the forebay and tailrace cuts they split off. This will allow for independent operation of the two power units that will be attached to each penstock on the powerhouse side. (Courtesy U.S. Army Corps of Engineers, Mobile District)

Fig. 7-37 Work on a temporary retaining wall high above the forebay cut is evident by the mounds of earth lying at the base near the penstock openings. (Courtesy U.S. Army Corps of Engineers, Mobile District)

Forebay Excavation and Intake Construction

Fig. 7-38 The wall was built to prevent earth and other debris from falling into the forebay area in front of the intake. It is Thursday, February 25, 1954. (Courtesy U.S. Army Corps of Engineers, Mobile District)

Fig. 7-41 Steel reinforcing for monolith no.1 is being set in place. It is Monday, March 15, 1954. (Courtesy U.S. Army Corps of Engineers, Mobile District)

Fig. 7-39 Workers are cleaning and removing fractured rock from the foundation area of monolith no. 1. (Courtesy U.S. Army Corps of Engineers, Mobile District)

Fig. 7-40 Engineers examine the foundation preparation for the sluice monolith. The sluice opening is divided into two sections. This is to preclude a vacuum from developing inside the sluice.[3] It is Tuesday, March 9, 1954. (Courtesy U.S. Army Corps of Engineers, Mobile District)

Fig. 7-42 You get an excellent view of the upper right forebay wall next to the face cut. You can see the different levels at which the cut was made. (Courtesy U.S. Army Corps of Engineers, Mobile District)

Lake Sidney Lanier "A Storybook Site"

Fig. 7-43 The concrete foundation for monolith no.1 has been poured. It is Wednesday, March 17, 1954. (Courtesy U.S. Army Corps of Engineers, Mobile District)

Fig. 7-45 With the foundation laid steel reinforcing for monolith no.1 is being set in place. (Courtesy U.S. Army Corps of Engineers, Mobile District)

Fig. 7-46 Foundation preparation for monolith no.2 is in progress. (Courtesy U.S. Army Corps of Engineers, Mobile District)

Fig. 7-44 Conduit for the heavy sluice gates is being set in place. The heavy gates that will open and close the sluice will rest between this conduit and another section behind this one. It is Thursday, March 25, 1954. (Courtesy U.S. Army Corps of Engineers, Mobile District)

Fig. 7-47 Concrete will be poured around these four sections of sluice conduit. The gates mentioned earlier will move up and down between these sections. It is Wednesday, March 31, 1954. The wooden frames for the concrete intake and powerhouse were constructed during the day and the concrete was poured at night. (Courtesy U.S. Army Corps of Engineers, Mobile District)

Fig. 7-48 A side view of the sluice conduit. (Courtesy U.S. Army Corps of Engineers, Mobile District)

Fig. 7-49 Concrete and steel framing for the sluice monolith no.3 is taking shape. It is Thursday, April 8, 1954. (Courtesy U.S. Army Corps of Engineers, Mobile District)

Fig. 7-50 Water entering this monolith will be partitioned off entering the sluice through two different openings. It is Wednesday, April 14, 1954. (Courtesy U.S. Army Corps of Engineers, Mobile District)

Fig. 7-51 Work on all three monoliths are at different phases as the infant intake structure begins to move up the forebay cut. It is Friday, April 23, 1954. (Courtesy U.S. Army Corps of Engineers, Mobile District)

Fig. 7-52 Gaze through the portal of monolith no.1 to the tailrace cut on the other side some 246 feet away. The concrete shows the faint outline of each stage of its framing. Although you can not see it this penstock splits off to the right about 100 feet inside creating two separate penstock openings on the tailrace side. It is Monday, May 3, 1954. (Courtesy U.S. Army Corps of Engineers, Mobile District)

Fig. 7-53 The long triangular partition that separates the flow of water through the sluice monolith is easily visible here on Monday, May 10, 1954. (Courtesy U.S. Army Corps of Engineers, Mobile District)

Forebay Excavation and Intake Construction

Fig. 7-54 On Monday, May 21, 1954 the intake structure is about a quarter of the way completed. When finished it will stretch well above the top of the forebay cut, some 190 feet from top to bottom. (Courtesy U.S. Army Corps of Engineers, Mobile District)

Fig. 7-55 The sluice intake monolith at left and a portion of monolith no.2 at right are moving slowly up the forebay walls. (Courtesy U.S. Army Corps of Engineers, Mobile District)

Fig. 7-56 Look through the penstock of monolith no.2 to the tailrace side. The long intersecting steel beams in front of the monolith opening, called trash guides, will house trash screens that trap large debris suspended in the water as it blasts through the penstocks. A trash hoist rake,

Fig. 7-57, located on top of the intake structure will periodically remove debris from the screens. Without these screens objects could move through the penstocks and damage the turbines. It is Friday, June 11, 1954. (Courtesy U.S. Army Corps of Engineers, Mobile District and RDC)

Fig. 7-58 The base of the intake structure on June 11, 1954. Today a photograph from this point would be nearly impossible because of the depth, some 150 feet below the surface of the water. (Courtesy U.S. Army Corps of Engineers, Mobile District)

Fig. 7-59 Upper construction of monoliths no.1 (background) and no.2 (foreground) show the unusual design of this station. The wide rectangular opening at bottom left is for the giant head gates that will seal off the entrance to the penstocks on the intake side. The narrow rectangular opening beside the head gate opening is for the emergency stop logs, Fig. 7-60,. In the event of an emergency, where the head gates could not be lowered to close the penstocks off, these gravity operated gates would be lowered into place to seal the penstock opening. During this period a strike caused by a trade union walk-out temporarily tied up construction and building for several months all over North Georgia. Iron and steel workers in the area walked off the job on July 1st which affected work on the intake structure. Enough work had been completed on the intake as to not affect work on the main earth dam directly adjacent to the forebay.⁴ (Courtesy U.S. Army Corps of Engineers, Mobile District and RDC)

Fig. 7-60.

Fig. 7-61 The Chattahoochee River has already been diverted from its original channel flow. In several years this photograph will be impossible as all but the high hills in the background will be inundated by the rising waters of Lake Lanier. (Courtesy U.S. Army Corps of Engineers, Mobile District)

Fig. 7-62 Same time and place but now you are looking downstream as water is flowing through the sluice and penstocks. It is circa mid 1954. (Courtesy U.S. Army Corps of Engineers, Mobile District)

Fig. 7-63 A closer view of framing work on the intake structure while the muddy water of the Chattahoochee passes by. (Courtesy U.S. Army Corps of Engineers, Mobile District)

Fig. 7-64 Construction atop monolith no.1 looms high above the flooded forebay cut. It is Friday, September 24, 1954. (Courtesy U.S. Army Corps of Engineers, Mobile District)

Fig. 7-65 The intake structure on Friday, September 24, 1954. The concrete wing walls located at the upper left and right are already being formed. (Courtesy U.S. Army Corps of Engineers, Mobile District)

Fig. 7-66 The forebay in late 1954. The intake structure can be seen at the lower right foreground. The Chattahoochee River is flowing into the forebay in the background. (Courtesy U.S. Army Corps of Engineers, Mobile District)

Fig. 7-67 The concrete batching and mixing plant that supplied concrete for construction of the intake monoliths. (Courtesy U.S. Army Corps of Engineers, Mobile District)

Fig. 7-69 The core trench is seen at right background as the monoliths move higher and higher. The wing walls left background are about half completed. (Courtesy U.S. Army Corps of Engineers, Mobile District)

Fig. 7-68 The plant has long since been removed. (RDC)

FOREBAY EXCAVATION AND INTAKE CONSTRUCTION

*Fig. 7-70 Turn 180 degrees to the left and you can see saddle dike no.2B at upper background. The trash rack guides stretch well above the present height of monolith no.1 It is Friday, November 5, 1954.
(Courtesy U.S. Army Corps of Engineers, Mobile District)*

*Fig. 7-73 The back of the intake structure and wing walls. This area will be filled in with earth and serve as a parking lot in the future. It is Friday, January 28, 1955.
(Courtesy U.S. Army Corps of Engineers, Mobile District)*

*Fig. 7-71 The intake structure on Wednesday, November 10, 1954.
(Courtesy U.S. Army Corps of Engineers, Mobile District)*

*Fig. 7-74 Trash and drifting debris collect up against the sluice and penstock monoliths. Even today all but the very top of this structure is underwater. It is Tuesday, February 8, 1955.
(Courtesy U.S. Army Corps of Engineers, Mobile District)*

*Fig. 7-72 Again on Friday, December 3, 1954. Before completion it will stretch above the hill in the background.
(Courtesy U.S. Army Corps of Engineers, Mobile District)*

Fig. 7-75 The intake structure is nearly completed on Thursday, April 28, 1955. The steps on the side allow workers to move from the top of the dam to the head gates and sluice work bays. (Courtesy U.S. Army Corps of Engineers, Mobile District)

Fig. 7-77 Today the largest portion of the intake structure is hidden beneath Lake Lanier. (RDC)

Fig. 7-76 The completed portion of the intake structure as it appeared on Thursday, April 28, 1955. It illustrates the tremendous size of the intake monoliths as they dwarf the forebay cut. (Courtesy U.S. Army Corps of Engineers, Mobile District)

Fig. 7-78 A double exposure gives you a good look at what lies under all that water. (Courtesy U.S. Army Corps of Engineers, Mobile District and RDC)

Forebay Excavation and Intake Construction

Fig. 7-79 James R. Johnston, one of many local men that worked on the dam over the years, looks out over the dam construction site. (Courtesy Mrs. James R. Johnston)

Fig. 7-80 Today you would only be able to see the lake in front of the intake. The Chatthahoochee River can be seen in the background. (Courtesy Mrs. James R. Johnston)

Fig. 7-81 At this time only the sluice tunnel at far left is allowing water to flow to the other side. (Courtesy Mrs. James R. Johnston)

Fig. 7-82 Visitors to the project look into the forebay cut from high atop the intake structure. The lake has yet to form in the background showing what is beneath all the water. (Courtesy U.S. Army Corps of Engineers, Mobile District)

Fig. 7-83 A contemporary photograph shows the lake's affect on the area. (Courtesy U.S. Army Corps of Engineers, Mobile District)

Notes

1. Gainesville Daily Times, 1957

2. Cecil Patterson, United States Army Corps of Engineers, Retired

3. Ibid.

4. Gainesville Daily Times, 1954

Congressman Landrum, General Holle, Mayor Hartsfield, and Congressman Davis pose for a photograph high above the tailrace cut during a visit to the project. (Courtesy William B. Hartsfield Papers, Special Collections, Robert W. Woodruff Library, Emory University) Colonel Fox, Charles Jackson, Congressman Davis, Congressman Landrum, and General Holle on the floor of the tailrace. (Courtesy William B. Hartsfield Papers, Special Collections, Robert W. Woodruff Library, Emory University)

CHAPTER EIGHT

Tailrace Excavation and Powerhouse Construction

The tailrace was etched out of solid rock very much the same way the forebay was created. The powerhouse, Fig. 8-1, like the intake is made of concrete and was built deep inside a rock gorge. After water has exited its base it flows down the tailrace and back into the Chattahoochee River below the main earth dam. The powerhouse is supplied water by three penstocks (penstocks no.2 and no.3 branch off and share a common opening on the intake side) 246 feet in length. Each one of these penstocks is connected to a power unit that produces electricity. The sluice, used for emergency releases of water, runs underneath the powerhouse but is not connected to a power unit.

Fig. 8-1 (RDC)

Fig. 8-3 It is circa 1950 and you are looking at the area that will someday be the tailrace. At this time the Chattahoochee River is a lazy slow moving river cutting through this wide river valley between Forsyth and Gwinnett Counties. (Courtesy U.S. Army Corps of Engineers, Mobile District)

Fig. 8-2 The Buford Dam site prior to construction in 1950. This rural setting was one of the primary economic reasons for building the dam at this location. (Courtesy U.S. Army Corps of Engineers, Mobile District)

Fig. 8-4 A panoramic view of the early excavation of the tailrace. The Chattahoochee River can be seen at left. The same methodical breaking away of rock will be affected here as was done on the forebay cut. It is Tuesday, January 29, 1952. (Courtesy U.S. Army Corps of Engineers, Mobile District)

Fig. 8-5 Once the overburden was removed excavation of the tailrace began. You are looking west and it is Wednesday, November 28, 1951. (Courtesy U.S. Army Corps of Engineers, Mobile District)

Fig. 8-7 The tailrace displays its distinctive shape even though there is a great deal of cutting and digging left to be accomplished. It is circa 1952.(Courtesy U.S. Army Corps of Engineers, Mobile District)

Fig. 8-6 The mass of protruding granite at right separates the powerhouse road from the main body of the tailrace. The gap between the rock will someday take you to a parking lot below the main earth dam. It is Tuesday, July 15, 1952. (Courtesy U.S. Army Corps of Engineers, Mobile District)

Fig. 8-8 On Monday, October 6, 1952 the tailrace cut appears much as it does today. (Courtesy U.S. Army Corps of Engineers, Mobile District)

Tailrace Excavation and Powerhouse Construction

Fig. 8-9 The large rock you saw in Fig. 8-6 appears longer and more pronounced. The tailrace unlike the forebay cut has changed very little over the course of time. Only the addition of the powerhouse and natural growth of the surrounding area have given it a different appearance. (Courtesy U.S. Army Corps of Engineers, Mobile District)

Fig. 8-10 This contemporary photograph gives you some idea as to the change time has made. (RDC)

Fig. 8-11 Excavation of the access tunnel is in progress. (Courtesy U.S. Army Corps of Engineers, Mobile District)

Fig. 8-12 The access tunnel on Wednesday, February 4, 1953. (Courtesy U.S. Army Corps of Engineers, Mobile District)

Fig. 8-13 The deepened tailrace cut looking downstream to the Chattahoochee River. The jagged rock sides appear this way even today. (Courtesy U.S. Army Corps of Engineers, Mobile District)

Fig. 8-14 Look sharply to the left and you can see the face cut. Even here you can see that an enormous amount of rock and earth will still have to be removed. (Courtesy U.S. Army Corps of Engineers, Mobile District)

Fig. 8-15 Excavation of the access tunnel continues. In the future a concrete porch with steps on both sides will be located below this tunnel. It is Tuesday, February 10, 1953. (Courtesy U.S. Army Corps of Engineers, Mobile District)

Fig. 8-16 The lower end of the tailrace cut in 1953. The depth of the tailrace has just about reached its present elevation. (Courtesy U.S. Army Corps of Engineers, Mobile District)

Fig. 8-17 (L-R) The Buford Dam Project's Resident Engineer, Charles A. Jackson; Chief of Army Engineers, General S.D. Sturgis; and Mobile District Chief, Colonel Walter K. Wilson pose for a picture on the access road leading to the dam site. (Courtesy U.S. Army Corps of Engineers, Mobile District)

Fig. 8-18 The penstocks wait for concrete and steel liners while workers continue cutting rock away at the floor of the tailrace to make room for the draft tubes. It is Friday, April 3, 1953. (Courtesy U.S. Army Corps of Engineers, Mobile District)

Tailrace Excavation and Powerhouse Construction

Fig. 8-19 On Monday, May 4, 1953 the tunnel excavations for the penstocks have been completed. You can see through penstock no.1 and the sluice to the forebay side. (Courtesy U.S. Army Corps of Engineers, Mobile District)

Fig. 8-20 Same day and time as Fig. 8-19 but your view is from the top of the right tailrace slope. The far right tunnel is the sluice. Penstock no.1 is to the left of the sluice, no.2 in the middle, and no.3 which is an off-shoot of no.2 is at far left. (Courtesy U.S. Army Corps of Engineers, Mobile District)

Fig. 8-21 Excavation in the powerhouse area has been completed and work on the temporary trestles has begun. These trestles will be used to move the steel liners into the penstocks where concrete will be blown in around them encasing them solidly against the rock. (Courtesy U.S. Army Corps of Engineers, Mobile District)

Fig. 8-22 From above the left tailrace slope you get a good look at the trestle work constructed for insertion of the penstock liners. (Courtesy U.S. Army Corps of Engineers, Mobile District)

Fig. 8-23 Construction of the concrete batching and mixing plant is underway. It is Friday, July 31, 1953. (Courtesy U.S. Army Corps of Engineers, Mobile District)

Fig. 8-24 and Fig. 8-25 Work continues as the penstocks are being prepared for their steel sleeves. It is Monday, August 10, 1953. (Courtesy U.S. Army Corps of Engineers, Mobile District)

Fig. 8-26 High above the tailrace slope you can see the progress below. (Courtesy U.S. Army Corps of Engineers, Mobile District)

Fig. 8-27 This aerial photograph shows the old river channel in relation to the forebay and tailrace cuts. The access bridge that spans the Chattahoochee River will remain here until work on the main earth dam begins. It is October, 1953. (Courtesy U.S. Army Corps of Engineers, Mobile District)

Fig. 8-28 A twenty-seven foot long section of the steel liner that will be encased in concrete inside penstocks no.1 and no.2 is shown on the floor of the tailrace. The liner will be set in penstock no.2 by rolling it on rails into the tunnel. Once secured tightly by concrete the thin metal spider rods will be removed. Until that time they will keep the liner from warping or flexing under its own weight. It is Tuesday, October 29, 1953. (Courtesy U.S. Army Corps of Engineers, Mobile District)

Fig. 8-29 It is Tuesday, November 13, 1953 and you are looking upstream at a section of the steel liner, for penstock no.2, being set in place inside the penstock excavation. Concrete will be pumped between the liner and rock effectively securing the liner in place. (Courtesy U.S. Army Corps of Engineers, Mobile District)

Fig. 8-31 Concrete framing has been set in place inside the sluice. Unlike the penstocks it will not be lined in steel. It is Tuesday, January 12, 1954. (Courtesy U.S. Army Corps of Engineers, Mobile District)

Fig. 8-30 Sections of the liner for penstock no.3 and no.2 are lying about the work area. The smaller diameter liners will be used in penstock No.3. It is Wednesday, December 16, 1953. (Courtesy U.S. Army Corps of Engineers, Mobile District)

Fig. 8-32 On Wednesday, January 27, 1954 a liner is being readied for entrance into the penstock. (Courtesy U.S. Army Corps of Engineers, Mobile District)

Fig. 8-33 On February 25, 1954 the steel liners have been encased in concrete, the sluice tunnel is finished, and removal of the trestles are in progress. (Courtesy U.S. Army Corps of Engineers, Mobile District)

Fig. 8-34 Forming for the sluice block is in progress. When completed it will simply become a concrete blocked extension of the sluice. It is Tuesday, April 5, 1954. (Courtesy U.S. Army Corps of Engineers, Mobile District)

Fig. 8-36 Here is a view of the stilling basin from the end sill or last section of framing. (Courtesy U.S. Army Corps of Engineers, Mobile District)

Fig. 8-35 This is a section of the right retaining wall of the stilling basin being framed for concrete. This stilling basin will fit up against the sluice block and a wall at the end of the structure will slow down the velocity of the water exiting the sluice. (Courtesy U.S. Army Corps of Engineers, Mobile District)

Fig. 8-37 You are looking downstream at the end sill which is the concrete wall constructed at the end of the stilling basin that will retard the speed of the water exiting the sluice. (Courtesy U.S. Army Corps of Engineers, Mobile District)

Tailrace Excavation and Powerhouse Construction

Fig. 8-38 On Monday, May 3, 1954 framing for the sluice block and stilling basin are nearly complete. (Courtesy U.S. Army Corps of Engineers, Mobile District)

Fig. 8-39 This is the end sill or concrete wall located across the lower end of the stilling basin. It is Friday, May 21, 1954. (Courtesy U.S. Army Corps of Engineers, Mobile District)

Fig. 8-40 On Friday, July 23, 1954 the stilling basin and sluice block were completed and taking on water. The training wall remains exposed today just as it does in this photograph. (Courtesy U.S. Army Corps of Engineers, Mobile District)

Fig. 8-41 Circa July, 1954 and water flowing through the forebay exits the penstocks and sluice and continues downstream to the river below the main earth dam site. When the powerhouse is ready for construction the penstocks (three tunnels left of the sluice block) will be sealed off. Water will continue to flow through the sluice block and down the stilling basin. With the help of a temporary cofferdam located near the end of the stilling basin's outside wall the foundation area of the powerhouse will remain dry. (Courtesy U.S. Army Corps of Engineers, Mobile District)

Lake Sidney Lanier "A Storybook Site"

Fig. 8-42 Again you see the penstocks and sluice releasing water downstream. (Courtesy U.S. Army Corps of Engineers, Mobile District)

Fig. 8-43 This is a photograph of the tailrace area before construction of the powerhouse or main earth dam. It is circa July, 1954. (Courtesy U.S. Army Corps of Engineers, Mobile District)

Fig. 8-44 A contemporary photograph shows the effects of time. (RDC)

Fig. 8-45 You are standing near the intake end of the access tunnel. It is Friday, July 23, 1954. (Courtesy U.S. Army Corps of Engineers, Mobile District)

Tailrace Excavation and Powerhouse Construction

Fig. 8-46 This contemporary photograph shows that very little has changed. (RDC)

Fig. 8-47 A pre-powerhouse photograph shows the penstocks, sluice block, and stilling basin releasing water. In about two years a huge concrete building will rest snugly in front of the penstocks and on top of the sluice block. Only the stilling basin will remain visible today. It is Tuesday, December 7, 1954. (Courtesy U.S. Army Corps of Engineers, Mobile District)

Fig. 8-48 The tailrace in flood. Even while construction was taking place the project was still subject to seasonal flooding and on Tuesday, February 8, 1955 you see just how bad it could be. (Courtesy U.S. Army Corps of Engineers, Mobile District)

Fig. 8-49 The cofferdam, that will keep the foundation area of the powerhouse dry, is being constructed beside the stilling basin. (Courtesy U.S. Army Corps of Engineers, Mobile District)

Fig. 8-50 The cofferdam is in place and the draft tube foundation area of the powerhouse can now dry out enough to begin construction. (Courtesy U.S. Army Corps of Engineers, Mobile District)

Fig. 8-51 The draft tube foundation for penstock no.2 is being prepared. (Courtesy U.S. Army Corps of Engineers, Mobile District)

Fig. 8-52 Wood framing put together by layering strips of one-by-four material over a wooden skeleton created the draft tube form that concrete would be poured over. When the concrete hardens the wood framing will be removed. (Courtesy Mrs. Mamie Waycaster)

Fig. 8-53 Draft tube framing continues. (Courtesy Mrs. Mamie Waycaster)

Fig. 8-54 Framing for the draft tube is complete. In time concrete will be poured over this wood frame creating the draft tube that will allow water to exit the powerhouse after generating electricity. (Courtesy U.S. Army Corps of Engineers, Mobile District)

Fig. 8-55 Many local residents like Jonnie R. Youngblood, shown here constructing a section of the draft tube framing, were hired by private contractors to build Buford Dam. (Courtesy Mrs. Mamie Waycaster)

Tailrace Excavation and Powerhouse Construction

Fig. 8-56 Completed sections of the draft tube framing. (Courtesy Mrs. Mamie Waycaster)

Fig. 8-57 The draft tube foundation for penstock no.1 on Friday, September 30, 1955. (Courtesy U.S. Army Corps of Engineers, Mobile District)

Fig. 8-58 Water is moving down the stilling basin while the draft tube framing for penstock no.2 is being completed. (Courtesy U.S. Army Corps of Engineers, Mobile District)

Fig. 8-59 On Friday, October 21, 1955 concrete continues to be poured in around the draft tube framing for penstock no.2. (Courtesy U.S. Army Corps of Engineers, Mobile District)

Fig. 8-60 This is a stay ring and will be mounted atop the draft tube. Water will move through the penstock entering the slats or vanes of this stay ring to turn a generator. (Courtesy U.S. Army Corps of Engineers, Mobile District)

Fig. 8-61 The stay ring is located to the left of the penstock opening. (Courtesy U.S. Army Corps of Engineers, Mobile District)

Fig. 8-62 On Wednesday, December 28, 1955 you can see the openings at the base of the powerhouse for the draft tubes. This is where water, having generated electricity, will exit the powerhouse and flow back into the river downstream. (Courtesy U.S. Army Corps of Engineers, Mobile District)

Fig. 8-63 This is the butterfly valve which is a device that will allow the third power unit to be operated independently from power unit no.2., since they share a common opening on the intake side. (Courtesy U.S. Army Corps of Engineers, Mobile District)

Tailrace Excavation and Powerhouse Construction

Fig. 8-64 The stay rings for power units no.1 and no.2 sit atop their draft tubes. Steel linings will be riveted around these stay rings creating scrolls that will carry water from the penstock to the stay rings. (Courtesy U.S. Army Corps of Engineers, Mobile District)

Fig. 8-65 The scroll is being riveted around the stay ring. It is Thursday, January 12, 1956. (Courtesy U.S. Army Corps of Engineers, Mobile District)

Fig. 8-66 You are looking at the stay ring and penstock for power unit no.1. It is Monday, February 6, 1956 and the gates of the intake structure were closed six days earlier. (Courtesy U.S. Army Corps of Engineers, Mobile District)

Fig. 8-67 The temporary cofferdam that was used to keep the powerhouse area dry is apparently doing the job it was constructed for. It is Monday, February 6, 1956. (Courtesy U.S. Army Corps of Engineers, Mobile District)

Fig. 8-68 On Thursday, February 9, 1956 water runs through the sluice as construction on the powerhouse continues. (Courtesy U.S. Army Corps of Engineers, Mobile District)

Fig. 8-69 The scroll case for power unit no.2 has been attached to the penstock. In time concrete will be poured over this area sealing the scroll in place and creating the second floor of the powerhouse. (Courtesy U.S. Army Corps of Engineers, Mobile District)

Fig. 8-70 The scroll case for power unit no.3. This scroll is smaller in diameter than the other two and also winds around the stay ring counter clockwise rather than the clockwise direction units no.1 and no.2 travel. It is Wednesday, February 22, 1956. (Courtesy U.S. Army Corps of Engineers, Mobile District)

Fig. 8-71 On Wednesday, February 22, 1956 the scroll is being attached to the stay ring of power unit no.1. (Courtesy U.S. Army Corps of Engineers, Mobile District)

Fig. 8-72 The process of attaching the scrolls to the power units is just about complete. It is Monday, April 9, 1956. (Courtesy U.S. Army Corps of Engineers, Mobile District)

Fig. 8-73 A pit liner has been placed above the stay ring of power unit no.2. It has steps to move down atop the stay ring. Concrete will be poured level with the top of the pit liner sealing the scroll in place. (Courtesy U.S. Army Corps of Engineers, Mobile District)

Fig. 8-74 The small door on the side of the scroll in this picture is about the only part of the scroll visible today. (Courtesy U.S. Army Corps of Engineers, Mobile District)

Fig. 8-75 The many different levels of the powerhouse are easily visible in this photograph. (Courtesy U.S. Army Corps of Engineers, Mobile District)

Fig. 8-76 A huge steel shaft attached to a generator above will run directly through the middle of this pit liner to a turbine runner inside the stay ring below. Water will strike the turbine runner and turn the generator. (Courtesy U.S. Army Corps of Engineers, Mobile District)

Tailrace Excavation and Powerhouse Construction

Fig. 8-77 On Friday, June 22, 1956 the pit liner for power unit no.2 has been encased in concrete. (Courtesy U.S. Army Corps of Engineers, Mobile District)

Fig. 8-78 Here you get a good look at the lower portion of the powerhouse. (Courtesy U.S. Army Corps of Engineers, Mobile District)

Fig. 8-80 Friday, July 20, 1956. (Courtesy U.S. Army Corps of Engineers, Mobile District)

Fig. 8-79 The concrete walls of the powerhouse slowly begin to take shape. (Courtesy U.S. Army Corps of Engineers, Mobile District)

Fig. 8-81 Wednesday, August 1, 1956. (Courtesy U.S. Army Corps of Engineers, Mobile District)

Fig. 8-82 The powerhouse is nearly finished. It is Monday, November 12, 1956. (Courtesy U.S. Army Corps of Engineers, Mobile District)

Fig. 8-83 This will become the generation bay where the generators will be located. Roof trusses for the west end of the powerhouse are being set in place on Tuesday, November 13, 1956. (Courtesy U.S. Army Corps of Engineers, Mobile District)

Fig. 8-84 Another view of truss placement atop the unfinished powerhouse roof. (Courtesy U.S. Army Corps of Engineers, Mobile District)

Fig. 8-85 The finished product nearly four decades later. (RDC)

Fig. 8-86 The switch yard located above the tailrace where power generated in the powerhouse is transferred via the transformer yard directly outside the powerhouse. (Courtesy U.S. Army Corps of Engineers, Mobile District)

Fig. 8-87 A contemporary photograph shows the same area. (RDC)

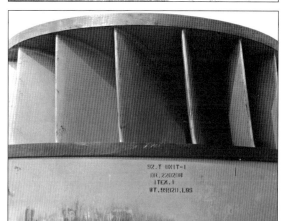

Fig. 8-88 This is the turbine runner for power unit no.1. This runner will be located inside the stay ring and water striking these vanes will turn a generator above. (Courtesy U.S. Army Corps of Engineers, Mobile District)

Fig. 8-89 These airfoil shaped devices are wicket gates and they will regulate the force the water, passing through the stay ring vanes, exerts on the turbine runner. (Courtesy U.S. Army Corps of Engineers, Mobile District)

Tailrace Excavation and Powerhouse Construction

Fig. 8-90 The wicket gates are in place between the stay ring and the turbine runner. Water passing through the scroll will enter the stay ring vanes and pass through these gates. The larger the opening between the gates the faster the turbine runner will rotate. As the wicket gates are closed the turbine runner will begin to slow down. (Courtesy U.S. Army Corps of Engineers, Mobile District)

Fig. 8-92 A dredge used in the cofferdam removal is seen on the floor of the tailrace. (Courtesy U.S. Army Corps of Engineers, Mobile District)

Fig. 8-91 On Wednesday, May 15, 1957 the removal of the cofferdam has begun. (Courtesy U.S. Army Corps of Engineers, Mobile District)

Fig. 8-93 The cofferdam seems a formidable task for removal. (Courtesy U.S. Army Corps of Engineers, Mobile District)

Fig. 8-94 On Wednesday, May 22, 1957 the powerhouse is nearly finished. In several months water will begin to flow through the draft tubes and out the bottom of the powerhouse as electricity is produced for the first time. Nearly forty years would pass before the Corps of Engineers would spend millions of dollars upgrading the power units in the late 1990s. (Courtesy U.S. Army Corps of Engineers, Mobile District)

Fig. 8-95 The flooded tailrace is a common site today. (RDC)

Fig. 8-98 Nearly a month later and the biggest portion of the dam is gone. (Courtesy U.S. Army Corps of Engineers, Mobile District)

Fig. 8-96 On Wednesday, May 29, 1957 water has begun to dismantle the cofferdam. (Courtesy U.S. Army Corps of Engineers, Mobile District)

Fig. 8-99 It has been many years since work on the powerhouse began but construction of this phase of the project is just about finished. Where this station rests was once solid rock. The old cars and trucks date the photograph, Wednesday, July 10, 1957. (Courtesy U.S. Army Corps of Engineers, Mobile District)

Fig. 8-97 The powerhouse is on-line on June 20, 1957 as water, having generated electrical power, exits power unit no. 2 (40,000 kw), enters the draft tube and flows down the tailrace for the river below. Unit no. 3 (6,000 kw) was placed in operation on July 26, 1957 and unit no. 1 started commercial operation on October 10, 1957. Power production would not go into full operation until July, 1958. Compare this photograph with the one taken shortly before construction of the powerhouse began, Fig. 8-41,.
It is sometimes hard to imagine just how much work was done.
(Courtesy U.S. Army Corps of Engineers, Mobile District)

Tailrace Excavation and Powerhouse Construction

A contemporary photograph, Fig. 8-102, shows the change that nearly 40 years has had on the area. (Courtesy U.S. Army Corps of Engineers, Mobile District) (RDC)

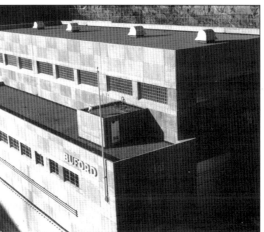

Fig. 8-103
The completed powerhouse on January 18, 1958. (Courtesy U.S. Army Corps of Engineers, Mobile District)

Fig. 8-100
A contemporary photograph shows the powerhouse decades after all the work has finished. (RDC)

Fig. 8-101
The tailrace and downstream area of the dam in late 1957. Compare this photograph with the one taken three years earlier, Fig. 8-43,. The main earth dam has yet to be constructed. (Courtesy U.S. Army Corps of Engineers, Mobile District)

Clearing on the Forsyth County side of the main earth dam site, the Gwinnett County side of the dam is in the background. (Courtesy James C. Davis Papers, Special Collections, Robert W. Woodruff Library, Emory University)

CHAPTER NINE

MAIN EARTH DAM CONSTRUCTION

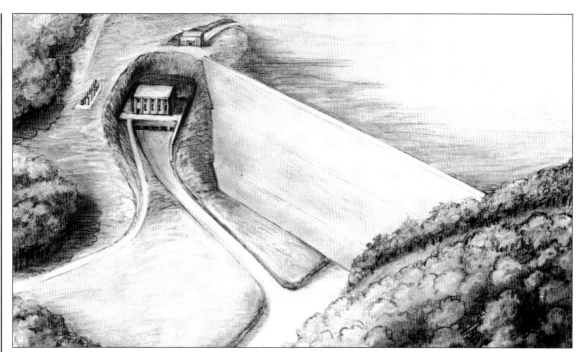

Fig. 9-1 (Courtesy U.S. Army Corps of Engineers, Mobile District)

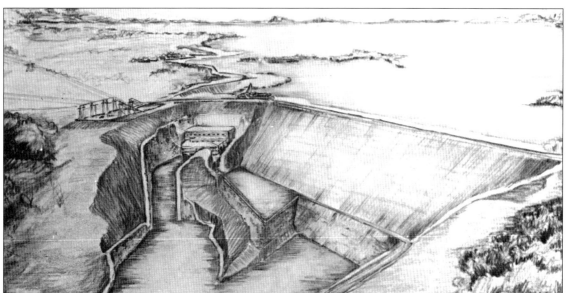

Fig. 9-2 (Courtesy U.S. Army Corps of Engineers, Mobile District)

There are many different kinds of dams in the U.S. and throughout the world and usually the type chosen is determined by the materials available, topography of the site, cost involved, and the reason for building the dam. Gravity dams are concrete types with steel reinforcing or stone. They rely on the weight of the structure to hold back the water. Arch dams are built of steel reinforced concrete, like gravity dams but are curved in shape. They are usually found in areas where a river flows through a narrow canyon. Hoover Dam on the Colorado River is an example of an arch dam. The curved design of these dams deflects the tremendous water pressure against the walls of the canyon it rests against. Buttress dams are like gravity dams except they are thin-walled concrete structures that rely on concrete supports spanning its length at regular intervals. Earth dams like the one at Buford are constructed by depositing earth and rock across a river in a triangular design. The lake side is usually draped with rocks or some type of water proof material to prevent erosion.[1]

Originally the plans for building a

Fig. 9-3 Location of the main earth dam at the southern end of Lake Lanier. (Courtesy U.S. Army Corps of Engineers, Mobile District, 1985 Lake Lanier Navigation Charts)

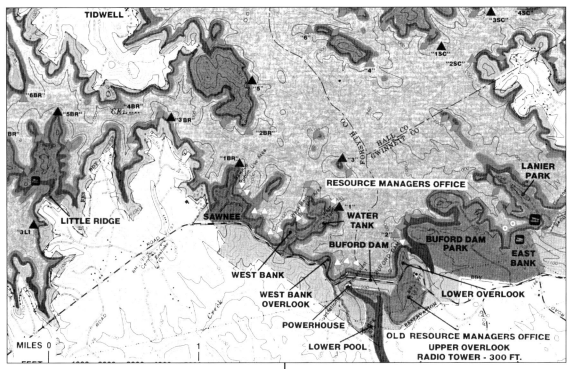

dam at the Buford site called for the construction of a concrete gravity dam 1,626 feet long with a top elevation of 1090.0, a 616 foot gated spillway with a crest elevation of 1061.0. In 1949 studies were made showing the Buford site was better suited for an earth filled type.[2] The availability of the necessary raw materials in this area and a projected savings of over 2 million dollars were the main reasons for the change in design. The government awarded the contract for building the dam to J.W. Moorman & Son of Muskoque, Oklahoma on February 12, 1954 for $1,487,425.00.[3]

The main earth dam on the Buford Project, *Fig. 9-3*, stretches across the Chattahoochee River at the southern most point of the reservoir. It is triangular in shape, much like an elongated pyramid, *Fig. 9-4*, and is comprised of a select fill (special quality of soil) in the center, with the slopes on either side made up of a random fill (combination of different mixtures of soil). The top elevation is 1106.0 above sea level with a maximum height of 200 feet. The upstream or lake side slope is made up of dumped granite rock with the downstream or river side slope seeded with grass. The dam is about 1630 feet in length, 2360 feet counting the intake structure, and was constructed in a river valley that separated Forsyth and Gwinnett Counties. A little over 3,751,000 cubic yards of earth were used to complete the dam as well as the three saddle dikes.[4] Bottom dump earth movers along with other heavy equipment and trucks, *Fig. 9-5*, were used to carry soil from the borrow area. (land directly in front of the present site of the dam now

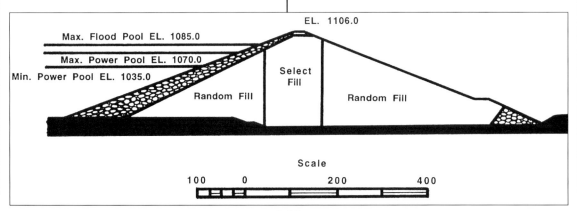

Fig. 9-4 The main earth dam (RDC)

Main Earth Dam Construction

underwater and an area east of the earth dam near the spillway to the main earth dam site) It took a little over three years worth of excavation and deposition of earth and rock to complete the dam and it still remains as one of the largest earth dams ever constructed by the United States Army Corps of Engineers. There is no spillway located on this dam. It was constructed several miles east near East Bank Park and is a long earth packed chute excavated out of granite with sloping sides layered with rocks.

Fig. 9-5 (Courtesy U.S. Army Corps of Engineers, Mobile District)

Fig. 9-6 The old Chattahoochee River channel at the dam site prior to construction of the main earth dam. (Courtesy U.S. Army Corps of Engineers, Mobile District)

Fig. 9-7 The materials used in building the earth dam would come from the borrow area or borrow pit which was the general area were Buford Dam Park is today. This view of the area was from saddle dike no. 3. (Courtesy U.S. Army Corps of Engineers, Mobile District)

Fig. 9-8 The Chattahoochee River flows quietly by as heavy vehicles move the rock and earth around on one of two stockpile areas. These stockpiles were used to collect rock and earth for later use on the main earth dam, saddle dikes, and bridge abutments. The dam will be constructed just to the right of this photograph in about two years. It is Tuesday, April 22, 1952. (Courtesy U.S. Army Corps of Engineers, Mobile District)

Fig. 9-9 Stockpile no.2 on Thursday, June 5, 1952. (Courtesy U.S. Army Corps of Engineers, Mobile District)

Main Earth Dam Construction

Fig. 9-10 Bulldozers move about the rock and earth of stockpile no.1. This stockpile is located on the riverside of the main earth dam. The road in the background is the powerhouse road today. You are looking south and it is Tuesday, October 14, 1952.(Courtesy U.S. Army Corps of Engineers, Mobile District)

Fig. 9-11 On Friday, December 26, 1952 stockpile no.2 has grown in size considerably from six months earlier, Fig. 9-9. (Courtesy U.S. Army Corps of Engineers, Mobile District)

Fig. 9-12 From high above a bluff on the Gwinnett County side of the dam you can see clearing in progress, the access bridge, and the construction of a cofferdam. This dam will block the flow of the Chattahoochee River here and force it to flow into the forebay cut. (Courtesy U.S. Army Corps of Engineers, Mobile District)

Fig. 9-13 Rock and earth are being deposited into the Chattahoochee River in order to construct the cofferdam mentioned in the previous photograph, Fig. 9-12. In the background between the trees you can see the forebay cut. In a little over a month work on the intake structure, penstocks, and sluice will have advanced to the stage that the river can be diverted into the forebay. At that time the gap between the rocks in this photograph will be closed. An earth plug constructed at the entrance to the forebay will be removed allowing water to flow into the forebay for the first time. It is Monday, May 3, 1954. (Courtesy U.S. Army Corps of Engineers, Mobile District)

Fig. 9-14 A Gainesville Daily Times article dated June 13, 1954 dealing with the Army's plans to divert the Chattahoochee River channel into the forebay. (Courtesy Gainesville Daily Times)

Main Earth Dam Construction

Fig. 9-15

Fig. 9-15 The camera has been positioned directly in front of the narrow gap in the cofferdam. The narrow opening is forcing the Chattahoochee River to rush through creating rapids. Very shortly now the life of the river at this spot and at this time will soon cease to exist. (Courtesy U.S. Army Corps of Engineers, Mobile District)

Fig. 9-16
At 1:10 PM on Wednesday, June 16, 1954 the Chattahoochee River had already begun to back up against the cofferdam and follow a new course. The triangular shaped hillside in the (cont.) background outlines the main earth dam. (Courtesy U.S. Army Corps of Engineers, Mobile District)

Fig. 9-17 From the access bridge, which will soon become a thing of the past, you can see the gap between opposing sides of the cofferdam is nearly closed. (Courtesy U.S. Army Corps of Engineers, Mobile District)

Fig. 9-16

Fig. 9-17

Fig. 9-18 Bulldozers push earth into place as they strengthen the cofferdam. The large mound of earth and rock in the background is one of two stockpile areas. (Courtesy U.S. Army Corps of Engineers, Mobile District)

Fig. 9-19 A bottom dump earth mover deposits its material as a bulldozer continues building up the middle of the cofferdam. (Courtesy U.S. Army Corps of Engineers, Mobile District)

Fig. 9-20 You are afforded an excellent opportunity to see just what the lake bottom looks like in front of the main earth dam. This is a photograph of the borrow area on Friday, May 21, 1954. Imagine today, all but the crest of the hills in the background underwater. (Courtesy U.S. Army Corps of Engineers, Mobile District)

Main Earth Dam Construction

Fig. 9-21 Removal of the earth at the site of the old river bed has begun. The old Resource Manager's Office will be constructed on top of the hill. Until the project is finished it will serve as the Resident Engineer's Office. At this time that office is located in Buford, Georgia, Fig. 9-22. It is Tuesday, June 29, 1954. (Courtesy U.S. Army Corps of Engineers, Mobile District)

Fig. 9-22

Fig. 9-23 A multitude of work is evident in this photograph. Behind the "V" shaped depression in the background work on the intake structure is taking place. The river bed will be cleared all the way to its granite base and then built back up from scratch. It is circa 1954. When foundation work was being completed here they found an old ship's anchor. They were not sure how the anchor got there but it was thought to have been an old barge anchor from an early river survey completed years before.(Courtesy U.S. Army Corps of Engineers, Mobile District)

Fig. 9-24 On Thursday, July 15, 1954 your view is east and you can see that work on the old river bed has reached the granite base. Work on the earth dam was not only carried on during the day but at night as well, as were other areas of the project's construction. (Courtesy U.S. Army Corps of Engineers, Mobile District)

Fig. 9-25 If you were at this spot today you would be buried under tons of earth. This is the base of the main earth dam which is also the old Chattahoochee River bed. It is Thursday, August 5, 1954 and Charles Jackson the Resident Engineer, at middle left and Mr. King a representative of the contractor, middle right, are discussing something atop the granite foundation. (Courtesy U.S. Army Corps of Engineers, Mobile District)

Fig. 9-26 Progress on the river bed clearing continues. Earth build-up to the left and right slopes of the dam has already begun. It will not be long now before the granite in the center will be covered over. Sawnee Mountain can be seen in the upper left background. It is Wednesday, August 11, 1954. (Courtesy U.S. Army Corps of Engineers, Mobile District)

Fig. 9-27 The river side slope of the infant dam. (Courtesy U.S. Army Corps of Engineers, Mobile District)

Fig. 9-28 A panoramic view of the intake and tailrace sides of the dam. Your view is west. Trucks and earth loaders move about the old river bed depositing their earth then move out for another run. It is Tuesday, August 24, 1954. (Courtesy U.S. Army Corps of Engineers, Mobile District)

Main Earth Dam Construction

Fig. 9-29 This panoramic photograph shows the east side of the dam taken the same day and time as the previous photograph. Buford Dam Road will run directly over this site but not before over 3,000,000 cubic yards of earth are set in place. (Courtesy U.S. Army Corps of Engineers, Mobile District)

Fig. 9-30 On Sunday, September 5, 1954 another panoramic view of the dam looking west again. This time though the area below the core trench is level and flat. From this point on the topography of the earth work here will begin to follow the outline of the hillside in the background. Eventually it will even cover the core trench. (Courtesy U.S. Army Corps of Engineers, Mobile District)

Fig. 9-31 This is an aerial view taken of the main earth dam site about the the same time as the previous photograph. You can clearly see the scarred borrow area and earth work section east of the dam where most of the earth used to build it came from. (Courtesy U.S. Army Corps of Engineers, Mobile District)

Main Earth Dam Construction

Fig. 9-32 Another aerial view, only you are looking downstream or south. You can see how the Chattahoochee River has been diverted into the forebay and continues flowing into the river behind the half completed dam. Forsyth County is on the right side of the dam, Gwinnett County on the left.(Courtesy U.S. Army Corps of Engineers, Mobile District)

Fig. 9-33 A similar photograph taken further upstream. (Courtesy U.S. Army Corps of Engineers, Mobile District)

Fig. 9-34 On Tuesday, October 12, 1954 this is what you would have seen had you traveled down the future powerhouse road. (Courtesy U.S. Army Corps of Engineers, Mobile District)

Main Earth Dam Construction

Fig. 9-35 Your looking to the Gwinnett County side of the main earth dam from the core trench on the Forsyth County side. (Courtesy U.S. Army Corps of Engineers, Mobile District)

Fig. 9-36 The main earth dam is beginning to take on its distinctive sloping design. The level area below the dam is where the powerhouse parking area will be located in the future. It is Friday, December 3, 1954. (Courtesy U.S. Army Corps of Engineers, Mobile District)

Fig. 9-37 Another panoramic view of the main earth dam site looking west to the Forsyth County side. (Courtesy U.S. Army Corps of Engineers, Mobile District)

Fig. 9-38 On Wednesday, March 2, 1955 the top of the earth dam looks like the surface of the moon. Tracks of heavy vehicles have scarred tightly packed earth. The operations office and water tower can be seen in the background. (Courtesy U.S. Army Corps of Engineers, Mobile District)

Main Earth Dam Construction

Fig. 9-39 The main earth dam on Thursday, April 28, 1955. (Courtesy U.S. Army Corps of Engineers, Mobile District)

Fig. 9-40 There is still work to be completed as you look at the flat surface of the unfinished dam and the back concrete portion of the intake structure. (Courtesy U.S. Army Corps of Engineers, Mobile District)

Fig. 9-41 You are looking east to the Gwinnett County side of the dam and the water at left is the Chattahoochee River. The forebay cut is seen at bottom foreground. (Courtesy U.S. Army Corps of Engineers, Mobile District)

Fig. 9-42 Your view is toward the Forsyth County side of the dam. (Courtesy U.S. Army Corps of Engineers, Mobile District)

Fig. 9-43 Dump trucks, scrapers, belly dump trucks, and pusher cats are parked on the main earth dam. (Courtesy U.S. Army Corps of Engineers, Mobile District)

Fig. 9-44 Seeding on the river side slope of the main earth dam is in progress. The rows were opened using a mule and plow and Bermuda sprigs were dropped in place by hand. It is Thursday, May 19, 1955. J.E. Hill of Decatur, Georgia was awarded a $6,300.00 contract for grassing and maintenance on the earth dam.[5] (Courtesy U.S. Army Corps of Engineers, Mobile District)

Fig. 9-45 The tailrace is in full view on Wednesday, June 1, 1955. The dam is nearly completed and the building located at the base of the dam will eventually be removed. It was a humidity controlled building which stored powerhouse equipment and also served as a field laboratory. (Courtesy U.S. Army Corps of Engineers, Mobile District)

Fig. 9-46 This contemporary photograph shows the same area. Not much has changed. Fig. 9-46 (RDC)

Fig. 9-47 The lake side slope of the dam is almost completely layered with rocks. This photograph was taken the same day and time as the previous shot of the tailrace slope. (Courtesy U.S. Army Corps of Engineers, Mobile District)

Fig. 9-48 Quite a change between then and now.(RDC)

Fig. 9-49 This aerial photograph was taken about the time that the earth dam was completed in late 1955.(Courtesy U.S. Army Corps of Engineers, Mobile District)

Main Earth Dam Construction

Fig. 9-50 The downstream side of the completed earth dam. (Courtesy U.S. Army Corps of Engineers, Mobile District)

Fig. 9-51 Another aerial view of the completed earth dam before the gates of the intake structure were closed and the lake began forming. (Courtesy U.S. Army Corps of Engineers, Mobile District)

Fig. 9-52 Several trees in the reservoir area will be left as fish shelters. Here you see reservoir clearing near the main earth dam.(Courtesy U.S. Army Corps of Engineers, Mobile District)

Fig. 9-53 The topography of the reservoir bottom is both hilly and flat.(Courtesy U.S. Army Corps of Engineers, Mobile District)

Fig. 9-54 A bulldozer effects reservoir clearing. (Courtesy U.S. Army Corps of Engineers, Mobile District)

Fig. 9-55 This aerial view shows the completed earth dam with the infant Lake Lanier forming in the background. It is circa 1956.(Courtesy U.S. Army Corps of Engineers, Mobile District)

Fig. 9-56 The water is taking over more and more land as the process of creating Lake Lanier continues. (Courtesy U.S. Army Corps of Engineers, Mobile District)

Fig. 9-57 The water depth here, next to the intake, has become fairly deep. (Courtesy U.S. Army Corps of Engineers, Mobile District)

Main Earth Dam Construction

Fig. 9-58 Minor grading work is being completed atop the finished earth dam.(Courtesy U.S. Army Corps of Engineers, Mobile District)

Fig. 9-59 It is circa 1957 and the lake has increased in size and depth. The river side slope of the dam has a good stand of grass and in a year or so the water will reach close to full pool. (Courtesy U.S. Army Corps of Engineers, Mobile District)

Fig. 9-60 A contemporary photograph from about the same place as the previous photograph. (RDC)

NOTES

1. U.S. Army Corps of Engineers, Mobile District

2. Apalachicola Basin Reservoir Regulation Manual, Appendix B, Buford Dam (Lake Sidney Lanier), Chattahoochee River, Georgia, February, 1991, pp. B1-5

3. Ibid., circa 1957.

4. U.S. Army Corps of Engineers, Mobile District

5. Gainesville Daily Times, July 27, 1956

Keith's Bridge (top) as it appeared in 1952 shortly before a fire destroyed the old covered bridge. (Courtesy Chestatee Regional Library from the Pictorial History of Hall County to 1950 by Sybil McRay)
After the fire (bottom) all that remained of the bridge were the stone pier supports. (Courtesy Chestatee Regional Library from the Pictorial History of Hall County to 1950 by Sybil McRay)

CHAPTER TEN

BRIDGE AND HIGHWAY RELOCATION AND CONSTRUCTION

In the early stages of planning for Buford Dam the Corps of Engineers heard the voices of concern over the relocation and upgrading of bridges, highways, and roads all over the proposed project. Citizens in every community directly effected by the lake were apprehensive about the plans for rerouting of highways, tearing down of bridges, and the building of new ones. At first a great deal of concern and opposition came from Hall County, which was understandable. An article appearing in the Gainesville Daily Times expressed that concern, **Fig. 10-1**,. All of the larger bridges, not to mention a number of smaller ones, located on Lake Lanier today are either in Hall County (Thompson, Longstreet and Lanier) or are the dividing boundary between Hall and other counties (Bolling, Browns, Wilkie). Hall County makes up the greatest acreage of surface water on the lake with a large number of peninsulas created by the erratic terrain in the area. So it is easy to see why they were so concerned about the Corps' relocation and replacement plans.

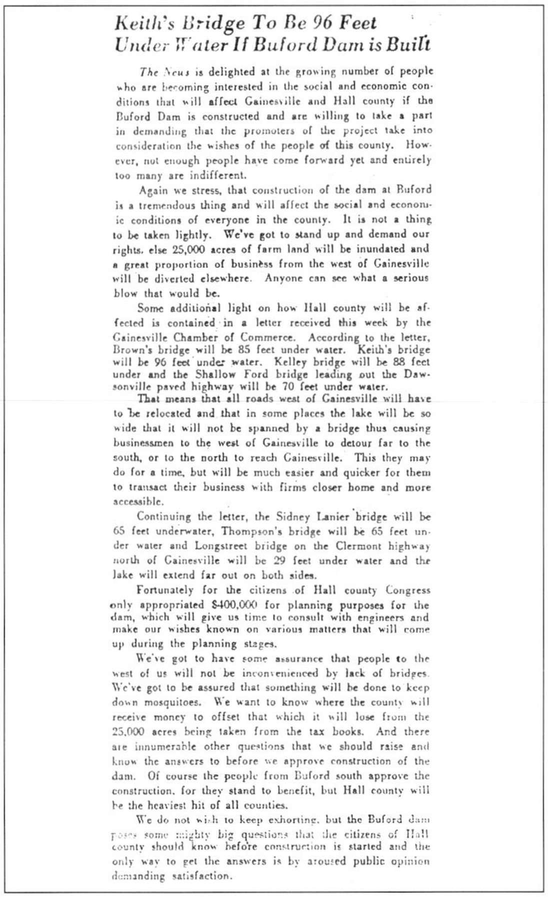

The highways and roads, crisscrossing the land that would become Lake Lanier, in many cases had to be relocated for obvious reasons. The elevation of the land the roads were located on would provide the government with an idea of those roads that would remain in use and those that would have to be removed or replaced. A number of factors were considered when determining whether or not bridges and highways below the flood line would be relocated. Early on, government officials would station men on or near bridges to get an indication as to how well they were traveled. These men conducting traffic surveys would count the number of vehicles traveling over them in a prescribed amount of time, usually a 24 hour period and during different times of the week. In this manner the government was given an idea as to just which routes were used the most. Armed with such data they could better determine which bridges and highways were a necessity to the people and needed to be replaced and those that would be inundated by the reservoir and not replaced.[1] In some instances the governments findings were not always warmly welcomed.

Fig. 10-1 A Gainesville Daily Times article, dated circa 1950 dealing with the relocation of bridges located in Hall County that will have to be replaced if Lake Lanier becomes a reality. (Courtesy Gainesville Daily Times)

Fig. 10-2 The New Bridge at Leather's Ford in Lumpkin County on the Chestatee River. It was one of many bridges not relocated by the Army Corps of Engineers when Lake Lanier began to form. (Courtesy U.S. Army Corps of Engineers, Mobile District)

In 1956 the United States Army Corps of Engineers notified the Lumpkin County Commissioners of Roads and Revenue that the New Bridge, **Fig. 10-2**, at Leather's Ford was not going to be relocated. It was determined that the bridge would have too high a cost in relation to benefits received to justify relocation. The Lumpkin County Commissioners asked the State Highway Department to conduct an "origin and destination" type traffic survey. In a 24 hour period from 6:00 AM to 6:00 PM on Thursday, May 10, 1956 the counter recorded 171 vehicles crossing the New Bridge. Fifty-seven percent of the traffic that day was stopped and asked origin and destination purpose. Forty percent used the route regularly, twenty-one percent going from home to work, fourteen percent for business, thirty-one percent for social and recreation, and thirty-four percent for shopping trips.[2]

The Corps of Engineers completed a forty-seven hour manned traffic count at the bridge from 12:00 noon Wednesday, July 11, 1956 continuously for 32 hours until 8:00 PM on Thursday, July 12th. A second count was made for another 15 hours from 5:00 AM, Thursday, July 13th, 1956 until 8:00 PM on the same day. The count recorded 185 vehicles (155 cars and 30 trucks). The average for a 24 hour period was 94 vehicles or 3.9 vehicles per hour.[3]

Because of the wide variance in traffic count figures the Lumpkin County Commissioners contested the Corps' findings and took the matter to court.[4] The Commissioners contention was that regardless of the findings that the Corps of Engineers was obligated to place the county in the same position or as good a position as it was in prior to construction of Buford Dam.[5] The Corps of Engineers took the stance that it would be "impractical" to replace every river crossing on such a large project. It was their contention that the State's own traffic count revealed that only forty percent or 68 of the 171 vehicles used the route on a "regular" basis and would suffer no inconvenience if the bridge was not available.[6] Both sides may have had

Fig. 10-3 The old Clark's Bridge (left) awaits the completion of the new bridge. (Gainesville Daily Times)

valid arguments but in April, 1958 a federal jury awarded the county $114,000.00 to replace the loss of the New Bridge.[7]

Clark's Bridge, *Fig. 10-3*, was another bridge that originally had been scraped for relocation. Hall County citizens requested the Army to reconsider replacing the old bridge as it was their contention that residents in the area would have to spend an additional $26,000.00 annually in extra mileage because they would have to use alternate routes. The county had an engineering firm complete a study which indicated an additional expense of $274,000.00 over 20 years to vehicle owners in the area which equated to only $13,700.00 annually. The Corps felt the county traffic survey showing extra travel figures was exaggerated and wanted to conduct another traffic destination and origin survey. After meeting with congressional officials and the county's attorney a compromise was reached. The Corps pledged some $285,000.00 toward the construction of a modern two-lane bridge. They said the county would have to provide the balance of between $40,000.00 and $90,000.00 to complete the structure which had an estimated cost at somewhere between $325,000.00 and $375,000.00. Eventually the State pledged Georgia funds to supplement the federal allocation to construct the new bridge. The old bridge was located downstream immediately adjacent to the present bridge site. *Fig. 10-142*.[8]

The Corps of Engineers contracted not to relocate Nix Bridge located on the Chestatee River in Dawson County. A relative of the bridge's namesake sought help from Senator Richard Russell in securing information concerning why the bridge was not being relocated.[9] The Corps of Engineers had contracted with the State of Georgia in May, 1954 to "relocate, rearrange or alter the state highway system at the Buford Project".[10] According to the contract they had agreed to relocate and provide for two crossings of the Chestatee River. One was Bolling Bridge about four miles downstream from Nix Bridge and the second was Wilkie Bridge about 3 miles upstream from Nix Bridge. For those people who used Nix Bridge to get to Dawsonville, which was the county seat and Gainesville these alternate routes were considered adequate.[11] When the state entered into the

Bridge and Highway Relocation and Construction

contract it agreed to "abandon all right, title, and interest in those facilities interfering with the project and to accept as full compensation there for the relocated facilities furnished by the government".[12] They also agreed to "save and hold the government harmless from any liability to owners or those possessing lands outside of the project who are or may be affected by the abandonment of roads set forth therein and further agreed to defend all said claims and to pay all damages and costs resulting therefore."[13]

Fig. 10-4 The temporary bridge that was constructed at the old Keith's Bridge site in 1953. Using the old stone piers that survived the fire a make-shift bridge was constructed by Forsyth and Hall Counties. It was eventually removed when the reservoir began to form in 1956. (Courtesy Chestatee Regional Library from the Pictorial History of Hall County to 1950 by Sybil McRay)

In some cases the bridges and highways that would be inundated by the water could not be relocated as in the case of Keith's Bridge, **Fig. 10-4**, which was destroyed by fire in 1952, rebuilt temporarily then removed when the reservoir began to form in 1956. Many bridges were not rebuilt or relocated because they were located in areas with too wide an expanse of water. Some highways all but completely disappeared and rerouting them over or around the lake would be too expensive or impractical. In many instances existing roads and available virgin land could substitute for their routes. In cases where bridges or roads were not relocated by the Army then the state could allocate the necessary money to continue the use of the facilities and contract to have them relocated.[14] In some instances the state contracted to oversee the construction of bridges having the Corps reimburse the state at a later date. An article appearing in the Gainesville Daily Times on Thursday, May 6, 1954 examined money the state was receiving for work they had completed on bridges in Forsyth and Hall Counties, **Fig. 10-5**,.

Fig. 10-5 An article by the Gainesville Daily Times concerning money given by the government to the state for bridge construction cost. (Courtesy Gainesville Daily Times)

Those roads located well above the flood elevation of 1085.0 would remain as they were and would become connecting points for relocated ones. A great many of the highways that would eventually dead end at or near the water's edge were used as boat ramp access points. Vans Tavern and

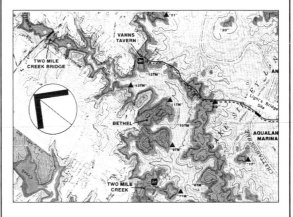

Fig. 10-6 Lake Lanier Navigation Map showing the location of old roads that are now covered by water. (Courtesy U.S. Army Corps of Engineers, Mobile District, 1985 Lake Lanier Navigation Charts)

Aqualand Marina were once connected by a road that traveled across Light's Bridge on the Chattahoochee River, **Fig. 10-6**. War Hill and Bolling Mill campgrounds are

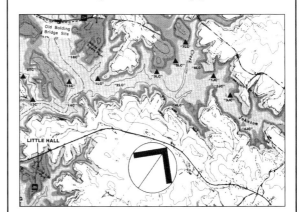

Fig. 10-7 Lake Lanier Navigation Map showing the location of old roads that are now covered by water. (Courtesy U.S. Army Corps of Engineers, Mobile District, 1985 Lake Lanier Navigation Charts)

connected by old Highway 53 that crossed over the old Bolding Bridge site which spanned the Chestatee River,

Fig. 10-7. Today when water levels drop to unusually low levels it is still possible to view some of these roads. An example would be Thompson Creek Park off of Highway 53. When water levels drop considerably you can see and walk out onto the paved road which use to be Highway 53. The old road is off to the left of the present boat ramp. There is a concrete culvert near the boat ramp running under the submerged road that use to allow creek water to flow underneath.

If you examine a map of the reservoir area before the lake then look at one after, you will see a considerable change. The pre-lake map shows the location of major bridges and highways in the area surrounding what would become Lake Lanier. *Fig. 10-8*,. The post-lake map shows the present day location of these bridges and highways, *Fig. 10-9*,. Most of Highway 53 from Dawsonville to Gainesville was relocated. The relocation was contracted by the Macon Construction Company of Franklin, North Carolina for $906,225.00.[15] Portions of 996, which would later become 369 and 141, which would become 306 were also relocated.[16] A section of the relocation for Highway 141 (now 369) was contracted by C.Y. Thomason Company of Greenville, South Carolina for $421,088.00.[17] A number of highways disappeared all together, one being 997 that ran from Cumming to Flowery Branch across what is now the southern end of Lake Lanier. On the pre-lake map Highway 400, Interstate 985 and McEver Road did not even exist as shown on the present map. Hall County sued the government in later years claiming that highways lost to the reservoir had not been adequately replaced. The 1.7 million won in federal court as compensation for the loss of roads helped pay for McEver Road's initial construction, which is simply an extention of Peachtree Industrial Boulevard.[18]

Fig. 10-8 Map of proposed reservoir. (Courtesy U.S. Army Corps of Engineers, Mobile District)

Fig. 10-10 You are looking east along a new section of Highway 53. Roads required a grade not to exceed six percent.[19] Traveling in this direction will take you to the new Bolling Bridge site, still under construction, that marks the boundary line between Forsyth and Hall Counties. (Courtesy U.S. Army Corps of Engineers, Mobile District)

Fig. 10-9 Post-lake map showing altered highway and road systems on Lake Lanier. (Courtesy U.S. Army Corps of Engineers, Mobile District and RDC)

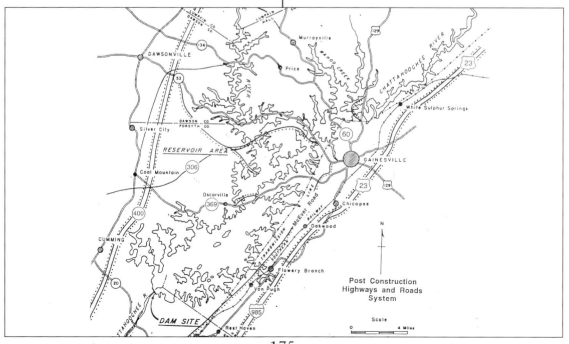

Bridge and Highway Relocation and Construction

Fig. 10-11 Moving your camera left you can see the long expanse of the relocated Highway 53. Your view is toward Dawson County. Continuing in this direction for several miles will take you to old Highway 53. (Courtesy U.S. Army Corps of Engineers, Mobile District)

Fig. 10-12 Relocated Highway 53 looking east toward Gainesville. (Courtesy U.S. Army Corps of Engineers, Mobile District)

Fig. 10-13 On Friday, June 24, 1955 your looking west to Dawson County. (Courtesy U.S. Army Corps of Engineers, Mobile District)

Fig. 10-15 A contemporary photograph looks somewhat different. (RDC)

Fig. 10-14 This portion of Highway 53 is located on a wide peninsula between Bolling and Lanier Bridge sites. Your view is east toward Gainesville. (Courtesy U.S. Army Corps of Engineers, Mobile District)

Fig. 10-16 On Thursday, August 2, 1956 you are looking at a section of the relocated Highway 129 in Hall County between Longstreet Bridge and Bell's Mill Bridge. The relocation of this highway was contracted by Ballenger Paving Company of Greenville, South Carolina for $269,703.00.[20] (Courtesy U.S. Army Corps of Engineers, Mobile District)

Lake Sidney Lanier "A Storybook Site"

Fig. 10-17 This is the approach roadway for Thompson Bridge looking west. You are on Highway 136 which will become Highway 60 in the future. It is Thursday, June 16, 1955. (Courtesy U.S. Army Corps of Engineers, Mobile District)

Fig. 10-20 You are looking along the axis of what will someday be the main earth dam. The left abutment of the main earth dam will rest against the end of this road. The Chattahoochee is barely visible between the trees. If you look closely in the background you can see work on the tailrace and forebay in progress some 1600 feet away. It is Thursday, August 2, 1951. (Courtesy U.S. Army Corps of Engineers, Mobile District)

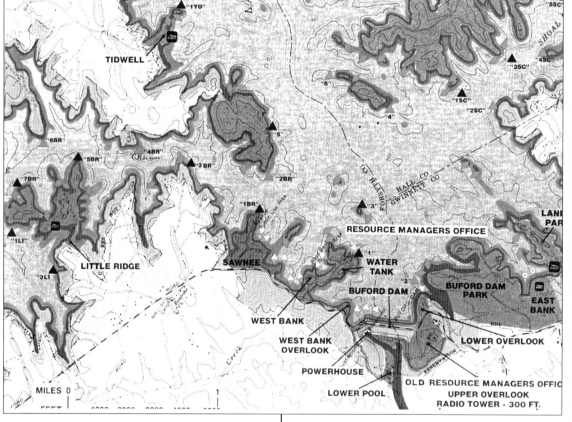

Fig. 10-18 Buford Dam Road runs along the southern edge of Lake Lanier. It was contracted by Groves, Lundin, and Cox Incorporated of Minneapolis, Minnesota for $2,836,712.00.[21] (Courtesy U.S. Army Corps of Engineers, Mobile District, 1985 Lake Lanier Navigation Charts)

Fig. 10-19 Buford Dam Road on Thursday, August 2, 1951 and you are standing in the entrance to the Lower Overlook. (Courtesy U.S. Army Corps of Engineers, Mobile District)

Fig. 10-21 Today the earth dam occupies the area of empty space seen in the previous picture. (RDC)

BRIDGE AND HIGHWAY RELOCATION AND CONSTRUCTION

Fig. 10-22 On Thursday, August 2, 1951 you are looking at what will be Buford Dam Road in the future. The ridge in the background is the site of the old operations building. The operations building, that would become the Resource Manager's Office in the future, will be constructed in about four years*. The ground breaking ceremony was held on the other side of this ridge 17 months earlier. The road leading off to the left is the powerhouse road. The road to the right will take you over the dam in the future. (Courtesy U.S. Army Corps of Engineers, Mobile District)

Fig. 10-23 The same area as the previous photograph, 13 months later on Tuesday, September 2, 1952. In the future a road will be constructed off to the right foreground of this photograph. This road will lead to the present Lanier Project Management Office and Visitor Center. (Courtesy U.S. Army Corps of Engineers, Mobile District)

Fig. 10-24 Quite a change from four decades ago. (RDC)

Fig. 10-25 Here is the road leading to the present Lanier Project Management Office mentioned in Fig. 10-23. (RDC)

Fig. 10-26 The present Lanier Project Management Office located atop a hilly peninsula on what use to be the western edge of Buford Dam Park, Fig. 10-18,. (RDC)

* *The title Resource Manager's Office was changed to Lanier Project Management Office in 1995*

Fig. 10-27 Looking south in the direction of Buford and in the opposite direction from Fig. 10-22 on Friday, June 27, 1952. (Courtesy U.S. Army Corps of Engineers, Mobile District)

Fig. 10-30 This area has changed dramatically over the years. (RDC)

Fig. 10-28 A stark contrast between then and now. (RDC)

Fig. 10-31 On Friday, June 27, 1952 this dirt road is an access road that will take you to an access bridge that spans the Chattahoochee River at the present site of the main earth dam. In the future it will be the powerhouse road that will take you to a parking lot below the dam. (Courtesy U.S. Army Corps of Engineers, Mobile District)

Fig. 10-29 What will become Buford Dam Road in the future was then a dirt access road. The intersection in the background is where Suwanee Dam Road and Buford Dam Road cross today. Turn left at the crossroads and you will end up in East Bank Park. (Courtesy U.S. Army Corps of Engineers, Mobile District)

BRIDGE AND HIGHWAY RELOCATION AND CONSTRUCTION

Fig. 10-32 The powerhouse road today. (RDC)

Fig. 10-33 On February 10, 1955 the old operations building located on top of a ridge overlooking the main earth dam, Fig. 10-18, is little more than a cinderblock shell. It was constructed by the Capital Construction Company of Atlanta, Georgia for $142,717.00.[22] This building served as the Resource Manager's Office for over 30 years before being moved to the site shown in Fig. 10-26. (Courtesy U.S. Army Corps of Engineers, Mobile District)

Fig. 10-33

Fig. 10-34, Fig. 10-35 and Fig. 10-36 are photographs of the operations building several years after construction. During the construction years this building served as the Resident Engineer's Office. After the project was completed it became the Resource Manager's Office and a visitor center. (Courtesy U.S. Army Corps of Engineers, Mobile District)

Fig. 10-34

Fig. 10-35

Fig. 10-36

Fig. 10-37 Today the building serves as an administrative office for a government contractor. (RDC)

Fig. 10-38 The motor pool construction. (Courtesy U.S. Army Corps of Engineers, Mobile District)

Fig. 10-39 The motor pool area is finished and ready for use. (Courtesy U.S. Army Corps of Engineers, Mobile District)

Fig. 10-40 In this contemporary photograph the water tower is gone and several additions to the complex have been completed. (RDC)

Fig. 10-41 On Monday, October 1, 1951 you see the access bridge constructed across the Chattahoochee River. (Courtesy U.S. Army Corps of Engineers, Mobile District)

Fig. 10-42 This aerial photograph of the dam site shows the location of the access bridge. (Courtesy U.S. Army Corps of Engineers, Mobile District)

Fig. 10-43 On Tuesday, February 10, 1953 the bridge allows access to stockpile no.2. The bridge will be removed in about a year and a half after the river is diverted into the forebay. (Courtesy U.S. Army Corps of Engineers, Mobile District)

Bridge and Highway Relocation and Construction

Fig. 10-44 On Monday, May 10, 1954 you are looking to the hillside that will become the left abutment of the main earth dam. (Courtesy U.S. Army Corps of Engineers, Mobile District)

Fig. 10-45 Brown's Bridge is located on Highway 369 and is the boundary line between Forsyth and Hall Counties. It was constructed a mile or so upstream from the old bridge. The substructure was built by C.Y. Thomason Company of Greenville, South Carolina for $421,088.00.[23] The superstructure was built by the Bristol Steel and Iron Works Incorporated of Bristol, Virginia for $461,921.00.[24] (Courtesy U.S. Army Corps of Engineers, Mobile District, 1985 Lake Lanier Navigation Charts)

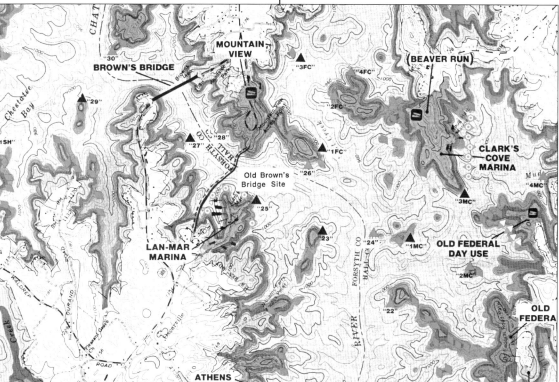

Fig. 10-46 This is a photograph taken of the old covered Brown's Bridge which was located a mile or so upstream from the present bridge and was destroyed during a flood in 1947. A Bailey steel military bridge was erected in its place and remained in use until the mid 1950's when the rising waters of Lake Lanier forced its removal. (Courtesy Gainsville Daily Times)

Fig. 10-47 The steep hillside in the background is the Hall County side of the Brown's Bridge site. Mountain View Park will be located in a wooded area at far right. The Chattahoochee River is flowing left to right. Workers are setting a steel cofferdam in place for the foundation of one of the concrete substructure piers. It is Wednesday, August 18, 1954. (Courtesy U.S. Army Corps of Engineers, Mobile District)

Fig. 10-48 On Sunday, October 10, 1954 you are looking at a portion of the relocated Highway 141 and the Hall County approach to Brown's Bridge. (Courtesy U.S. Army Corps of Engineers, Mobile District)

Fig. 10-49 The Forsyth County abutment of Brown's Bridge on Tuesday, October 19, 1954. (Courtesy U.S. Army Corps of Engineers, Mobile District)

Fig. 10-50 Same view nearly a month later. (Courtesy U.S. Army Corps of Engineers, Mobile District)

Fig. 10-52 Pier no.3 reaches further and further up as the right abutment slope rises in the background. (Courtesy U.S. Army Corps of Engineers, Mobile District)

Fig. 10-51 The same day as the previous photograph and you get a close up view of framing for pier no.4. (Courtesy U.S. Army Corps of Engineers, Mobile District)

Fig. 10-53 It is Tuesday, December 7, 1954 and pier no.4 has grown considerably in size. (Courtesy U.S. Army Corps of Engineers, Mobile District)

Bridge and Highway Relocation and Construction

*Fig. 10-54
On Wednesday, January 26, 1955 the pier substructures are nearing completion.
(Courtesy U.S. Army Corps of Engineers, Mobile District)*

*Fig. 10-57
Turn around 180 degrees and you see the Hall County abutment.
(Courtesy U.S. Army Corps of Engineers, Mobile District)*

*Fig. 10-55
A little over a month later on Wednesday, March 3, 1955.
(Courtesy U.S. Army Corps of Engineers, Mobile District)*

*Fig. 10-58
It is Thursday, June 16, 1955 and you get a downstream view of the superstructure work.
(Courtesy U.S. Army Corps of Engineers, Mobile District)*

*Fig. 10-56
You are looking at the completed pier substructure work on Friday, May 6, 1955. Your view is toward the Forsyth County abutment.
(Courtesy U.S. Army Corps of Engineers, Mobile District)*

Fig. 10-59 An upstream look shows a portion of the superstructure being transported across the bridge. (Courtesy U.S. Army Corps of Engineers, Mobile District)

Fig. 10-60 This photograph shows that construction of the superstructure was accomplished from both ends of the bridge simultaneously. It is Monday, July 6, 1955. (Courtesy U.S. Army Corps of Engineers, Mobile District)

Fig. 10-62 The view is from the Hall County side on Wednesday, November 9, 1955 and the steel decking for the floor of the bridge has been set in place. (Courtesy U.S. Army Corps of Engineers, Mobile District)

Fig. 10-63 The completed Brown's Bridge on Thursday, February 9, 1956. The gates of the intake structure were closed nine days ago and soon the river channel here will begin to swell over its banks and start the long process of creating Lake Lanier. (Courtesy U.S. Army Corps of Engineers, Mobile District)

Fig. 10-61 The steel superstructure now runs the length of the substructure piers and you are able to gauge the tremendous depth of the lake at this bridge site. (Courtesy U.S. Army Corps of Engineers, Mobile District)

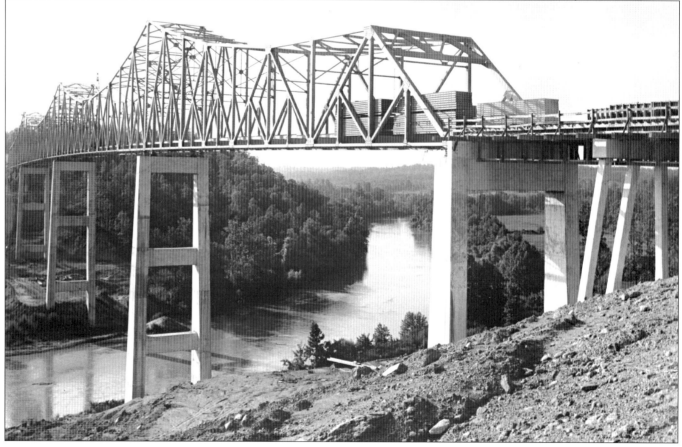

Bridge and Highway Relocation and Construction

Fig. 10-64 Brown's Bridge as it appears today. (RDC)

Fig. 10-67 The camera is looking east toward Brown's Bridge. (Courtesy U.S. Army Corps of Engineers, Mobile District)

Fig. 10-65 This photograph shows a portion of the 150 tons of steel salvaged from the old Brown's Bridge that was shipped to San Luis Obispo, California. (Courtesy Gainesville Daily Times)

Fig. 10-68 It is Wednesday, January 26, 1955 and you get a good look at the construction site. Your view is west away from Brown's Bridge construction. (Courtesy U.S. Army Corps of Engineers, Mobile District)

Fig. 10-66 Two-Mile Creek Bridge is also located on Highway 369 in Forsyth County. It is similar in construction to Wilkie Bridge and Bell's Mill Bridge. It was constructed by the Henry Newton Company of Decatur, Georgia for $93,479.00.[25] (Courtesy U.S. Army Corps of Engineers, Mobile District, 1985 Lake Lanier Navigational Charts)

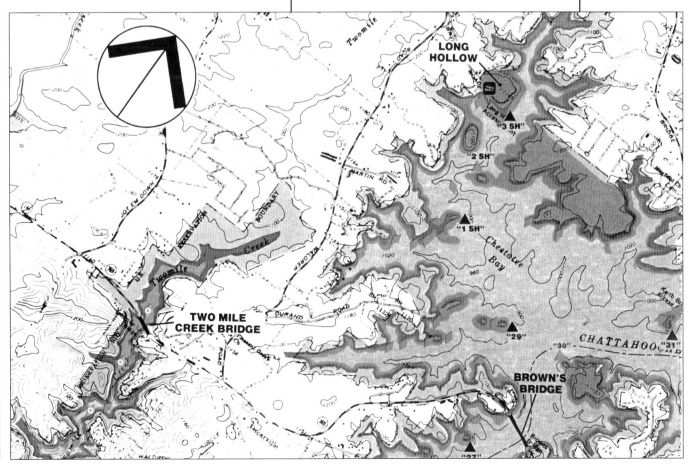

*Fig. 10-69
On Friday, May 6, 1955 the bridge's substructure piers have been completed and steel now spans the top. (Courtesy U.S. Army Corps of Engineers, Mobile District)*

*Fig. 10-70
Work atop the bridge continues on Wednesday, July 6, 1955. (Courtesy U.S. Army Corps of Engineers, Mobile District)*

*Fig. 10-71
Again you see work on the bridge on the same day and time as the previous photograph. Your view is west from the left abutment and water will move in under the bridge from the left in several years creating a small cove to the right of this photograph. (Courtesy U.S. Army Corps of Engineers, Mobile District)*

*Fig. 10-72
Now you see what the completed bridge looked like on Wednesday, November 9, 1955. (Courtesy U.S. Army Corps of Engineers, Mobile District)*

*Fig. 10-73
Today aside from the water very little has changed. (RDC)*

Bridge and Highway Relocation and Construction

Fig. 10-74 Lanier Bridge is located on Highway 53 in Hall County. Moving up the old Chattahoochee River channel it is the next bridge past Brown's Bridge. In the mid 1990's the bridge's name was changed to the Jerry D. Jackson bridge. It was built by the Oman Construction Company Incorporated of Nashville, Tennessee for $164,195.00.[26] The superstructure was built by Bristol Steel and Iron Works of Bristol, Virginia for $494,064.00.[27] (Courtesy U.S. Army Corps of Engineers, Mobile District, 1985 Lake Lanier Navigational Charts)

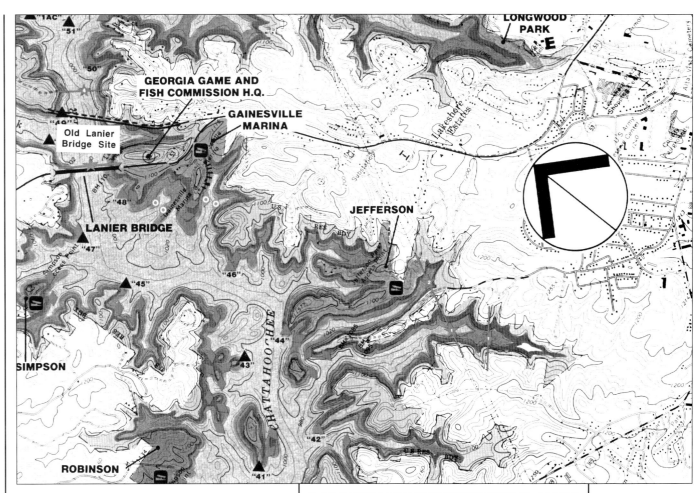

Fig. 10-75 This is the site chosen for Lanier Bridge. Your view is toward the right abutment with the Chattahoochee River flowing right to left. It is Thursday, March 3, 1955. (Courtesy U.S. Army Corps of Engineers, Mobile District)

Fig. 10-76 On Friday, March 4, 1955 you can see the flood plain adjacent to the left abutment of the bridge site. (Courtesy U.S. Army Corps of Engineers, Mobile District)

Fig. 10-77 On Friday, April 29, 1955 framing for pier no.2 is well underway. (Courtesy U.S. Army Corps of Engineers, Mobile District)

Fig. 10-78 On the same day you can see the early stages of pier substructure framing on the other side of the river. Your view is to the right abutment away from Gainesville. (Courtesy U.S. Army Corps of Engineers, Mobile District)

*Fig. 10-79
On Tuesday, May 31, 1955 the bridge site is busy with activity.
(Courtesy U.S. Army Corps of Engineers, Mobile District)*

*Fig. 10-80
Notice that the left abutment of Lanier Bridge is not as steep as the right, as seen in Fig. 10-79. Your view is toward Gainesville. In about three years in April, 1958 this site will spark the "Lady of the Lake" mystery. A car driven by a Gainesville woman, Susie Roberts, will skid off the right abutment of the bridge at approximately this location and come to rest some 90 feet below the water. The vehicle with the remains of Ms. Roberts was not discovered until November, 1990 when a bridge construction crew began dredging operations for another bridge at this site. About a year or so after the accident a body was found in the lake but authorities were unable to identify the remains. After finding the vehicle in 1990 investigators believed this body to have been Delia Mae Parker Young a passenger in Ms. Robert's car that night.[28]
(Courtesy U.S. Army Corps of Engineers, Mobile District)*

*Fig. 10-81
Lanier Bridge on Wednesday, November 9, 1955.
(Courtesy U.S. Army Corps of Engineers, Mobile District)*

Bridge and Highway Relocation and Construction

Fig. 10-82 Two months later and steel has begun to span the concrete piers. (Courtesy U.S. Army Corps of Engineers, Mobile District)

Fig. 10-83 Quite a difference between then an now. Like Thompson's Bridge, Lanier Bridge also received a second bridge at this site. (RDC)

Fig. 10-85 In this old newspaper photograph you can see the steel superstructure has almost reached the entire length of the bridge. (Courtesy Atlanta Journal and Atlanta Constitution)

Fig. 10-84 Today there are two bridges where until recently there was only one. (RDC)

Fig. 10-86 Water has nearly covered the road in the foreground as the completed Lanier Bridge rises high above Lake Lanier. This is an upstream view of the bridge taken from a portion of old Highway 53 that will not survive the rising waters of Lake Lanier. (Courtesy U.S. Army Corps of Engineers, Mobile District)

Fig. 10-87 This is a downstream view of Lanier Bridge taken about the same time as the previous photograph, Fig. 10-86. (Courtesy U.S. Army Corps of Engineers, Mobile District)

Fig. 10-88 A photograph of Lanier Bridge is seen here hanging in a local store. This photograph was made in April, 1958 and is a downstream view of the bridge while the lake was forming. (Courtesy U.S. Army Corps of Engineers, Mobile District)

Fig. 10-89 On Thursday, February 28, 1957 Lanier Bridge spans the rising waters of Lake Lanier. Your view is in the direction of Gainesville. (Courtesy U.S. Army Corps of Engineers, Mobile District)

Fig. 10-90 In 1990 construction of the second bridge has already begun. (RDC)

Fig. 10-91 Today you see two bridges standing side by side. (RDC)

Bridge and Highway Relocation and Construction

Fig. 10-92 Lake Lanier has begun to surround Lanier Bridge. (Courtesy Gainesville Daily Times)

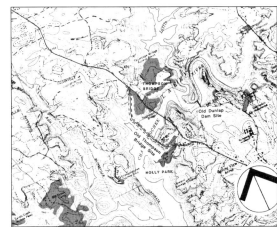

Fig. 10-95 Thompson's Bridge is located several miles outside of Gainesville on Highway 60 over the main river channel of the Chattahoochee River. It is the next bridge past Lanier Bridge moving up the old river channel and was constructed by two different companies. The substructure was contracted by Wright Contracting Company of Columbus, Georgia for $246,671.00, which also included the approach road.[29] The superstructure was contracted by C.Y. Thomason Company of Greenville, South Carolina for $411,518.00.[30] (Courtesy U.S. Army Corps of Engineers, Mobile District, 1985 Lake Lanier Navigation Charts)

Fig. 10-93 Vehicles begin to travel over the completed bridge. (Courtesy Gainesville Daily Times)

Fig. 10-94 Old Lanier Bridge is being blasted away. Although the bridge was removed there was still considerable value to the structure as there was to most of the bridges removed on the project. The salvagable steel here was worth between $40,000.00 and $50,000.00 with the inital salvage operation conducted after the lake had already inundated the structure. (Courtesy Gainseville Daily Times)

Fig. 10-96 This is a photograph of the old covered Thompson's Bridge taken in 1932. This bridge was replaced in 1939 by a bridge that remained in use until 1957 when the present bridge was built. (Courtesy Chestatee Regional Library from the Pictorial History of Hall County to 1950 by Sybil McRay)

Fig. 10-97 Here is another view of the old covered Thompson's Bridge taken in 1932. (Courtesy Gainesville Daily Times)

Fig. 10-100 Framing for one of the substructure piers is in progress. (Courtesy U.S. Army Corps of Engineers, Mobile District)

Fig. 10-98 This is the Thompson's Bridge site on Tuesday, May 31, 1955. The view is toward the right abutment and the river stream is flowing right to left. (Courtesy U.S. Army Corps of Engineers, Mobile District)

Fig. 10-101 On Thursday, August 18, 1955 several of the substructure piers have been completed. (Courtesy U.S. Army Corps of Engineers, Mobile District)

Fig. 10-99 Here you see the left abutment of the bridge. (Courtesy U.S. Army Corps of Engineers, Mobile District)

BRIDGE AND HIGHWAY RELOCATION AND CONSTRUCTION

Fig. 10-102 Your view is in the direction of Gainesville on Thursday, September 15, 1955. (Courtesy U.S. Army Corps of Engineers, Mobile District)

Fig. 10-105 Here you see the second bridge adjacent to the original one constructed in the late 1950's. (RDC)

Fig. 10-103 The concrete substructure piers of Thompson's Bridge are finished as you gaze across the vast expanse toward Gainesville on Wednesday, November 9, 1955. (Courtesy U.S. Army Corps of Engineers, Mobile District)

Fig. 10-104 The photograph shows Thompson's Bridge in the late 1980's as construction of a second bridge has started in the background. Because of increased traffic patterns it was necessary to build this second bridge. (RDC)

Fig. 10-106 Steel sections of the bridge have been inundated by cresting flood waters. It is Tuesday, April 17, 1956. Working on bridges could sometimes be hazardous as was the case on this bridge. On Wednesday, May 29, 1956 a little over a month after this photograph was taken a young man removing scaffolding from below the steel decking would fall 90 feet to his death in the shallow water below.[31] (Courtesy U.S. Army Corps of Engineers, Mobile District)

Fig. 10-107 The completed bridge in the summer of 1956. (Courtesy U.S. Army Corps of Engineers, Mobile District)

Fig. 10-108 This is old Thompson's Bridge as it appeared just before the new bridge was opened for traffic. The rising waters of Lake Lanier caused a postponement of the impoundment until the new bridge was finished. (Courtesy Chestatee Regional Library from the Pictorial History of Hall County to 1950 by Sybil McRay)

THE WATERS of the lake slowly lap under the supports of the Thompson Bridge here, and on the other side the lake has just about covered the road. It was expected last night, that the Thompson Bridge Road would be closed to traffic past the north side of the bridge. The new bridge going up several hundred yards from the old structure is incomplete, and it will probably be some time before the traffic can be routed over it.

Fig. 10-109 Water from the rising lake is just about to crest the roadway leading to the old Thompson's Bridge. Unusually heavy rains coupled with impoundment of water nearly flooded over this portion of the highway too early. (Courtesy Gainesville Daily Times)

Fig. 10-111 The new Thompson's Bridge is finished and taking on traffic. It is Thursday, August 2, 1956. (Courtesy U.S. Army Corps of Engineers, Mobile District)

Fig. 10-110 Old Thompson's Bridge is being dismantled for salvage. It was sold to J.D. Morse of Calhoun, Georgia for $2,501.00.[32] (Courtesy Gainesville Daily Times)

Fig. 10-112 Another contemporary photograph taken in the late 1980's showing the second bridge construction. (RDC)

Fig. 10-113 The completed second bridge. (RDC)

Fig. 10-114 Bolling Bridge is located on Highway 53 and is the first bridge spanning the old river channel of the Chestatee River. Like Brown's Bridge it is the dividing line between Forsyth and Hall Counties. It was constructed by R.G. Foster and Company of Wadley, Georgia for $538,261.00.³³ (Courtesy U.S. Army Corps of Engineers, Mobile District, 1985 Lake Lanier Navigational Charts)

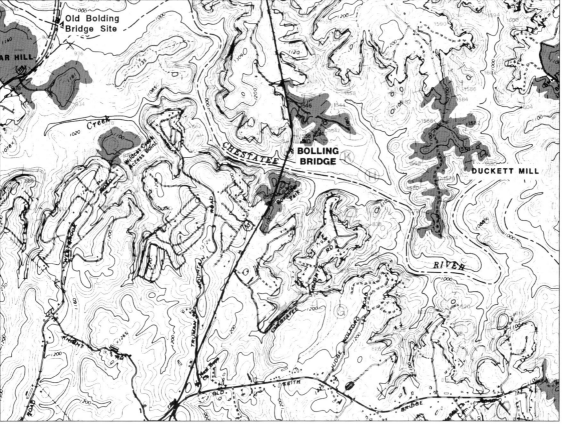

Fig. 10-115 This is a photograph taken of the old Bolding Covered Bridge that was located further upstream from the present bridge. It was a dangerous bridge because of the robbers who would hide up in the rafters waiting for unsuspecting travelers to come by. This bridge preceded the old Bolding Bridge, Fig. 10-129, that was torn down in 1954 when a new site for the bridge was chosen. It is not known why the old bridge bares the name Bolding and the present bridge Bolling, in all likelihood it was probably just a mistake in spelling that was never corrected. (Courtesy Chestatee Regional Library from the Pictorial History of Hall County to 1950 by Sybil McRay)

Bridge and Highway Relocation and Construction

Fig. 10-116 The steep escarpment of the Forsyth County side of the Bolling Bridge site can be seen from the Hall County side on Friday, June 24, 1955. (Courtesy U.S. Army Corps of Engineers, Mobile District)

Fig. 10-118 The process of clearing the bridge site for construction is nearing completion. (Courtesy U.S. Army Corps of Engineers, Mobile District)

Fig. 10-117 On the same date as the previous photograph you can see the Hall County side of the bridge site. (Courtesy U.S. Army Corps of Engineers, Mobile District)

Fig. 10-119 Concrete substructure pier construction is well underway in this photograph taken on Thursday, September 15, 1955. (Courtesy U.S. Army Corps of Engineers, Mobile District)

Fig. 10-120 The afternoon sun creates a hard glare on the camera lens as you look to the Forsyth County side of Bolling Bridge. Soon the steel superstructure will begin to cross over these piers. It is Tuesday, January 17, 1956. (Courtesy U.S. Army Corps of Engineers, Mobile District)

Fig. 10-121 The steel superstructure on the Hall County side is easily visible in this photograph taken nine days after the gates of the intake structure were closed on Thursday, February 9, 1956. (Courtesy U.S. Army Corps of Engineers, Mobile District)

Fig. 10-122 On Wednesday, April 18, 1956 the erection of the bridge's steel superstructure is nearly completed. If you look closely you can see that the middle of the bridge is missing as the two sides have yet to meet one another. (Courtesy U.S. Army Corps of Engineers, Mobile District)

Fig. 10-123 Here is a contemporary photograph taken from the same spot as the previous photograph. (RDC)

Fig. 10-124 This is another photograph taken on Wednesday, April 18, 1956 and the absent middle portion of the steel superstructure is easily visible. (Courtesy U.S. Army Corps of Engineers, Mobile District)

Fig. 10-125 The same date again but this time from the Forsyth County side of the bridge looking to the vast area of land at right that will be inundated by the rising waters of Lake Lanier. (Courtesy U.S. Army Corps of Engineers, Mobile District)

Fig. 10-126 Today the water changes things quite a bit. (RDC)

Fig. 10-127 With the gates of the intake structure closed the lake slowly begins to climb up the substructure piers of Bolling Bridge. (Courtesy U.S. Army Corps of Engineers, Mobile District)

Fig. 10-128 It is easy to see the effect Lake Lanier has on the bridge. (Courtesy U.S. Army Corps of Engineers, Mobile District)

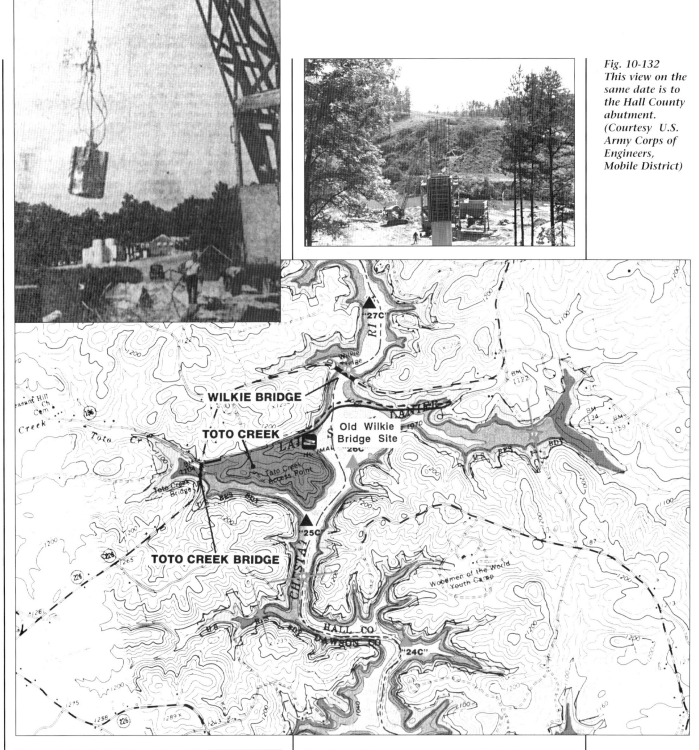

Fig. 10-129 Dynamite blasts and a one ton blockbuster make quick work of a section of the old Bolding Bridge as workers move to salvage the steel. (Courtesy Gainesville Daily Times)

Fig. 10-132 This view on the same date is to the Hall County abutment. (Courtesy U.S. Army Corps of Engineers, Mobile District)

Fig. 10-130 Wilkie Bridge is located on Highway 136 and is the next bridge up from Bolling Bridge on the old Chestatee River channel. It was constructed by the Ballenger Paving Company and Inland Bridge Company Incorporated of Greenville, South Carolina for $428,515.00. This contract price also included Toto Creek Bridge and the relocation of Highway 136.[34] The bridge marks the boundary line between Dawson and Hall Counties. (Courtesy U.S. Army Corps of Engineers, Mobile District, 1985 Lake Lanier Navigational Charts)

Fig. 10-131 It is Thursday, September 15, 1955 and you are looking at the Wilkie Bridge site as substructure pier work is in progress. The view is toward the Dawson County abutment. (Courtesy U.S. Army Corps of Engineers, Mobile District)

Fig. 10-133 The work area below the substructure piers will be underwater in several years. It is Wednesday, November 9, 1955. (Courtesy U.S. Army Corps of Engineers, Mobile District)

BRIDGE AND HIGHWAY RELOCATION AND CONSTRUCTION

Fig. 10-134 On Wednesday, April 18, 1956 debris has collected against the base of one of the substructure piers. (Courtesy U.S. Army Corps of Engineers, Mobile District)

Fig. 10-135 Workers move across the steel I-beams set across the bridge on Thursday, August 2, 1956. Your view is to the Hall County abutment. (Courtesy U.S. Army Corps of Engineers, Mobile District)

Fig. 10-136 Today water covers a good deal of the bridge work. (RDC)

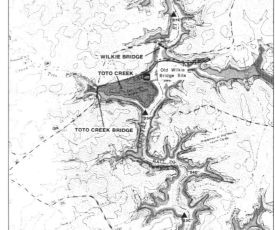

Fig. 10-130 Toto Creek Bridge, also located on Highway 136, is west of Wilkie Bridge in Dawson County. It too was constructed by the Ballenger Paving Company and the Inland Bridge Company Inc. of Greenville, South Carolina for $428,515.00. This contract price also included Wilkie Bridge and the relocation of Highway 136.[35] (Courtesy U.S. Army Corps of Engineers, Mobile District, 1985 Lake Lanier Navigational Charts)

Fig. 10-137 This is the Toto Creek Bridge site on Thursday, February 9, 1956. The gates of the intake structure were closed nine days before. Because this area is so far north of the dam site it will be several years before the lake appears here. (Courtesy U.S. Army Corps of Engineers, Mobile District)

Lake Sidney Lanier "A Storybook Site"

Fig. 10-138 Bridge construction on Wednesday, April 18, 1956. (Courtesy U.S. Army Corps of Engineers, Mobile District)

Fig. 10-139 On Thursday, October 11, 1956 the bridge has been completed. Your view is east in the direction of Gainesville. (Courtesy U.S. Army Corps of Engineers, Mobile District)

Fig. 10-142 Bell's Mill Bridge is located on Highway 129 north of Gainesville in Hall County. It was constructed by the Tidwell Construction Company of Douglasville, Georgia for $590,322.00. This contract price included the road approach and construction of Longstreet Bridge.[36] (Courtesy U.S. Army Corps of Engineers, Mobile District, 1985 Lake lanier Navigation Charts)

Fig. 10-140 You are standing on the side of Highway 136 and looking in the direction of Gainesville on Thursday, October 11, 1956. (Courtesy U.S. Army Corps of Engineers, Mobile District)

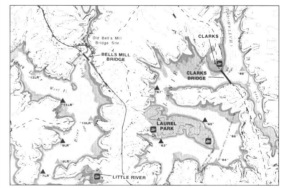

Fig. 10-141 Time and use, have taken their toll over the years. (RDC)

Fig. 10-143 This is old Bell's Mill Bridge on Friday, February 22, 1957. The lake elevation at this site would put this bridge underwater at normal pool. Removal of this bridge was contracted by the Columbus Construction Company of Columbus, Georgia for $11,000.00. This contract price also included the demolition of the old Longstreet Bridge.[37] (Courtesy U.S. Army Corps of Engineers, Mobile District)

Bridge and Highway Relocation and Construction

Fig. 10-144 This is a photograph taken of the old Bell's Mill Bridge taken in 1932. (Courtesy Chestatee Regional Library from Windows of Memory, The Hall County That Was, A Photographic History by Sybil McRay and James E. Dorsey)

Fig. 10-145 Old Bell's Mill Bridge is gone. Only the concrete substructure piers remain. (Courtesy U.S. Army Corps of Engineers, Mobile District)

Fig. 10-146 On Thursday, April 19, 1956 you are standing on the right abutment of Bell's Mill Bridge looking in the direction of Gainesville. (Courtesy U.S. Army Corps of Engineers, Mobile District)

Fig. 10-147 Pier substructure work is nearing completion when this photo was taken on Thursday, April 19, 1956. (Courtesy U.S. Army Corps of Engineers, Mobile District)

Fig. 10-148 On Thursday, June 21, 1956 steel I-beams are being set in place above the concrete substructure piers. (Courtesy U.S. Army Corps of Engineers, Mobile District)

Fig. 10-150 You are looking up at the completed bridge from the left side of the right abutment. (Courtesy U.S. Army Corps of Engineers, Mobile District)

Fig. 10-149 In a little over a month most of the steel I-beams are in place. (Courtesy U.S. Army Corps of Engineers, Mobile District)

Fig. 10-151 It is Thursday, November 29, 1956 and you are looking to the left abutment of Bell's Mill Bridge. (Courtesy U.S. Army Corps of Engineers, Mobile District)

BRIDGE AND HIGHWAY RELOCATION AND CONSTRUCTION

Fig. 10-152 This contemporary photograph shows you the bridge surrounded by Lake Lanier. (RDC)

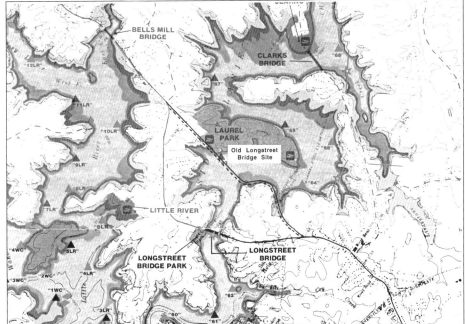

Fig. 10-153 Longstreet Bridge is also located on Highway 129 north of Gainesville. (Courtesy U.S. Army Corps of Engineers, Mobile District, 1985 Lake Lanier Navigation Charts) It was constructed over the main river channel of the Chattahoochee River and was named after Confederate General James Longstreet, Fig. 10-154,. (Courtesy Chestatee Regional Library from the pictorial History of Hall County to 1950 by Sybil McRay) The old bridge was located a mile or so upstream from its present site, Fig. 10-155. (Courtesy Gainesville Daily Times) It was constructed by the same company that built Bell's Mill Bridge, the Tidwell Construction Company of Douglasville, Georgia.[38]

Fig. 10-154

Fig. 10-155

Fig. 10-156 On Thursday, April 19, 1956 the huge substructure piers tower above the wide river plain below. (Courtesy U.S. Army Corps of Engineers, Mobile District)

Fig. 10-157 You are looking across the wide expanse of the Longstreet Bridge site. (Courtesy U.S. Army Corps of Engineers, Mobile District)

Fig. 10-158 On Thursday, August 2, 1956 the substructure piers of Longstreet Bridge are finished. (Courtesy U.S. Army Corps of Engineers, Mobile District)

BRIDGE AND HIGHWAY RELOCATION AND CONSTRUCTION

Fig. 10-159 Longstreet Bridge on Thursday, November 29, 1956. (Courtesy U.S. Army Corps of Engineers, Mobile District)

Fig. 10-160 You are looking to the left abutment of Longstreet Bridge as construction continues. This photograph gives you an excellent view of what lies beneath the water. (Courtesy U.S. Army Corps of Engineers, Mobile District)

Fig. 10-161 Today much of the work completed beneath the bridge has long since disappeared. (RDC)

Fig. 10-162 This was the memorial marker located at the old Longstreet Bridge site. It was placed there by the Longstreet Chapter of the United Daughters Confederacy in 1935. The old bridge site was located a half mile or so, Fig. 10-155, upstream from the present site. It was contracted for removal by the Columbus Construction Company of Columbus, Georgia for $11,000.00. This contract price also included the removal of the old Bell's Mill Bridge.[39] (Courtesy U.S. Army Corps of Engineers, Mobile District)

Fig. 10-163 The right abutment of the old Longstreet Bridge on Friday, February 22, 1957. (Courtesy U.S. Army Corps of Engineers, Mobile District)

Fig. 10-164 A plaque honoring General Longstreet. (Courtesy U.S. Army Corps of Engineers, Mobile District)

Fig. 10-165 One month later and the bridge has been removed. (Courtesy U.S. Army Corps of Engineers, Mobile District)

Lake Sidney Lanier "A Storybook Site"

Fig. 10-166 This unusual photograph shows you an old bridge pier support for a bridge that proceeded the old Longstreet Bridge. (Courtesy U.S. Army Corps of Engineers, Mobile District)

Fig. 10-167 This 1932 photograph shows the older bridge, that preceded the old Longstreet Bridge, before it was removed. (Courtesy Chestatee Regional Library from Windows of Memory, The Hall County That Was, A Photographic History by Sybil McRay and James E. Dorsey)

Fig. 10-168 The left abutment of old Longstreet Bridge just before removal. (Courtesy U.S. Army Corps of Engineers, Mobile District)

Fig. 10-169 Within the month on Wednesday, March 27, 1957 the bridge is gone. (Courtesy U.S. Army Corps of Engineers, Mobile District)

Notes

1. General File, Series XI, Sub-Series C, Richard B. Russell Collection, Richard B. Russell Library, University of Georgia Libraries, Athens, Georgia. Letters from Lumpkin County Commissioners of Roads and Revenue and Brigadier General J.L. Person, Assistant Chief of Engineers for Civil Works, United States Army Corps of Engineers to Senator Richard B. Russell Jr., December 28, 1956 and March 7, 1957.

2. Ibid., Letter from the State Highway Department of Georgia to Attorney A.R. Kenyon, June 19, 1956.

3. Ibid., Letter from F.G. Turner Assistant Chief, Engineers Division, United States Army Corps of Engineers to Attorney A.R. Kenyon, November 29, 1956.

4. Ibid., Letter from Attorney A.R. Kenyon to United States Army Corps of Engineers, Office of the District Engineer, December 3, 1956.

5. Ibid., Letter from the Lumpkin County Commissioners of Roads and Revenue to Senator Richard B. Russell Jr., December 28, 1956.

6. Ibid., Letter from Brigadier General, Assistant Chief of Engineers for Civil Works to Senator Richard B. Russell Jr., March 7, 1957.

7. Gainesville Daily Times, April, 1958.

8. Ibid., 1955-56.

9. General File, Series XI, Sub-Series C, Richard B. Russell Collection, Richard B. Russell Library, University of Georgia Libraries, Athens, Georgia. Letter from Mrs. Arthur J. Nix relative of the namesake of Nix Bridge to Senator Richard B. Russell Jr., February 9, 1956.

10. Ibid., Letter from Major General E.C. Itchner, Assistant Chief of Engineers for Civil Works to Senator Richard B. Russell Jr., March 6, 1956.

11. Ibid.

12. Ibid.

13. Ibid.

14. Ibid.

15. Gainesville Daily Times, 1957.

16. Ibid.

17. Ibid.

18. Ibid., Sunday, March 23, 1969.

19. Cecil Patterson, United States Army Corps of Engineers, Retired.

20. Gainesville Daily Times, 1957.

21. Ibid.

22. Ibid.

23. Ibid.

24. Ibid.

25. Ibid.

26. Ibid.

27. Ibid.

28. Atlanta Journal Constitution, November 3, 1990.

29. Gainesville Daily Times, 1957.

30. Ibid.

31. Ibid., May 30, 1956.

32. Ibid., June 10, 1956.

33. Ibid., 1957.

34. Ibid.

35. Ibid.

36. Ibid.

37. Ibid.

38. Ibid.

39. Ibid.

In the early 1950's Lake Lanier existed in words only.

CHAPTER ELEVEN

CONTRIBUTION OF A GEORGIA POET

An artist's sketch of the birthplace, located in Macon, Georgia, of Sidney Clopton Lanier, author of Song of The Chattahoochee and namesake of Lake Lanier. (Courtesy Georgia Department of Archives and History)

Buford Dam was authorized by Congress in the late 1940's and construction began not long afterwards but it was not until the late 1950's that the reservoir was officially named. For the most part newspaper and magazine articles referred to the lake simply as Buford Lake. Perhaps it was a foregone conclusion, at least early on, that the dam and lake would share the same name after all it was a common practice. This was not to say that there were not plenty of suggestions concerning the name of the lake. It would seem that just about everyone had their own idea on the subject. Atlanta Mayor William B. Hartsfield felt that the lake should be named after Senator Richard B. Russell. Hartsfield felt this a fitting tribute to a major figure in the project's early approval and funding battles on Capitol Hill.[1] Hartsfield himself was considered by many to be a prime candidate for lending his name to the lake, *Fig. 11-1*,.[2]

There was even a suggestion that the lake bear the name of Georgia Tech Football Coach Bobby Dodd and for many this was an idea that had considerable merit. That was until someone noted that "Dodd Dam" might be perceived as an inappropriate comment to make over the radio. You have to remember we are talking about the 1950's.[3]

As the project, and the lake it would soon create, became more and more of a reality so to did the idea of providing a suitable name for the reservoir. The news media picked up on the issue and a number of stories appeared in local newspapers throughout the area. One such story appeared in the Atlanta Journal and Constitution on Sunday, January 31, 1954 more than two years before the lake was officially named. The article was entitled "Will Rogers' Lake" by Harold Martin and it examined the suggestion of a Mr. A.S.

Fig. 11-1 Letter to Senator Russell from Jess Baggett concerning naming the Buford Dam reservoir. (Courtesy Joe Baggett)

Furcron a geologist who felt the lake should be named after Will Rogers. Mr. Furcron explained that such an act would be a fitting tribute to the popular humorist who was killed in an airplane crash in 1935. According to Mr. Furcron when the lake was formed it would "bury forever a section of Georgia hill country that is rich in Indian history. The trails the Cherokees traveled, the wooded glades where they hunted, the springs they drank from, and the little farms they cultivated, before, under pressure of white population they left their lands and moved to the West, will be lost to the historian and archaeologist forever."[4]

Furcron used genealogical research to point out that Will Rogers was a descendent of a family of Rogerses living on the Chattahoochee River near the site where Buford Dam is today. They were three-quarters Indian and one-quarter white but like most of the Cherokees of this region had long sense developed European ways of living. They farmed the land, owned slaves, could read and write English, and knew how to spin and weave. It was Furcron's opinion that because Will Roger's descendants were Cherokees from Georgia he could see no better way to pay tribute to both a culture that had lived on the land long before Europeans came to the new world and one of America's greatest humorists and homespun philosophers.[5]

There were still others who made their suggestions known usually in the form of a letter or personal contact with their representatives in Washington. The sons of Confederate Veterans, the John B. Gordon Camp no.46 out of Atlanta, drafted a letter to Senator Richard Russell Jr., himself a

SONS OF CONFEDERATE VETERANS
JOHN B. GORDON CAMP No. 46
P. O. BOX 1895
ATLANTA, GEORGIA

May 3, 1954

Senator Richard B. Russell
Washington D. C.

Dear Senator Russell:

At a meeting of the John B. Gordon Camp No. 46 of the Sons of Confederate Veterans, a resolution was unanimously adopted, suggesting the name of "lake Sidney Lanier" for the big body of water that will be formed by the Buford Dam across the Chattahoochee River.

While Sidney Lanier has always been honored and loved throughout the South, to the best of our knowledge, this would be the first time that an honor, national in scope, would be given to him. To give the name of the poet who wrote the beautiful "Song of the Chattahoochee" to a lake formed by this river, seems to us to be a fitting memorial to Georgia's Sidney Lanier.

We will greatly appreciate your efforts to help us make this resolution a reality.

Yours very truly

Clyde A. Boynton, Commander Camp #46 S.C.V.

By: John E. Summer, Adjutant

Fig. 11-2 Letter from the Sons of Confederate Veterans, John B. Gordon Camp no. 46 concerning naming the Buford Dam reservoir. (Courtesy Sons of Confederate Veterans)

suggested namesake for the lake, on May 3, 1954, **Fig. 11-2**. In the letter they believed that the reservoir that would be created by Buford Dam should be called Lake Sidney Lanier in honor of the Georgia poet. To the groups knowledge Lanier had never had his name used in such a manner and it seemed fitting that the man who brought such fame to the Chattahoochee River be honored in such a manner.[6] This idea gained considerable support as that same year the Georgia General Assembly passed a proposal asking the U.S. Congress to name the reservoir after the Georgia poet.

A small bit of irony can be noted here as it seems at least one objection to naming the lake after Sidney Lanier came from a rather unusual source, one of his own descendants. Apparently J. Smith Lanier of West Point a civic leader and a kinsman of the late Georgia poet, opposed to the lake being named after his relative. Mr. Lanier was not opposed to the use of his name but to what the name was being used for. Evidently, according to Mr. Lanier, Lake Sidney Lanier was supposed to be given to a proposed Georgia Power Company dam just above his hometown of West Point. It was Mr. Lanier's belief that had the Great Depression not crippled the economy the dam would have been constructed as originally planned and his ancestor's name

Fig. 11-3 5th District Congressman Phil Landrum. (Courtesy of the Library of Congress)

would have been used for that project.[7] Official records indicate that, at least in part Mr. Lanier's claim was correct. In a report issued to Congress by the Secretary of War from the Chief of Army Engineers on the ACF River System development a hydroelectric power dam north of West Point called Lanier Dam was proposed. It was a concrete gravity type dam with earth dike abutments that was supposed to provide 196,000 acre feet of flood storage. Although Lanier Dam never became a reality, West Point Lake Dam did. The present Corps facility was constructed in approximately the same area the 1939 survey map, developed by the Army, had the proposed Lanier dam located.[8]

Congressional involvement in providing a name for the Buford reservoir was necessitated by the fact that the Buford Dam was a federal public works project and it would take the creation of a public law to officially name the lake. Phil Landrum, *Fig. 11-3*, the 5th District Representative sponsored a bill in the U.S. House of Representatives to name the reservoir. This bill, H.R. 9045, designated the lake created by Buford Dam as Lake Sidney Lanier in honor of the Georgia poet who immortalized the Chattahoochee River in a poem he wrote in 1879 entitled "Song of the Chattahoochee.[9]

On May 6, 1954 during the second session of the 83rd Congress H.R. 9045 was introduced into the record under Public Bills and Resolutions. It was referred to the Committee on Public Works for consideration.[10] All bills even ones of this nature must go through similar legislative procedures. Apparently, because the bill was introduced so late in the session it never really had the time to move through committee for consideration by the entire House. There is no evidence that the bill was deliberately stalled or held up in committee as some bills are to prevent them from being discussed or voted on by the entire body. It simply lacked the time needed to exit the committee. Mr. Landrum was laying the ground work for the next Congress where he knew the bill could be given the time and consideration it would need to move through the legislative process effectively.

When the 1st session of the 84th Congress convened the following year Mr. Landrum again introduced the bill. The bill to designate the Buford reservoir as Lake Sidney Lanier was now H.R. 6961.[11] On the 22nd of June, 1955 after Mr. Landrum had introduced the bill it was referred, just as it had been the year before, to the Committee on Public Works for consideration.[12] The difference being, it now had two separate sessions of the same Congress in which to move from a bill to a law. A little over a month later on July 25th the Committee on Public Works referred H.R. 6961, House report no.1401, to the House Calender without amendments which meant the committee was not changing the wording of the text and the bill would be referred to the House floor as introduced.[13] Five days later on July 30th H.R. 6961, having been referred to the House Calender, was brought to the floor of the House for discussion. The following are minutes recorded in the United States Congressional Record concerning the bill's discussion.

The Clerk called the bill, H.R. 6961, to designate the lake created by Buford Dam in the State of Georgia as Lake Sidney Lanier.

The Clerk read the title of the bill

The SPEAKER. Is there objection to the present consideration of the bill?

Mr. CUNNINGHAM. Mr. Speaker, reserving the right to object, I would like to inquire of the author of the bill or some

Fig. 11-4 Sidney Clopton Lanier (Courtesy of the Library of Congress)

member of the committee, a question which will apply also to the next bill. Can he tell me why the views of the Board of Geographic Names was not secured? I note in the report there is a letter from the Secretary of the Army stating that the Army has no objection to this bill, but it goes on to say that the Board of Geographic Names may have an interest in the bill and recommends that their views be secured. According to the report, their views were not secured.

Mr. LANDRUM. Mr. Speaker, if the gentleman will yield, there was no objection. They did not desire to file a report or to make any recommendation about it.

Mr. CUNNINGHAM. In other words, they were considered?

Mr. LANDRUM. That is true.

Mr. CUNNINGHAM. I withdraw my reservation of objection of the bill?

There being no objection, the Clerk read the bill, as follows:

Be it enacted, etc., That the lake created by the Buford Dam, now being constructed on the Chattahoochee River about 35 miles northeast of Atlanta, Georgia shall be known and designated as Lake Sidney Lanier in honor of the late Sidney Lanier, author of the poem Song of the Chattahoochee. Any law, regulation, document, or record of the United States in which such lake is referred to under any other name or designation, shall be held to refer to such lake as Lake Sidney Lanier.

The bill was ordered to be engrossed and read a third time, was read the third time and passed and a motion to reconsider was laid on the table.[14]

On August 1st the bill appears in the Senate Record and is referred to the Committee of Public Works.[15] The process in the Senate would be similar to what happened in the House. The committee

Fig. 11-5 Eight cent commemorative stamp of Sidney Clopton Lanier issued by the U.S. Postal Service in 1972. (U.S. Postal Service)

would make its recommendations on the bill and if favorable, which it was, would refer it to the floor of the Senate for discussion. The first session of the 84th Congress ended with the bill having passed the House and standing in committee in the Senate. When the next session of the 84th Congress convened it would continue its path through the Senate committee work and beyond.

On March 7, 1956 the Senate Public Works Committee reported on H.R. 6961, Senate no. 1638.[16] Twelve days later on March 19th, the Senate considered H.R. 6961. It was ordered to a third reading and on the third reading passed.[17] One day later on the 20th, the Speaker pro tempore in the Senate affixed his signature to the bill and it was signed by Vice President Richard M. Nixon who was President of the Senate.[18]

On the same day in the House the Speaker, Sam Rayburn, put his signature on H.R. 6961 as the path through the House and Senate was just about complete. All that it lacked now was a trip to the White House.[19]

On March 21st the House Committee on Administration reported that the committee presented President Eisenhower a number of bills and joint resolutions of the House. (resolutions put together by the House and Senate concurrently). One of those bills was H.R. 6961.[20] It would be up to President Eisenhower to sign the bills before they could become law. On April 9th the President communicated a message to the House of Representatives that on March 29th he had approved and signed H.R. 6961.[21] With the President's signature H.R. 6961 designating the reservoir at Buford Dam as Lake Sidney Lanier, became Public Law 56-457 passed by the second session of the 84th Congress. The reservoir at Buford Dam would now have an official name when finally created it would be known as Lake Sidney Lanier.

When Public Law 56-457 was signed by President Eisenhower the lake was not even two months old. The gates of the intake structure had only recently been closed and the Chattahoochee River was slowly beginning to give ground to a 38,000 acre lake. The life of the Chattahoochee River at this site and in this form would soon be a thing of the past. A musician and poet many years before had put to pen a verse about the river now creating this lake. It captured his imagination and so endeared him to this area that Congress had seen fit to name this soon to be body of water after him. Who was this man and what legacy did he leave behind that would want the people of Georgia to have one of their most prized resources bear his name?

Sidney Clopton Lanier, **Fig. 11-4**, was born to Robert Sampson and Mary Jane Lanier in Macon, Georgia on Thursday, February 3, 1842.[22] His father was a lawyer and like most fathers wished his son to travel in his footsteps. His mother the former Mary Jane Anderson saw to it that her son's education did not lack the finer tones. Along with his scholarly interests she also encouraged him to pursue music and literature at a very young age. This must have been an easy task as the young Lanier showed an avid interest in both music and literature. He was a self taught musician and exhibited this talent on a wide range of instruments. At a young age he used to imitate bird calls with homemade flutes he fashioned from river weeds that were in great abundance near his home.[23] He was just as prolific with the guitar, violin, piano, and organ. His childhood was normal for that time in history growing up in antebellum middle Georgia with his younger brother Clifford and sister Gertrude*. He enjoyed the outdoors and perfected his gifts in music and literature that would someday define what his life had been all about.[24]

When he was 14 he entered Oglethorpe College which was a Presbyterian school near Midway, Georgia. It is a commonly accepted myth that he attended Oglethorpe University in Atlanta. Undoubtedly the similarity in the two institution's names is the reason. Unfortunately Lanier's alma mater did not have many years left as it would not be able to survive the destruction and carnage of the Civil War.[25] Lanier excelled in his chosen field graduating at the top of his class in 1860, this despite the fact that he spent nearly a year as a postal clerk in Macon. It was during his years in college that he began to sport the beard that would forever define his appearance in portraits, one being his picture on an eight cent commemorative stamp, **Fig.11-5**, issued by the U.S. Postal Service in 1972.[26] Upon graduating from college he had mapped out elaborate plans to travel to Europe and study abroad in the classics and see what up until now he had only read about. As fate would have it though, his life took a rather unusual twist and spun off in an entirely different direction. The political climate and tension in the United States that sparked the Civil War changed all his grand plans.[27] In April, 1861 at the age of 19 and fresh out of college he volunteered for service with the Macon Volunteers of the Second Georgia Battalion. With all his talents and education Lanier was still wrapped up in the Southern mystique and lifestyle of the South prior to the Civil War. His ideals were not uncommon for young men of his generation in the South that saw it as a duty to defend their way of life. He charged into

---

* It is not known if Gertrude was younger or older than Sidney.

the light with the strong belief that he was defending a simple way of life. It would take four years of war before most of this came crashing down upon him and plant the seed that would eventually claim his life at such a tender age.

Lanier was part of a group of soldiers that were the first men to leave the state for Virginia. He entered service as a private and remained at this rank, despite his education, until the last year of the war. His failure to gain rank more rapidly than he did was due in part to his refusal to be separated from his younger brother Clifford.[28] His first year in the service was the calm before the storm. He was assigned to a regiment just outside of Norfolk, Virginia. Because the Northern markets had been cut off by the war there were a great deal of goods available to the untold thousands of soldiers stationed in Norfolk. It was a good time to be had by all as Lanier would later remember having an abundance of leisure time to devote to his music and studying German, Spanish, and French. Like most, he believed the conflict would not last long and he could soon return to his life's plans. Despite the comfort he experienced during his first year of service Lanier would be a part of some of the most fierce infantry battles fought during the Civil War. He would see action at Seven Pines, Drewry's Bluffs, The Seven Days Battles, Malvern Hill, Chancellorsville, and would even serve in defense of Petersburg. In Petersburg while serving in the signal corps he had access to a small library that he managed to put to good use. By his own admission it was during this time that he first began to feel the consumption that he would feel for the rest of his life. His transfer to the signal corps though might have been a blessing in disguise. The constant playing required by the flute in all likelihood added years to his life. In 1863 his company was on the move and he saw service again in North Carolina and Virginia.[29]

In 1864 Sidney and Clifford were both given duty aboard their own blockade runners. While serving on the blockade runner "LUCY" Sidney was captured by Union forces and imprisoned at Point Lookout, Maryland.[30] For Lanier the war had become two sides of the same coin. He had come to enjoy the free life of living off the land and sleeping under the stars but the price was the war and all its tyranny. In later years he would comment on how foolish it was to have struck out for war with such high ideals of conquest. While imprisoned in Maryland Lanier had time to think of his life before the war and what he would do when the day came that it was over. In the long months held captive he had decided that if he ever got out of this alive he intended to make poetry his life's work.[31]

In February, 1865 he was finally released from prison. With the war over, in poor health, and broke, with the exception of one twenty-dollar gold piece and his flute, he made his way back to his home State of Georgia. It was a long hard trip back, mostly on foot, with his brother Clifford making it home several months after he did. It must have been a joy for Lanier to be back in a familiar place, where he had spent his youth and had such vivid memories but the event was marred by the death of his mother from the very consumption that would someday take her eldest son's life.[32]

Sidney had been home less than six weeks before his mother died and after her death, and perhaps feeling he needed to get away, he traveled to Point Clear, Mobile Bay to stay with his uncle. Several months of outdoor living improved his health but it was never a cure. The pattern seen here would remain the same throughout his short life. There would be periods of calm between agonizing periods of congestion and hemorrhaging of the lungs. He did many things and visited many places in the ensuing years. He was a clerk in Montgomery, Alabama for two years and made a trip to New York in an attempt to publish Tiger Lilies which he had written in April, 1867.[33] In September of that same year he became the headmaster of an academy of some one hundred students in Prattville, Alabama. By the years end he had met and married Mary Day the daughter of Charles Day of Macon, Georgia.[34]

In January, 1868 he had his first problem with hemorrhaging of the lungs causing his return to Macon, his health somewhat of a concern. He would remain in Macon practicing law with his father for five years. By now he exhibited a constant cough and was forced to travel about the United States in search of anything that would improve his condition. In New York he found his general health had improved and after several months returned to Macon only to find a rapid decline again. In December, 1872 he was on the road again, this time to San Antonio, Texas. Lanier was going to establish a home in the dry climate but this did not seem to help and he returned home several months later.[35]

Lanier began to feel that the struggle with his consumption would only lead to the inevitable. He began to believe that he had been placed on this earth, be it ever so short a period of time, with special talents. In a letter to his wife from Texas he explained his feelings about his life and what remained of it. "Were it not for some circumstances which make such a proposition seem absurd in the highest degree, I would think that I am shortly to die, and that my spirit hath been singing its swan song before dissolution. All day my soul hath been cutting swiftly into the great space of subtle, unspeakable deep driven by wind after wind of heavenly melody. The very inner spirit and essence of all wind songs, bird songs, passion songs, folk songs, country songs, sex songs, soul songs and body songs hath blown upon me in quick gusts like the breath of passion and sailed me into a sea of vast dreams, whereof each wave is at once a vision and a melody."[36]

He moved to Baltimore, Maryland in December, 1873. The move was partly because of the climate but also because he wished to pursue his poetry and a chance to use his flute outside of his own enjoyment. He could take advantage of the culture and learning, all the while earning a living for his family. It was something that would have been difficult for him to do, at the time, in his native South. He eventually became the first flute for the Peabody Symphony.

Sidney's father requested that he return to Macon in late 1873 to help him with his law practice. It was evident that he wanted his son to live a comfortable life not wanting for anything and at the same time knowing life for him would be short. The younger Lanier replied in a letter written on Saturday, November 29, 1873. "I have given your last letter the fullest and most careful consideration. After doing so I feel sure that Macon is not the place for me. If you could taste the delicious crystalline air and the champagne breeze that I've just been rushing about in, I am equally sure that in point of climate you would agree with me that my chance for life is ten times as great here as in Macon. Then, as to business, why should I, nay, how can I, settle myself down to be a third-rate struggling lawyer for the balance of my little life, as long as there is a certainty almost absolute that I can do some other things so much better? Several persons, from whose judgment in such matters there can be no appeal, have told me, for instance, that I am the greatest flute-player in the world; and several others, of equally authoritative judgment, have given me an almost equal encouragement to work with my pen. Of course I protest against the necessity which makes me write such things about myself. I only do so because I so appreciate the love and tenderness which prompt you to desire me with you that I will make the fullest explanation possible of my course, out of reciprocal honor and respect for the motives which lead you to think differently from me. My dear father, think how for twenty years, through poverty, through pain, through weariness, through sickness, through the uncongenial atmosphere of a farcical college and of a bare army and then of an exacting business life, through all the discouragement of being wholly unacquainted with literary people and literary ways___ I say, think how, in spite of all these depressing circumstances, and of a thousand more which I could enumerate, these two figures of music and of poetry have steadily kept in my heart so that I could not banish them. Does it not seem to you as to me, that I begin to have the right to enroll myself among the devotees of these two sublime arts, after having followed them so long and so humbly and through so much bitterness?"[38]

Robert Lanier accepted his son's decision as best he could and would continue to help him. Even though Lanier was playing in the symphony his health was making it difficult to pursue his writing and music. In his later years he would often be unable to work for months on end. He would travel to Texas again, to Florida, Pennsylvania, and North Carolina in search for a cure for his sickness. He would try anything and everything from pine breaths to clover blossoms but nothing seemed to give him lasting relief from the tuberculosis. Through all this he still managed to produce literature that would be popular even today. He drowned himself in the intense study of English literature and the mastering of the formal verse. Music became an important part of his life in his later years but it would never have the same importance as his poetry.[39]

In 1874 he traveled to Florida to write a book for a railroad company. He was able to spend some time with his family at Sunnyside, Georgia. It was while he was there that he wrote "Corn". The poem was featured in Lippincott's Magazine which caught the eye of Baynard Taylor who played a significant role in having Lanier commissioned to write the cantata for the opening of the Centennial Exposition in Philadelphia.[40]

Between 1874 and 1876 he would produce such works as "Symphony", "Psalm of the West", "Nine from Eight", "Jones Private Argument" and "Thar's More in the Man Than Thar is in the Land". These works were accomplished even while continuing his work with the symphony. He was supposed to write the "Life of Charlotte Cushman" an early American actress who would become the first member of the Theatrical Hall of Fame but the work stopped when a friend of the Cushman family, who was to provide the bulk of the biographical material, became ill.

By now Sidney's health had deteriorated to the point that the doctors told him that if he did not seek a warmer climate he would not live much longer. He went to Tampa but by April of the next year he was back in Baltimore and with the Peabody Symphony. It was a tribute to his resolute energy and desire to continue to live his life as he wished despite his illness.[41] His English literature studies and Elizabethan Verse lectures opened the door to another accomplishment as he was appointed a lecturer on literature at John Hopkins University. He was given the news of his appointment on his 37th birthday. It also marked the first time since his marriage in 1867 that he had a steady income. "A Song of the Future", "The Revenge of Hamish", "The Song of the Chattahoochee" and "A Song of Love", were all written during this period. It was also during this time that he wrote "The Marshes of Glynn" which he had intended to follow with a series of poems called the "Hymns of the Marshes". This never developed as his health declined even further and although not really knowing it at the time he was nearing the end of his life. He would continue to work on his literature and lecture as well as perform constant rehearsals with the symphony except when illness would drive him to his bed.[42]

In August, 1880 while in West Chester, Pennsylvania with his wife and her father his fourth son was born but the climate there soon became intolerable and he returned to Baltimore in early September of that same year. For much of that winter he fought the constant disease for his very life. In December of that same year fighting a fever of over 104 degrees and almost to weak to eat he finished his last and what many consider his greatest poem, "Sunrise," which was one of the series of "Hymns of the Marshes,". In February, 1881 he decided to begin a series of lectures and by April despite the consumption he had finished twelve. There were to be more, some twenty or so, but his health would not permit this.[43]

Earlier that same year he made his last trip to New York for talks with Charles Scribner's Sons about his upcoming publication of the King Arthur series of books. His doctors advised him that his only hope of prolonging his life was to take to tent life in the high clean, pure, climate of the mountains. With his brother Clifford's help he moved and set up tent near Asheville, North Carolina.[44] Now nearing the end he was perhaps blown some fair wind of economic luck in that he was commissioned by the railroad for an account of the region as he had done in Florida. Lanier was able to get together source materials and a working outline in his mind for the book but because of his illness, which would render him even unable to dictate to his wife, he never finished the work.

On Thursday, August 4, 1881 he went on a ride with his wife to Lynn, North Carolina which is located in Polk County. He wanted to see if the climate there would be any better for his fever and hemorrhaging. This trip proved to be the final round in his struggle to beat the consumption that had afflicted him for the largest portion of his life. He was unable to return to the encampment they had set up at Richmond Hill near Asheville. Receiving a telegram concerning his brother's condition Clifford assisted his father in moving the encampment to Lynn where he stayed until August 24th when he returned home. Robert Lanier who had accompanied Clifford left the incampment five days later on August 29th. Although they were not aware of it at the time it would be the last time either man would see him alive. On Monday evening, September 7, 1881 a week and one day after his father left the encampment Lanier finally gave up the fight and passed away.[45] He was buried in Greenmount Cemetery in Baltimore, Maryland. A huge pink colored boulder from the State of Georgia was placed at the burial site with an inscription from one of his poems "Sunrise" "I am lit with the sun".

Sidney Lanier was only 39 years old when he died and because most of his best works were produced so late in life he only managed to reach minor poetic status when compared with other notable poets. Many historians believe had he lived longer he would have become a major American poet not to mention what impact his music would have had. He was a talented individual who lived and worked during argumentively some of the most turbulent times in our history, as well as his own. He was a talented musician and although his music was a very special part of his personality he is best remembered for his poems such as "The Marshes of Glynn" and perhaps the one that insured his legacy as a native Georgian poet, "The Song of the Chattahoochee".

Song of the Chattahoochee

    Out of the hills of Habersham
    Down the valleys of Hall
I hurry amain to reach the plain
Run the rapid and leap the fall,
Split at the rock and together again,
Accept my bed, or narrow or wide,
And flee from folly on every side
With a lover's pain to attain the plain
    Far from the hills of Habersham
    Far from the valleys of Hall.

    All down the hills of Habersham
    All through the valleys of Hall,
The rushes cried Abide, abide,
The willful waterweeds held me thrall,
The laving laurel turned my tide,
The ferns and the fondling grass said stay,
The dewberry dipped for to work delay,
And the little reeds sighed Abide, abide,
    Here in the hills of Habersham
    Here in the valleys of Hall.

    High o'er the hills of Habersham
    Veiling the valleys of Hall
The hickory told me manifold
Fair tales of shade, the poplar tall
Wrought me her shadow self to hold,
The chestnut, the oak, the walnut, the pine,
Overleaning, with flickering meaning and sign,
Said, Pass not, so cold, these manifold
    Deep shades of the hills of Habersham
    These glades in the valleys of Hall.

    And oft in the hills of Habersham,
    And oft in the valleys of Hall,
The white quartz shone, and the smooth brook-stone
did bare me of passage with friendly brawl,
And many a luminous jewel lone
-Crystals clear or a -cloud with mist,
Ruby, garnet and amethyst-
Made lures with the lights of streaming stone
    In the clefts of the hills of Habersham,
    In the beds of the valleys of Hall.

    But oh, not the hills of Habersham
    And oh, not the valleys of Hall
Avail: I am fain for to water the plain.
Downward the voices of Duty call-
Downward, to toil and be mixed with the main;
The dry fields burn, and the mills are to turn,
And a myriad flowers mortally yearn,
And the lordly main from beyond the plain
    Call o'er the hills of Habersham,
    Call through the valleys of Hall.[46]

Notes

1. Martin, H. (1978). William Berry Hartsfield. (p. 198). Athens: University of Georgia Press.

2. General File, Series XI, Sub-Series C, Richard B. Russell Collection, Richard B. Russell Library, University of Georgia Libraries, Athens, Georgia, Letter from Jess Baggett, Lawrenceville, Georgia to Senator Richard Russell.

3. Martin, H. (1978) William Berry Hartsfield. (p. 198). Athens: University of Georgia Press.

4. Atlanta Journal Constitution, January 31, 1954, From an article by Harold H. Martin, Will Rogers' Name Seems Apt for Lake That Will Cover Georgia's Cherokee Cities.

5. Ibid.

6. General File, Series XI, Sub-Series C, Richard B. Russell Collection, Richard B. Russell Library, University of Georgia Libraries, Athens, Georgia, Letter from the Sons of Confederate Veterans in Atlanta to Senator Richard B. Russell Jr.

7. Untitled newspaper article

8. Letter from The Secretary of War from the Chief of Engineers to the U.S. House of Representatives Committee on Rivers and Harbors, U.S. House Document no.342, 1st Session, 76th Congress, p. 66.

9. The United States Congressional Record, 83rd Congress, Second Session, Volume 100, Index, p.719.

10. Ibid., Part 5, p.6175, May 6, 1954.

11. Ibid., 84th Congress, First Session, Volume 101, Index, p.880

12. Ibid., Part 7, p. 9035, June 22, 1955.

13. Ibid., Part 9, p. 11424-11425, July 25, 1955.

14. Ibid., Part 10, p. 12402, July 30, 1955.

15. Ibid., p. 12532, August 1, 1955.

16. Ibid., Second Session, Volume 102, Part 3, p. 4113, March 7, 1956.

17. Ibid., Part 4, p. 5022, March 19, 1956.

18. Ibid., p. 5166, March 20, 1956.

19. Ibid., p. 5211, March 20, 1956.

20. Ibid., p. 5301, March 21, 1956.

21. Ibid., Part 5, p. 5953, April 9, 1956.

22. The Encyclopedia Americana, 1961, Volume 16, pp. 730-731.

23. Gainesville Daily Times, October 2, 1994, Special 175th Anniversary Issue contributed by Ruth Waters.

24. Ibid.

25. Day, M. (1981). Poems of Sidney Lanier. (p. xiii). Athens: University of Georgia Press. Reprint of the 1906 edition published by Scribner, New York.

26. Gainesville Daily Times, October 2, 1994, Special 175th Anniversary Issue contributed by Ruth Waters.

27. Day, M. (1981). Poems of Sidney Lanier. (p. xiii). Athens: University of Georgia Press. Reprint of the 1906 edition published by Scribner, New York.

28. Ibid., p. xv.

29. Ibid., p. xvi.

30. The Encyclopedia Americana, 1961, Volume 16, p. 731.

31. Day, M. (1981). Poems of Sidney Lanier. (p. xvii). Athens: University of Georgia Press. Reprint of the 1906 edition published by Scribner, New York.

32. Famous Georgians. Georgia Department of Archives, Atlanta, Georgia.

33. Day, M. (1981). Poems of Sidney Lanier. (p. xvii). Athens: University of Georgia Press. Reprint of the 1906 edition published by Scribner, New York.

34.. Ibid., p. xviii.

35. bid.

36. Ibid., p. xix.

37. Ibid., p. xix.

38. Ibid., p. xx & xxi.

39. Ibid., p. xxi.

40. Ibid., p. xxiv.

41. Ibid., p. xxvi.

42. Ibid., p. xxvii.

43. Ibid., p. xxviii.

44. bid., p. xxix.

45. Ibid., p. xxx.

46. Ibid., p. 24.

Lake Sidney Lanier "A Storybook Site"

THE BUFORD DAM BEGINS OPERATIONS

PROGRAM

PROGRAM CHAIRMAN—H. Weldon Gardner, First President of Upper Chattahoochee Development Association.

11:30 A. M.—Music by the Third Army Band of Fort McPherson, Ga. Band Master, Chief Warrant Officer, Wilmont N. Trumbull.

DEDICATORY PRAYER—Rev. Jack Tatum, pastor of the Buford First Baptist Church

WELCOME—H. Weldon Gardner

LOWERING OF THE GATES—Conducted by Charles A. Jackson, Jr., Resident Engineer

Congressman James C. Davis	Robert M. Holder	James E. Jackson
Mayor William B. Hartsfield	Col. Harold E. Bisbort	Carl Lawson
General H. J. Hoeffer	J. C. Dover	John M. Cooper
H. Weldon Gardner	Roy Otwell	Frank K. Shaw

GIFT TO THE CITY OF ATLANTA—First gallon of water taken from Lake Lanier presented by Weldon Gardner to Paul Weir, Manager of Atlanta Water Works Association.

MOTORCADE FROM DAM TO CITY OF BUFORD PUBLIC SQUARE

12:30 P. M.

MUSIC—Third Army Band

WELCOME—Lionel Drake, Chairman of the Buford City Commission

MASTER OF CEREMONIES—H. Weldon Gardner

Unveiling of bronze tablets mounted on granite test core taken by rotary drilling 192 feet below the surface at the Buford Dam site.

READING OF INSCRIPTION ON TABLETS—Paul Weir,

Tablet No. 1—Congressman James C. Davis, Atlanta

Tablet No. 2—General H. J. Hoeffer, Division Engineer

Tablet No. 3—Carl Lawson, President of the UCDA

Tablet No. 4—Mayor William B. Hartsfield, Atlanta

Following the unveiling 200 invited guests will go to the High school cafetorium for a luncheon.

1.00 P. M.—Luncheon—Carl Lawson, Presiding

MUSIC—Third Army Band

INVOCATION—Rev. Lester M. James, Pastor of the Buford Presbyterian Church

RECOGNITION OF DISTINGUISHED GUESTS—Col. Joseph E. Cheeley, Jr., Secretary of UCDA

MASTER OF CEREMONIES—Mayor William B. Hartsfield, Atlanta

BRIEF REMARKS BY DISTINGUISHED GUESTS:

Congressman James C. Davis.	Col. Harold E. Bisbort, District Engineer
Gen. H. J. Hoeffer, Division Engineer	Charles A. Jackson, Resident Engineer
Paul Weir, Manager of Atlanta Water Works Association	John Quillian, State Highway Department AND OTHERS

Events scheduled for the gate closing as they appeared on the program.
(Courtesy Mrs. Weldon Gardner)

CHAPTER TWELVE

LAKE SIDNEY LANIER

Shortly before noon on Wednesday, February 1, 1956, one month shy of six years from the ground breaking ceremony, the gates of the intake structure at Buford Dam were closed. In a ceremony atop the left bank of the main earth dam the intake gate switches were simultaneously thrown by Mrs. Viola Davis, the 85 year old mother of Congressman James C. Davis, 5th District, who could not attend because of business in Washington, D.C.; Atlanta Mayor, William B. Hartsfield; John M. Cooper of the Atlanta Freight Bureau; General H.J. Hoeffner, Division Engineer for the South Atlantic Division; Frank Shaw, Industrial manager of the Atlanta Chamber of Commerce; James E. Jackson, Chairman of the Atlanta Aldermanic Board; Colonel H.E. Bisbort, District Engineer of the Mobile District; Roy P. Otwell, Mayor of Cumming; H. Weldon Gardner, past President of the Upper Chattahoochee Development Association; Carl Lawson President of the Upper Chattahoochee Development Association and Buford City Manager, J.C. Dover, *Fig. 12-1*,.[1] Lake Sidney Lanier was born at that moment.

After the gates were closed a bucket of water was drawn and presented to Atlanta Waterworks Manager Paul Weir as a symbolic gesture denoting the beginning of a new era in the regulation of the Chattahoochee River. Following the gate closing the ceremony was moved to Buford City Park where an unveiling ceremony took place. Four bronze plaques honoring those persons who worked tirelessly to get the dam funded and constructed were officially dedicated. The plaques were mounted on a cylindrical monument bored out of solid rock by a rotary drill some 192 feet below the present site of the intake structure.[2] Atlanta's Mayor William B. Hartsfield unveiled the plaque that carried the names of city officials and Atlanta citizens that helped see the project completed, *Fig. 12-2*,. Congressman Davis' Mother Viola Davis, unveiled the plaque which contained statistical data about the project, *Fig. 12-3*,. General H.J. Hoeffner, Division Engineer of the South Atlantic Division unveiled a plague honoring the United States Senators, Congressmen, and Corps of Engineer officials responsible for

Fig. 12-1 Dignitaries gather at the dam site to officially close the gates of the intake structure. (Courtesy William B. Hartsfield Papers, Special Collections, Robert W. Woodruff Library, Emory University)

Fig. 12-2 Recognizing the City of Atlanta. (RDC)

Fig. 12-3 Recognizing the Buford Dam Project. (RDC)

Fig. 12-4 Recognizing the U.S. Army Corps of Engineers. (RDC)

the projects construction, **Fig. 12-4** and **Fig.12-5**,. Weldon Gardner a past president

Fig. 12-5 General Hoeffner unveils the plaque recognizing the efforts put forth by Congress and the U.S. Army Corps of Engineers in constructing Buford Dam. (Courtesy Mrs. Weldon Gardner)

Fig. 12-7 Photograph of the core plug shortly after being placed in Buford City Park, circa 1957. (Courtesy Mrs. Weldon Gardner)

Fig. 12-8 The same core plug in Buford City Park today. (RDC)

of the Upper Chattahoochee Development Association unveiled a plaque honoring the UCDA, City of Buford, Gwinnett County Commissioners, Counties in the lake area, and the press for the work they gave to the eventual construction of the dam, **Fig.12-6**.

Following the unveiling ceremony some 200 guest were invited to a luncheon at the same high school cafetorium, where six

Fig. 12-6 Recognizing the local cities and counties involved in getting the project approved then funded. (RDC)

years before the ground breaking dinner was held. **Fig. 12-9**.

Fig. 12-9 A luncheon held after the gate closing in honor of the occasion. (Courtesy William B. Hartsfield Papers, Special Collections, Robert W. Woodruff Library, Emory University)

Fig. 12-10 Six days after the gates of the intake structure were closed you could see that the lake had started to take over larger and larger sections of the land directly in front of the dam. (Courtesy U.S. Army Corps of Engineers, Mobile District)

Fig. 12-11 On the same date as the previous photograph you can see the end of the forebay cut at left and the future site of West Bank Park which is the line of trees at upper left. (Courtesy U.S. Army Corps of Engineers, Mobile District)

Original estimates, based on amounts of rainfall predicted and general contract work on bridges, roads, and other facilities, were for the lake to fill to near capacity within a year.[3] Although this would not be the case the reservoir did fill to near capacity in a little over two years.[4] During this period there would only be two major interruptions in the impoundment schedule but there were smaller temporary impoundment limitations set during the lengthy process of creating the lake. These limitations were imposed when there was a danger of inundating areas that were not ready for flooding. One such limitation occurred barely two weeks after the gates were closed. Removal of a cemetery in Forsyth County, work on a power line, and salvage work on old Brown's Bridge caused the elevation of the lake to be held at 965.0 for a little over six hours.[5] Electrical power would be generated once the elevation rose above 1035.0 which is the bottom of the power pool elevation. This is the lowest the lake is ever expected to fall for generating electricity. Below this elevation is considered the permanent pool area.[6]

Not long after the gates of the intake structure were closed the Army Corps of Engineers was faced with a rumor spreading like wildfire that the dam was leaking. As the rumor mill went around it was reported that the leak was so bad that the infant lake would need to be drained to repair the damage. Someone had even reported a great deal of water and even a pump in the powerhouse construction area to deal with the leak. If people listened to the stories, a great deal of water, a pump, stands to reason that there must be a leak. The fact was there was a leak but it was something that was expected. The Corps of Engineers had a paradox of sorts, or at least it seemed that way. The very water that was causing the leak would eventually stop it. The resident engineer dispelled the rumors explaining that this was expected. The massive gates of the intake were constructed on a pressure seal principle meaning the intense water pressure that would be present when the lake filled up would eventually seal the leak. He also explained the abundance of water at the powerhouse construction area. A good deal of the water present was a designed flow as it was needed to keep newly poured concrete wet during the curing process. So even, if there had not been a leak they still would have pumped water in to wet the concrete.[7]

In March, 1956 one month after impoundment began the lake had grown nearly 48 1/2 feet in depth to an elevation of 976.72 and nearly 20 miles in length.[8] Several creeks near the dam that were tributaries of the Chattahoochee had seen their mouths all but disappear. Big Creek whose mouth was located at elevation 930 was just such a stream.[9] The river covered at least four major bridge sites in this time period. Lights Bridge, located on highway 997 between Flowery Branch and Forsyth County; Old Brown's Bridge on highway 141; Keith's Bridge at the confluence of the Chattahoochee and Chestatee Rivers; and Kelly's Bridge upstream from Keith's Bridge.[10] Keith's Bridge, Lights Bridge, and Kelly's Bridge were not relocated. Keith's Bridge was rebuilt temporarily after being destroyed by a fire, Fig. 10-4, but eventually removed again when the lake began to form.

Early on, the process of creating a lake attracted its share of both the curious and adventureous at heart. A 38,000 acre body of water was actually forming in their own backyard and for many it was too much of a temptation to resist. Bridge sites, roads or just about anywhere someone could walk or drive to see the rising water were popular gathering places. It would probably spark as much curiosity today as it did in the 1950's. The residents of this area were seeing a dramatic change to their homes, churches, schools, businesses, everyday places they had seen and visited many times before. Bridge sites were popular places as people would gather near those that were being inudated by the rising water in a chance to tempt fate. They would usually choose sites where the river and lake had met and drive over the old bridges there. There were reports of vehicles traveling highway 997 between Flowery Branch and Cumming. They would navigate their way across old Light's Bridge to the other side where lake water was beginning to overtake the area then turn around in the mud and drive back across. In time the impoundment process would prevent this type of activity as the roads leading to these bridges would be cut off by water filling the low lying dips or swales in the road preventing any travel at all.

Other groups would gather near the dam to watch the rising water creep over the banks of the channel as debris of all kinds would float downstream eventually coming to rest up against the intake. This debris would swirl around in the erractic and temporary eddies formed by the varied topography of this area. Traffic jams along the narrow roads were created by people flocking to the area to get a glimpse of something that would disappear forever. Locals would gather at familiar landmarks such as a bridge or building watching contractors dismantle them before the water claimed what was left, which was usually a bridge support pier or foundation of a house. Scenes like this were common all over the lake and would continue for several years to come especially further north where the water was not as wide or deep and more imulated the river channels.[11]

Although contemporary landmarks such as bridges, roads, homes even things like impoundment dams built for irrigation and as a water source for farms were more noticeable they were not the only things being affected by the rising water. A great deal of local history was disappearing as well. One example was a century old home located in Hall County near the Chattahoochee River that was being saved from a watery grave. The property, owned by Mr. and Mrs. R.C. Estes of Atlanta, had originally been awarded to Jonathan Pope in 1819 as one of the last known land lotteries held in the State of Georgia. The original log portion of the house had been constructed in 1825 by Thomas Mufford who had purchased a tract of the original land from Pope. As bystanders watched workers jacked up the old structure placing it onto steel girders as the infant lake had moved up to a corner of the house. The property had remained in the Mufford family until the turn of the century when it was purchased by M.L. Light of Gainesville. In 1934 Estes purchased the farm that his wife had been born in and had briefly lived in as a child. Apparently the house was not the only historical artifact being moved. On a hillside adjacent to the house contractors were also moving the graves of Jonathan Bufford, the builder of the original log home and the graves of his family and slaves.[12]

There were still other pieces of history soon to disappear. The many old ferry sites where travelers would cross the Chattahoochee and Chestatee Rivers would soon disappear as well. Pirkle's Ferry, Williams Ferry, Thornton, (later known as Shadburn's) Ferry, Huckby's (later known as Knuckoll's) Ferry, Light's Ferry, Winn's Ferry, and Keith's Ferry were all local and well known sites on the river.[13] A number of old mills, some ten in all, had been located near the dam in what would become the reservoir. Of these ten or more mills only three remained in the mid-1950's. Scales Mill on the Baldridge Creek, old Phillips Mill, and the Rice Mill on Four-Mile Creek. Old Phillip's Mill owned by S.A. Mangum formerly had a wheat mill but at the time the dam was being constructed it was no longer in use. The Rice Mill had a cotton gin and saw mill. One of the many that had not survived was an old cotton mill built by Minor Brown around 1880 on Four Mile Creek which spun thread for weaving filling, when people still used hand looms all over America. Brown sold the mill to a company out of Gainesville which became the Green Cotton Mills.[14]

Another example of the history that would soon vanish was the historic Vann's

Tavern building, *Fig. 12-12* and *Fig. 12-13*, and the site of the ferry that crossed the

Fig. 12-12 Photograph taken by the U.S. Army Corps of Engineers during property inventory for the Real Estate Project Office. (Pictorial History of Hall County To 1950, Sybil McRay)

Fig. 12-13 Vann's Tavern being dismantled in 1956 to avoid the rising waters of Lake Lanier. The building was moved to New Echota. (Pictorial History of Hall County To 1950, Sybil McRay)

Chattahoochee River there. The tavern built in 1805, on the Old Federal Pike road from Augusta to Nashville, was located on a section of Lake Lanier that is today adjacent to Athens and Vann Tavern Parks. Around the turn of the century James Vann a local Cherokee Indian Chief owned the tavern and ferry. He was shot and killed by a man whose friend was killed in a duel with Vann. At the time of construction the tavern and surrounding property was the home of the Frank Boyd family. It was purchased by a Boyd ancestor with gold brought back from the California gold rush in the 1800's. The building, an historic landmark, was spared the fate of impoundment and taken apart a log at a time then moved to New Echota, in Gordon County.[15]

At the end of March the water elevation was at 992.28. The depth at the intake structure had risen to 71 feet, rising 16.16 feet during this one month period.[16] By the 1st of April the lake had claimed nearly 8,500 acres of land. An old Georgia Power Company dam site located on the Chattahoochee River in Hall County near elevation 990 and old Bolding Mill on the Chestatee River had met the same fate as the many bridges in the area.[17] The rising water level was slowly creeping up on the approaches of the old Lanier Bridge, *Fig. 10-94*, and Thompson Bridge sites, *Fig. 10-108*,.[18] In early April, 1956 the lake elevation was at 996.92 feet above sea level. The deck of the old Lanier Bridge was at 1000.09, old Bolding Bridge over the Chestatee, *Fig. 10-129*, was at 1009.70, old Thompson Bridge over the Chattahoochee was at 1010.0, and old Longstreet Bridge, *Fig. 10-168*, over the Chattahoochee, was at 1046.90.[19]

With the lake inundating more and more dry land its affect on the wildlife population and vast forest land became more evident. This region of North Georgia was teeming with an abundance of wildlife. Rabbits, deer, quail, doves, rodents, snakes, etc. that lived on or even in the land began to flee the rising water. Their natural habitat was disappearing and they moved to higher elevations to stave off drowning and remain dry. This migration of wildlife, although expected by many, caught a great deal of the local residents as well as visitors to the area off guard. Even so, this area was still very much rural and vast enough for the natural ecosystem to absorb the migration up and outward. The impoundment of water was necessary for the lake to form and although the duration was longer and at a slower rate impounding the waters of the Chattahoochee and Chestatee Rivers was basically flooding dry land. Another strange sight, especially in the summer months, were the trees and whole forest that had been partially overtaken by the lake. They were standing in the shallow water drowning and their leaves changing colors. It seemed strange to see the bright fall like colors in the middle of a steamy hot afternoon. Just about anywhere you went on the lake or near the shoreline where there were trees you could see a multitude of autumn golds, yellows, reds, and browns. The ever changing bands of color followed the water's path and would continue to do so until the lake fully formed and its shoreline became more stable.

When the lake elevation reached 1002.5 sometime in mid April, 1956 there was over 11,000 acres of surface water. About this time the Corps of Engineers stopped the impoundment process to allow for the continued use of the old Thompson Bridge. It would have been necessary to reroute traffic a great distance north and west had the water been allowed to inundate the bridge. Even with the elevation stopped at 1002.5 there was a chance following heavy rains that the bridge

Fig. 12-14 Thompson Bridge approach. (Courtesy U.S. Army Corps of Engineers, Mobile District)

approach roadway, **Fig. 12-14**, could be overcome by rising waters.[20] The present Thompson Bridge built over the relocated highway 136 (now Highway 60) was not completed until July, 1956. When the bridge was finished and traffic detoured the impounding of the reservoir was allowed to continue. At that time the lake had 33 feet to go before reaching the minimum power pool and 68 feet to reach normal pool of 1070.0, **Fig. 12-15**,.[21]

Fig. 12-15 Article concerning opening the new Thompson Bridge for traffic. (Courtesy Gainesville Daily Times)

[**Fig. 12-16 and Fig. 12-17**]
Bolding Dam, **Fig. 12-18** and Bolding Mill (Glover's Mill), **Fig. 12-19**, sites had

Fig. 12-16 Before too long the topping of trees and the rising elevation of the lake would cause scenes like this to disappear. (Courtesy U.S. Army Corps of Engineers, Mobile District)

Fig. 12-17 The lake is slowly beginning to overtake more and more land in front of the main earth dam. (Courtesy U.S. Army Corps of Engineers, Mobile District)

Fig. 12-18 Bolding Dam on the Chestatee River. This portion of the Chestatee River is now part of Lake Lanier. The mill was located just to the right of this photograph. (Pictorial History of Hall County To 1950, Sybil McRay)

Fig. 12-19 Bolding Mill was constructed in the 1890's by Margaret Wooley. In later years it was owned by Joe Gover and known as Gover's Mill. (Pictorial History of Hall County To 1950, Sybil McRay)

become victims of the lake as the Chestatee River here had already begun to overflow its banks. The mill was originally constructed by Margaret Wooley. In later years it was operated by W.R. Bolding.[22] Nix Bridge located at elevation 1019.20 would become only a memory as it was one of a number of smaller bridges that would not be relocated. The old Dunlap Dam site, *Fig. 12-20*, an early turn of the century dam, *Fig. 12-21*

Fig. 12-20 Location of the old Dunlap Dam abandoned some years before the lake formed. (Courtesy U.S. Army Corps of Engineers, Mobile District, 1988 Lake Lanier Navigation Charts)

Fig. 12-21 Dunlap Dam (Courtesy Chestatee Regional Library)

Fig. 12-22 Dunlap Dam Power Station. (Courtesy Chestatee Regional Library)

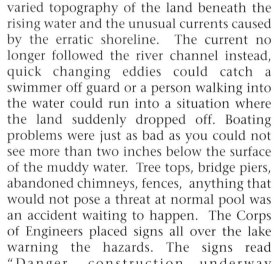

Fig. 12-23 Lake Warner (Courtesy Chestatee Regional Library)

Fig. 12-24 Group photograph taken in front of Dunlap Dam at the turn of the century. (Courtesy Gainesville Daily Times)

and *12-22*, then abandoned, that created Lake Warner, *Fig. 12-23*, would also disappear from the scene. The dam and lake not only provided electricity but a sandy beach during an era when power and recreational activities of this type were new and at somewhat of a high premium, *Fig. 12-24*,. The lake was named for General A.J. Warner a congressman from Marietta, Ohio. He came to Hall County and built a power plant on the Chestatee River near Leather's Ford.[23] The power plant's location was not far from the New Bridge site.

During this period safety concerns began to develop for the Corps of Engineers as boating and other water activities were on the rise. There were problems with swimming such as the murky water or the varied topography of the land beneath the rising water and the unusual currents caused by the erratic shoreline. The current no longer followed the river channel instead, quick changing eddies could catch a swimmer off guard or a person walking into the water could run into a situation where the land suddenly dropped off. Boating problems were just as bad as you could not see more than two inches below the surface of the muddy water. Tree tops, bridge piers, abandoned chimneys, fences, anything that would not pose a threat at normal pool was an accident waiting to happen. The Corps of Engineers placed signs all over the lake warning the hazards. The signs read "Danger, construction underway throughout Lake Lanier during 1956. Lake unsafe for boating, water skiing, swimming, and other water sports." The fact of the matter was that the government considered any use of the water, aside from fishing on the banks, trespassing on government property because the lake had not fully formed.[24] Boundary lines on the shore

Fig. 12-25 On Tuesday, March 20, 1956 more and more land begins to disappear. (Courtesy U.S. Army Corps of Engineers, Mobile District)

Fig. 12-26 Hundreds of small islands appear in the background but in time they will be unable to escape the inevitable inundation of water. (Courtesy U.S. Army Corps of Engineers, Mobile District)

began to change daily as more and more land was overcome by the rising water.

Fig. 12-25 and Fig. 12-26
Several months earlier with the surface area of the lake beginning to take up a greater amount of land a problem developed with mosquitoes. This was considered serious because mosquitoes could spread diseases including malaria. Two 16 foot utility boats were used to collect specimens of the mosquito population on the rising lake. The concern on the government's part was with the anopheles type of mosquito which transmitted malaria. Using an airplane DDT was sprayed over infected areas. The boats moved about the lake during the day, when the insects were less active, collecting specimens to examine the effect the spraying was having on the rising population. This program took place over a three month period with the full cooperation of the Georgia Public Health Service. Although considered inappropriate today, the use of DDT was considered common practice in the 1950's when dealing with mosquitoes and other pests especially those that transmitted diseases. Scientists eventually found a health hazard linked to the use of the chemical

and banned its use in the United States in 1972.[25] [**Fig. 12-27** and **Fig. 12-28**]

In March, 1957 water impoundment was again stopped. With the lake at elevation 1033.0 the clearing of trees and other obstructions would begin, **Fig. 12-29**

and **Fig. 12-30**,. Several crews in boats moved over the reservoir cutting down trees that were above the water. This would provide a comfortable safety margin for boaters, skiers, and general water recreation when the elevation reached normal pool of 1070.0. About 9,390 acres of trees were

Fig. 12-27 Modified clearing operations. (Courtesy U.S. Army Corps of Engineers, Mobile District)

Fig. 12-28 On Wednesday, December 5, 1956 clearing operations near the shoreline continue. (Courtesy U.S. Army Corps of Engineers, Mobile District)

Fig. 12-29 (Courtesy Gainesville Daily Times)

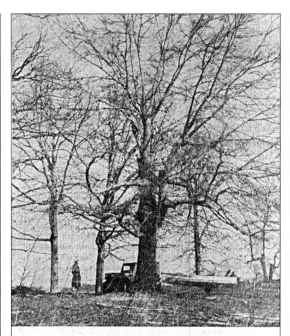

Tree Will Remain as 'Fish Attractor'

A few oaks with large, spreading crowns, such as this one being inspected by Charles White, US Corps of Engineer clearing inspector, will be left in coves and bays of the lake as "fish attractors." The tops of the attractor trees will extend above the water in protected spots where they will not be a danger to boating.

Fig. 12-30 (Courtesy Gainesville Daily Times)

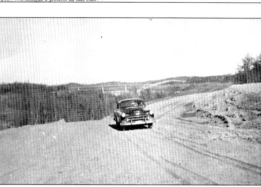

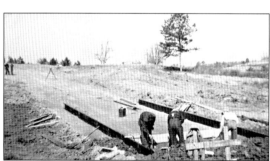

topped at elevation 1035.0 Between elevations 1035.0 and 1070.0 some 14,156 acres of land, around what would become the shoreline of the lake, were cleared.[26]

Things were made difficult by unusually heavy rains over many months that drove the lake elevation up.[27] Today divers have reported seeing large areas of trees underwater that clearly show the markings of having been cut off at the same level. An article appearing in the Gainesville Daily Times addressed the delays in water impoundment, ***Fig. 12-31***, ***Fig. 12-32***, ***Fig. 12-33***.

On Friday, May 24, 1957 the lake elevation was recorded at 1032.22 and the old Wilkie Bridge site was disappearing.[28] As was the case a year earlier the warm weather began to pose another recreational problem. The surface of the water was still filled with all types of debris that could become hazardous to boaters as well as other water recreation such as swimming or skiing. Large numbers of tree tops were still barely underneath the surface of the lake and posed their own types of problems. Warnings continued to be issued by the Corps that until the elevation rose another six or seven feet boating and swimming of any kind would be extremely dangerous.

On Thursday, June 13, 1957 the lake elevation was recorded at 1033.70.[29] "E" day as it was called was initiated on Monday, June 17th which was the first day that electrical power was generated for commercial use. The powerhouse had been producing electricity for several weeks but only to dry out insulators in the generators. This was the first day that power had actually been transferred to the high-tension wires outside the powerhouse.[30]

With the lake elevation at 1033.70 the water's journey was just about halfway complete. Another ten feet would do the

THE DAILY TIMES, GAINESVILLE, GA.- WED MAY 9, 1956—6

What's Delaying Impoundment of Water?

All Northeast Georgians are fascinated by the slowly rising waters of Lake Lanier and all of us enjoy seeing the lake level gradually creep higher and higher, slowly submerging old landmarks, slowly spreading acre after acre of water over the countryside.

As much fun as this may be and as eager as we may be to see and enjoy the waters of the lake, we should realize that from a practical point of view there are good reasons for holding up impoundment now. For one thing, the city of Gainesville feels it has a legal right to demand recognition of the fact that the lake is covering what is now a city street. Undoubtedly, the city hopes to bargain this street off for further considerations by the federal government of either cash of replacement facilities.

For another, if the water is allowed to come up, Gainesville's traffic movement to and from other cities in this area will be hampered. The Cleveland Road already is blocked by construction of a new bridge at Bell's Mill, although it seems to us unnecessary to detour around the entire road just for that one project. The Bolding Bridge on the Chestatee, an important link in direct traffic to Dawsonville from Gainesville, is not yet complete although the old bridge is still open. If the water rose it would close that artery.

If the new Lanier Bridge (Dawsonville highway) had been finished a few weeks earlier, the state would have begun removing steel from the old bridge before the water covered it. Even now if dropping the lake two or three feet would save $50,000 worth of steel and would not delay the eventual production of power, we would be willing to relinquish that saved water.

And we can only wonder about the timing on bridge building in the reservoir. If the new Lanier Bridge had been finished earlier we would have avoided submerging the old one; if the new Thompson Bridge had been finished earlier, we could have saved the old Bailey bridge and not interefered with traffic flow on the Dahlonega Road. Are we to have similar problems when the water reaches the old Longstreet Bridge on the Cleveland Road?

The new Clark's Bridge Road hasn't even been let yet. Will there be a problem on that road?

This all reminds us that Hall County and the Corps of Engineers haven't reached agreement yet on a list of bridge and road replacement projects. As the water rises the difficulty of shipping materials and building bridges will increase.

So far Buford Dam and its reservoir represent an investment by the people of the United States in excess of $35,000,000. It is only right that this money begin to produce a return in power income, flood control and navigation as soon as possible. Therefore, we can see the economic reasons for wanting to fill the lake and use the water without delay.

Schedules call for recreation on the lake by summer of 1957. They call for power on the line December 1 of this year. We understand that strikes in Northern industrial plants have delayed equipment for the powerhouse and might delay the power on line date.

Everything considered, then, if we can save money and move traffic more easily by holding the water level for a short time, reducing it if necessary, we should not complain when the Engineers do so. On the other hand, we should comment that through the untrained eyeball it appears the bridge builders failed to make their schedules.

Fig. 12-31 Article concerning delaying impoundment of Lake Lanier. (Courtesy Gainesville Daily Times)

Fig. 12-32 On January 2, 1957 a Corps vehicle makes its way along a boat ramp approach near Oscarville. Browns Bridge can be seen in the distant background. (Courtesy U.S. Army Corps of Engineers, Mobile District)

Fig. 12-33 Again on January 2, 1957 workers are busy setting the framing for a boat ramp. The water here has yet to inundate the ramp area. On a few occassions the lake rose faster than expected and the engineers would have to construct the ramps on higher ground and push them into the water. (Courtesy U.S. Army Corps of Engineers, Mobile District)

trick as the elevation of the lake would reach 1043.0 and the reservoir would be half full. Engineers explained that the top 27 feet of the reservoir's depth would contain as much water as all of the reservoir below this level. To many people this seemed hard to believe and they could not understand why it was taking the lake so long to fill up. Army engineers noted that as the reservoir filled up the rising water spread out covering more and more of the dry earth, which soaked up millions of gallons of water. As the surface area of the lake spread outward that increased the evaporation of water and increased the area that needed to be inundated.[31] [*Fig. 12-34* and *Fig. 12-35*]

The lake was continuing its trek up the Chattahoochee River wiping clean all traces of the old Bell's Mill which had been dismantled over a year before. Old Bell's Mill Bridge located at elevation 1051.75, which was adjacent to the old mill, had been torn down, *Fig. 10-145*, and relocated on higher ground close by.

Another local landmark in Hall County was giving way to the rising waters of Lake Lanier. An area just off 129, which was the road approach to the old Longstreet Bridge, known as Haynes Bottom or Looper Speedway, *Fig. 12-36*, *Fig. 12-37*, *Fig. 12-38*,

Fig. 12-34 This photograph taken from approximately where the Upper Overlook is located today shows the rising water of Lake Lanier. (Courtesy U.S. Army Corps of Engineers, Mobile District)

Fig. 12-35 Today you see Lake Lanier at normal pool. (Courtesy U.S. Army Corps of Engineers, Mobile District)

Fig. 12-39, *Fig. 12-40*, would soon become a narrow channel surrounding what would eventually become Laurel Park. The facility had long been a popular dirt track speedway for weekend race enthusiasts. Participants in these races would vie for several hundred dollars in prize money and were the forerunners to the popular stock car races of today. The events have long since passed into local history but the physical infrastructure of the facility is still present, although hidden under the waters of Lake Lanier.[32]

This regions more recent history would not be the only historical resources that would be effected by rising waters of

Fig. 12-36 The entrance gate where visitors paid their two dollars to watch the races. (Official Army Photograph Courtesy U.S. Army Corps of Engineers, Mobile District)

Fig. 12-37 Concessions area (Official Army Photograph Courtesy U.S. Army Corps of Engineers, Mobile District)

Fig. 12-38 The 1/2 mile dirt track. It could possibly have been a 1/4 mile track as source information varies. (Official Army Photograph Courtesy U.S. Army Corps of Engineers, Mobile District)

Fig. 12-39 Concrete portions of the bleachers have been seen by divers and above water during extremely low lake levels. (Official Army Photograph Courtesy U.S. Army Corps of Engineers, Mobile District)

Fig. 12-40 An observation platform. (Official Army Photograph Courtesy U.S. Army Corps of Engineers, Mobile District)

the lake. In the 1930's the Works Progress Administration under the direction of Robert Wauchope identified 24 archeological and prehistoric sites in the five county area that would become Lake Lanier. During early construction of the dam 60 prehistoric sites were identified when River Basin Surveys were conducted by the Smithsonian Institution. In 1954 Clemens de Baillou an archeologist with the Georgia Historical Commission excavated historical artifacts from "Summerour" an archeological dig in the Oscarville Community. The site was an ancient Indian family's home located on the Chattahoochee River near the old Chief Vanns ferry site in Forsyth County. de Baillou was working under the direction of Dr. Arthur R. Kelly then the head of the Archeology Department at the University of Georgia. A number of items including an old grindstone used to grind maize for meals, posthole remnants, and an ancient fireplace were found at this site.[33]

Continued diggings over nearly two years at a presumed mound found some 100 yards from the river revealed evidence of former occupants of the area dating back some 8,000 years. The mounds were believed to have been constructed using baskets to carry earth. Thousands of years of erosion and plowing reduced the height of the mounds by nearly ten feet. At the time it was suggested that they were temple mounds used for religious rites and ceremony.[34]

Decades later in 1978 the University of Georgia continued this work when it began cultural resource studies of government owned lands on the project. About one third of the land was surveyed and some 540 archeological and historic sites were found. Fifty-three of these sites were eventually recommended as potentially eligible for the National Register of Historic Places. In years to follow the Corps of Engineers in cooperation with the Georgia State Historic Preservation Officer (SHPO) determined that about 18 of these sites were non-significant.[35] An area located near Flowery Branch, Georgia known as "Booger Bottom" was reported to have yielded pottery fragments from a mound about 250 feet long, several hundred feet wide, and about seven feet high. The mound was located on property owned by J. B. Whiting and C. B. Romberg. At one time gold was even mined near where the Old Federal Highway once ran. Archeologists suspect the mounds were built by people whose ancestors lived in the East thousands of years ago. This culture had developed considerably having utilized the process of agriculture, growing tobacco, and making bows and arrows. [36]

On Wednesday, January 1, 1958 the lake elevation was recorded at 1047.08 With each passing day regions further north were being affected by the rising elevations of the reservoir and as Lake Lanier contined to move up the fingers of the Chattahoochee and Chestatee River channels old bridge sites continued to disappear. Old Clark's Bridge on the Chattahoochee which stood at elevation 1049.00, **Fig. 10-3**, was seeing a new bridge being constructed immediately adjacent to the old one while the New Bridge on the Chestatee River at elevation 1065.0 was becoming only a memory as it would not be relocated.

On Friday, August 1, 1958 the lake was measured at 1068.77. Seasonal fluctuation of the lake showed the elevation back down to 1060.68 on Wednesday, January 21, 1959. At 7:00 pm, Monday, May 25, 1959 the lake elevation reached 1070.0 for the first time which was considered normal pool*. The elevation of Lake Lanier changes depending on the weather and the seasons, which is what caused the drop in elevation from August 1, 1958 through January 21, 1959. Officially the lake did not reach normal pool for three and a half years but it did reach close to what could be considered full pool in about two and a half years.[37]
Fig. 12-41, **Fig. 12-42**, and **Fig. 12-43**. Over the years the lake elevation has fluctuated up and down depending on seasonal conditions and other factors. Since the lake reached full pool for the first time the lowest elevation ever recorded was 1052.68 in December, 1981. The highest elevation to date was 1077.19 which occurred on April 14, 1964.

The lake's creation drastically altered the physical appearance of the area and buried portions of its history in the process. To tell every story, every event or place affected would be an impossible task, there is just to many of them. Hundreds of families lost land and property to the lake and just as many local landmarks or the sites they once occupied were lost to the waters of Lake Lanier. The history told here in all likelihood only scratches the surface of the story and what was left behind. Over the years the stories of what life and the area was like before the lake was formed have been passed on from one generation to the next. In many cases it is the only history we have of the area and what took place all those years ago.

Fig. 12-42 Sailboats move about the water near the main earth dam while Lake Lanier continues to rise, circa 1958. (Courtesy U.S. Army Corps of Engineers, Mobile District)

Fig. 12-43 The completed dam with Lake Lanier filling up in the background. (Courtesy U.S. Army Corps of Engineers, Mobile District)

Fig. 12-41 Lake Lanier continues to fill. (Courtesy U.S. Army Corps of Engineers, Mobile District)

---

* Originally the conservation pool level was set at 1065.0 with a top flood control elevation of 1080.0. In 1953 the Mobile District presented studies to the Chief of Engineers that raising the conservation pool to 1070.0 and the top flood control pool to 1085 would benefit power production. They also noted that this increase would have no adverse effects on flood control protection. The Chief of Engineers approved the increase on September 11, 1953. In the 1980's the conservation pool elevation was again raised one foot to 1071.0

Notes

1. Atlanta Journal, February 1, 1956

2. Ibid.

3. Ibid.

4. "Fact Sheet" courtesy navigation chart developed by the United States Army Corps of Engineers, 1985.

5. Gainesville Daily Times, February 14, 1956

6. Lake Sidney Lanier Visitation Phamplet, 1989

7. Gainesville Daily Times, 1956

8. Ibid., March 2, 1956

9. Ibid., February 15, 1956

10. Ibid., March 2, 1956

11. Ibid., February 6, 1956

12. Ibid.,

13. Ibid., May 26, 1955

14. Ibid.

15. Pictorial History of Hall County To 1950, Sybil McRay, p. 133

16. Gainesville Daily Times, April 1, 1956

17. Ibid., April 1, 1956

18. Ibid., April 3, 1956

19. Ibid., April 12, 1956

20. Ibid., April 19, 1956

21. Ibid., July, 1956

22. Pictorial History of Hall County To 1950, Sybil McRay, p. 12

23. Ibid., p. 19

24. Atlanta Journal Constitution, 1956

25. Gainesville Daily Times, April 12, 1956

26. Updating of The Master Plan, Lake Sidney Lanier, Chattahoochee River, GA, Volume 1, United States Army Corps of Engineers, Mobile District, Mobile Alabama, June, 1987, p.2-02.

27. Ibid., March 19, 1957

28. Ibid., May 24, 1957

29. Ibid., June 13, 1957

30. Ibid., June 14, 1957

31. Gainesville Daily Times, May 6, 1957

32. Lakeside on Lanier, June 21, 1995

33. Gainesville Daily Times, February 14, 1954

34. Ibid., December 26, 1955

35. Updating the Master Plan, Lake Sidney Lanier, Chattahoochee River, GA, Volume 1, United States Army Corps of Engineers, Mobile District, Mobile, Alabama, June, 1987, p. 3-01

36. Gainesville Daily Times, October 2, 1994, Special 175th Anniversary Issue

37. "Fact Sheet" courtesy navigation chart developed by the United States Army Corps of Engineers, 1985

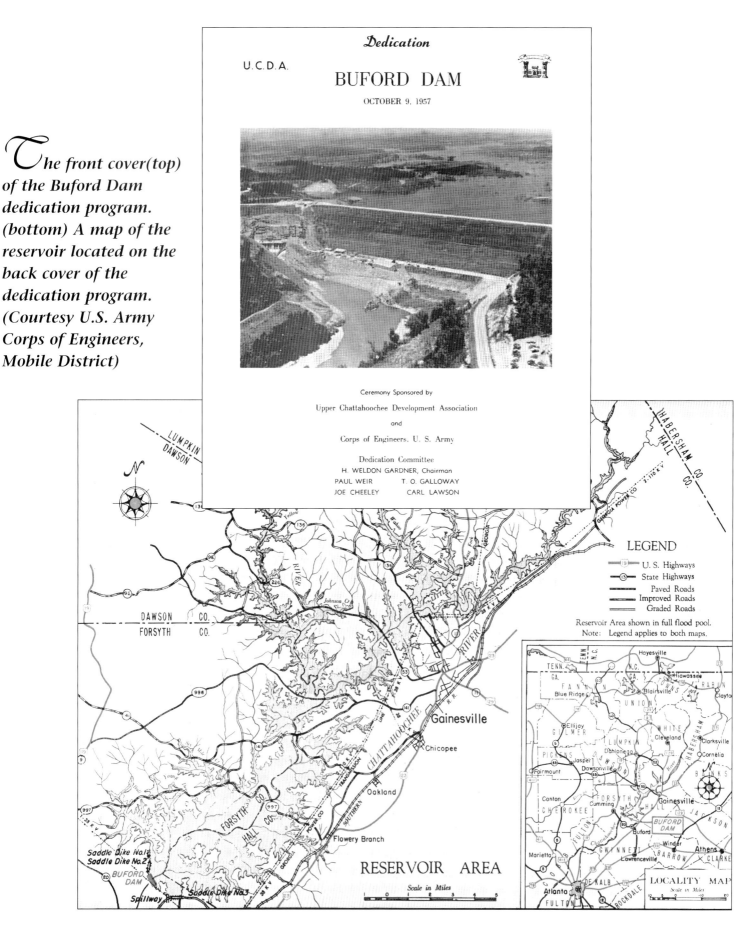

The front cover (top) of the Buford Dam dedication program. (bottom) A map of the reservoir located on the back cover of the dedication program. (Courtesy U.S. Army Corps of Engineers, Mobile District)

CHAPTER THIRTEEN

DEDICATION - OCTOBER 9, 1957

Shortly after noon on Wednesday, October 9, 1957 the dedication for Buford Dam took place. The ceremony, *Fig. 13-1*, was held on top of the intake structure in a parking lot overlooking the lake that had already grown to nearly 30,000 acres of surface water. People from all walks of life including representatives of the United States Army Corps of Engineers, the United States Congress, and city and county officials from a dozen counties and several states gathered atop the huge dam to join in the ceremony that officially dedicated the 44 million dollar project,

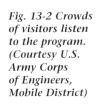

Fig. 13-1 The schedule of events for the dedication. (Courtesy U.S. Army Corps of Engineers, Mobile District)

Fig. 13-2 Crowds of visitors listen to the program. (Courtesy U.S. Army Corps of Engineers, Mobile District)

Fig. 13-3 Buses that brought the many out of town guest to the dedication are parked along Buford Dam Road adjacent to the parking lot atop the intake structure where the dedication ceremony was held. (Courtesy U.S. Army Corps of Engineers, Mobile District)

Fig. 13-4 The parking lot area today. (RDC)

Fig. 13-5 The boatcade that brought a number of dignitaries to the ceremony powers by the main earth dam. (Courtesy U.S. Army Corps of Engineers, Mobile District)

Fig. 13-6 C-130's making a pass over the top of the dam in honor of the occasion. (Courtesy U.S. Army Corps of Engineers, Mobile District)

Fig. 13-7 Weldon Gardner (Courtesy U.S. Army Corps of Engineers, Mobile District)

Fig. 13-8 Mayor Hartsfield (Courtesy U.S. Army Corps of Engineers, Mobile District)

Fig. 13-2 and *Fig. 13-3*. The weather seemed to be tailormade for the event,

unlike the ground breaking ceremony seven years earlier, as the skies overhead were clear blue and very accommodating. The long hard years of first acquiring approval, then finding the funding for the project, and finally construction were over.

A motorcade, similar to the one that had made the trek to the dam site many years before to break ground, left Buford bringing hundreds of people to the top of the dam. Visitors were not limited to the Buford entourage as they flocked from seemingly every direction and place to take part in the ceremony. They would not have to brave the cold and wet conditions that had plagued the ground breaking all those years before. One mode of transportation that was not present at the ground breaking probably drew the most attention. A boatcade, *Fig. 13-5*, of some fifty or so small vessels powered their way past the main earth dam before beaching and allowing their passengers to attend the dedication. It seemed a fitting way to ring in a new era for this region as well as all of Georgia. The air travel to the ceremony was equally represented as nine Lockheed C-130 transports, *Fig. 13-6*, and three Navy bombers streaked by overhead in honor of the occasion. The promoters of the event left nothing to chance as they wanted the dedication to be a grand extravaganza.[1]

Weldon Gardner, *Fig. 13-7*, of Buford,

President of the UCDA (Upper Chattahoochee Development Association) and one of the dignitaries that broke ground seven years earlier, opened the ceremony by presenting Williams B. Hartsfield, *Fig. 13-8*,

Dedication - October 9, 1957

Mayor of Atlanta to the crowds.[2] Hartsfield, himself a shoveler at the ground breaking was once again in his element. As master of ceremonies he would officially christen the project and although he was near the end of his political career participating in this event was very important to him. It culminated years of often times frustrating work to see the project become a reality. He had been a long time proponent of the project and probably been involved in getting its construction approved and started more than anyone. Hartsfield noted the work of others and the affect Lake Lanier would have on the future development of the Chattahoochee River and this area as well as those individuals and groups that would benefit from its construction.[3] Considering the tremendous growth and development this region of North Georgia has experienced since, you can not help but wonder just how far his vision stretched.

The United States Army Corps of Engineers was well represented as a host of Corps officials addressed the crowds. General Albrecht, **Fig. 13-9**, who succeeded

Fig. 13-9 General Albrecht (Courtesy U.S. Army Corps of Engineers, Mobile District)

Major General H. Hoeffner, **Fig. 13-10**, as the South Atlantic Division Chief spoke of the navigation benefits linked to the project, ironic as they may seem today.[4] It is probably important to note here that at the time of the dedication navigation on the river probably played more of a role in the overall scheme of things when considering the benefits that would be derived from this and other planned projects on the Chattahoochee River. As noted earlier it was assumed by many at that time that eventually Atlanta would become a major cog in the huge machine that would become augmented river navigation. We know that not to be true today. For whatever the reasons, economic or political, the river's

Fig. 13-10 General Hoeffner (Courtesy U.S. Army Corps of Engineers, Mobile District)

full navigation potential was never developed.

The officer directly in charge of the Buford Project was Colonel Harold E. Bisbort, **Fig. 13-11**,. His comments were

Fig. 13-11 Colonel Bisbort (Courtesy U.S. Army Corps of Engineers, Mobile District)

directed at the immediate benefits the people of this area had already gained as a result of the projects completion. "The Buford Project has already prevented some $375,000.00 in flood damage losses as well as generated limited amounts of electrical power since June."[5]

Major General Walter K. Wilson, **Fig. 13-12**, who was the Mobile District

Fig. 13-12 General Wilson (Courtesy U.S. Army Corps of Engineers, Mobile District)

Chief when the ground breaking took place and also one of the nine persons who broke ground that day, represented the Washington delegation of the United States Army Corps of Engineers.[6] During the project's construction years he served as the District and Division Chief. He was one of many rising stars in the Corps of Engineers and four years later in 1961 President Kennedy would name him Chief of Army Engineers.

Jim Woodruff Sr., **Fig. 13-13**, considered by many as the father of resource

Fig. 13-13 Jim Woodruff Sr. (Courtesy U.S. Army Corps of Engineers, Mobile District)

and water development on the lower portion of the Chattahoochee spoke this day. His son Jim Woodruff Jr., **Fig. 13-14**,

Fig. 13-14 Jim Woodruff Jr. (Courtesy U.S. Army Corps of Engineers, Mobile District)

who was head of the Three River Development Association and an honorary member of the UCDA accompanied his father to the ceremony and expressed his thoughts on the occasion.[7] The senior Woodruff already had his name on the first project constructed on the river, the Jim Woodruff Lock and Dam, **Fig. I-1**, **Fig. I-5** and **Fig. I-6**, located at the convergence of the Chattahoochee, Flint Rivers which created Lake Seminole.

Georgia Representatives James C. Davis, **Fig. 13-15**, and Phil Landrum,

Fig. 13-15 James C. Davis (Courtesy U.S. Army Corps of Engineers, Mobile District)

Fig. 13-16 Phil Landrum (Courtesy U.S. Army Corps of Engineers, Mobile District)

Fig. 13-16, were also present at the ceremony.[8] Landrum who had replaced John S. Wood as the 9th District Representative after the project began, represented the people living in counties where Lake Lanier was located. Davis, who had spearheaded the early battles in Congress for approval then funding, represented the people South of the dam, in Atlanta and surrounding areas, who would greatly benefit from the project's existence.

Georgia's Governor Marvin Griffin, **Fig. 13-17**, and former Governor and now

Fig. 13-17 Governor Griffin (Courtesy U.S. Army Corps of Engineers, Mobile District)

the State's Junior Senator Herman Talmadge, **Fig. 13-18** took to the podium.[9] Talmadge had succeeded long time Georgia statesman Senator Walter F. George, who had passed

Dedication - October 9, 1957

Fig. 13-18 Senator Talmadge (Courtesy U.S. Army Corps of Engineers, Mobile District)

Fig. 13-19 Senator Russell at the podium. (Courtesy U.S. Army Corps of Engineers, Mobile District)

away several months before the dedication. As governor he was the keynote speaker at the ground breaking ceremony and recalled a day not long since passed when he stood atop a hillside some 1600 feet away overlooking the Chattahoochee and broke ground for the project he was now dedicating. After he spoke he introduced the keynote speaker, the States Senior Senator Richard B. Russell Jr., *Fig. 13-19*,.

Russell had led the fight in the Senate and later in a conference committee to obtain the original money for construction in the late 1940's.

Senator Russell reminded those present that the nation's use of one of its most valuable resources, water, was increasing daily. "Our greatest challenge will be to develop and harness our streams to secure the maximum advantage for water resources." He noted that several things stood in the way of realizing that end. "One was the policies of the Bureau of the Budget and second, the constant attacking of public works bills as being wasteful. The Bureau of the Budget is ill equipped to be a policy making body in this field.... its complication of simple procedures throws clouds of doubt over many civil works projects now under construction." Russell stated that the Bureau had actually held back funds appropriated by Congress for such projects. "Congress must find the means to take the withering hands of the Bureau off the efforts of the Board of Engineers and for Congress to develop our land and water resources."

Russell also attacked those who claimed that public works projects are only useful in their own community. He stated that champions of foreign aid are the most avid and vigorous objectors to domestic resource development. He explained that many of the projects such as Buford Dam are "self-liquidating", that the benefits reaped from their construction would eventually pay for themselves many times over.[10]

William B. Hartsfield, the master of ceremonies, was chosen to christen the $44,000,000.00 public works project. With the speeches over he stepped to the front of the grandstand next to a concrete block to complete the ceremony. His right hand draped with a rubber glove, he christened the concrete ceremonial block with Coca Cola bottles containing water from each of the three rivers in the water development system, *Fig. 13-20* and *Fig. 13-21*,.[11] It is

Fig. 13-20 Mayor Hartsfield dedicates the project. (Courtesy U.S. Army Corps of Engineers, Mobile District)

Fig. 13-21 Mayor Hartsfield dedicates the project. (Courtesy U.S. Army Corps of Engineers, Mobile District)

Fig. 13-22 Honorary Commodores (Courtesy U.S. Army Corps of Engineers, Mobile District)

Fig. 13-23 The United States Army band that played at the dedication ceremony. (Courtesy U.S. Army Corps of Engineers, Mobile District)

Fig. 13-24 Atlanta Mayor William B. Hartsfield at the podium. (Courtesy U.S. Army Corps of Engineers, Mobile District)

suggested that the particular bottles chosen were a direct result of the close friendship that Mayor Hartsfield had with Atlanta entrepreneur Robert W. Woodruff, the CEO of the Coca Cola Corporation.

After the christening ceremony the Commodore of the University Yacht Club, Lamar Swift, donned the visiting "VIP's" with caps dubbing them honorary "Commodores", *Fig. 13-22*, for their work and dedication in seeing a dream become a reality.[12]

Fig. 13-25 General Wilson speaking to the guests. (Courtesy U.S. Army Corps of Engineers, Mobile District)

Dedication - October 9, 1957

Fig. 13-26 (L-R) Weldon Gardner, Senator Russell, Colonel Bisbort, Governor Marvin Griffin, Representative Phil Landrum. (Courtesy U.S. Army Corps of Engineers, Mobile District)

Fig. 13-27 (L-R) General Albrecht, Jim Woodruff Sr., _____, General Wilson, Senator Herman Talmadge. (Courtesy U.S. Army Corps of Engineers, Mobile District)

Fig. 13-28 Senator Russell (Courtesy U.S. Army Corps of Engineers, Mobile District)

Fig. 13-29 (L-R) General Wilson, General Albrecht and Colonel Bisbort. (Courtesy U.S. Army Corps of Engineers, Mobile District)

Fig. 13-30 (L-R) Senator Talmadge, General Albrecht, Representative Davis, Governor Griffin, and _____ at a luncheon held after the dedication ceremony. (Courtesy U.S. Army Corps of Engineers, Mobile District)

Fig. 13-31 (L-R) Jim Woodruff Sr. and General Wilson at the luncheon. (Courtesy U.S. Army Corps of Engineers, Mobile District)

Fig. 13-32 (L-R) F.M. Byrd, Senator Russell, Mayor Hartsfield, and Curtis Bryant at the luncheon. (Courtesy U.S. Army Corps of Engineers, Mobile District)

Fig. 13-33 Mayor Hartsfield on a boat en route to the dedication. (Courtesy William B. Hartsfield Papers, Special Collections, Robert W. Woodruff Library, Emory University)

NOTES

1. Gainesville Daily Times
2. Ibid.
3. Ibid.
4. Ibid.
5. Ibid.
6. Ibid.
7. Ibid.
8. Ibid.
9. Ibid.
10. Ibid.
11. Ibid.
12. Ibid.

The headstone and marker of William B. Hartsfield's burial site. The inscription on the marker tells all, "Mayor". His interment is in West View Cemetery in Atlanta, Georgia. (RDC)

CHAPTER FOURTEEN

BIOGRAPHY

On May 25, 1959 normal pool of elevation 1070.0 for Lake Lanier was recorded for the first time.[1] An additional foot of elevation was added to the reservoir in 1976 bringing the present mark to 1071.0. There would be minor construction yet to be completed but for the most part the majority of the work was finished. With the lake now fully developed the benefits presupposed by its early planners could now be implemented. It had been nearly 35 years, since before the second world war, that development of this region had been proposed and studied. Local, state, and federal officials ceased upon the political and economic climate of the time in getting this project approved and constructed. Many believed that the dam and its reservoir would determine the future of the entire intracoastal waterway of Georgia and beyond and well it has. Decisions concerning regulation and use of water from Lake Lanier have an enormous impact on those regions south of the dam all the way to the Gulf of Mexico.

Those individuals who helped usher in a new era of economic growth and seemingly limitless potential for this area would leave their legacy of political action behind. Operations and continued development of the project's resources would be left to the future to manage. Each generation would place its own importance on what resources it would choose to develop. At the same time they would have to come to grips with problems, some of which did not even exist at the time the project was completed, that could and would arise from the expanded use and abuse of the reservoir. Whether or not the early planner's goals of what the project would provide for the people of this region ever developed, in part or in whole, is argumentative. That the project has had an economic impact on this region of enormous proportion, is not. How that impact is perceived, either good or bad, again is up for debate. There were many people involved with the Buford Dam Project. Some of them were in the forefront of the fight while others moved about quietly behind the scenes their impact more subtle and indirect. Equated in man hours the development of the reservoir did not come cheap but overall they were just as important as the dollars spent to see the project through. Many foresaw a not so distant future when resources derived from the reservoir would benefit not only them but generations to come.

The man probably most involved politically at all levels of the fight to win both approval then funding for the project

Fig. 14-1 William B. Hartsfield (Courtesy U.S. Army Corps of Engineers, Mobile District)

was then Atlanta Mayor, William Berry Hartsfield, *Fig. 14-1,*. With the dam completed Hartsfield continued on with the job of politics and running a city. In 1962 he stepped down as the city's chief executive ending nearly three decades of service to the City of Atlanta. He was first elected mayor in 1936 and with the exception of a one year war time period in the 1940's he held the office for 26 years. After retiring from public life he traveled and became the President of the Southeastern Fair Association. This position would afford him the opportunity to travel all over the world as an official spokesman for the organization in its never ending search for new and unusual talent. He continued to be active in the community and charities and was an advisor to the Ford Foundation on Urban Problems. In 1968 he became the recipient of the Great Georgian Award for a lifetime of service to his state.[2]

In December of 1970 he suffered a heart attack and although it appeared as if he might weather the worst of the storm he never fully recovered. He died at St. Josephs Hospital in Atlanta on Monday, February 22, 1971 at the age of 80. Interment is at Westview Cemetery in Atlanta where the single word "Mayor" is on the headstone.[3]

Fig. 14-2 James C. Davis (Courtesy U.S. Army Corps of Engineers, Mobile District)

James C. Davis, **Fig. 14-2**, the 5th District Representative who was at the forefront of the battle in Congress for the project's approval and funding continued on as Georgia's 5th District Representative until the early 1960's.[4] He was defeated for re-election in 1962 after serving 16 years in the House of Representatives as a member of the Post Office and Civil Service Committee and the District of Columbia Committee.[5] After his unsuccessful attempt at a ninth term he returned to his home in Georgia to practice law. He was the publisher of the Atlanta (Ga.) Times from 1963 to 1965. He was a member of the Board of Directors of Salem Campground and the DeKalb Federal Savings and Loan Association in Atlanta, Georgia. He died at the age of 86 on Monday, December 28, 1981. Interment is in the Oak Hill Cemetery, Newnan, Georgia.[6]

Senator Richard B. Russell, **Fig. 14-3**, who was very instrumental in acquiring first monies for construction to begin, would continue to serve in the Senate for another

Fig. 14-3 Richard B. Russell Jr. (Courtesy Library of Congress)

14 years. About the only major or national recognition he obtained during this period was his appointment to the Warren Commission, which investigated the assassination of President John F. Kennedy.[7] His bid for the presidency, in the mid 1950's and serving as the President Pro Tempore of the Senate during the 91st and 92nd Congress would be the pinnacle of his national prominence. In his years in the Senate he would serve as Chairman of the Committee of Immigration (75th through 79th Congress), Committee on Manufactures (79th Congress), Committee on Armed Services (82nd and 84th through 89th Congress) and the Committee on Appropriations (91st Congress).[8] He spent the latter years of his service in the Senate concentrating his energies as a politician for the betterment of Georgia. He would become an excellent behind the scenes force in the Senate, using his power and political savvy to influence legislation. Russell was considered by many of his colleagues to be a complex individual who believed deeply in and fought hard for his principles. He shunned the bright lights and clamor of Capitol Hill living as a bachelor in a small apartment in Washington, D.C.[9] In later years his health declined as he was plagued with emphysema and then cancer. He died of respiratory failure at Walter Reed Army Medical Center on Thursday, January 21, 1971 at the age of 73 after serving 38 years

Fig. 14-4 John S. Wood (Courtesy Library of Congress)

Fig. 14-5 Phil Landrum (Courtesy Library of Congress)

Fig. 14-6 Walter F. George (Courtesy Library of Congress)

in the Senate.[10] Interment is in the Russell Memorial Park, Winder, Georgia.[11]

John Stephens Wood, **Fig. 14-4**, was the 9th District Representative from Cherokee County at the time the project won approval then received appropriations for construction to begin. Several years after the ground breaking he announced that he would not be a candidate for renomination in 1952 and left the Congress after serving five terms (March 4, 1931 through January 3, 1935 and January 3, 1945 through January 3, 1953). After he left Washington he returned to Canton, Georgia and resumed his law practice until health problems forced him to retire. He was 83 when he died in Marietta, Georgia on Thursday, September 12, 1968. Interment is in Arlington Cemetery, Sandy Springs, Georgia.[12]

Phil Landrum, **Fig. 14-5**, would remain in Congress as the 9th District Representative until his retirement from active political life in 1976. He would serve twelve terms in the House of Representatives totaling twenty-four years of service. At one time he was the fourth ranking member of the powerful House Ways and Means Committee. He co-sponsored the Landrum-Griffin Act which controlled union corruption. The National Vocational Education Act, Library Services Act, and the Appalachian Regional Development Program were all bills he played an active part in passing. He would become the senior member of the representatives serving in the House from Georgia, paving the way for a former law partner and aid, Representative Ed Jenkins, to take his place. He lived for many years after his retirement on his farm in Jasper, Georgia. He died at Pickens General Hospital on Monday, November 19, 1990 at the age of 83.[13]

Senator Walter F. George, **Fig. 14-6**, was a long time member of the United States Senate. He was first elected to the office in

1922 while serving as a Justice on the Georgia State Supreme Court.[14] He was elected to succeed Rebecca Latimer Felton who was appointed to the unexpired term of Thomas E. Watson. In 1956 a youthful Herman Talmadge having served as Governor used his experience and political savvy along with the networking and organization left to him by his father to win the senatorial democratic primary. Senator George having lost major supporters withdrew from the primary when it became evident that Talmadge had acquired the political and corporate backing that he himself had once enjoyed.[15] He served thirty-five years in the Senate chairing and serving on many important and influential committees during that time. He was the President pro tempore of the Senate during the 84th Congress; Chairman of the Committee on Privileges and Elections (73rd through 76th Congress); Committee on Foreign Relations (76th, 77th and 84th Congress); Committee on Finance (77th through 79th, 81st and 82nd Congress); Joint Committee on Internal Revenue Taxation (81st and 82nd Congress); Select Committee on Case Influence (84th Congress) and Special Committee on Foreign Assistance (84th Congress).[16] After leaving the Senate he served for a short time in the Eisenhower administration as first a NATO ambassador then as a foreign policy advisor. On Sunday, August 4, 1957, two months shy of the Buford Dam Dedication, he died of heart related problems at his home in Vienna, Georgia. He was 79 years old.[17] Interment is in Vienna Cemetery, Vienna, Georgia.[18]

Senator Herman Eugene Talmadge, *Fig. 14-7*, would continue to serve Georgia throughout the 1960's and 70's. He was the Chairman of the Committee on Agriculture and Forestry (92nd through the 95th Congress) and the Committee on Agriculture, Nutrition and Forestry (95th and 96th Congress). He would serve on the Senate Select Sub-Committee investigation of the Watergate scandal that would eventually lead to the resignation of Richard M. Nixon as President of the United States in 1974. His own political career ran into trouble when he was investigated for financial improprieties in the late 1970's. In 1979 he was denounced by the Senate for

Fig. 14-7 Herman Talmadge (Courtesy U.S. Army Corps of Engineers, Mobile District)

financial misconduct and in 1980 he was defeated for re-election by Mack Mattingly. He left the Senate after serving 24 years in the office and returned to Hampton, Georgia to practice law. He died at his home on March 21, 2002.[19]

Fig. 14-8 Mason J. Young (Courtesy U.S. Army Corps of Engineers, Mobile District)

Colonel Mason James Young, *Fig. 14-8*, who was a classmate at West Point with President Eisenhower and General Omar N. Bradley, was the South Atlantic Division Chief when early planning and funding for the project took place. At the time he was the South Atlantic Chief he had more river and harbor duty than any other

Corps officer. After leaving the South Atlantic Division he was the first commander (1949-52) of the Communications Zone across France set up to supply forces in Germany. He retired from active military service as a Brigadier General in 1953. After retirement he worked for the engineering firm of Faye, Spofford and Thordike in Boston supervising airfield construction and other engineering projects until 1961. He died at the age of 88 on Wednesday, October 27, 1982 in Newport News, Virginia. Interment is in Glenwood Cemetery, Londonderry, New Hampshire.[20]

Fig. 14-9 Raymond A. Wheeler (Courtesy U.S. Army Corps of Engineers, Mobile District)

General Raymond Albert Wheeler, *Fig. 14-9*, was the Chief of Engineers during the early years of funding and planning for the dam. He held this post from 1946 to 1949. He retired that year as a Major General after 42 years of active military service. After retirement he organized and headed an engineering staff and a department of Technical Operations for the International Bank for Reconstruction and Development (World Bank) in Washington, D.C. He acted as an engineering consultant and a staff member of the World Bank and after leaving the organization he became an engineering consultant for special projects. From 1956-57 he headed an international task force in the clearing operation of the Suez Canal after the Arab-Israel War of 1956. From 1957-58 he headed a United Nations group of engineers to prepare a program of studies for comprehensive development of the Lower MeKong River Basin in Indochina. From 1964 to 1971 he was a member of the Engineering Board of Review which oversaw the design and construction of projects on the Columbia River in Canada which had been authorized by a treaty between the United States and Canada. He died on Friday, February 8, 1974 at Walter Reed Army Medical Center in Washington, D.C. at the age of 88. Interment is in Arlington National Cemetery, Arlington, Virginia.[21]

Fig. 14-10 Bernard L. Robinson (Courtesy U.S. Army Corps of Engineers, Mobile District)

Colonel Bernard Linn Robinson, *Fig. 14-10*, who was Chief of the South Atlantic Division from 1949 to 1951 was one of three Corps officers who broke earth at the ground breaking ceremony that officially started the project in March, 1950. He was promoted to Major General in 1948 and from 1951-52 he was the Engineer Commissioner for the District of Columbia. From 1953-55 he served as the Deputy Chief of Engineers and Director of the Joint Construction Agency in France from 1955-57.[22] He retired from active duty with the rank of Major General in 1957. He lived out his latter years in Manchester, Missouri, passing away at the age of 92 on January 6, 1994.[23]

General Lewis Andrew Pick, *Fig. 14-11*, was Chief of Engineers at the time the ground breaking ceremony was

Fig. 14-11 Lewis Pick (Courtesy U.S. Army Corps of Engineers, Mobile District)

Fig. 14-12 Walter K. Wilson (Courtesy U.S. Army Corps of Engineers, Mobile District)

held and during the first few years of construction from March 1, 1949 to January 26, 1953. He retired from active duty with the rank of Lieutenant General in 1953. After retirement he devoted a great deal of his time to state and national politics. He lobbied hard for congressional approval of certain engineering projects he was interested in, one being the completion of the dams and reservoirs of the Pick-Sloan Plan. He accepted the position of Vice-Chairman of Georgia Pacific Plywood Company that same year. In 1954 he became a consultant to the John J. Harte Company in Atlanta, Georgia on the construction of a power plant in Quito, Ecuador. In 1955 he accepted the position of Chairman of the Board for the company. He died on Sunday, December 2, 1956 in Washington, D.C. at the age of 66.[24]

Walter K. Wilson Jr., *Fig. 14-12*, who was a Colonel and the District Engineer for the Mobile District during the project's early planning and construction and another of the Army officers who broke ground in 1950 would become the South Atlantic Division Chief in 1952. President John F. Kennedy would make him the Chief of Engineers in 1961 and he would remain in that post until his retirement on June 30, 1965 at the rank of Lieutenant General after 36 years of active military service. From 1965-71 he was Vice President of Southern Industries Corporation in Mobile, Alabama. From 1966-73 he was that companies Director and Chairman of the Task Force 200 in Mobile, Alabama. From 1971-75 he served as a member of the U.S. Military Academy Planning Board which advised the Department of the Army on the Academy's construction and expansion program.[25] He lived out his retirement years in Mobile, Alabama where he died on Friday, December 6, 1985.[26]

Lester W. Hosch, *Fig. 14-13*, continued as a business and civic leader in Gainesville,

Fig. 14-13 Lester Hosch (Courtesy Chestatee Regional Library)

Biography

Georgia for many years following the completion of Buford Dam. He had accepted the invitation of Mayor Hartsfield along with many other local officials and civic leaders during the early years of funding for the project to travel to Washington, D.C. in order to obtain badly needed appropriations for completion of the dam. As a member and officer in the Rotary Club he was named man of the year in 1968 and a Paul Harris Fellow in 1971. He was also a life member of the Jaycee's. For his affiliation and work in the Rotary Club the mayor of Gainesville proclaimed March 15, 1971 as Lester Hosch Day. He was 89 when he died at his home in Gainesville, Georgia on Tuesday, May 3, 1977. Interment is in Alta Vista Cemetery, Gainesville, Georgia.[27]

Fig. 14-14 J. Larry Kleckley (Courtesy Mrs. Weldon Gardner)

J. Larry Kleckley, **Fig. 14-14**, another Gainesville resident who was one of nine who broke ground at the ground breaking ceremony in the early 1950's was actively involved in the politics of acquiring early funding and eventual construction of the project. He was President of the Upper Chattahoochee Development Association (UCDA) and like his fellow Hall Countian continued to be active after the project's completion in the business community and civic area in the North Georgia city for many years. He was a 32 degree Scottish Rite Free Mason and a member of the Elks Lodge. He served as a member of the Service Corps of Retired Executives (SCORE) which was an affiliate of the Small Business Administration. He also wrote a regular column for the Gainesville Daily Times under the name of "Mountain Willie". After battling a lengthy illness he died on Saturday, August 28, 1982 at Lanier Park Hospital just three days after celebrating his 82nd birthday. Interment is in Memorial Park, Gainesville, Georgia.[28]

Fig. 14-15 Charles A. Jackson (Courtesy U.S. Army Corps of Engineers, Mobile District)

Charles A. Jackson, **Fig. 14-15**, was the project's resident engineer. He had a long and distinguished career with the Army Corps of Engineers having seen the completion of several dams in Georgia and South Carolina. He had been the resident engineer for the Allatoona Dam and when it was completed he came to the Buford Project. In 1956 he became the resident engineer for the Hartwell Dam. With the dam at Hartwell complete he began work on NASA's rocket testing facilities on the Pearl River in Hancock County, Mississippi. He was the Area Engineer in charge of design and construction of the test facilities. He retired after 35 years of government service in 1965. He lived out his retirement years on Lake Hartwell where he died in Anderson, South Carolina on June 24, 1974.[29]

L.D. Ewing, **Fig. 14-16**, of Norcross who served as Secretary of the Gwinnett County Chamber of Commerce was another local official who went to Washington with

Fig. 14-16 L.D. Ewing (Courtesy Mrs. Jo Ann Weathers)

Mayor Hartsfield in hopes of drumming up support for their cause. Testifying before congressional appropriations committees he implored the committee members to give the project the money it desperately needed. He was a charter officer of the Upper Chattahoochee Development Association and would eventually become the UCDA's President. He was also an instrumental figure in seeing the development of the Lake Lanier Islands Authority in the mid 1960's. He died on Friday, September 2, 1983 with

Fig. 14-17 Weldon Gardner (Courtesy Mrs. Jo Ann Weathers)

interment in Peachtree Memorial Cemetery Norcross, Georgia.[30]

Weldon Gardner, **Fig. 14-17**, an insurance agent for over 30 years and a long time Gwinnett County resident who lived in Buford was a very active local citizen involved in the early funding battles for the project. He was one of the nine people chosen to break earth at the ground breaking ceremony and like his fellow Gwinnett Countian, L.D. Ewing, was a charter member of the UCDA becoming the first president of the organization. Gardner worked closely with Mayor Hartsfield in getting the project approved, funded and then constructed. He made several trips with the Atlanta Mayor along with others of the region to Washington to lobby for the project's completion. After the project was finished he continued his work with the UCDA as well as the community. He was Chairman of the Gwinnett County Industrial Development Authority and would also hold that position with the Gwinnett Hospital Authority. He was seen as a driving force in developing and planning a central hospital system in Gwinnett County and would also continue to lend his name and support for many causes and organizations over the years in Buford as well as Gwinnett County. He died on Wednesday, August 22, 1973 at the age of 69. Interment is in Alta Vista Cemetery, Gainesville, Georgia.[31]

Jess Baggett, **Fig. 14-18**, was a former

Fig. 14-18 Jess Baggett (Courtesy Jack Baggett,)

Mayor of Lawrenceville and state senator. He also accompanied Mayor Hartsfield to Washington, D.C. on more than one occassion to win original approval then

Biography

funding for the dam. He was one of the founders and the first president of Gwinnett Federal Savings and Loan Association. A prominent business leader he owned and operated an automobile dealership and oil company in Lawrenceville. He was a charter member and president of the Kiwanis Club and very active in the Gwinnett County Chamber of Commerce. In 1961 he received a sliver plaque from the county for his many years of outstanding service to the people of Gwinnett County. He passed away, following a lengthy illness, on Sunday, January 17, 1965. Interment is in Gwinnett Memorial Gardens.[32]

*Fig. 14-19
Roy P. Otwell
(Courtesy Mrs. Jo Ann Weathers)*

Roy P. Otwell, *Fig. 14-19*, known to the citizenry of Forsyth County as "Mr. Roy" was a stalwart business and political leader in the county for over 60 years. He served as the Mayor of Cumming for 30 years. An entrepreneur of the first caliber he owned and operated numerous businesses including a drugstore, car dealership, newspaper, bank and was even a commercial and residential builder. The Lions Club, Kiwanis Club and the local Chamber of Commerce all benefited from his support. Otwell helped establish the Georgia Baptist Hospital and served on the Board of Trustees for Truett-McConnell Junior College in Cleveland, Georgia. Otwell had been a long time proponent for the project and for many years afterwords would refer to the project as the "Cumming-Buford Dam". He made the trek to Washington, D.C. with Mayor Hartsfield on more than one occasion to testify before both the House and Senate Appropriations Committee for support and funding for the dam. When the project officially began he was one of the men picked to break ground that day. He was also very active with the UCDA serving as a Vice President for the Forsyth County chapter of the organization. With the project's completion he would remain an active civic and political figure in Forsyth County for over 30 years. He was 93 when he died on Monday, February 8, 1988. Interment is in Sawnee View Gardens in Cumming, Georgia.[33]

Notes

1. "Fact Sheet" from a Lake Sidney Lanier navigation chart produced by the United States Army Corps of Engineers, 1985.

2. Dictionary of Georgia biography by Kenneth Coleman and Charles Stephen Gurr.

3. Atlanta Constitution, February 23, 1971

4. Biographical Directory of the United States Congress: 1774-1989, Bicentennial Edition, p. 878-879.

5. Georgia Democratic Party, Atlanta, Georgia

6. Atlanta Constitution, December 29, 1981

7. Dictionary of Georgia Biography by Kenneth Coleman and Charles Stephen Gurr.

8. Biographical Directory of the United States Congress: 1774-1989, Bicentennial Edition, p. 1754.

9. Dictionary of Georgia Biography by Kenneth Coleman and Charles Stephen Gurr.

10. Richard B. Russell Jr., Senator from Georgia by Gilbert C. Fite.

11. Biographical Directory of the United States Congress: 1774-1989, Bicentennial Edition, p. 1754.

12. Ibid., p. 2082

13. Gwinnett Daily News, November 21, 1990

14. Biographical Directory of the United States Congress: 1774-1989, Bicentennial Edition, p. 1052-1053

15. Dictionary of Georgia Biography by Kenneth Coleman and Charles Stephen Gurr.

16. Biographical Directory of the United States Congress: 1774-1989, Bicentennial Edition, p.1053

17. Dictionary of Georgia Biography by Kenneth Coleman and Charles Stephen Gurr

18. Biographical Directory of the United States Congress: 1774-1989, Bicentennial Edition, p. 1053

19. Ibid., p. 1910

20. From the magazine the "Assembly", Volume XLIII, No.3, published quarterly by the Association of Graduates, U.S.M.A., West Point, New York

21. Ibid., Volume XXXIII, No.3

22. From historical information provided by Reference Historian Dale E. Floyd, U.S. Army Corps of Engineers, Fort Belvoir, Virginia

23. West Point Military Academy, West Point, New York

24. From historical information provided by Reference Historian Dale E. Floyd, U.S. Army Corps of Engineers, Fort Belvoir, Virginia

25. Memoirs of General Walter K. Wilson, produced by U.S. Army Corps of Engineers, Mobile District, Mobile, Alabama

26. West Point Military Academy, West Point, New York

27. Gainesville Daily Times, May 4, 1977

28. Ibid., August 29, 1982

29. Anderson Independent, June 25, 1974

30. Gwinnett Daily News, September 3, 1983

31. Gwinnett Daily News, August 23, 1973

32. Ibid., January 18, 1965

33. Forsyth County News, February 10, 1988

Appendix I.
Appropriations and Contractorial Statistics

Private companies were awarded contracts by the United States Army Corps of Engineers to complete the construction phase of the project. Although the Corps of Engineers oversaw the construction and Congress provided funding the actual work was completed by the private sector. Bids were accepted by the Corps of Engineers based on specifications drawn up by government engineers. These contracts were filed as part of public record. The majority of the contracted work listed here fell under the category of design and construction.

Buford Dam Appropriations

Year	Appropriations to Date	Budget Estimate	House Allowance	Senate Allowance	Conference Allowance
1947	.00	.00	.00	.00	.00
1948	.00	.00	.00	.00	.00
1949	$250,000.00	.00	.00	$1,000,000.00	.00
1950	$650,000.00	$67,000.00	.00	$2,261,000.00	$750,000.00
1951	$1,400,000.00	$1,000,000.00	$400,000.00	$900,000.00	$900,000.00
1952	$2,300,000.00	$900,000.00	.00	$900,000.00	$900,000.00
1953	$3,200,000.00	$3,000,000.00	$3,000,000.00	$3,000,000.00	$3,000,000.00
1954	$6,181,000.00	$8,500,000.00	$5,000,000.00	$8,000,000.00	$7,500,000.00
1955	$13,681,000.00	$5,800,000.00	$5,800,000.00	$9,500,000.00	$9,300,000.00
1956	$22,981,000.00	$11,830,000.00	$11,830,000.00	$11,830,000.00	$11,830,000.00
1957	$34,811,000.00	$4,553,000.00	$4,553,000.00	$4,553,000.00	$4,553,000.00
1958	$39,364,000.00	$572,000.00	$572,000.00	$572,000.00	$572,000.00
1959	$39,936,000.00	$2,560,902.00	$2,560,902.00	$2,560,902.00	$2,560,902.00
1960	$42,496,902.00	$1,524,613.00	$1,524,613.00	$1,524,613.00	$1,524,613.00
1961	$44,021,515.00 [1]				

Contractorial Statistics

Job	Contractor	Cost	Date
Saddle Dike no.3 and Spillway	H.M. Rodgers and Son, Memphis, Tennessee	$297,627.00	03-01-50
Forebay, tailrace tunnels, saddle dikes no.1&2 and access road	Groves, Lundin and Cox, Inc. Minneapolis, Minnesota	$2,836,712.00	06-07-51
Hydraulic turbine and butterfly valve	James Leffer and Company Springfield, Ohio	$212,024.00	02-15-57
Hydraulic turbines	Newport News Shipbuilding and Dry Dock Company Newport News, Virginia	$1,224,295.00	11-02-51
Alternating current generators	Westinghouse Electric Corp. East Pittsburgh, Pennsylvania	$2,276,512.00	02-25-52
Power and sluice tunnels	L.A. Tvedt Contractors Memphis, Tennessee	$552,179.00	03-16-53

Appendix I. Appropriations and Contractorial Statistics

Sluice and service gates	Phillips and Davies Inc. Kenton, Ohio	$178,500.00	03-13-53
Gate hoist	Armstrong and Hand Inc. Houston, Texas	$153,990.00	01-15-55
Head gate, stop logs and trash racks	Guy F. Atkinson Company and DBA Williamette Iron and Steel Company Portland, Oregon	$222,783.00	03-16-53
Intake structure and sluice	J.A. Jones Construction Co. Charlotte, North Carolina	$2,011,402.00	10-22-53
Main earth dam	J.W. Moorman and Son Muskogee, Oklahoma	$1,487,425.00	03-01-54
Trash rake, hoist and car	Milwaukee Crane and Service Co. Cudahy, Wisconsin	$14,750.00	06-30-54
Brown's Bridge (substructure) and relocation no.141	C.Y. Thomason Company Greenville, South Carolina	$421,088.00	07-14-54
Wells for operation area	Virginia Supply and Well Co. Atlanta, Georgia	$5,400.00	08-03-54
Reservoir operations building, utilities and appurtenances	Capital Construction Company Atlanta, Georgia	$142,717.00	11-26-54
Construction of Two-Mile Creek Bridge	Henry Newton Company Decatur, Georgia	$93,479.00	12-10-54
Construction of superstructure for Brown's Bridge	Bristol Steel and Iron Works Inc. Bristol, Virginia	$461,921.00	12-20-54
Construction of substructure for Lanier Bridge	Oman Construction Co. Inc. Nashville, Tennessee	$164,195.00	02-25-55
Carbon dioxide fire extinguishing equipment for powerhouse	Walter Kidde and Co. Inc. Bellville, N.J.	$21,821.00	04-22-55
Construction of substructure and approach roads, Thompson's Bridge (schedule A)	Wright Contracting Co. Columbus, Georgia	$246,671.00	04-25-55
Relocation of Georgia State Route no.53	Macon Construction Company Franklin, North Carolina	$906,225.00	04-25-55
Construction of superstructure Thompson's Bridge (schedule B)	C.Y. Thomason Company Greenville, South Carolina	$411,518.00	04-27-55
Powerhouse switch yard and and transformer yard	Ivey Brothers Const. Co. Inc. Atlanta, Georgia	$3,076,138.00	05-09-55

Superstructure for Lanier Bridge	Bristol Steel and Iron Works Bristol, Virginia	$494,064.00	05-17-55
Bolling Bridge	R.G. Foster and Company Wadley, Georgia	$538,261.00	05-24-55
Power transformers	Westinghouse Electric Corp. Mobile, Alabama	$253,367.00	06-10-55
Switch gear and equipment	Westinghouse Electric Corp. Mobile, Alabama	$225,300.00	06-23-55
Oil circuit breakers	Federal Pacific Electric Co. San Francisco, California	$127,699.00	06-10-55
300 ton electric motor operated overhead trolley crane	Harnischfeger Corporation Milwaukee, Wisconsin	$186,340.00	05-25-55
Switch gear and equipment	Zinsco Electrical Production Los Angeles, California	$19,240.00	06-23-55
Switch gear and equipment	General Electric Company Mobile, Alabama	$99,795.00	06-23-55
Turbine governing equipment	The Pelton Water Wheel Co. Inc. San Francisco, California	$88,702.00	06-14-55
Switch yard equipment	Southern States Equipment Corp. Hampton, Georgia	$107,091.00	06-24-55
Reservoir clearing parcels 1-4	Wade Lahar Construction Co. Mountain Home, Arkansas	$1,611,560.00	07-01-55
Sewerage treatment plant	City of Gainesville Gainesville, Georgia	$1,465,000.00	07-22-55
Construction of Wilkie Bridge, Toto Creek and relocation of Georgia State Route 136	Ballenger Paving Co. and Inland Bridge Co. Inc. (joint venture) Greenville, South Carolina	$428,515.00	08-13-55
Construction of Longstreet Bridge and Bell's Mill Bridge (schedule A and B)	Tidwell Construction Company Douglasville, Georgia	$590,322.00	10-20-55
State Route no.11 (schedule C)	Ballenger Paving Company Greenville, South Carolina	$269,703.00	10-21-55
Relocation of Squirrel Creek Road (Georgia State Route 115)	Ballenger Paving Company Greenville, South Carolina	$53,235.00	01-19-56
Relocate electric line facilities	Sawnee Electric Membership Sawnee, Georgia	$169,019.00	01-30-56

Appendix I. Appropriations and Contractorial Statistics

Removal of Old Brown's Bridge (Bailey Type M-1) Georgia State no.141	Inland Bridge Co. Inc. Chester, South Carolina	$3,250.00	02-08-56
18 ton draft tube gantry crane	Cyclops Iron Works San Francisco, California	$29,969.00	04-17-56
Relocation of cemeteries	Julius A. Schwerin Jr. Aiken, South Carolina	$5,348.00	02-10-56
Relocation of cemeteries	Julius A. Schwerin Jr. Aiken, South Carolina	$5,900.00	05-16-56
Grassing, repair and maintenance of down stream slope of the main earth dam and tailrace	J.E. Hill Decatur, Georgia	$6,300.00	07-24-56
Repair and resurfacing of left bank access roads and parking areas	Ballenger Paving Company Greenville, South Carolina	$22,941.00	08-06-56
Relocation of telephone line facilities	Southern Bell Telephone and Telegraph Company	$51,734.00	11-01-56
Relocation, rearrangement or alteration of Forsyth County, Georgia roads	Forsyth County, Georgia	$128,450.00	12-10-56
Fabricated structural steel	American Bridge Division U.S. Steel Corporation Birmingham, Alabama	$19,897.00	12-19-56
Alteration of Houser's Mill Bridge and road	Hall County, Georgia	$5,500.00	12-20-56
Wahoo Creek Road relocation	Ed Smith and Sons Atlanta, Georgia	$166,668.00	01-08-57
Relocation of cemeteries in Buford reservoir area at Buford Dam, Chattahoochee River	Little-Davenport Funeral Home Inc. Gainesville, Georgia	$34,406.00	01-17-57
Sales contract Longstreet Bridge (sales)	Victory Wrecking Company Columbus, Georgia	$200.00	02-25-57
Sales contract Clark's Bridge (sales)	Gainesville Auto Wrecking Company Gainesville, Georgia	$325.00	02-26-57
Demolition of Longstreet relief and Bell's Mill Bridges	Columbus Construction Company Columbus, Georgia [2]	$11,000.00	03-12-57

Notes

1. Congressional Record, United States Army Civil Functions and Public Works Appropriations Fiscal Years 1947-1961.

2. Gainesville Daily Times 1957.

Appendix II. Impoundment Statistics

Statistics of Reservoir Flooding for Lake Sidney Lanier

Date	Elevation
February 01, 1956	928.25 (Gates closed)
February 22, 1956	971.67
February 29, 1956	976.12

47.87 foot increase in lake elevation since gates were closed on February 1, 1956.

Date	Elevation
March 01, 1956	976.72
March 06, 1956	978.92
March 12, 1956	980.58
March 24, 1956	990.00
March 31, 1956	992.28

16.16 foot increase in lake elevation for the month of March, 1956.

Date	Elevation
April 05, 1956	993.45
April 11, 1956	996.92
April 18, 1956	1002.50

Impoundment temporarily stopped to complete construction of Thompson Bridge. Lake elevation would remain at 1002.50 for nearly three months.

Date	Elevation
July 14, 1956	1002.52
July 25, 1956	1003.67
July 31, 1956	1004.08

1.58 foot increase in lake elevation for the month of July, 1956.

Date	Elevation
August 01, 1956	1004.16
August 30, 1956	1004.86

.70 foot increase in lake elevation for the month of August, 1956.

Date	Elevation
September 02, 1956	1004.95
September 30, 1956	1006.51

1.56 foot increase in lake elevation for the month of September, 1956.

Date	Elevation
October 01, 1956	1006.55
November 01, 1956	1007.57
December 01, 1956	1008.39
December 31, 1956	1013.62

84.37 foot increase in lake elevation since gates closed February 1, 1956.

January 01, 1957	1013.71
February 02, 1957	1020.22
March 03, 1957	1028.00

Impoundment stopped for reservoir clearing. Heavy rains in early April, 1957 drove lake elevation to 1031.30. Difficulties with intake gate controls caused lake elevation to drop to 1029.95 on May 3, 1957. Impoundment resumed in late June, 1957.

June 01, 1957	1032.67
July 01, 1957	1035.00
August 01, 1957	1036.00
September 01, 1957	1036.11
October 01, 1957	1036.69
November 01, 1957	1038.30
December 01, 1957	1042.91
December 31, 1957	1047.00

33.38 foot increase in lake elevation for 1957 and 117.75 foot increase since gate closing on February 1, 1956.

January 01, 1958	1047.08
February 01, 1958	1050.02
March 01, 1958	1053.42
April 01, 1958	1057.74
May 01, 1958	1061.80
June 01, 1958	1064.67
July 01, 1958	1065.45
August 01, 1958	1068.77

21.77 foot increase in lake elevation would represent the highest level of the lake for 1958.[1] Lake elevation is normally dropped in late summer and fall to allow the reservoir to catch winter and spring rains. Normal pool of elevation 1070.0 would not be obtained for the first time until May 25, 1959.[2]

APPENDIX II. IMPOUNDMENT STATISTICS

NOTES

1. Lake elevations as found in the Gainesville Daily Times from February 1, 1956 to August 1, 1958.

2. "Fact Sheet" courtesy navigation chart developed by the United States Army Corps of Engineers, 1985.

Appendix III - Land Acquisitions Information

The information that follows is an abridged collection of data on land sales statistics taken from promissory deed records and segment maps of Lake Lanier provided by the United States Army Corps of Engineers. It represents the best available record of land sales for Buford Dam and is intended to provide general information about land sales for the project. The tract numbers indicate the county(ies) where the land was located. Skips in sequential order of the tracts represent land that was not purchased by the government which usually meant it was located above elevation 1085.0, future easement purchases, or absent research information. The prices shown for each tract of land represents what was considered the fair market value of the land at the time it was purchased. It does not include any additional money the owner may have received through the courts. The date shown is when the government took possession of the land. A brief description of the land's topography, potential use, and other characteristics are also provided.

Dawson County

Tract	Property Owner	Acres	Price	Date
L-1226-E-1	Taylor, J. Henry	14.56	324.00	12-14-56
Mountainous and steeply rolling with a small amount of bottom land				
L-1226-E-2	Taylor, J. Henry	.50	10.00	12-14-56
Topography is gently rolling and suitable for cropland if desired				
L-1227-E	Gazaway, Mrs. George			12-06-57
Perpetual flowing easement				
L-1228	Clarke, Ima (aka Ima Clark Hamby)	16.12	800.00	07-23-56
Cropland and woodland				
L-1229-E	Pugh, George S.	12.47	700.00	08-02-55
Idle with various vegetation growing a few scattered pines				
L-1230-E	Pugh, George S.	3.48	165.00	12-07-56
Cut over woodland and improved pasture				
L-1231-E	Rome Kraft Co.	1.81	70.00	02-13-57
Wooded tract, topography is medium to steeply rolling				
L-1253	Taylor, J. Henry	7.35	600.00	12-14-56
Wooded land and homesites				
L-1255	Wilson, Odell	1.75	1,725.00	12-12-57
The highest and best use is thought to be for a homesite, front lots and agriculture				
L-1256	Woody, Van J.; Mrs. van J.	1.40	160.00	02-24-56
Gently rolling land most of which is open and used for pasture				
L-1259	Anderson, Irma	33.10	3,750.00	04-05-56
Best use agricultural				
L-1259-E-1-2	Anderson, Irma	.55		04-05-56
Best use agricultural				

L-1262 Woodliff, T. J. .31 100.00 04-05-56
Wooded road front

L-1263 Anderson, C. C. 6.88 47,500.00 04-05-56
Suited for present use

Fig. A-III-1 L-1263 (Courtesy U.S. Army Corps of Engineers, Mobile District, Official U.S. Army Photograph)

Fig. A-III-2 L-1263 (Courtesy U.S. Army Corps of Engineers, Mobile District, Official U.S. Army Photograph)

L-1264-1-2-3 Martin, Charlie I. 193.80 12,300.00 04-20-56
Highest and best use being agricultural and forestry purposes

L-1265 Horne Jr., T. L.; Scott Jr., G.B. .39 100.00 07-23-56
Highest and best use is residential

L-1266 Skinner, Maude Dobbs .78 200.00 05-05-56
The land slopes medium up from the highway and has a few pine trees on it

L-1267 Smith, R. G. .78 200.00 12-01-55
Highest and best use is residential

L-1268 Whitmire, G. T. 30.31 2,375.00 12-10-55
Best suited for building lots and forestry

L-1271 Garmon, James L. 2.73 9,150.00 12-10-55
Highest and best use is considered to be residential

L-1272 Barrett, J. G. 7.09 400.00 03-28-56
Medium to steeply rolling and only a small area suited for cropping

L-1273 Wilson, J. C 2.53 290.00 04-13-56
Woodland

L-1275 Whitmire, G. T. 1.24 275.00 08-31-56
Best suited for building purposes

L-1276   Wilson, Odell   2.48   3,175.00   12-01-55
Best suited for buildings lots

Fig. A-III-3 L-1276 (Courtesy U.S. Army Corps of Engineers, Mobile District, Official U.S. Army Photograph)

Fig. A-III-4 L-1276 (Courtesy U.S. Army Corps of Engineers, Mobile District, Official U.S. Army Photograph)

L-1277   Burdett, James C.   2.48   550.00   12-01-55
Best suited for residential

L-1278   Taylor, J. Henry   5.44   650.00   12-10-55
Best suited for building lots

L-1284-1-2   McClure, J. C.   59.00   4,425.00   12-10-55
Adapted to general crops, pasture and timber production

L-1286-1-2   Cox, Vada   36.15   3,150.00   08-13-56
Adapted to general crops, pasture and/or meadow and timber production

L-1287   Whitmire, G. T.   120.00   5,150.00   12-29-55
Farm land and forestry

L-1288   Hamby, Mattie Effie   43.60   2,250.00   08-08-56
Topography is level to medium rolling

L-1290   Pirkle, Glen E.   56.70   4,275.00   01-14-56
Gently to medium rolling except woodland which is steeply rolling

L-1292   Smith, Charles W.   .92   90.00   03-09-56
Adapted best to a country homesite

L-1293-E   Fouts, Taft   .01
Perpetual flowing easement

L-1294   Whitmire, G. T.   1.72   1,100.00   12-10-55
Cropland

L-1295   Townsend, George R.;   10.08   675.00   12-10-55
                 Mrs. George R.
Adapted to pasture and timber

L-1296   Garrett, J. E.   36.66   2,050.00   07-07-56
Best suited for home and/or poultry production purposes

L-1297-1-2   Dockery, Homer   52.98   3,750.00   04-05-56
General farm unit

L-1298   Sams, L. R.   23.25   3,050.00   04-05-56
Best use is forestry

Fig. A-III-5 L-1298 (Courtesy U.S. Army Corps of Engineers, Mobile District, Official U.S. Army Photograph)

Fig. A-III-6 L-1298 (Courtesy U.S. Army Corps of Engineers, Mobile District, Official U.S. Army Photograph)

M-1301   Hughes, T. F.   5.50   365.00   03-02-56
The topography for open land is undulating with medium rolling for woodland

M-1301-E-1 and E-4   Hughes, T. F.   9.15   45.00   03-02-56
The topography for open land is undulating with medium rolling for woodland

M-1301-E-2 and E-3   Hughes, T. F.   1.00   250.00   03-02-56
This forms a considerable portion of the front yard

M-1303   Hughes, H. G.   19.80   1,100.00   03-09-56
The topography is level to undulating for bottom lands and gently to medium rolling upland

M-1303-E-1-2   Hughes, H. G.   7.16   685.00   03-09-56
Level to medium rolling

M-1303-E-3-4   Hughes, H. G.   2.30   15.00   03-09-56
The topography is level to undulating for bottom lands and gently to medium rolling upland

M-1304   Smith, Glen E.   42.00   2,375.00   02-24-56
Adapted to growing of crops and small grain

M-1304-E-1-2   Smith, Glen E.   3.33   25.00   02-24-56
Adapted to growing of crops and small grain

M-1306   Martin, Eallar   7.81   550.00   12-28-56
Good agricultural section

M-1306   Bennett, Lyman; Mrs. Lyman   2.53   165.00   04-28-56
Gently to medium rolling land and most of the land in cultivation or pasture

M-1306-E   Bennett, Lyman; Mrs. Lyman   2.29   15.00   04-28-56
Gently to medium rolling

M-1309-E   Rome Kraft Company   .83   10.00   10-24-58
The topography is undulating and is adapted to woodland

M-1310   Smith, Dessie   10.00   3,650.00   04-20-56
Best use is agricultural

M-1311   Hughes, H. G.   69.50   7,050.00   06-01-56
Gently to medium rolling land with about 60% cleared and a large part is improved pasture

M-1312-E   Collins, E. J.   5.74   100.00   12-12-57
The highest and best use for the subject tract is for forest products

M-1313   Elliott, A. W.   7.69   450.00   09-10-56
Agricultural purposes

M-1314   Smith, Clay   33.80   2,200.00   04-28-56
Suited for crops and pasture

M-1315-E-1-2   Bettis, R. T.   5.81   120.00   08-03-57
Consists of reverting creek bottoms

M-1316   Sparrow, Frances A.   .14
Perpetual flowing easement

M-1317   Pirkle, Thomas P.   53.50   4,720.00   12-28-56
Medium rolling and adapted to general crops, pasture and timber

Fig. A-III-7 M-1317 (Courtesy U.S. Army Corps of Engineers, Mobile District, Official U.S. Army Photograph)

Fig. A-III-8 M-1317 (Courtesy U.S. Army Corps of Engineers, Mobile District, Official U.S. Army Photograph)

M-1317-E-1-2-3   Pirkle, Thomas P.   3.07   30.00   12-28-56
Adapted to general and truck crops, pasture and timber

M-1320   King, James P.   .10   06-30-56
Perpetual flowing easement

M-1321   Whitmire, J. T.   1.90   175.00   05-08-56
Level to medium rolling and adapted to pasture and timber

M-1321-E   Whitmire, J. T.   .23   10.00   05-08-56
Medium rolling and adapted to present use

M-1322   Barker, Mrs. J. R.   79.90   15,650.00   05-23-56
Highest and best use is agricultural

M-1322-E-1-2   Barker, Mrs. J. R.   2.97   1,300.00   05-23-56
Highest and best use is agricultural

M-1323-1-2	Elliott, Ruby Hughes	19.68	5,200.00	12-28-56
Best suited for agricultural use				
M-1323-E	Elliott, Ruby Hughes	2.60	50.00	12-28-56
Best suited for agricultural use				
M-1324	Owen, J. C.	35.82	2,175.00	07-23-56
Agricultural and forestry				
M-1325	Bryson, Howard Luther	9.56	900.00	07-23-56
Best suited for agricultural purposes				
M-1325-E	Bryson, Howard Luther	1.00	30.00	07-23-56
Best suited for agricultural purposes				
M-1326	Jenkins, Roy E.	12.40	6,000.00	12-28-56
Medium rolling				
M-1327-1-2	Bennett, Lannie; Gladys	15.60	1,075.00	12-28-56
Best suited for agricultural purposes				
M-1328	Townley, H. C.	19.74	6,690.00	09-06-56
Grazing, building purposes and good grazing land				
M-1329-1-2	Owens, Alma	2.08	200.00	06-30-56
The best use of the tract is believed to be agriculture				
M-1329-E-1-2	Owens, Alma	1.45	325.00	06-30-56
Best use is pastureland				
M-1331-E	Spier, Wesley	.20		06-30-56
Perpetual flowing easement				
M-1332-E	Pair, J. Ronald	.15		06-30-56
Perpetual flowing easement				
M-1333-E	Bagheri, M.T.	.13		06-30-56
Perpetual flowing easement				
M-1334-E	Hendrix, Harold M.	.02		06-30-56
Perpetual flowing easement				
M-1335-1-2	Barker, Floyd	26.16	4,850.00	12-28-56
Pine woodland				
M-1335-E	Barker, Floyd	.46	10.00	12-28-56
Well suited for agricultural purposes				
M-1336	Wallace, Hazel E.	40.00	3,740.00	06-30-56
Best suited for agricultural uses				
M-1337-1-2	Robertson, Wilbert	56.43	7,400.00	07-23-56
Best suited for agricultural purposes				

M-1337-E-1-2   Robertson, Wilbert   3.71   100.00   07-23-56
Cropland

M-1338   Duncan, Lee   61.00   3,150.00   07-23-56
Agriculture and forestry

M-1339   Duncan, Thomas P.   61.00   7,100.00   07-23-56
Chicken raising, subsistence farming, timber sales and homesite

M-1340   Smith, Rufus G.   69.50   7,500.00   07-02-56
Suited for cultivation or pasture

Fig. A-III-9 M-1340 (Courtesy U.S. Army Corps of Engineers, Mobile District, Official U.S. Army Photograph)

Fig. A-III-10 M-1340 (Courtesy U.S. Army Corps of Engineers, Mobile District, Official U.S. Army Photograph)

M-1344   Godfrey, A. J.   37.00   2,200.00   04-20-56
Medium rolling land and best suited for agriculture and forestry

M-1345   Tatum, Elizabeth   66.80   3,850.00   05-11-56
Level to medium rolling and adapted to crops, pasture and timber

M-1346   Duncan, Robert L.   16.70   2,015.00   04-28-56
Medium rolling and best use of the property is agricultural and forestry

M-1346-E   Duncan, Robert L.   .46   10.00   04-28-56
Medium rolling land best suited for agriculture and forestry

M-1348   Nix, Pearl Grace   3.47   225.00   06-01-56
Woodland

M-1349   Bruce, Ralph   62.60   4,600.00   07-23-56
General farming

M-1349-E-1-2   Bruce, Ralph   2.37   120.00   07-23-56
General crops

M-1350   Duncan, Wilma   19.75   1,175.00   05-31-56
Pasture, woodland and homesite

M-1351   Reeves, Mrs. Eugene   14.16   675.00   12-07-56
Agricultural and forestry

M-1351-E   Reeves, Mrs. Eugene   .84   10.00   12-07-56
Agricultural and forestry purposes

Appendix III - Land Acquisitions Information

M-1352-1-2 McClure, J. C. 48.79 2,500.00 08-31-56
Medium to steeply rolling land with some flat land along the tract

M-1352-E McClure, J. C. .30 10.00 08-31-56
Best use is forestry

M-1356 Duncan, Emma E. 78.50 1,400.00 04-13-56
Adapted to general crops

Fig. A-III-11 M-1356 (Courtesy U.S. Army Corps of Engineers, Mobile District, Official U.S. Army Photograph)

Fig. A-III-12 M-1356 (Courtesy U.S. Army Corps of Engineers, Mobile District, Official U.S. Army Photograph)

M-1357-1-2-3 Wehunt, Butha 27.55 3,700.00 06-05-56
Cultivable and woodland

M-1358 McKinney, Leila 33.00 1,400.00 06-01-56
Level to medium rolling and adapted to timber production

M-1359 Duncan, T. P. 30.54 1,400.00 04-05-56
Adapted to pasture and timber

M-1359-E Duncan, T. P. .20 10.00 04-05-56
Pine woodland

M-1360-1-2 Georgia Power Company 159.76 6,425.00 04-05-56
Adapted to general crops

M-1361 Nix, Pearl Grace 68.00 4,150.00 07-23-56
Cropland, woodland and idle and reverting upland cropland

M-1362-1-2 Duncan, Silvie 52.36 2,650.00 07-23-56
Woodland

M-1362-E Duncan, Silvie .38 10.00 07-23-56
Adapted to cropland

M-1363 Duncan, Elizabeth 15.00 5,150.00 04-20-56
Level to medium rolling and adapted to present use

M-1364 Tatum, Elizabeth 129.00 5,700.00 02-20-56
Topography is level to steeply rolling and best adapted to timber production

M-1365 Garrett, Hiram R. 121.00 7,300.00 12-29-55
Adapted to general crops, pasture and woodland

M-1366 Pethel Jr., D. T. 8.00 9,150.00 08-31-56
Gently to steeply rolling and adapted to timber and country homesite

M-1379-E Arthur Pugh Const. Co. Inc. .17
Perpetual flowing easement

Q-1703 Moss, Emmett D.

Q-1704 Grant, V. M. 55.50 5,750.00 03-27-57
Best use is for homesite and timber growing

Fig. A-III-13 Q-1704 (Courtesy U.S. Army Corps of Engineers, Mobile District, Official U.S. Army Photograph)

Fig. A-III-14 Q-1704 (Courtesy U.S. Army Corps of Engineers, Mobile District, Official U.S. Army Photograph)

Q-1705 Wehunt, Butha Sosebee 23.70 3,375.00 12-31-56
Pasture and timber

Q-1705-E Wehunt, Butha Sosebee 1.38 20.00 12-31-56
Improved pasture

Q-1708-E Hughes, J. C. 3.52 540.00 10-26-56
Upland improved pasture

Q-1709-E Couch, Glen 4.38 500.00 03-16-56
Fescue, clover and lespedeza land

Q-1710-E Whelchel, Rilla 3.68 265.00 03-16-56
Pine and bushland

Q-1713-E Helton, R. C. .27 10.00 04-21-56
Sparce growth of mixed hardwoods

Q-1714 Richards, Evelyn I. 13.30 750.00 04-11-56
Topography is gently to medium rolling and best adapted to growth of timber

Q-1714-E Richards, Evelyn I. 6.35 250.00 04-11-56
Topography is gently to steeply rolling

Q-1715 Moss, K. C. 31.20 1,600.00 08-02-55
Topography is gently to medium rolling

Appendix III - Land Acquisitions Information

Q-1715-E-1   Moss, K. C.   1.20   90.00   08-02-55
Some open land, a portion with very little growth

Q-1715-E-2-3   Moss, K. C.   1.30   10.00   08-02-55
Adaptable to growth of timber

Q-1716-E   Helton, Mrs. J. W.   2.83   130.00   09-01-55
Woodland

Q-1717-1-2   Moss, Emmett D.   118.72   5,500.00   08-13-56
Topography is gently to steeply rolling

Q-1717-E   Moss, Emmett D.   7.70   235.00   08-13-56
Land best suited to timber growth

Q-1718   Garmon, C. L.   2.00   3,050.00   08-13-56
Soil is Cecil Clay Loam, medium to steeply rolling and adapted as homesite

Fig. A-III-15 Q-1718 (Courtesy U.S. Army Corps of Engineers, Mobile District, Official U.S. Army Photograph)

Fig. A-III-16 Q-1718 (Courtesy U.S. Army Corps of Engineers, Mobile District, Official U.S. Army Photograph)

Q-1719   Noblin, Edna A.   27.50   1,400.00   08-02-55
Woodland

Q-1719-E   Noblin, Edna A.   2.99   180.00   08-02-55
Topography ranges from 1st bottom to steeply rolling woodland

Q-1729-1-2-3-4   Noblin, Edna A.   15.15   1,050.00   09-24-56
Highest and best use is for timber raising

Q-1729-E   Noblin, Edna A.   .46   10.00   09-24-56
Highest and best use is timber raising

Q-1730   Grant, V. M.   9.18   400.00   12-31-56
Timber growing

Q-1731   Liveright, Addie E.   190.00   8,900.00   09-24-56
Gently to steeply rolling land with 60 acres of bottom land which is growing up with brush

Q-1733   Evans, F. W.   40.90   4,400.00   07-06-56
Gently to medium rolling best suited for crops and pasture

Q-1734   Reeves, Laura Belle   34.80   3,685.00   06-22-56
Level to medium rolling and are adapted to truck and general crops

Tract	Property Owner	Acres	Price	Date
Q-1735	Sosebee, Minnie	36.70	2,500.00	09-18-56
Gently to steeply rolling land				
Q-1736	Reeves, Albert	6.12	600.00	12-14-56
Agriculture and forestry				

Forsyth County

Tract	Property Owner	Acres	Price	Date
A-100	Scales, E.W.; Mrs. E.W.	184.68	11,500.00	09-20-54
Undulating to steeply rolling				

Fig. A-III-17 A-100 (Courtesy U.S. Army Corps of Engineers, Mobile District, Official U.S. Army Photograph)

Fig. A-III-18 A-100 (Courtesy U.S. Army Corps of Engineers, Mobile District, Official U.S. Army Photograph)

Tract	Property Owner	Acres	Price	Date
A-101	Hamner Lumber Co.	72.00	1,450.00	09-20-54
Steeply rolling ranging from gently rolling to steeply rolling				
A-102	Mullinax, W.A.	82.77	2,850.00	09-20-54
Best adapted to growing timber				
A-103	Shadburn, H.E.	99.24	4,100.00	04-13-54
Undulating on bottom land to medium rolling on some of the cultivable land				
A-104	Shadburn, M.E.	120.0	4,200.00	09-20-54
Best adapted to growing timber				
A-105	Fowler, Alam K.	150.30	3,200.00	12-07-54
Best adapted for growing timber				
A-106-1-2-3-4	Otwell, Roy P.	441.00	4,400.00	08-02-55
No description				
A-106-E-1 &E-2	Otwell, Roy P.	.80	10.00	08-02-55
Topography is medium rolling				
A-107	Mashburn Sr., Marcus	395.69	18,850.00	04-18-55
Topography is rolling and rough				
A-107-E	Mashburn Sr., Marcus	2.70	10.00	04-18-55
Topography is rolling and rough				

Appendix III - Land Acquisitions Information

A-108   Nuckolls, T.L.   13.09   300.00   04-04-55
Best use is timber growing

A-110   Unamed Cemetery   .25   10.00   01-17-56
Best adapted for burial site

A-111   Shadburn Cemetery   .23
Best use for burial site (lone burial site of William Shadburn)

A-112   Hendrick Cemetery   .25   1.00   01-17-56
Cemetery

A-114-1-2   Williams, H.A.   6.80
No description

A-115-1-2   Mashburn, Dr. Marcus   462.00   34,515.00   12-01-55
Adaptable to growing of timber and partically for grazing

A-115-E-1,2,3   Mashburn, Dr. Marcus   8.57   50.00   12-01-55
Best use is grazing, pasturing, and growing timber

A-120   Day, Thurston   15.00   850.00   05-27-55
Topography is gently to medium rolling

A-121-1 & 2   Pruitt, G.L.   31.61   1,875.00   07-26-55
Some woodland, small scale with row and cultivated land

A-122   Phillips, Harry R.   56.00   3,475.00   09-13-55
Suitable for pasture and grazing project and growing timber

A-125   Williams, Arnold   58.30   3,500.00   04-28-55
Best use for reforestation

A-126   Williams, Mercer   54.85   6,825.00   04-28-55
Best suited to timber or grazing area

Fig. A-III-19 A-126 (Courtesy U.S. Army Corps of Engineers, Mobile District, Official U.S. Army Photograph)

Fig. A-III-20 A-126 (Courtesy U.S. Army Corps of Engineers, Mobile District, Official U.S. Army Photograph)

A-127   Kemp Cemetery   .02
Best use for burial site

A-130   Williams, Richard R.   1.00   500.00   02-10-55
Gently rolling

Tract	Owner	Acres	Amount	Date
A-131	Williams, Arnold	102.00	7,925.00	12-23-54
Gently rolling to steeply rolling				
A-132	Williams, Ralph I.	3.00	950.00	11-29-54
Gently rolling				
A-133	Williams, H.C.	60.00	5,875.00	12-23-54
Mostly used for grazing				
A-134	Babb Jr., G.B.	110.00	5,700.00	08-02-55
It is suitable for timber growing				
A-135	Pirkle, Willie J.	134.40	8,050.00	05-27-55
Topography is from bottom lands to mountainous, open lands are mostly classed as bottom to gently rolling				
A-136	Shadburn, J.E.	40.00	800.00	08-02-55
Woodland				
A-137	Holtzclaw, J.G.	48.40	1,700.00	06-03-55
Topography is medium rolling to steeply rolling				
A-138	Holtzclaw, J.G.	29.30	2,100.00	04-16-56
Row crops, small grain, and timberland				
A-138-E	Holtzclaw, J.G.	1.38	10.00	04-16-56
Woodland pasture				
A-139	Smith, Annie	8.04	200.00	05-05-55
Gently to medium rolling				
A-139-E-1 & E-2	Smith, Annie	.86	10.00	05-05-55
Gently to medium rolling				
A-141	McGee, James H.	53.50	1,985.00	09-06-55
Gently to medium rolling				
A-142	Smith, Jason	10.56	315.00	06-16-55
Gently to medium rolling				
A-142-E	Smith, Jason	.44	10.00	06-16-55
Gently to medium rolling				
A-143	Barrett, Eula Mae	16.00	1,900.00	09-30-55
Suitable for small farm unit and timber growing				
A-144	Otwell, Roy P.	56.60	18,500.00	08-02-55
Bottom land level to undulating, idle land medium rolling with woodland to steeply rolling rough				

Appendix III - Land Acquisitions Information

A-145   Smith, Eli   120.00   6,000.00   03-18-55
Gently rolling to medium rolling with portion of woodland steeply rolling

Fig. A-III-21 A-145 (Courtesy U.S. Army Corps of Engineers, Mobile District, Official U.S. Army Photograph)

Fig. A-III-22 A-145 (Courtesy U.S. Army Corps of Engineers, Mobile District, Official U.S. Army Photograph)

A-146   Shadburn, J.E.   175.70   6,100.00   08-02-55
Topography is undualating to level for bottom land, open land and idle land medium rolling and gently rolling and woodland gently rolling to steeply rolling

A-147-1-2-3   Merritt, George L.   267.08   9,250.00   12-31-55
                                 (deceased)
Best use for growing timber

A-148   Old Beaver Ruin Cemetery   1.00   50.00   01-17-56
Best adapted to cemetery site

A-150   Samples, George L.   78.20   2,500.00   06-11-56
The topography of this tract is gently rolling and best use is timber growing

A-150-E   Samples, George L.   1.70   10.00   06-11-56
Topography is gently rolling

A-151   Merritt, James F.   4.82   140.00   11-18-55
Best suitable for timber growing

A-152-1-2   Otwell, Roy P.   114.00   3,400.00   08-02-55
The best use of this tract is timber growing

A-152-E-1,2,3   Otwell, Roy P.   2.37   15.00   08-02-55
Highest and best use is growing timber

A-153   Davis, T.J.   42.70   1,550.00   09-23-55
Suitable for timber growing

A-154-1-2-3-4-5   Bragg, Jewell   25.02   1,400.00   07-21-55
Gently rolling, medium rolling to steeply rolling

A-154-E   Bragg, Jewell   .10   10.00   07-21-55
Used for timber growing

A-155-1 & 2   Kocurek, Ernest   31.45   1,200.00   08-02-55
Best use is timber growing

A-156   Ellis, L.J.   18.02   650.00   08-02-55
Best use is for timber growing

A-156-E-1 & E-2   Ellis, L.J.   1.38   10.00   08-02-55
Best use is timber growing

A-157   Tate, Guy   51.06   3,700.00   09-06-55
Suitable for a general cotton and poultry unit

A-157-E   Tate, Guy   2.53   25.00   09-06-55
Open field for row crops

A-160-1-2   Henderson, T.W.   8.84   450.00   06-17-55
Best use subsistence farming where there is a supplemental income

Fig. A-III-23 A-160-1-2 (Courtesy U.S. Army Corps of Engineers, Mobile District, Official U.S. Army Photograph)

Fig. A-III-24 A-160-1-2 (Courtesy U.S. Army Corps of Engineers, Mobile District, Official U.S. Army Photograph)

A-160-E-1 & E-2   Henderson, T.W.   2.69   15.00   06-17-55
Gently to medium rolling

A-161-E-1 & E-2   Henderson, Cleburne   .51   10.00   08-11-55
Best use is timber growing

A-162   Henderson, A.B.   25.60   1,550.00   08-02-55
Parcel 1 crops and pasture, parcel 2 & 3 forestry

A-163   Hammond, Daniel C.   4.91   125.00   05-21-55
Medium rolling to gently rolling

A-164   Hammond, L.O.   31.90   1,450.00   05-21-55
Gently rolling to medium rolling

A-166-E   Davis, C.E.   9.87   75.00   11-25-55
Six acres suitable for cultivation, balance for woodland

A-167-E   Holtsclaw, J.J.   6.20   50.00   08-02-55
Woodland

A-168   Davis, T.J.   26.40   1,168.00   12-22-55
Open land upland with balance is woodland

A-168-E   Davis, T.J.   1.10   10.00   12-22-55
Timber growing

A-170-E   Tiner, Ralph   .76   10.00   03-09-56
Idle land suitable for cultivation

Appendix III - Land Acquisitions Information

A-171 Burruss, George E. 25.93 1,000.00 06-29-55
The topography is level to undulating and gently rolling to medium rolling

A-173 Tiner, George F. 25.80 2,450.00 09-06-55
General farming

A-173-E Tiner, George F. .92 10.00 09-06-55
Woodland

A-174 Stanford, Lewis C. 18.18 725.00 08-26-55
The topography is level for bottom and gently rolling to medium rolling for upland

A-174-E-1 & E-2 Stanford, Lewis C. 2.22 10.00 08-26-55
Best use is woodland pasture

A-175 Mashburn, Dr. Marcus 347.00 16,375.00 08-26-55
Part farming row crops and grazing

Fig. A-III-25 A-175 (Courtesy U.S. Army Corps of Engineers, Mobile District, Official U.S. Army Photograph)

Fig. A-III-26 A-175 (Courtesy U.S. Army Corps of Engineers, Mobile District, Official U.S. Army Photograph)

A-176 Shadburn, M.E. 64.40 4,425.00 12-22-54
Adapted to row farming

A-177-1 & 2 Holland, Montie Thompson 92.72 16,800.00 11-18-55
Best use for pasturing and raising stock

A-177-E-1 & E-2 Holland, Montie Thompson 11.25 175.00 11-18-55
Best adapted to grasses and grazing

A-178-1 & 2 Holland, Howard M. 59.87 6,300.00 09-16-55
Best use is for pasturing

A-178-E Holland, Howard M. 1.45 25.00 09-16-55
Pasture grazing and grasses

A-181 Henderson, Gladstone 32.00 7,075.00 06-24-55
General farm and poultry unit

A-181-E Henderson, Gladstone 2.68 75.00 06-24-55
Topography is gently rolling

A-182 Payne, Berlin D. 24.80 2,840.00 08-12-55
Small farm and home unit

A-183	Heard, Hoyt	63.50	5,000.00	06-24-55

Undulating for bottom lands and second bottoms with upland gently rolling to medium rolling

A-183-E	Heard, Hoyt	1.07	10.00	06-24-55

Present use is woodland and pasture

A-184	Heard, Clarence	11.94	500.00	07-21-55

Used for timber growing

A-185-1-2	Smith, Bill	12.40	450.00	07-21-55

Tract has been row croped with poultry and small grain with timber growing

A-186-E	Heard, Nettie	1.38	10.00	08-02-55

Timber growing

A-187	Otwell, Edwin	11.25	935.00	06-30-55

Best use is farmland and forest

A-188-1 & 2	Robbs Jr., J.L.	12.30	1,225.00	08-25-55

Best use is as an adjunct to a small general and dairy farm and poultry unit

A-188-E	Robbs Jr., J.L.	1.60	10.00	08-25-55

Pine reproduction

A-190-1-2-3-4-5	Mashburn Jr., Marcus; James	1.88		

No description

A-192	Davies, M.C.	101.00	4,700.00	06-03-55

Woodland

A-193	Mashburn Sr., Marcus	56.10	3,500.00	09-06-55

Best use is part farming and grazing

Fig. A-III-27 A-193 (Courtesy U.S. Army Corps of Engineers, Mobile District, Official U.S. Army Photograph)

Fig. A-III-28 A-193 (Courtesy U.S. Army Corps of Engineers, Mobile District, Official U.S. Army Photograph)

A-194-1-2	Burruss, Ralph W.	26.20	1,650.00	09-01-55

Woodland areas and the upland cropland

A-195	Turner, W.M.	16.45	1,200.00	08-02-55

Farmland

A-195-E   Turner, W.M.   1.15   10.00   08-02-55
Farmland, woodland

A-196   Reinero, Clara Allen   7.30   640.00   08-02-55
Best use is timber growing

A-196-E   Reinero, Clara Allen   1.35   10.00   08-02-55
Best use is timber growing

A-197   Youngblood, Herschell   2.75   160.00   05-28-55
Best use is as a woodland adjunct to a good farm and poultry unit

A-197-E   Youngblood, Herschell   2.76   25.00   05-28-55
Best use is as a woodland adjunct to a good farm and poultry unit

C-301-E   Good, Jack   .02
No description

C-302   Phillips Cemetery   .25   20.00   01-17-56
Best adapted to cemetery site

C-303   Woodcliff, T.J.   2.50   100.00   10-01-54
Best adapted to tree growth

C-304   Hamner, J.C.   316.00   8,000.00   09-20-54
Best adapted to growing timber

C-305   Allen Inc., Bona   1102.00   35,000.00   06-27-55
The highest and best use of this tract is for timber growing and pastureland

Fig. A-III-29 C-305 (Courtesy U.S. Army Corps of Engineers, Mobile District, Official U.S. Army Photograph)

Fig. A-III-30 C-305 (Courtesy U.S. Army Corps of Engineers, Mobile District, Official U.S. Army Photograph)

C-306   Woodliff, T.J.   116.75   2,300.00   10-01-54
Adapted only to growing timber

C-307   Fraser, J.C.   117.00   3,000.00   07-12-54
Undulating to steeply rolling from gently to medium rolling

C-308   Hamner Lumber Co.   180.00   5,650.00   09-20-54
Best suited to growing timber

C-309   Brogdon, Frank   238.00   5,000.00   09-20-54
Best adapted to growing timber

Tract	Owner	Acres	Amount	Date
C-311-E	Mullins, J.R.; Bussey, Virginia	.03		
No description				
C-316	Nuckolls, Nila	96.00	2,300.00	06-30-54
Steeply rolling				
C-317	Orr, H.W.	91.10	3,000.00	06-05-54
Medium rolling to steeply rolling				
C-318	Light, Frances J.	82.00	3,160.00	05-17-54
Undulating to steeply rolling				
C-319	Light, Frances J.	120.00	3,150.00	05-17-54
Gently rolling to medium steeply rolling				
C-321	Orr, Maude S.	40.00	1,000.00	12-17-55
Adapted to growing timber				
C-322	Otwell, Roy P.	80.70	2,600.00	12-07-54
Undulating to gently rolling to steeply rolling				
C-325	Nuckolls, E.D.	94.90	2,000.00	12-22-54
Best adapted to growing timber				
C-326	Hamner, J.C.	325.00	12,500.00	09-20-54
Best suited to timber and growing timber				
C-327	Allen Jr., Bona	80.00	1,700.00	06-13-55
Suitable for timber growing				
C-328	Driskell, G.D.	60.00	1,100.00	08-02-55
Best adapted to growing timber				
C-329	Bragg, G.W.	41.00	5,385.00	11-30-54
Best suited for broiler production				
C-330	Sams Jr., Hansford	3.44	225.00	03-02-56
Reverting cropland and woodland				
C-331	Driskell, G.D.	6.00	635.00	08-02-55
Highest and best use is for growing timber				
C-333-1-2-3	Treadway Jr., T. Foley	25.31	1,300.00	10-03-55
Highest and best use is believed to be agricultural and forestry				
C-334	Williams, John R.	55.30	2,120.00	08-02-55
Rolling				
C-335	Vance, W.A.	45.10	2,800.00	06-16-55
About 30 acres are open and the other rather steeply rolling medium land				
C-335-E	Vance, W.A.	.08	10.00	06-16-55
Best use is forestry				

C-336 Best suited for timber	Heard, Annie Odell	8.26	310.00	12-03-55
C-336 E-1 & E-2 Best use forestry	Heard, Annie Odell	.38	10.00	12-03-55
C-337 Reverting cropland, some woodland	Heard, Hoyt	33.90	1,000.00	08-03-55
C-338 Adapted only to growing timber	Hamner, W.B.	40.00	1,000.00	06-13-55
C-340 Best use chicken raising with row cropping	Morgan, Jessie	40.00	4,003.00	12-28-55

Fig. A-III-31 C-340 (Courtesy U.S. Army Corps of Engineers, Mobile District, Official U.S. Army Photograph)

Fig. A-III-32 C-340 (Courtesy U.S. Army Corps of Engineers, Mobile District, Official U.S. Army Photograph)

C-344-1-2 Gently to medium rolling	Cagle, N.R.	22.09	1,325.00	07-21-55
C-345 Neighborhood is fairly well settled by small tract owners	Morgan, Leon B.	120.00	10,720.00	07-29-55
C-346 HIghest and best use is farmland and woodland	Robbs Jr., J.L.	7.95	450.00	10-31-55
C-347 Best use would be row crops and grazing	Henderson Jr., A.B.	86.00	7,334.00	06-17-55
C-348 Wooded	Driskell, J.B.	48.64	4,100.00	08-02-55
C-349-E Best use is growing timber	Heard, Luther	.53	10.00	07-25-55
C-350 Medium to steeply rolling woodland	Driskell, John C.	12.74	765.00	08-02-55
C-350-E Perpetual flowing easement	Driskell, John C.	.68		08-02-55
C-353 The topography is medium to steeply rolling	Chadwick, Pauline	10.28	690.00	06-16-55

C-354	Manston, C.A.	31.10	1,160.00	08-22-55
Open cropland, woodland and small forest product				
C-355	Otwell, Edwin	6.54	275.00	09-29-55
Highest and best use is for the production of wood and timber				
C-356	Sams Jr., Hansford	18.75	1,800.00	10-06-55
Small farm unit				
C-356-E	Sams Jr., Hansford	.15	10.00	10-06-55
Mixed woodland				
C-357	Youngblood, Herbert; Phillips, R.H.	38.25	5,850.00	03-07-55
Best use of combination row crops, pasture and chicken raising unit				
C-358	Collins, Troy E.	86.80	4,800.00	08-15-55
Good cropland				
C-359	Mangum, Walter	120.00	3,500.00	12-21-54
Best adapted to tree growth				
C-360	Mangum, S.A.	6.00	4,700.00	12-07-54
Principally for mill and water holdings are for operation of water mill				

Fig. A-III-33 C-360 (Courtesy U.S. Army Corps of Engineers, Mobile District, Official U.S. Army Photograph)

Fig. A-III-34 C-360 (Courtesy U.S. Army Corps of Engineers, Mobile District, Official U.S. Army Photograph)

C-361	Mangum, S.A.	55.00	3,500.00	12-07-54
Steeply rolling				
C-362	Strayhorn, J.L.	21.60	850.00	06-16-56
The highest and best use for this tract is forestry				
C-362-E	Strayhorn, J.L.	.46	10.00	06-16-56
Area is a branch bottom used as woodland pastures				
C-363	Orr, C.F.	14.92	802.00	06-27-55
Woodland pasture				
C-363-E	Orr, C.F.	1.61	15.00	06-27-55
Best use for crops, pasture and woodland				
C-364	Ghegan, Drury W.	27.50	1,400.00	07-25-55
The community is only fair and sparsely settled by general and poultry farmers				

Appendix III - Land Acquisitions Information

C-365 Kelley, Mrs. F.W. 63.80 2,525.00 08-09-55
Highest and best use for this tract is a low grade farm and as forestry

C-366-1-2-3 Millwood, Virgil C. 161.18 16,155.00 10-29-55
General farm and poultry unit including cropland and woodland also pasture

C-366-E-1 & E-2 Millwood, Virgil C. 1.89 25.00 10-29-55
Highest and best use is for cropping and woodland

C-367-1-2 Millwood, Virgil C. 139.30 10,692.00 09-15-55
Highest and best use is farming and forestry

C-367-E Millwood, Virgil C. 2.90 40.00 09-15-55
Highest and best use is agricultural

C-368 Millwood, C.E. 100.70 3,250.00 12-08-54
Fair for all type farming

C-369 Turner, W.M. 96.70 12,040.00 08-02-55
Gently to medium rolling

C-370 Floyd, W.L. 73.74 11,747.00 08-19-55
Gently rolling to steeply rolling the rougher lands being in the woodland area

C-372 Millwood, Beulah 1.15 60.00 12-28-56
Highest and best use is for timber growing

C-374 Morgan, W.E. 70.00 4,500.00 08-02-55
Topography is gently to steeply rolling

C-375 Long, Ferrell 4.36 234.00 08-19-55
Woodland

C-375-E Long, Ferrell .70 25.00 08-19-55
Grazing and grasses

C-376 Bowen, Cecil E. 6.34 350.00 10-27-56
Small scale farming and forestry

Fig. A-III-35 C-376 (Courtesy U.S. Army Corps of Engineers, Mobile District, Official U.S. Army Photograph)

Fig. A-III-36 C-376 (Courtesy U.S. Army Corps of Engineers, Mobile District, Official U.S. Army Photograph)

C-376-E Bowen, Cecil E. 2.00 50.00 10-27-56
Small scale farming and forestry

C-377 Mashburn, Maynard 9.75 245.00 06-30-55
The highest and best use is forestry

C-378	Bennett, R.R.; Hubert J.	27.20	950.00	08-24-55
Woodland				
C-379	Cain, S.H.	106.30	7,500.00	08-03-55
Best adapted to growing timber and part time farming				
C-380	Kellogg, W.T.	165.50	15,600.00	10-06-55
Best suited to row farming and raise some boilers				
C-383	Raines, Morris T.	4.90	425.00	08-22-55
Topography is hilly				
C-384	Rieves, A.B.	12.63	410.00	08-02-55
Forestry				
C-385	Floyd, W.L.	4.85	300.00	08-05-55
Highest and best use would be growing timber				
C-386-1-2-3	Fouts, Claud	33.96	4,585.00	07-26-55
Small quantity of merchantable forest product				

Fig. A-III-37 C-386-1-2-3 (Courtesy U.S. Army Corps of Engineers, Mobile District, Official U.S. Army Photograph)

Fig. A-III-38 C-386-1-2-3 (Courtesy U.S. Army Corps of Engineers, Mobile District, Official U.S. Army Photograph)

C-386-E-1, E-2, E-3, E-4	Fouts, Claud	7.00	85.00	07-26-55
Small quantity of merchantable forest product and improved pasture				
C-387-E	Ledford, A.S.	.92	10.00	05-26-56
Forestry				
C-388	Ledford, J.A.	2.00	185.00	08-22-55
Home and or business development				
C-389	Lawson, Clyde W.	85.70	14,950.00	08-02-55
Mediocre farm				
C-389-E-1-2	Lawson, Clyde W.	14.33		08-02-55
No description				
C-390	Shoemake, J.W.	1.20	350.00	07-29-55
Best use for the tract is for home purposes and a small poultry (broiler) unit				
C-391	Woodliff, T.J.	35.60	1,700.00	08-02-55
Best use is forestry				

Appendix III - Land Acquisitions Information

C-391-E-1-2-3   Woodliff, T.J.   12.40   65.00   08-02-55
Reverting cropland and mixed woodland

C-394   Mathis, Mary Jane   34.75   3,277.00   07-22-55
HIghest and best use is as part of a small and well developed livestock farm

C-395   Smith, H.L.   40.00   2,750.00   06-17-55
Highest and best use is small farm and home unit

C-395-E   Smith, H.L.   .70   10.00   06-17-55
Highest and best use is small farm and home unit

C-396   Gee, A.J.   74.00   7,025.00   04-11-55
Best for general farming and production of poultry

C-397   Woodliff, M.B.   29.50   2,650.00   08-02-55
Best for agricultural and forestry

C-397-E-1 & E-2   Woodliff, M.B.   11.25   250.00   08-02-55
Cropland and bushy

E-500   Rieves, A.B.   69.00   3,600.00   11-18-54
Portion of bottom land could be cultivated in crops

E-501   Bagby, F.F.   697.00   33,100.00   08-20-54
Various types of soils

E-502   Rieves, A.B.   261.00   28,500.00   11-18-54
Principal income now appears to be hogs and cattle, supplemented by small sawmill

Fig. A-III-39 E-502 (Courtesy U.S. Army Corps of Engineers, Mobile District, Official U.S. Army Photograph)

Fig. A-III-40 E-502 (Courtesy U.S. Army Corps of Engineers, Mobile District, Official U.S. Army Photograph)

E-503   Castleberry, James T;   48.25   5,825.00   06-29-54
                      Mrs. James T.
Gently rolling

E-504   Liles, J.B.   95.75   4,200.00   06-13-55
Tract is best adapted to subsistence farming and growing timber

E-505   Summerour, H.W.   111.60   14,000.00   11-18-54
Best adapted to general farming and growing chickens

E-506   Boyd, James F.   97.00   13,000.00   09-20-54
Adapted to row cropping

E-507	Fouts, J. Claud	390.60	23,250.00	08-02-54
Best adapted to growing timber and dairy farm				
E-510	Pinson, Wilburn; Floy	111.00	9,720.00	01-26-55
Best suited to growing of grasses and pasturing				
E-511	Allen, Ann Wallis	95.00	4,700.00	12-16-54
Best adapted to raising broilers and subsistence farming				
E-512	Mathis, Dewey	85.58	19,290.00	10-26-54
Land is adaptable to row cropping and also pasturing				
E-512-E	Mathis, Dewey	.34	25.00	10-26-54
Best suited for woodland pasture				
E-513	Waldrip, Ray V.	119.40	7,100.00	12-17-54
Best adapted to growing timber				
E-514	Durand, John W.	109.30	5,200.00	08-02-55
Topography is undulating along streams with uplands of gently to medium rolling				
E-514-E-1-2-3-4-5	Durand, John W.	1.88	10.00	08-02-55
Woodland and timber growing				
E-515-1-2-3-4	Allen, Mrs. L.C.	51.23	2,100.00	08-31-54
Forestry and subsistence farming				
E-515-E-1 & E-2	Allen, Mrs. L.C.	8.57	625.00	08-31-54
Cropland and woodland				
E-516	Boyd, James F.	39.73	1,950.00	08-02-55
Forestry				
E-517	Crow, Nora	4.30	175.00	07-14-54
Gently to steeply rolling				
E-517-E	Crow, Nora	1.33	125.00	07-14-54
Gently to steeply rolling				
E-518	Reynolds, P.B.	3.90	240.00	11-18-55
Steeply rolling woodland				
E-518-E	Reynolds, P.B.	.23	10.00	11-18-55
Wooded				
E-519-1-2	Crow, Guy	9.10	800.00	12-05-55
Best suited for timber growing				
E-519-E	Crow, Guy	1.29	10.00	12-05-55
Suited best for growing timber				
E-520	Cagle, L.H.	32.60	975.00	09-07-55
Medium to steeply rolling woodland				
E-520-E	Cagle, L.H.	.61	10.00	09-07-55
Woodland				

Appendix III - Land Acquisitions Information

E-523-E   Allen, Mrs. Willie   .57   250.00   08-09-56
Adapted to farming

E-524   Mathis, Glenn   10.56   615.00   06-27-55
The land lies gently to medium rolling

E-524-E   Mathis, Glenn   .69   10.00   06-27-55
Best use is growing timber

E-525   Woodliff, T.J.   30.00   2,675.00   10-01-54
Lands reverted to Alder and other bush type growth

Fig. A-III-41 E-525 (Courtesy U.S. Army Corps of Engineers, Mobile District, Official U.S. Army Photograph)

Fig. A-III-42 E-525 (Courtesy U.S. Army Corps of Engineers, Mobile District, Official U.S. Army Photograph)

E-526   Welch, W.F.   11.70   650.00   08-02-54
Best adapted for growing timber

E-527   Hemphill, Minnie C.   11.00   500.00   07-14-54
Best use is for growing timber

E-528   Bennett, Jim   32.64   2,000.00   08-12-54
Best adapted for growing timber

E-528-E   Bennett, Jim   .36   50.00   08-12-54
Best adapted for growing timber

E-529   Bennett, Ralph   2.30   150.00   08-27-54
Best adapted to woodland

E-529-E   Bennett, Ralph   .85   1,550.00   08-27-54
Best adapted to woodland

E-530   Bennett, Addie   12.30   600.00   07-14-54
Bottom land have reverted to timber

Fig. A-III-43 E-530 (Courtesy U.S. Army Corps of Engineers, Mobile District, Official U.S. Army Photograph)

Fig. A-III-44 E-530 (Courtesy U.S. Army Corps of Engineers, Mobile District, Official U.S. Army Photograph)

Tract	Owner	Acres	Amount	Date
E-531	Bennett, Viola	47.39	2,650.00	07-14-54
Greater portion of land idle with some of it reverting				
E-531-E	Bennett, Viola	.31	25.00	07-14-54
Gently rolling				
E-532	Duran, J.H.	19.51	1,300.00	07-21-55
Subsistence farming and timber				
E-532-E	Duran, J.H.	.07	10.00	07-21-55
Adapted to timber production				
E-533	Bennett, Brice	78.00	3,675.00	09-24-55
Best suited for forestry				
E-534-E	Robbs, W.V.	.99	10.00	01-12-57
Pasture				
E-535	Crow, Emory	13.50	900.00	08-16-55
Level to medium rolling				
E-536-E	Rieves, A.B.	.39	10.00	12-28-56
Wooded land best use forestry				
E-537	Waldrip, Clyde	4.82	425.00	09-23-55
Creek bottom, idle cropland and some timber				
E-537-E	Waldrip, Clyde	2.07	20.00	09-23-55
Wooded				
E-538	Bennett, Brice	5.74	335.00	04-26-56
The tract is all woodland with a rather steep slope leading down to a creek				
E-538-E	Bennett, Brice	.92	10.00	04-26-56
Gentle to medium rolling with a small branch running through				
E-539	Porter, F.M.	24.92	820.00	09-07-55
Wooded				
E-541-E	Orr, Clarence	.60	10.00	03-26-57
Timber growing				
E-542	Cain, W.M.	3.67	290.00	08-25-55
Wooded				
E-542-E	Cain, W.M.	.46	10.00	08-25-55
Wooded				
E-543	Bennett, Ralph	35.00	1,900.00	08-31-55
Woodland				
E-544-E	Waldrip, E.C.	2.84		06-14-57
Perpetual flowing easement				

Appendix III - Land Acquisitions Information

Tract	Owner	Acres	Price	Date
E-545	Crow, Bessie B; Mathis, Claudie; Johnson, Cleo; Fannie, Gaines T.; Guy, D.; Waldrip, E.C.	19.52	1,265.00	10-01-55

Mostly timberland

E-545-E-1 & E-2	Crow, Bessie B; Mathis, Claudie; Johnson, Cleo; Fannie, Gaines T.; Guy, D.; Waldrip, E.C.	1.15	10.00	10-01-55

Wooded

E-546	Orr, Kenneth	12.40	1,300.00	12-17-55

Gently to medium rolling, best suited for farm land

E-547	Waldrip, C.F.	20.80	860.00	10-07-55

Suited for timber growing

E-548	Orr, Mrs. L.C.	61.21	5,180.00	09-09-55

Highest and best use is farm unit

Fig. A-III-45 E-548 (Courtesy U.S. Army Corps of Engineers, Mobile District, Official U.S. Army Photograph)

Fig. A-III-46 E-548 (Courtesy U.S. Army Corps of Engineers, Mobile District, Official U.S. Army Photograph)

E-549	Jordan, C.G.	21.80	800.00	08-02-55

Forestry

E-550	Bagby, F.F.	40.00	1,300.00	12-21-54

Reverting to bushes and small tree growth

E-551	Bagby, F.F.	40.00	900.00	05-28-55

Best adapted to timber

E-552	Bagby, F.F.	36.00	950.00	05-05-55

Mostly steeply rolling, best used for grazing

E-553	Thompson, Ralph C.	94.75	11,650.00	10-29-55

Best adapted for small farm unit and growing timber

E-556	Orr, W.F., Mrs.	77.93	3,300.00	12-08-55

Reverting to woodland

E-557	Unknown Cemetery	.25	15.00	01-17-56

Cemetery site

E-558	Duran, G.L.	30.30	4,845.00	08-05-55

Topography is gently to steeply rolling and best use is for farming and chicken raising

E-559   Orr, C.F.   113.00   5,200.00   08-11-55
Best use is timber growing

E-560   Durand, Egbert L.   35.00   2,250.00   11-12-55
Rolling and better suited for grazing

E-561   Manston, C.A.; Townsend   40.00   2,200.00   08-22-55
                W.L.; Hathcock, W.C.;
                Collins, Troy B.
Best suited for growing timber

E-562-1-2   Manston, C.A.; Townsend,   105.82   4,000.00   08-22-55
                W.L.; Hathcock, W.C.;
                Collins, Troy B.
Best used for growing timber

E-563   Light, Francis J.   197.50   14,447.00   08-20-55
Well balanced farm with good improved pasture and open land and timber growing land

Fig. A-III-47 E-563 (Courtesy U.S. Army Corps of Engineers, Mobile District, Official U.S. Army Photograph)

Fig. A-III-48 E-563 (Courtesy U.S. Army Corps of Engineers, Mobile District, Official U.S. Army Photograph)

E-564   Light, Francis J.   68.20   1,611.00   08-20-55
The topography is from gently to steeply rolling and best use is for timber growing

E-565-E-2   Barrett, Mrs. E.M.   1.15   50.00   12-17-57
Used for cultivation and pasture

E-570   Thompson, Annie   93.51   5,400.00   08-02-55
General farming and growing timber

E-570-E   Thompson, Annie   .69   10.00   08-02-55
General farming and growing timber

E-571-E   Bethel Baptist Church   2.53   15.00   12-13-56
Woodland

E-590-1-2-3   Anderson, Charles   1.79
No description

G-701   Smith, E.A.   155.00   17,850.00   07-28-54
Best adaptable to row crops and grazing

G-702   Byers, Aaron L.   47.75   6,595.00   06-26-54
Cultivation of crops or pastures

Appendix III - Land Acquisitions Information

G-703　　　　　　　Hayes, M.R.　　　　　　58.00　　　　7,350.00　　　06-30-54
Best adapted for grazing and raising feed stuff

G-704　　　　　　　Brogdon, Martha　　　　79.00　　　　4,200.00　　　08-02-55
Best use is subsistence farming

G-705　　　　　　　Martin, Mrs. Mignon　　45.20　　　　2,700.00　　　09-15-55
Topography is better than average and soil is Cecil Sandy Clay Loam

G-706　　　　　　　Martin, H.V.　　　　　　39.80　　　　5,450.00　　　08-20-55
General farming and broiler raising

G-707　　　　　　　Egbert, Keith　　　　　　68.60　　　　5,200.00　　　09-02-55
Best use is subsistence farming

G-710　　　　　　　Parks, Hoke　　　　　　28.75　　　　2,300.00　　　09-20-54
Principally for grazing lands

G-711　　　　　　　Parks, Hoke S.　　　　　50.00　　　　6,500.00　　　09-20-54
Bottom lands pasture grazing, upland has some row crops

G-712　　　　　　　Brogdon, E.D.　　　　　34.00　　　　5,075.00　　　09-02-54
Upland is medium to steeply rolling

G-713　　　　　　　Whitlow, Clifford A.　　50.00　　　　5,400.00　　　09-29-54
Bottom lands are cropped, rougher area is fenced for grazing

G-714　　　　　　　Whiltlow, W.S.　　　　　50.00　　　　3,065.00　　　07-30-54
Best adapted for row crops

G-715　　　　　　　Chastain, Mrs. C.A.　　138.00　　　　9,100.00　　　11-23-54
Best adapted to subsistence farming, raising broilers and timber growing

G-716　　　　　　　McNeal, W.W.　　　　　61.00　　　　7,350.00　　　09-27-54
Best adapted to grazing

G-717　　　　　　　Pruitt, Ora　　　　　　　61.00　　　　5,000.00　　　09-20-54
Adapted to both grazing and crops

Fig. A-III-49 G-717 (Courtesy U.S. Army Corps of Engineers, Mobile District, Official U.S. Army Photograph)

Fig. A-III-50 G-717 (Courtesy U.S. Army Corps of Engineers, Mobile District, Official U.S. Army Photograph)

G-720　　　　　　　Hardeman, R.A.　　　　101.00　　　12,500.00　　　09-20-54
Upland is pastured. Portion is rough and mountainous

G-721　　　　　　　Pierce, A.D.　　　　　　90.00　　　　4,595.00　　　05-13-55
Woodland

Tract	Owner	Acres	Amount	Date
G-722	Beyers, X. T.	110.00	12,500.00	08-25-55
Diversified farming operation				
G-725	Bryant, Annie Mae	10.00	1,440.00	05-09-55
Merchantable forest product				
G-726	Smith, W.T.	28.00	4,925.00	08-24-55
Best use is general farming				
G-727	Grier, W.H.	38.00	3,550.00	08-12-55
The topography is mostly medium rolling in the fields to steeply rolling in the woodland				
G-728	Darracott, T.A.	54.00	6,350.00	03-01-55
Well terraced with medium erosion				
G-729	McNeal, Mrs. Willie Bell	8.15	325.00	09-22-55
Best adapted for growing timber				
G-730	Whitlow, W.S.	15.38	925.00	09-30-55
Best adapted to pasture and timber production				
G-734-1-2-3	McConnell, Jonathan E.	26.57	2,175.00	08-30-55
Woodland and woodland pasture				
G-735	Ivey, C.E.	50.10	2,000.00	12-31-55
Adapted to general crops and woodland				
G-736-1-2	Porter, Mrs. S.W.; Starling	24.53	1,570.00	05-12-56
Cropland, pasture and woodland				
G-737	Martin, Clifton; Ida Bell	30.10	1,300.00	06-04-56
Highest and best use is general crops and timber growing				
G-739	Greer, Ernest	21.60	1,525.00	12-17-55
Best suited for row crops, pasture, and timber growing				
G-739-E-1 & E-2	Greer, Ernest	2.57	35.00	12-17-55
Woodland				
G-741	Mitchell, Etta	17.89	1,000.00	08-02-55
Growing timber				
G-741-E	Mitchell, Etta	.45	10.00	08-02-55
Topography is steeply rolling and is adapted to the use of growing timber				
G-744	Martin Jr., H.V.	82.00	4,475.00	11-18-55
Best suited for farming but needs some clearing				

Appendix III - Land Acquisitions Information

G-745   Jones, Thurman V.   113.00   11,725.00   09-22-55
Adapted to general farming, livestock and timber production

Fig. A-III-51 G-745 (Courtesy U.S. Army Corps of Engineers, Mobile District, Official U.S. Army Photograph)

Fig. A-III-52 G-745 (Courtesy U.S. Army Corps of Engineers, Mobile District, Official U.S. Army Photograph)

G-746   Freeland, W.H.   40.80   3,430.00   09-15-55
Adapted for farming and raising of poultry

G-747   Bagwell, C.A.   60.00   4,700.00   09-15-55
Best use is timber growing

G-748   Hinson, Mrs. F.B.   38.50   2,300.00   08-02-55
Timber production

G-749   Morris, Maxie; Fay Mathis   30.30   1,800.00   08-12-55
Gently rolling to medium rolling

G-750   Tatum, E.E.   3.00   200.00   09-30-55
Best suited for forestry and pasture

G-754   Freeland, C.D.   2.98   1,830.00   08-30-55
Open pasture and woodland

G-755   Martin, M. M.   12.40   800.00   08-02-55
General crops, pasture and timber

G-755-E   Martin, M. M.   .13   100.00   08-02-55
Idle cropland and reverting pines

C-757   Pinson, W.A.   5.13   320.00   12-01-55
Best use of this is chicken raising, subsistence farming, and timber production

G-758   Freeman, Nellie   24.80   1,250.00   09-29-55
Best adapted for timber

G-759-E   Harris Estate, J. Homer   5.42   08-02-55
Perpetual flowing easement

G-760   Mooney, J.E.   1.74   100.00   08-23-55
Soil is Gecil Sandy Loam medium rolling and adapted to timber production

G-760-E   Mooney, J.E.   .11   10.00   08-23-55
This is woodland tract consisting of a narrow comparatively level valley along the left bank of a small creek

G-764	Bagwell, Billy	12.63	730.00	09-15-55

HIghest and best use is timber

G-765	Bagwell, C.A.	53.10	2,900.00	12-05-55

Level to steeply rolling and adapted to pasture, crops, and woodland

G-767	Jones, Amanda; Oscar; Herschel; Hubert; Skinner, Grace; Brown, Mertice	70.48	6,150.00	04-16-56

Topography is undulating for bottom land with gently rolling to medium rolling for upland

Fig. A-III-53 G-767 (Courtesy U.S. Army Corps of Engineers, Mobile District, Official U.S. Army Photograph)

Fig. A-III-54 G-767 (Courtesy U.S. Army Corps of Engineers, Mobile District, Official U.S. Army Photograph)

G-768	Bryant, Rufus	1.00	135.00	12-05-55

Woodland

G-769	Carlisle, Grover	49.00	2,690.00	11-18-55

Adapted to general crops, pasture and timber

G-770	Smith, Herschell T.	7.58	260.00	08-31-55

Adapted to timber production and pasture

G-771-1-2-3	Smith, O.J.	8.89	800.00	10-04-55

Woodland

G-773	Jones, Lester C.	1.15	55.00	09-02-55

Woodland and topography is steeply rolling

G-773-E	Jones, Lester C.	.30	10.00	09-02-55

Woodland

G-774-E	Ivey, R.F.	1.15	10.00	08-23-55

Gently rolling

G-775	Ivey, G. E.	28.70	1,160.00	08-09-56

Cropland, timber and pasture

G-776	Barron, H. F.	4.13	250.00	08-26-55

Cropland, pastureland and mixed woodland

G-778-1-2	Barron, Emily	49.40	3,300.00	04-12-56

Woodland

G-778-E-1 & E-2	Barron, Emily	1.19	10.00	04-12-56

Woodland

Appendix III - Land Acquisitions Information

G-779-1-2   Barron, L. T.   15.16   1,225.00   05-04-56
Cropland and woodland

G-780   Henderson, Mary V.   64.50   3,030.00   04-26-56
Best adapted to pasture and timber production

G-781   Woolfolk, W. W.   44.60   2,550.00   05-26-56
General crops and/or pasture and timber production

G-783-E   Meredith, Malcolm J.   .02
Perpetual flowing easement

J-1023   Unknown Cemetery   .25
No description

J-1081   Conner, H. E.   .67   4,525.00   12-23-54
Adapted to use of homesite

Fig. A-III-55 J-1081 (Courtesy U.S. Army Corps of Engineers, Mobile District, Official U.S. Army Photograph)

Fig. A-III-56 J-1081 (Courtesy U.S. Army Corps of Engineers, Mobile District, Official U.S. Army Photograph)

L-1201   Pierce, A. D.   261.00   10,750.00   10-12-55
Best use for growing timber and cultivation of corn and grain

L-1201-E-1   Pierce, A. D.   16.30   700.00   10-12-55
Wooded

L-1201-E-2-3-4-5-6 Pierce, A. D.   3.00   25.00   10-12-55
Wooded

L-1202-1-2-3   Woolfolk, W. W.   13.14   425.00   10-12-55
Best use is growing timber

L-1202-E   Woolfolk, W. W.   5.00   100.00   10-12-55
Steeply rolling

L-1203-E   Martin, W. E.   2.90   72.00   10-10-55
Best suited to woodland

L-1204 E   Westbrook, M. H.;   1.54   138.00   04-17-56
                   Presnell, Alma
Topography is gently rolling

L-1205-E   Westbrook, Hubert M.   5.55   470.00   05-19-55
Topography is gently to medium rolling

L-1206-E-1-2	Westbrook, W. P.	.21	36.00	05-20-55

Tract L-1206-E-1 all woodland, L-1206-E-2, is cultivable land

L-1207-E Orr, Clarence E. 4.18 520.00 05-05-55
Utilized for grain interplanting and cutting of hay crops

L-1208-E Smith, Jamie 1.00 200.00 05-05-55
Gently rolling

L-1209 Pittard, Francis W.; Joel C.
No description

L-1211-E Smith, Tate 1.67 825.00 05-05-55
Gently to steeply rolling

L-1212-E Martin, B. E. 1.48 85.00 06-24-55
Woodland

L-1213-E Burtz, W. N. 2.40 135.00 05-06-55
Medium rolling land

L-1214-E Westbrook, Cynthy C. 4.50 1,830.00 06-17-55
Cultivable and open pastureland

L-1216-E Burtz, Flora 3.06 685.00 06-03-55
Best suited for homesite, pasture, garden and growing of timber

L-1217-E Bennett, Estil 3.65 1,000.00 05-27-55
Gently rolling topography

L-1218-E Bennett, Laura 4.70 335.00 05-13-55
Principally open land, small portion being in woodland

L-1221-E-1-2 Burdett, J. C. .59 86.00 08-05-55
Woodland and homesite

L-1222-E Evans, John T. 4.99 1,950.00 06-03-55
Topography is gently to steeply rolling

L-1223-E Day, Alvious 2.34 410.00 05-27-55
Topography is gently rolling

Fig. A-III-57 L-1223-E (Courtesy U.S. Army Corps of Engineers, Mobile District, Official U.S. Army Photograph)

Fig. A-III-58 L-1223-E (Courtesy U.S. Army Corps of Engineers, Mobile District, Official U.S. Army Photograph)

Appendix III - Land Acquisitions Information

L-1224-E	Day, A. M.; Cynthia	8.36	435.00	05-13-55

Woodland is rough and steeply rolling, open areas are fair topography

L-1225-E	Evans, John T.	.83	33.00	05-27-55

Woodland

L-1226-E-1	Taylor, J. Henry	14.56	324.00	12-14-56

Mountainous and steeply rolling with a small amount of bottom land

L-1232-E	Wilson, J.C.			12-06-57

Perpetual flowing easement

L-1233	Nix, Arthur E.	5.74	550.00	12-01-55

Highest and best use is forestry

L-1234	Hudgins, Otto	17.40	1,050.00	12-03-55

Woodland

L-1235	Hudgins, Otto	26.90	1,550.00	12-03-55

Woodland

L-1236	Martin, Charlie I.	12.47	1,250.00	12-01-55

Wooded

L-1237-1-2	Anderson, C. C.	13.32	700.00	12-10-55

Best suited for small scale farming and forestry

L-1238	Woolfolk, W. W.	19.30	600.00	05-26-56

Woodland

L-1238-E	Woolfolk, W. W.	.76	10.00	05-26-56

Woodland

L-1239	Day, Winifred	14.92	625.00	12-01-55

Woodland

L-1240	Unknown Grave	.017	10.00	01-17-56

Grave site

L-1241	Pierce, A. D.	11.48	575.00	04-05-56

Adapted to timber production

L-1242-1-2	Coons, Forrest H.; Marie A.	9.86	400.00	12-01-55

Adapted to timber production

L-1243-1-2	Stewart, Leon; C. D.	65.55	4,500.00	04-05-56

The highest and best use is agricultural and forestry

L-1243-E	Stewart, Leon; C. D.	1.45	5,535.00	04-05-56

Medium to steeply rolling land best suited for agricultural purposes

L-1244	McClure, J. A.	268.00	28,500.00	04-07-56

Topography is level to medium rolling

L-1245   Jones, C. E.; Ruby Flossie;   167.00   13,000.00   02-20-56
                 Ora; Edwin L.; Hoyt M.
Level to steeply rolling and adapted to general crops, pasture and timber

Fig. A-III-59 L-1245 (Courtesy U.S. Army Corps of Engineers, Mobile District, Official U.S. Army Photograph)

Fig. A-III-60 L-1245 (Courtesy U.S. Army Corps of Engineers, Mobile District, Official U.S. Army Photograph)

L-1246   Anderson, C. C.   55.00   3,600.00
Well adapted to agricultural purposes

L-1247   Woolfolk, W. W.   21.90   875.00   05-26-56
Cropland and woodland

L-1248   Anderson, C. C.   29.50   1,050.00   04-05-56
Best use is forestry

L-1251   Skinner, L. C.   52.25   4,500.00   12-03-55
A desirable farm unit

L-1252   Jewell, Edith Lilly   90.00   6,600.00   01-05-57
Agricultural purposes

L-1255   Wilson, Odell   1.75   1,725.00   12-12-57
The highest and best use is thought to be for a homesite, front lots and agricultural

L-1256   Woody, Van J.;   1.40   160.00   02-24-56
                 Mrs. Van J.
Gently rolling land most of which is open and used for pasture

L-1259   Anderson, Irma   33.10   3,750.00   04-05-56
Best use is agricultural

Fig. A-III-61 L-1245 (Courtesy U.S. Army Corps of Engineers, Mobile District, Official U.S. Army Photograph)

Fig. A-III-62 L-1245 (Courtesy U.S. Army Corps of Engineers, Mobile District, Official U.S. Army Photograph)

Appendix III - Land Acquisitions Information

Gwinnett County

Tract	Property Owner	Acres	Price	Date
B-214	Smith, Cora	38.00	1,150.00	11-18-54
Suitable for timber growing				
B-216	Robinson, E.E.	8.24		
No description				
B-217	Pugh, Ora L.	1.40	60.00	08-13-56
Best use is timber growing				
B-218	Green, H.G.	97.30	3,000.00	12-09-54
Gently to steeply rolling to mountainous				
B-236	Bagwell, Rosa Lou	25.70	925.00	07-25-55
Timber growing				
B-255	Hamilton, Alma Mae	9.00	900.00	03-24-56
Best use is growing timber				
B-256	Hughes, C.D.	30.80	1,550.00	10-20-55
Highest and best use is timber growing				
B-257	Pugh, Agnes M.	5.40	240.00	06-30-55
Highest and best use is timber growing				
B-258	Bagwell, Rosa Lou; Mrs. Bowman	5.30	250.00	07-25-55
Highest and best use is timber growing				
B-259	Toney, Emma	6.00	225.00	07-25-55
Best use is for timber growing				
B-260-E	Martin, Lee	.20	10.00	04-10-56
Topography is gently rolling and best use is for timber growing				
B-261-E	Pugh, Agnes M.	.46	10.00	09-06-55
Topography is gently rolling and best use is for timber growing				
B-262	Toney, Emma	8.30	935.00	07-25-55
Best use is timber growing				
B-263	Kennedy, Idus; Eloise	7.40	260.00	07-09-55
Topography is gently rolling				

B-264 Crain, Roy M. 15.50 1,000.00
Highest and best use for this tract would be as that of growing timber

Fig. A-III-63 B-264 (Courtesy U.S. Army Corps of Engineers, Mobile District, Official U.S. Army Photograph)

Fig. A-III-64 B-264 (Courtesy U.S. Army Corps of Engineers, Mobile District, Official U.S. Army Photograph)

B-265-1-2 Hughes, Felton C. 37.90 1,600.00 09-19-55
Tract has been used for timber growing

B-266 Bowman, Lucian 1.38 65.00 12-08-55
Being used for timber growing

B-266-E-1 & E-2 Bowman, Lucian .57 10.00 12-08-55
Timber growing

B-267 Hughes, Clifford D. 5.20 375.00 10-20-55
Best and highest use for growing timber

B-268 Hughes, Alton I. 3.70 129.50 09-10-55
Best use is timber growing

B-269 Tuggle, Quillian 8.73 400.00 09-10-55
Timber growing is best use

B-270 Phillips, L.J. 11.98 500.00 04-28-56
The best use is believed to be small scale farming and forestry

B-271 Hamilton, J. Paul; Alma, Mae B 17.00 700.00 03-24-56
Wooded land with very little cleared

B-272 Dolvin, Lane 10.79 400.00 03-24-56
Highest and best use is for growing timber

B-273 Puckett, Crawford 8.50 400.00 03-23-56
Best suited for forestry

B-274-1-2 Pass, Daisey Mae (Bruce B. as guardian) 70.30 3,375.00 04-06-57
Topography is gently rolling to steeply rolling

B-283 Bagby, T.E. 2.75 165.00 03-23-56
Pasture and woodland

B-283-E-1 & E-2 Bagby, T.E. 1.95 10.00 03-23-56
Wooded brushland

Tract	Property Owner	Acres	Price	Date
BL-201 Homesite	Robinson, Ralph	2.58	500.00	08-13-56
BL-202 Homesite	Robinson, Frank	2.40	500.00	08-13-56
BL-203 Homesite	Robinson, Tom Ed	2.18	500.00	08-13-56
W-2301-E Woodland	McDonald, H. S.	4.97	60.00	06-15-57
W-2303-E Used for agricultural purposes	Pugh, W. R.	34.25	700.00	12-19-57
W-2304-E Best adapted to row crops, pasture and growing timber	Pugh, Freda B.	10.00	150.00	12-19-58
W-2306-E Woodland	Grogan, W. D.	15.00	225.00	06-17-57

Hall County

Tract	Property Owner	Acres	Price	Date
B-200 Adapted to growing timber	Georgia Railway and Power Co.	153.00	2,550.00	09-20-54
B-201 Most adaptable to growing timber	Hamner, J.C.	100.00	2,600.00	09-20-54
B-202 Medium to steeply rolling woodland	Nuckolls, T.L.	50.00	1,300.00	05-19-54
B-203 Woodland	Hammer, W.B.	176.75	3,200.00	09-20-54
B-204 Steeply rolling and suitable for growing timber	Compton, H.E.	185.00	4,000.00	09-20-54
B-205 Best adapted to growing timber	Allen Inc., Bona	158.00	4,000.00	06-16-55
B-206 Best adapted to growing timber	Patterson, Zack	132.00	3,600.00	11-18-54
B-207 Undulating to steeply rolling	Johnson Estate, Hershiel	237.85	9,400.00	09-24-54
B-208 Adapted only for timber growing	Hamner, J.C.	99.33	2,400.00	09-20-54
B-209 Undulating to mostly steeply rolling	Hamner, J.C.	119.69	3,650.00	09-20-54

B-210   Rowe, Fred O.   125.00   3,125.00   07-23-56
Topography is roughly to steeply rolling to mountainous

B-211   Brogdon, Frank   176.00   4,500.00   04-12-55
Best adapted to growing timber

B-212   Bartlett, Mildred Irene   353.80   8,000.00   11-18-54
Best adapted to growing timber

B-213   Peppers, Eston   100.00   2,250.00   09-20-54
Most adaptable for timber growing

B-215   Shoal Creek Baptist   4.00   4,000.00   03-24-56
                Church and Cemetery
Church and cemetery site

Fig. A-III-65 B-215 (Courtesy U.S. Army Corps of Engineers, Mobile District, Official U.S. Army Photograph)

Fig. A-III-66 B-215 (Courtesy U.S. Army Corps of Engineers, Mobile District, Official U.S. Army Photograph)

Fig. A-III-67 B-215 (Courtesy U.S. Army Corps of Engineers, Mobile District, Official U.S. Army Photograph)

Fig. A-III-68 B-215 (Courtesy U.S. Army Corps of Engineers, Mobile District, Official U.S. Army Photograph)

B-218   Green, H.G.   97.30   3,000.00   12-09-54
Gently to steeply rolling to mountainous

B-219   Garrett, Leonard   40.00   1,750.00   10-18-54
Best to growing timber and grazing

B-220   Garrett, Mae   85.00   2,350.00   09-20-54
Best adapted to growing timber

B-221   Kingloff, Mildred L.;   132.00   4,450.00   12-16-54
                Crain, Roy M.; Richards,
                Gordon, R.
Steep and rolling for anything except growing timber

APPENDIX III - LAND ACQUISITIONS INFORMATION

B-222   Chambers, Edgar   175.00   5,225.00   05-20-55
Best adapted to growing timber

B-223   Ashcraft, Gus   176.00   4,000.00   06-13-55
Suited mostly for growing timber

B-224   Dollar, Vera M.   98.00   17,000.00   11-18-54
Best adapted to subsistence farming and growing timber

Fig. A-III-69 B-224 (Courtesy U.S. Army Corps of Engineers, Mobile District, Official U.S. Army Photograph)

Fig. A-III-70 B-224 (Courtesy U.S. Army Corps of Engineers, Mobile District, Official U.S. Army Photograph)

B-225   Robinson, E.E   .25   3,000.00   11-18-54
Suited mostly for growing timber

B-226   Spencer Hill Baptist   .92   1.00   01-17-57
                         Church and Cemetery,
                         Trustees
Spencer Hill Cemetery

B-227   Spencer Hill Baptist   .43
                         Church
No description

B-228   Hamner, J.C.   626.07   20,000.00   09-20-54
Most adaptable to timber growing

B-229   Harrington, W.A.   84.85   6,000.00   09-02-55
Best use is growing timber

B-230   Brogdon, Frank   119.60   5,500.00   09-20-54
Reverting to woodland

B-231   Hamner, J.C.   70.00   4,800.00   09-20-54
Best adapted to growing timber

B-232   Crane, B.B.; Griffin, Mood   50.40   1,370.00   12-21-54
Medium rolling for most part and logging is generally satisfactory

B-233   Brown, Alberta   60.00   2,500.00   07-14-56
Highest and best use is forestry, neglected farm unit

B-234   Brogdon, Frank   23.60   965.00   01-20-56
Best use is forestry

B-235	Thornton, J.J.; Brown, Annie T.	194.00	7,400.00	10-28-54

Best adapted for growing timber

B-237	Butler White Cemetery	.02	1.00	01-17-57

Cut over woodland and the topography is undulating

B-238	Mundy Cemetery	.25	1.00	01-17-57

Cut over woodland and the topography is gently rolling

B-239	Thornton Cemetery	.25	1.00	01-17-57

Cut over woodland and the topography is gently rolling

B-240	Unknown and unnamed Cemetery	.13	1.00	01-17-57

Cut over woodland and the topography is gently rolling

B-241	Bryant Cemetery	.06	1.00	01-17-57

Cut over woodland and the topography is gently rolling

B-242	Unknown and unamed Cemetery	.06	1.00	01-17-57

Cut over woodland and the topography is medium rolling

B-243	Unknown and unamed Cemetery	.06	1.00	01-17-57

The topography is undulating

B-244   Johnson, Ella
Kuckolls Cemetery

B-245	Beard Cemetery	.25	1.00	01-17-57

Cut over woodland and the topography is gently rolling

B-246	Unknown and Unamed Cemetery	.23	1.00	01-17-57

Cut over woodland and the topography is gently rolling

B-247	Unknown Cemetery Formerly Wilson Cemetery	.25		

B-248   Thornton, J.J.; Brown Annie T.
Unnamed Cemetery

B-251	Allen, Stanley	39.13	1,800.00	04-10-56

Subject tract is entirely wooded and the best use is forestry

Appendix III - Land Acquisitions Information

B-252   Tuggle, Homer H.   40.27   1,700.00   10-10-55
Highest and best use is forestry

Fig. A-III-71 B-252 (Courtesy U.S. Army Corps of Engineers, Mobile District, Official U.S. Army Photograph)

Fig. A-III-72 B-252 (Courtesy U.S. Army Corps of Engineers, Mobile District, Official U.S. Army Photograph)

B-253   Buice, Kate   145.00   7,500.00   11-15-56
Best suited for timber growing

B-254   Brown, Rosa   69.90   3,700.00   11-19-55
Highest and best use is for timber growing

B-256   Hughes, C.D.   30.80   1,550.00   10-20-55
Highest and best use is timber growing

B-257   Pugh, Agnes M.   5.40   240.00   06-30-55
Highest and best use is timber growing

B-258   Bagwell, Rosa Lou; Mrs. Bowman   5.30   250.00   07-25-55
Highest and best use is timber growing

B-260-1-2   Martin, Lee   46.60   1,925.00   04-10-56
Best use is timber growing

B-274-1-2   Pass, Daisey Mae (Bruce B. as guardian)   70.30   3,375.00   04-06-57
Topography is gently rolling to steeply rolling

B-275   Pass, R.V.; Duncan, R.F.   37.40   2,000.00   05-05-55
Best use is for forestry

B-276   Pass, Bruce B.   79.20   5,475.00   12-17-55
Best suited for agriculture, poultry and timber

Fig. A-III-73 B-276 (Courtesy U.S. Army Corps of Engineers, Mobile District, Official U.S. Army Photograph)

Fig. A-III-74 B-276 (Courtesy U.S. Army Corps of Engineers, Mobile District, Official U.S. Army Photograph)

Tract	Owner	Acres	Amount	Date
B-277	Brown, Jack	1.80	180.00	10-22-55
Highest and best use is for a homesite				
B-278-1-2	Crain, Roy M.	34.90	5,150.00	12-05-55
Best use is agricultural				
B-278-E	Crain, Roy M.	.90	15.00	12-05-55
Upland idle				
B-279	Sears, Berthel P.	4.02	230.00	12-05-55
Best use, timber growing				
B-279-E	Sears, Berthel P.	2.10	262.50	12-05-55
Fishing and picnicing area				
B-280	Patterson, Howard	.87	100.00	11-05-55
Best suited for residential and poultry raising				
B-281	Merritt, J. Ray	4.16	225.00	10-20-55
The area is well settled along the highway but little farming is done				
B-282	Camp, C.C.; Rowe, Winfield	4.96	250.00	10-22-55
Woodland				
B-285	Camp, C.C.	39.20	2,775.00	04-07-56
Best use agricultural				
B-285-E	Camp, C.C.	2.50	25.00	04-07-56
Best use grazing purposes				
B-286	Camp, C.C.	1.10	100.00	11-07-55
Best use is homesite				
B-287	Robinson, E.E.	18.00	1,375.00	
Best use is forestry				
B-288-1-2	Pass, Elizabeth	84.00	4,000.00	12-05-55
General farm unit				
B-289	Whidby, Mrs. Newton	72.90	4,350.00	12-05-55
Best use is agricultural and forestry				
B-289-E	Whidby, Mrs. Newton	.20	10.00	12-05-55
Best use forestry and part time farming				
B-290	Milam, Walter G.	6.00	400.00	12-28-55
Best use of this tract is for a low grade home development site and forestry				
B-291	Rowe, W.	7.30		
No description				
B-292	Brogdon, Frank; Row, W.	14.30	675.00	11-15-55
Best use for low grade home development and forestry				

Appendix III - Land Acquisitions Information

B-293   Erwin, J.B.   12.70   650.00   11-15-55
Best use for home development and forestry

B-295   Robinson, E.E.   16.00   1,000.00   06-13-55
Highest and best use is for the development of a small farm unit

B-296   Cox, Hubert   10.60   600.00   12-28-55
Woodland

B-297-1-2   Brown, J.A.   53.50   3,735.00   09-08-55
Best suited to poultry raising

B-298   Hendrix Cemetery   .25   1.00   01-17-57
Tract is on a small knoll above a branch of Shoal Creek

B-299   Sears, Berthel P.   10.38   1,400.00   07-23-56
Topography is gently rolling to medium rolling

BI-204   Shoal Creek Baptist Church
Formerly Shoal Creek Church Cemetery

D-400-E   Whitaker, Dan S.   .02
Perpetual flowing easement

D-401   Georgia Power Company   438.00   10,300.00   09-20-54
Best adapted to growing timber

D-402   Hamner, J.C.   324.88   14,500.00   09-20-54
Woodland and some acreage pasture land

Fig. A-III-75 D-402 (Courtesy U.S. Army Corps of Engineers, Mobile District, Official U.S. Army Photograph)

Fig. A-III-76 D-402 (Courtesy U.S. Army Corps of Engineers, Mobile District, Official U.S. Army Photograph)

D-403   Estes, R.C.   299.00   18,500.00   09-20-54
Utilized for any general crop

D-404   Meaders, Barney R.   101.00   5,450.00   07-19-54
                   Polly Stargel
Undulating to steeply rolling

D-405   Smith, G.W.   100.00   16,300.00   05-25-54
Undulating to steeply rolling

D-406   Hunt, Lewis K.   93.00   6,150.00   09-28-55
Best use is considered general farming with poultry raising

D-407	Old Chattahoochee Baptist Church Cemetery	1.00	1.00	01-17-57

Cut over woodland and the topography is gently rolling

D-408	Hutchin Burial Site, Barry	1.00	25.00	01-17-56

Best adapted to growing timber

D-409-1-2-3	Hamner, J.C.	612.10	33,000.00	06-13-55

Principally for pasturing

D-410	Hamner, J.C.	56.50	3,250.00	11-18-54

Tract best adapted to growing timber

D-411	Chattahoochee Baptist Church	2.13	9,000.00	06-16-56

The tract is situated on a knoll and is best suited as a church and cemetery site

Fig. A-III-77 D-411 (Courtesy U.S. Army Corps of Engineers, Mobile District, Official U.S. Army Photograph)

Fig. A-III-78 D-411 (Courtesy U.S. Army Corps of Engineers, Mobile District, Official U.S. Army Photograph)

D-412	Old Chattahoochee Baptist Church Cemetery	.62	

Cemetery

D-414-E	Stewart, Peggy M.	.01	

Perpetual flowing easement

D-415	Hamner, A.E.	325.70	15,000.00	11-18-54

Best adapted to subsistence farming and growing timber

D-416	Gaines, I.P.	229.00	18,000.00	06-26-54

Best adapted to growth of timber

D-417	Pugh Burial Site, Martin	1.00	1.00	01-17-57

Cut over woodland area and the topography is gently rolling

D-418	Bagby, W.E.	189.00	17,650.00	06-05-54

Upland gently and medium rolling

D-419	Greer, Pat	48.00	2,100.00	04-27-54

Gently rolling to medium to steeply rollling

D-420	Pugh, W.H.	85.00	5,870.00	06-26-54

Hilly or rough

Appendix III - Land Acquisitions Information

Tract	Owner	Acres	Price	Date
D-421	Fraser, Aurora G.; Virginia, G.; Gaines, Felton	86.00	6,750.00	12-23-54

Best suited for growth of corn, chickens as a main money crop

D-422	Gaines, Ellie	86.00	4,750.00	12-05-55

Highest and best use part time farm and for forestry

D-423	Holman, Lester	58.00	3,900.00	08-03-55

Small general and poultry farm

D-424-1-2	General Capital Corp.	76.00	4,600.00	12-14-55

Best use is agricultural and forestry

D-425-1-2	Beard, Mrs. Parilee	29.60	1,500.00	12-28-55

Best use is home tract and forestry

D-426-E	Johnson, Bernard C.	.04		

Perpetual flowing easement

D-427	Carlisle Cemetery	.25	1.00	05-15-56

Cemetery

D-428	Unknown Cemetery	.002	1.00	01-17-57

Topography is gently rolling

D-429	Unknown and Unnamed Cemetery	.23	1.00	01-17-57

Topography is gently rolling

D-430	Cape, Reba; Grover C.	2.49		

No description

D-431-E	Mann, E.V.	.17		

Perpetual flowing easement

D-432	Clark, A.C.	8.95	425.00	12-31-55

Gently to medium rolling in open lands

D-433-1-2	Stringer, Idell	157.90	7,800.00	10-06-54

Gently to medium to steeply rolling

D-434	Clark, A.C.	100.00	9,075.00	12-23-54

Undulating to gently to medium rolling

Fig. A-III-79 D-434 (Courtesy U.S. Army Corps of Engineers, Mobile District, Official U.S. Army Photograph)

Fig. A-III-80 D-434 (Courtesy U.S. Army Corps of Engineers, Mobile District, Official U.S. Army Photograph)

Tract	Owner	Acres	Amount	Date
D-435	Chambers, Edgar	77.75	4,150.00	09-07-54
Best suited for woodland and is beginning to revert thereto				
D-436	Martin, Mrs. E.G.	30.00	2,800.00	09-16-55
Growing timber and used for hay crops				
D-437	Pruitt, P.W.	85.00	3,750.00	11-15-55
Best adapted to timber growing				
D-438	Puckett, Henry A.	64.20	1,980.00	11-07-55
Best adapted to timber production				
D-438-E	Puckett, Henry A.	.70	10.00	11-07-55
Best adapted to timber production				
D-439	Kimbrell, Agnes	9.40	425.00	09-08-55
Gently to medium rolling				
D-440-1-2	Dorsey, J.D.	4.82	225.00	09-21-55
Suitable for farming				
D-440-E	Dorsey, J.D.	.97	10.00	09-21-55
Gently sloping and adapted to pasture				
D-441-E	Humphrey, J.C.	.06		
Perpetual flowing easement				
D-442-1-2	Whidby, Mrs. H.L.	3.26		
No description				
D-443-E	University Yacht Club Inc.			
Perpetual flowing easement				
D-444	City of Buford	32.00		
No description				
D-446-1-2	Stone, John E.	93.51	4,500.00	12-31-56
Development of lake front property				
D-447-1-2	Holland, A.H.	44.55	2,425.00	04-21-56
Improved pasture, cultivable and woodland				
D-448-1-2	Clark, R.J.	81.50	4,200.00	09-16-55
The highest and best use is row cropping and pasture				

Appendix III - Land Acquisitions Information

D-449   Hughes, Vernon   110.50   13,600.00   11-15-55
Best use is subsistence farming

Fig. A-III-81 D-449 (Courtesy U.S. Army Corps of Engineers, Mobile District, Official U.S. Army Photograph)

Fig. A-III-82 D-449 (Courtesy U.S. Army Corps of Engineers, Mobile District, Official U.S. Army Photograph)

D-450   Cline, Mrs. P.M.   37.70   1,850.00   10-06-55
Highest and best use is growing timber

D-453-E   Cauthon, M.   .08
Perpetual flowing easement

D-454   Whiting, J.G.   1.60   200.00   05-03-57
The topography is medium rolling and highest and best use is forestry

D-455-1-2   Hudgins, Otto   31.53   1,850.00   09-28-55
Best adapted to subsistence farming and growing timber

D-456   Kilgore, T.R.   2.66   225.00   09-06-55
Highest and best use is growing timber

D-457-E   Tanner, M.   .03
Perpetual flowing easement

D-458   Phagan, Evie L.   13.58   850.00   10-21-55
The topography is from undulating in the bottom to medium rolling and the highest and best use is for subsistence farming

D-459-1-2   Humphrey, Minnie Sims;   48.29   2,800.00   02-28-56
                            Paralee, Edwin; Eugene,
                            Henry Ford; Strickland,
                            Winnie Nell; Smith, Ida
                            Doris
The land is medium to steeply rolling and best use being agriculture and forestry

D-460-1thru 8   Estes, Mrs. Artrue H.   38.90   1,650.00   09-06-55
Reproduction of timber

D-463   Nuckolls, A.B.   4.59   260.00   12-07-55
Timber growing or wooded pasturelands

D-463-E   Nuckolls, A.B.   2.0   10.00   12-07-55
Wooded pasture

D-464   Morrow, Jewell T.;   1.81   145.00   11-26-55
                            Flora Carlisle
Woodland

D-464-E-1 & E-2   Morrow, Jewell T.;   2.39   15.00   11-26-55
                   Flora Carlisle
Woodland

D-465   Jones, Clark T.   57.90   17,860.00   11-26-55
Gently to medium rolling land, well adapted as a dairy unit

D-465-E   Jones, Clark T.   8.72   275.00   11-26-55
Gently to medium rolling land well adapted as an open pasture

D-466   Orr, William E.   3.90   7,910.00   10-27-55
Highest and best use would be for homesite and growing timber

D-467   Town of Flowery Branch   68.10   7,500.00   10-27-55
The immediate vicinity is agricultural, but some housing development is taking place nearby

D-468   Martin, Henry Herbert   3.00   900.00   03-24-56
Suited for residential purposes

D-469   Strayhorn, Mrs. M.N.   37.60   21,000.00   12-05-55
Best use forestry

D-469-E-1 & E-2   Strayhorn, Mrs. M.N.   3.45   6,000.00   12-05-55
Best use is residential or business property

D-470   Wayne, Lena M.   7.58   4,625.00   05-31-56
Cropland and wooded land

Fig. A-III-83 D-470 (Courtesy U.S. Army Corps of Engineers, Mobile District, Official U.S. Army Photograph)

Fig. A-III-84 D-470 (Courtesy U.S. Army Corps of Engineers, Mobile District, Official U.S. Army Photograph)

D-470-E   Wayne, Lena M.   2.53   5,000.00   05-31-56
Wooded and cropland

D-471   Wayne, Frances M.   3.58   425.00   03-13-56
Tract is gently to steeply rolling with about 50% cleared

D-472-E   Clark, H.E.   9.30   90.00   07-10-57
The highest and best use is for agricultural purposes

D-473-E   Clark, Don   5.43   12-06-57
Perpetual flowing easement

D-474   Lee, T.J.   5.74   650.00   11-16-55
Steeply rolling land

Appendix III - Land Acquisitions Information

ID	Name	Acres	Price	Date
D-476	Bell, Cecil C.	4.59	600.00	04-06-56
Well adapted to small scale farming				
D-477-1-2	Bell, G.C.	20.88	3,300.00	12-08-55
Agricultural				
D-478	Bailey, G. W.	6.35	1,535.00	09-13-57
Agricultural				
D-478-E	Bailey, G.W.	9.41	2,155.00	09-13-57
Highly improved lands, buildings and land, recreational use				
D-479	Johnson, Herbert M.	9.64	500.00	09-26-55
Open land of good quality which lies medium to gently rolling				
D-479-E	Johnson, Herbert M.	.69	10.00	09-26-55
Highest and best use is growing timber				
D-480	Lake, G.V.	39.00	2,800.00	12-07-55
Agricultural with timber growing				
D-481-E	Black, W.A.	3.82	168.00	06-17-57
Agriculture				
D-483-E	Clark, Carl N.	.45	25.00	07-10-57
The highest and best use is for agricultural purposes				
D-484	Compton, Hubert	81.20	3,000.00	11-15-55
Best suited to growing timber				
D-485-E	Brady, William A.	.01		
Perpetual flowing easement				
D-486	Lee, Booker C.	1.72	150.00	05-05-56
Uncultivated land, adaptable to crops or pasture grasses				
D-486-E	Lee, Booker C.	2.98	40.00	05-05-56
Bottom idle land				
D-487	Sibley, William Hart	25.70	1,350.00	05-04-56
Highest and best use is growing timber				
D-487-E-1 & E-2	Sibley, William Hart	2.85	15.00	05-04-56
Woodland				
D-488-1-2-3	Black, C.M.	37.73	2,200.00	05-23-56
Highest and best use is pasture and woodland				
D-488-E-1 & E-2	Black, C.M.	5.12	15.00	05-23-56
Woodland				

D-489	Snellings, H.F.	40.18	6,000.00	11-15-55

Growing timber and country store site best use

Fig. A-III-85 D-489 (Courtesy U.S. Army Corps of Engineers, Mobile District, Official U.S. Army Photograph)

Fig. A-III-86 D-489 (Courtesy U.S. Army Corps of Engineers, Mobile District, Official U.S. Army Photograph)

D-489-E	Snellings, H.F.	1.61	10.00	11-15-55

Suitable only for woodland

D-490-1-2	Johnson, Fletcher M.	26.65	3,650.00	01-27-56

Wooded and contains a quantity of merchantable forest products

D-490-E-1 & E-2	Johnson, Fletcher M.	9.92	50.00	01-27-56

Mixed woodland

D-492-E	Brown, Hannah B.	.04		

Perpetual flowing easement

D-493-E	Fraser, G.G.	2.76	138.00	08-12-57

Creek bottom land suited to agriculture only

D-494-E	Fraser, J.C.	1.84	10.00	03-16-57

Creek bottoms and pasture

D-495-E	Fraser, T.L.	4.82	212.00	06-08-57

Creek pasture and reverting

D-496	Carter, L.B.	7.40	1,800.00	12-05-55

Pastureland

D-496-E	Carter, L.B.	3.36	100.00	12-05-55

Pastureland

D-498-E	Georgia Shoe Manufacturing Co.	1.00	500.00	12-13-57

Building lot

D-499-E	Parsons Jr., Calvin M.	.72	375.00	08-16-57

Building lot

F-600-E	Smith, Cecil M.	.003		

No description

F-601	Romberg, C.J.	382.00	31,000.00	03-22-55

Pasturing and raising of supporting feed crops

F-602   Pruett, Azalee L.   70.00   5,175.00   12-22-54
Adaptable to row crops and pasturing

F-603   Romberg, C.J.   286.00   9,700.00   08-03-54
Best adapted to growing of timber or woodland

F-604   Propes, W.W.   86.00   6,800.00   08-06-54
Gently to steeply rolling

Fig. A-III-87 F-604 (Courtesy U.S. Army Corps of Engineers, Mobile District, Official U.S. Army Photograph)

Fig. A-III-88 F-604 (Courtesy U.S. Army Corps of Engineers, Mobile District, Official U.S. Army Photograph)

F-605   Couch, C.A.   123.50   7,085.00   09-10-54
Best adapted for cultivation and some grazing land

F-606   Walden, Euzelia   50.00   1,815.00   07-23-54
Poor

F-607   Banks Jr., R.   372.00   24,815.00   12-01-56
Raising chickens and pasture

F-607-E   Banks Jr., R.   49   10.00   12-01-56
Adapted to growing timber

F-608-E   Schultz, A.C.;   .003
              Mannie E.
No description

F-609-1-2-3   DeFoor Properties Inc.   .08
No description

F-610   Hamner, J.C.   101.90   4,500.00   06-13-55
The topography is mostly medium rolling and is mostly suited to growing timber

F-611   Johnson & Johnson Inc.   63.60
No description

F-612   Johnson & Johnson Inc.   1.00
No description

F-613   McConnell, R.G.   197.00   25,825.00   08-04-55
Best suited to growing broilers, subsistence farming and growing timber

F-614   Barrett, R.H.   230.00   13,775.00   08-11-55
Best adapted to growing timber and subsistence farming

Tract	Owner	Acres	Value	Date
F-615 Best adapted to growing timber	Reed, L.O.	89.40	3,250.00	11-18-54
F-616 Best adapted to growing timber	Reed, L.O.	32.00	900.00	11-18-54
F-617 Best use forestry	Hood, W.E.	.76	50.00	11-09-55
F-618 Reverting to woodland	Coley, G.F.; Vernie B.	150.50	5,450.00	11-23-54
F-619 Reverting to woodland	Coley, G.F; Vernie B.	226.40	12,500.00	11-24-54
F-620-1-2 Farm unit	Propes, B.H.	108.38	7,300.00	12-05-55
F-620-E Best use is grazing	Propes, B.H.	.34	10.00	12-05-55
F-621 Suitable for use as forestry only	Abercrombie, Robert M.	44.20	2,000.00	02-01-55
F-622 Best suited for forestry	Pethel, Lessie Crain	2.07	100.00	10-12-55
F-623 Best adapted to growing timber	Whitmire, Ralph	144.60	5,000.00	09-30-54
F-624 Best adapted to growing timber	Elliott, Rufus	1.40	100.00	12-21-54
F-624-E Best adapted to growing timber	Elliott, Rufus	.97	1,500.00	12-21-54
F-625 Best adapted to growing timber	Hulsey, Mrs. Frankline	20.64	875.00	10-06-54
F-626 Best adapted to growing timber	Phillips, W.J.	101.52	3,750.00	07-14-54

Fig. A-III-89 F-626 (Courtesy U.S. Army Corps of Engineers, Mobile District, Official U.S. Army Photograph)

Fig. A-III-90 F-626 (Courtesy U.S. Army Corps of Engineers, Mobile District, Official U.S. Army Photograph)

Appendix III - Land Acquisitions Information

ID	Name	Acres	Price	Date
F-626-E	Phillips, W.J.	2.52		07-14-54
Best adapted to growing timber				
F-627	Georgia Power Company	42.14	1,000.00	06-13-55
Best adapted to growing timber				
F-628	McConnell, R.G.	2.00	200.00	03-03-55
Best use is for agricultural purposes				
F-629	Robinson, L.B.	2.91	250.00	04-06-56
Best use is forestry				
F-630	Doolittle, Edna	262.30	10,000.00	07-14-54
Best adapted to growing timber				
F-630-E	Doolittle, Edna	1.90	125.00	07-14-54
Medium to steeply rolling				
F-631	Orr, W.L.	110.00	5,000.00	09-30-54
Steeply rolling				
F-632	Skinner, Olin H.	4.36	175.00	10-13-55
Rolling woodland				
F-633	Unknown and Unnamed Cemetery	.25	1.00	01-17-57
Topography is gently rolling				
F-634	Whitmire, Ralph	.05		
No description				
F-635	Winn Cemetery	.25	1.00	05-15-56
Cemetery				
F-636-1-2	Taylor, Mark; Mrs. Loma	15.61	575.00	03-16-56
Medium rolling woodland and best use is believed to be forestry				
F-637	Pirkle, Frank; Chambers, Bob	28.20	1,300.00	10-21-55
Best suited for forestry				
F-638	Weatherford Jr., Lewis M.	18.75		
No description				
F-639	Wetherford, E.B.	17.45	925.00	11-08-55
Very good cropland and rolling woodland				
F-640-1-2-3	Eades, Eston; Hudgins, Otto; Reed, John R.	28.31	1,800.00	12-23-55
Woodland and cropland				
F-641-1-2	Holland, Lizzie,	6.40	475.00	04-18-56
Medium to steeply rolling with a small amount of merchantable timber				

F-642	Smith, Clyde	15.98	800.00	10-06-55

Best suited for homesites and forestry

F-643-1-2	Crow, Lee,	7.58	360.00	03-14-56

A few acres are cleared but most of the tract is medium to steeply rolling woodland

F-644	Reed, R.H.	23.40	1,250.00	10-21-55

Best suited for growing timber

F-645	Waldrip, C.F.	22.27	1,350.00	10-22-55

Best suited for residential purposes and timber growing

F-646	Whitmire, R.A.	.52	50.00	03-02-56

Best suited for growing timber

F-646-E	Whitmire, R.A.	2.30	25.00	03-02-56

Semi-cleared pasture

F-647	Smith, Arnold	5.51	450.00	03-13-56

The area is situated at the back of the tract and is medium rolling woodland

F-647-E	Smith, Arnold	.69	10.00	03-13-56

Medium rolling woodland

F-649	O'Kelley, Mrs. Frankie Lord	50.00	10,215.00	10-22-55

Cropland and woodland

Fig. A-III-91 F-649 (Courtesy U.S. Army Corps of Engineers, Mobile District, Official U.S. Army Photograph)

Fig. A-III-92 F-649 (Courtesy U.S. Army Corps of Engineers, Mobile District, Official U.S. Army Photograph)

F-649-E	O'Kelley, Mrs. Frankie Lord	.91	10.00	10-22-55

Wooded

F-650	Brown, Eva Ruby	1.00	80.00	12-05-55

Best suited for agriculture

F-652	Merritt, E.J.	7.34	400.00	03-07-56

This tract is adapted to small scale farming and poultry raising

F-653	Merritt, Velma	14.24	800.00	11-19-55

Best suited for agricultural purposes

F-655	Whiting, John H.	12.63	900.00	12-08-55

Suited for agricultural uses

Appendix III - Land Acquisitions Information

Tract	Owner	Acres	Price	Date
F-655-E	Whiting, John H.	1.15	10.00	12-08-55
Suited for agricultural uses				
F-657	Bagwell, Myrtle Brown	17.76	800.00	10-26-56
Highest and best use is believed to be forestry				
F-657-E	Bagwell, Myrtle Brown	.46	10.00	10-26-56
Highest and best use is believed to be forestry				
F-658	Moore, Travis	229.00	14,475.00	02-10-56
Gently to steeply rolling				
F-658-E-1 & E-2	Moore, Travis	3.20	30.00	02-10-56
Open and wooded pasture				
F-659	Propes, Lawton B.	7.35	1,500.00	03-30-57
Best use is road frontage potential homesite				
F-660-1-2	Mundy, E.C.	20.90	2,150.00	03-16-56
Some improved pasture with the remainder being steeply to medium rolling woodland				
F-661	Little, M.H.	13.00	750.00	03-01-56
The topography is rather rolling and rough and is all wooded with no improvements				
F-662	McNeal, Lillie Brown	7.29	350.00	12-05-55
Best suited for growing timber				
F-663-1-2	Propes, Lawton B.	27.83	3,950.00	02-03-56
Cropland and woodland				
F-664	Odell Jr., U.S..	22.70	850.00	02-29-56
Adapted to general crops				
F-665-1-2	Bagwell, J.W.	19.51	1,300.00	04-13-56
Tract of land is level to steeply rolling and adapted to general crops and timber production				
F-666	Bagwell, A.D.	25.60	1,400.00	03-20-56
Medium rolling and best use is for general crops, pasture and timber production				
F-667-E	Bagwell Farms Inc.	5.28	100.00	09-05-56
Adapted to general crops, pasture and/or meadow				
F-669	Odell Jr., U.S.	18.37	850.00	02-29-56
Adapted to general crops, pasture and timber				
F-670	Morris, E.C.	1.15	75.00	09-29-55
Woodland				
F-671	Weatherford, Paul	4.52		
No description				
F-672	Holland, Mrs. Lou Dell	.69	50.00	04-07-56
Best use is for homesite				

F-673   Jackson, Corine Bertha   1.29   75.00   10-10-55
and Charlie M.
Woodland

F-674-1-2   Waldrip, Anna B.   7.12   212.00   06-15-57
Timber production highest and best use

F-675-1-2   Odell Jr., U.S.   15.15   5,980.00   03-01-56
Best adapted to truck crops, pasture and timber production

Fig. A-III-93 F-675-1-2 (Courtesy U.S. Army Corps of Engineers, Mobile District, Official U.S. Army Photograph)

Fig. A-III-94 F-675-1-2 (Courtesy U.S. Army Corps of Engineers, Mobile District, Official U.S. Army Photograph)

F-676   Byers, Sanford   3.44   150.00   12-05-55
Medium to steeply rolling and adapted to timber production

F-678   Reed, U.S.   1.61   60.00   12-05-55
Timber production is best use

F-678-E   Reed, U.S.   .46
Perpetual flowing easement

F-679   Gilleland, Irene R.; Reed,   2.53   250.00   12-06-55
Luther A.; Reed, Mrs.
Belle Luther; Wilson,
Marinel Reed; Reed, Lloyd
H.; Coleman, T.
Woodland

F-679-E   Gilleland, Irene R.; Reed,   .69   10.00   12-06-55
Luther A.; Reed, Mrs.
Belle Luther; Wilson,
Marinel Reed; Reed, Lloyd
H.; Coleman, T.
Woodland

F-680-E   Mooney, George R.   3.90   15.00   02-27-57
Woodland

F-681   Reed, Monia   9.18   475.00   03-19-56
All woodland except a small idle field of about 2 1/2 or 3 acres

F-682   Umprey, John W.;   4.82   200.00   06-02-56
Bunnel, Florida
It is all woodland, gently to medium rolling and soil is Madison Sandy Clay Loam

Appendix III - Land Acquisitions Information

F-684 Woodland	McKinzey, G.M.	6.43	360.00	11-21-55
F-685 Woodland	Cleveland, R.C.	8.17	500.00	11-21-55
F-686 Part time farm land	Walding, Ella W.	16.00	2,600.00	10-31-55
F-687-1-2-3-4 Poultry farm	Crow, G.C.	71.22	4,700.00	12-16-55

Fig. A-III-95 F-687-1-2-3-4 (Courtesy U.S. Army Corps of Engineers, Mobile District, Official U.S. Army Photograph)

Fig. A-III-96 F-687-1-2-3-4 (Courtesy U.S. Army Corps of Engineers, Mobile District, Official U.S. Army Photograph)

F-688-1-2 Fairly good home and part time farm unit	Clark, C.C.	31.45	2,300.00	11-19-55
F-690-1-2 A part time farm	Vickers, Hershel; Barnes, Joe	49.14	2,500.00	08-27-56
F-690-E Semi-open pasture	Vickers, Hershel; Barnes, Joe	.46	10.00	08-27-56
F-691 Fairly well improved general and poultry farm	Phagan, Homer T.	56.73	4,450.00	12-20-55
F-692 Topography is gently to medium rolling	Banks Jr., R.	20.00	Donation	05-17-57
H-801 Best adapted to growing timber	Bennett, Jackson	72.30	2,750.00	10-04-54
H-802 Best adapted to growing timber	Haynes, Hollis	71.60	2,850.00	11-18-54
H-803 Woodland	Cagle, Mrs. T.S.; Mrs. Katie Lou Cagle Jones	41.40	1,000.00	09-09-54
H-804 Bottom land is undulating on the upland, medium to steeply rolling	Almond, Henry	112.80	5,375.00	08-27-54

H-805   Cagle, Mrs. T.S.; Mrs.   6.00   575.00   09-09-54
Katie Lou Cagle Jones
Best adapted for timber growing

H-806   Roper, Parks   23.00   9,175.00   08-20-54
Best adapted for farm land

Fig. A-III-97 H-806 (Courtesy U.S. Army Corps of Engineers, Mobile District, Official U.S. Army Photograph)

Fig. A-III-98 H-806 (Courtesy U.S. Army Corps of Engineers, Mobile District, Official U.S. Army Photograph)

H-807   Georgia Power Company   1,439.00   47,500.00   06-10-55
Best use is growing timber

H-808   Prater Cemetery   .25   10.00   01-17-56
Cemetery site

H-809   McCleskey Cemetery   .25   1.00   01-17-57
The topography is steeply rolling

H-810   Pethel Jr., D.T.   70.00   4,900.00   04-04-55
Topography ranges from bottom lands to steeply rolling

H-814   Golden Jr., Mrs. D.E.   102.00   4,450.00   11-23-55
Best use is forestry

H-815   Wright's Ice Cream Co.   432.60   20,000.00   06-13-55
Highest and best use is growing timber

H-817   Shiretzki, Mrs. D.S.   40.64   3,500.00   11-30-55
Best use is to be agriculture and forestry

H-818   Robinson Cemetery   .04   1.00   01-17-57
The tract is part of an old farm unit that has reverted to woodland

H-819   Waldrip, Ray V.   216.00   8,400.00   12-03-55
Agricultural and forestry

H-820   Roper, C.E.   123.00   11,965.00   03-06-56
Open bottom and rolling upland suitable for cultivation or pasture

H-822-1-2   Abercrombie, R.M.   59.06   3,500.00   11-30-55
Used for pasture and is suited for agriculture and forestry

H-823   Robinson Cemetery   .25   1.00   01-17-57
The topography is medium rolling

H-824   Robinson, Ben H.   130.0   7,350.00   03-24-56
Cropland and woodland

Fig. A-III-99 H-824 (Courtesy U.S. Army Corps of Engineers, Mobile District, Official U.S. Army Photograph)

Fig. A-III-100 H-824 (Courtesy U.S. Army Corps of Engineers, Mobile District, Official U.S. Army Photograph)

H-825   Smith, Monroe C.   63.00   2,250.00   12-09-55
Woodland

H-825-E   Smith, Monroe C.   1.38   10.00   12-09-55
Woodland

H-826   Parks, Perry F.   6.50   390.00   08-25-56
Heavily wooded tract, medium to steeply rolling

H-827   Bryant, Willie   54.40   1,200.00   05-07-56
Best suited to growing timber

H-827-E   Bryant, Willie   6.73   30.00   05-07-56
Woodland

H-828   Banks Jr., R.   10.30   250.00   11-24-56
Forestry

H-830   Bryant Cemetery   .25   1.00   01-17-57
The topography is medium rolling

H-834   Cook, Robert Lee   20.95   1,150.00   08-03-56
Highest and best use for the land acquired is woodland forestry

H-834-E   Cook, Robert Lee   .09   10.00   08-03-56
Mixed woodland of gently rolling topography and highest and best use is for forestry

H-835-E   Mead, Howard N.   1.08   10.00   10-23-57
Woodland branch bottom suited best for forestry

H-836   Cain, O.D.   8.50   500.00   12-03-55
Forestry

H-836-E   Cain, O.D.   .92   10.00   12-03-55
Highest and best use is forestry

H-838-1-2   Bruce, E.C.   62.00   3,250.00   03-03-56
Best for subsistence farming

| H-839-1-2 | Jett, A.H. | 11.39 | 600.00 | 12-10-55 |

Best use is producing timber

| H-839-E | Jett, A.H. | 1.45 | 15.00 | 12-10-55 |

Best use is agricultural and forestry

| H-840 | Simpson, Mrs. Will Ella; W.H.; Buice, R.A. | 29.39 | 2,750.00 | 03-01-56 |

Highest and best use is for residential and forestry purposes

Fig. A-III-101 H-840 (Courtesy U.S. Army Corps of Engineers, Mobile District, Official U.S. Army Photograph)

Fig. A-III-102 H-840 (Courtesy U.S. Army Corps of Engineers, Mobile District, Official U.S. Army Photograph)

| H-844 | Robinson, Mrs. John | 40.40 | 3,000.00 | 03-01-56 |

Best us general farm and poultry units

| H-845 | Smith, Lillie Gertrude | 50.90 | 2,125.00 | 05-17-57 |

Forestry

| H-846 | Stovall, Mabel E. | 143.00 | 4,400.00 | 03-20-57 |

Best use for tract is forestry

| H-847-1-2 | Garner, Lee W.; Inez | 7.91 | 325.00 | 09-14-56 |

The highest and best use for the land is forestry

| H-847-E | Garner, Lee W.; Inez | .30 | 10.00 | 09-14-56 |

The highest and best use is forestry

| H-848 | Waldrip, Ray V. | 87.00 | 3,475.00 | 10-21-55 |

Adapted to general crops, pasture and timber production

| H-849 | Trubey, Jessie F. | 12.65 | 525.00 | 12-02-55 |

Woodland

| H-850 | Doss, S.E. | 4.60 | 185.00 | 11-14-55 |

Wooded

| H-853-E | Williams, Marcus | .46 | 15.00 | 06-08-57 |

Woodland

| H-854 | Mathis, Carl | 8.50 | 375.00 | 11-21-55 |

Woodland

| H-855 | Aiken, Mrs. Dewey | 3.90 | 150.00 | 12-14-55 |

Wooded

Appendix III - Land Acquisitions Information

H-856-E Woodland	Wingo, R.L.	.39	10.00	12-02-55
H-857 Pasture and woodland	Barnes, J. Alvin	15.73	1,075.00	04-27-56
H-857-E Woodland	Barnes, J. Alvin	.30	10.00	04-27-56
H-858 Crops, pasture and/or meadow, timber production	Hulsey, D.C.	88.60	7,000.00	11-30-55
H-859 Highest and best use is growing timber	Parks, A.P.	2.58	90.00	04-27-56
H-860-1-2 Gently to medium rolling	Powell, Eldridge C.	42.03	4,750.00	11-17-55
H-861 Adapted to general crops, pasture, and timber production	Smith, Henrietta	9.41	635.00	10-13-55
H-861-E-1 & E-2 Wooded	Smith, Henrietta	1.38	10.00	10-13-55
H-862 Wooded	Waldrip, Ray V.	1.38	90.00	10-21-55
H-863 Adapted to pasture and woodland	Jones, Burl R.	2.30	150.00	12-03-55
H-864 Adapted to timber production	Frix, Anna	10.90	600.00	10-22-55
H-865 Adapted to timber production	Reed Jr., James M.	8.95	525.00	10-13-55
H-866 Level to steeply rolling and adapted to timber growing	Ivey, Balus	38.30	2,250.00	03-27-56
H-866-E Area lies along and on each side of a wooded ravine and adapted to timber production	Ivey, Balus	.46	10.00	03-27-56
H-867-1-2 Adapted to growth of timber	Long, William B.; Luna I.	14.17	900.00	11-10-55
H-868 Adapted to timber	Smith, Henrietta; Frix, Anna; Tanner, Rosie Lee; Smith, Elsie Mae	2.30	135.00	12-07-55

H-869	Parks, Perry E.	78.18	32,000.00	08-25-56

Best use is thought to be for chicken production and livestock

Fig. A-III-103 H-869 (Courtesy U.S. Army Corps of Engineers, Mobile District, Official U.S. Army Photograph)

Fig. A-III-104 H-869 (Courtesy U.S. Army Corps of Engineers, Mobile District, Official U.S. Army Photograph)

H-869-E-1-2-3	Parks, Perry E.	1.00	10.00	08-25-56

Best use is considered to be woodland and growing of timber

H-870	McNeal, W.H.	34.10	1,850.00	12-05-55

Suited to pasturing and grazing

H-871	Chapman, Harry R.	2.76	125.00	12-05-55

Best adapted to timberland

H-872	Red Hen Farms (West, James W.; Travis, L. Edd)	6.43	260.00	05-25-56

Reverting woodland best suited to forestry

H-875-1-2-3	Stringer, Fred	179.93	10,500.00	04-05-56

Adaptable to row cropping and grazing

Fig. A-III-105 H-875-1-2-3 (Courtesy U.S. Army Corps of Engineers, Mobile District, Official U.S. Army Photograph)

Fig. A-III-106 H-875-1-2-3 (Courtesy U.S. Army Corps of Engineers, Mobile District, Official U.S. Army Photograph)

H-875-E-1-2	Stringer, Fred	2.52	25.00	04-05-56

Wooded and semi-improved pasture

H-876-1-2	Gould, Jay S.	20.57	1,650.00	12-05-55

Best use is pasture and grazing

H-877	Stringer, Charles	43.00	2,000.00	04-05-56

Cut over woodland

H-877-E	Stringer, Charles C.; Glenn G.	.70		04-05-56

Perpetual flowing easement

Appendix III - Land Acquisitions Information

H-879	Moon, S.C.; Griffin, M.	14.00	750.00	12-28-56
Land best adaptable to growing of timber				
I-901	Nix, Pearl Grace	39.07	10,175.00	02-29-56
Woodland				
I-901-E-1-2	Nix, Pearl Grace	.84		02-28-56
Perpetual flowing easement				
I-902	City of Gainesville	137.00		
No description				
I-902-E	City of Gainesville	1.15		12-29-55
Perpetual flowing easement				
I-903-E	Plaginos, Paul C.	1.38	250.00	07-10-57
Creek bottom				
I-910	Johnson Jr., Hammond W.; Plaginos, Paul C.	9.68	4,500.00	08-17-56
Topography medium to steeply rolling and adapted to residential sites				
I-910-E-1 & E-2	Johnson Jr., Hammond W.; Plaginos, Paul C.	1.36	45.00	08-17-56
Best adapted to woodland				
I-912-1-2	Puckett, Carl L.	2.25	450.00	04-05-56
Woodland				
I-912-E	Puckett, Carl L.	.16	10.00	04-05-56
Woodland				
I-913	Jewell, J.D.	2.98	600.00	07-07-56
This tract is all woodland and slopes down to a small stream best use is for timber growing				
I-913-E-1 & E-2	Jewell, J.D.	.92	20.00	07-07-56
These easements tracts are wooded and are the slopes to a branch				
I-914	Burns, Dr. J.K.	49.13	17,575.00	01-12-56
Woodland and cropland				
I-914-E	Burns, Dr. J.K.	.62	15.00	01-12-56
Woodland and cropland				
I-915	Wofford, George W.	27.32	5,750.00	02-29-56
Growing timber and abattoir headquarters best use				
I-915-E	Wofford, Mrs. DorothyWall	01.15		02-28-56
Perpetual flowing easement				
I-918-1-2-3	Carter, Linton C.	54.02	10,000.00	01-17-56
Timberland				

ID	Name	Acres	Amount	Date
I-918-E Woodland	Carter, Linton C.	.69	20.00	01-17-56
I-919 General Farming	Duncan, W.D.	66.20	10,425.00	11-24-57
I-920 Best use for woodland and housesites	Quillian, Roxie	18.37	1,975.00	02-29-56
I-921 Woodland or housesites best use	Strickland, Devada	18.20	5,950.00	02-29-56

Fig. A-III-107 I-921 (Courtesy U.S. Army Corps of Engineers, Mobile District, Official U.S. Army Photograph)

Fig. A-III-108 I-921 (Courtesy U.S. Army Corps of Engineers, Mobile District, Official U.S. Army Photograph)

ID	Name	Acres	Amount	Date
I-922 Woodland or housesite	Anderson, Zephyr	15.73	1,875.00	02-29-56
I-922-E Perpetual flowing easement	Anderson, Zephyr	.15		02-28-56
I-923 Best adapted for woodland or housesites	Whelchel, E. M.	24.90	2,900.00	02-29-56
I-923-E Perpetual flowing easement	Whelchel, Julia Bell	.15		02-28-56
I-924 Topography is medium rolling	Fulford, Bert	3.45	750.00	04-14-56
I-925 Highest and best use is cabin site and growing of timber	Orschel, J. E.; Mrs. J.E.	4.33	1,000.00	09-18-55
I-926 Adapted for woodland or housesites	Spinner, Hazel Quillian	14.24	1,500.00	02-29-56
I-927 Best adapted for woodland or housesites	Anderson, Zephyr Rine	11.48	1,225.00	02-29-56
I-928 Best adapted for woodland and homesites	Dunnaville, Bessie	10.10	1,050.00	02-29-56
I-929 No description	Duvall, H.A.	38.60		

Appendix III - Land Acquisitions Information

I-930-1-2	Duvall Jr., Harley	1.44	150.00	08-17-56
The highest and best use of the part taken is for timber growing				
I-932	Houser, E. F.	77.00	23,500.00	02-29-56
Best adapted for general row crop farming				
I-933	Pinson, J. H.	45.20	12,350.00	11-15-55
Undulating in the bottoms and medium to steeply rolling in the woodland				
I-935-E	Lenderman, H. B.	.23	50.00	08-04-55
Some cleared and some having brush edges				
I-936	Minor, H. M.	8.15	11,000.00	02-29-56
Suited for homesites				
I-937	Dunagan Cemetery	.25		
No description				
I-938	Cook, J. A.	1.38	1,200.00	03-30-57
The highest and best use is building lots				
I-939	Lenderman, H. B.	1.18	1,200.00	08-20-56
Highest and best use is building lots				
I-940	Minor, Toy	.81	80.00	04-26-55
Best use is for timber growing or grazing area				
I-940-E	Minor, Toy	1.51	200.00	04-26-55
Best use is for growing of timber or grazing area				
I-941	Roper, W. A.	71.0	10,000.00	11-10-56
Grazing				
I-941-E-1 & E-2	Roper, W. A.	4.85	1,275.00	11-10-56
Woodland				
I-942	Lenderman, H. B.	83.00	35,000.00	01-25-57
Homesite and development into building lots				
I-943-E	Higgins, S. T.	.30	600.00	08-12-55
The area is used for parking and entrance to a wood working shop				
I-944-E	Allison, J. A.	.08	50.00	08-11-55
Improved pasture slopes gently				

I-945   Pinson, Vista M.   80.80   20,000.00   11-15-55
Best use for subdivision lots

Fig. A-III-109 I-945 (Courtesy U.S. Army Corps of Engineers, Mobile District, Official U.S. Army Photograph)

Fig. A-III-110 I-945 (Courtesy U.S. Army Corps of Engineers, Mobile District, Official U.S. Army Photograph)

I-947   Jay, Theo   60.00   11,550.00   11-17-56
Agricultural purposes.   Due to location some parts would sell readily as building sites

I-948-E   Roper, W. A.   1.15   200.00   10-07-57
Woodland

I-949   Grindle, H. E.   36.32   6,350.00   05-17-55
The highest and best use of this tract is a homesite, farming and growing timber

I-951   Riverside Military   1.61   400.00   12-15-56
                 Academy Inc.
Timber growing and could be used for recreational purposes

I-951-E   Riverside Military   .69   25.00   12-15-56
                 Academy Inc.
Timber

I-952   City of Gainesville   17.00
Fomerly Gainesville Water Works

I-953   Georgia Power Company   116.00   45,700.00   02-29-56
Best suited for recreational purposes and pastureland

I-953-E-1-2   Georgia Power Company   3.12   02-29-56
Perpetual flowing easement

I-954-E   Hall, Charles H.; Mamie   1.58   350.00   09-04-56
Woodland

I-955-E   McCarver, W.C.   .43   12-22-56
Perpetual flowing easement

I-956   Smithgall, Charles   7.09   1,800.00   08-03-56
The entire tract is woodland and the highest and best use is for subdivision purposes

I-956-E   Smithgall, Charles   1.50   65.00   08-03-56
Level to medium rolling and the highest and best use is for subdivision purposes

I-958   Davies, G. L.   57.60   10.00   11-15-55
Best adapted to timber growing

Appendix III - Land Acquisitions Information

I-958-E-1 & E-2 Woodland	Davies, G. L.	6.82	1,625.00	11-15-55
I-958-E-3 Best use is timber growing	Davies, G. L.	.69	10.00	11-15-55
I-960-E-1 & E-2 Building sites	Waters, Albert L.	1.00	675.00	11-15-55
I-961-E Homesite and store location	Smith, Calvin Floyd	.37	10,665.00	12-29-55

Fig. A-III-111 I-961-E (Courtesy U.S. Army Corps of Engineers, Mobile District, Official U.S. Army Photograph)

Fig. A-III-112 I-961-E (Courtesy U.S. Army Corps of Engineers, Mobile District, Official U.S. Army Photograph)

I-965 Gently to medium rolling of which the greater part is wooded	Harrington, Y. J.	5.05	1,300.00	07-06-56
I-965-E Gently to medium rolling of which the greater part is wooded	Harrington, Y. J.	2.36	2,350.00	07-06-56
I-967-1-2 Topography is level to steeply rolling and adapted to crops, pasture and/or meadow	Stephens, J. Fred	55.77	13,500.00	09-17-56
I-968 Dairy unit	Culpepper, Charles O.	31.20	6,575.00	04-05-56
I-968-E Improved upland pasture	Culpepper, Charles O.	1.90	200.00	04-05-56
I-969 Cropland and pasture	Westmoreland Jr., Charles C.	105.00	10,000.00	04-05-56

ID	Owner	Acres	Value	Date
I-970	Waters, P. D.	69.10	12,000.00	04-05-56

Best use is rural homesite lots

Fig. A-III-113 I-970 (Courtesy U.S. Army Corps of Engineers, Mobile District, Official U.S. Army Photograph)

Fig. A-III-114 I-970 (Courtesy U.S. Army Corps of Engineers, Mobile District, Official U.S. Army Photograph)

ID	Owner	Acres	Value	Date
I-970-E	Waters, P. D.	.69	100.00	04-05-56

Idle cropland

I-971	Blue Ridge Broadcasting Co.	7.58	850.00	04-15-57

Timber growing

I-971-E-1 & E-2	Blue Ridge Broadcasting Co.	.99	50.00	04-15-57

Timber growing

I-972	Hudgins, Mrs. Avie	32.00	5,000.00	08-03-56

Best suited to residential lots

I-973-E	Shockley, Sherman	.03	150.00	12-16-57

Building lots

I-974-E	Wiley, Harold	.20		03-09-58

Perpetual flowing easement

I-975	Ellis, James H.	.37	100.00	11-24-56

Woodland suitable for rural homesite

I-976	Hudgins, Raymond	1.82	400.00	01-26-57

Topography is level to medium rolling

I-976-E	Hudgins, Raymond	.18	10.00	01-26-57

Topography is level to medium rolling

I-977	Kitchens, Myrtle	1.84	450.00	11-24-56

Pasture and woodland

I-978	Waters, Clyde F.	.55	125.00	12-28-56

Highest and best use is for a building site

I-979	Hollifield, Monroe J.	.92	300.00	04-14-56

Bottomland

I-980-1-2	Waters, Clyde F.	11.71	3,450.00	12-30-55

Highest and best use is for farming and pasture

Appendix III - Land Acquisitions Information

I-981 Kemp, Cordie 1.61 400.00 04-09-56
Best use is country homesite with subsistence farming

I-982 Moore, Ernest 21.50 5,150.00 12-28-56
Adapted to general crops and woodland

I-982-E-1 & E-2 Moore, Ernest 29.16 350.00 12-28-56
Woodland and cropland

I-983 Ellis, L. B.; Mrs. L. B. 3.57 700.00 12-28-56
Level to medium rolling and the highest and best use is for a country homesite

I-984 Waters, A. L. 2.52 358.00 12-29-56
Woodland could be used for subdivision

I-985 Wiley, Robert L. 1.22 225.00 12-28-56
Woodland and country homesite

I-986-E Blue Ridge Broadcasting Company 1.00   08-14-58
Perpetual flowing easement

I-988 Ellis, Frances Puett 11.02 2,350.00 08-03-56
Potential subdivision land

I-990-E-1-2-3-4 Waldrep, R.M. 9.41   12-24-57
Perpetual flowing easement

I-991-E Mabry, A.J. 2.59   12-13-57
Perpetual flowing easement

J-1000 Jackson Cemetery .50 35.00 01-17-56
Cemetery site

J-1001 Conner, Clifton H. 159.05 26,030.00 10-26-55
The best use is pasture with some general farming, poultry raising and livestock

Fig. A-III-115 J-1001 (Courtesy U.S. Army Corps of Engineers, Mobile District, Official U.S. Army Photograph)

Fig. A-III-116 J-1001 (Courtesy U.S. Army Corps of Engineers, Mobile District, Official U.S. Army Photograph)

J-1002 Robinson, H. C. 71.78 27,500.00 02-10-56
Highest and best use is pasture

J-1003 Martin, R. T. 46.00 5,550.00 12-13-55
Best use of this tract is homesite and general farming

J-1004	Martin, R. T.	45.25	9,784.00	12-13-55
Best use is a homesite and general farming				
J-1005	Martin, Jay	38.00	9,550.00	12-29-55
Suitable for pasture				
J-1006	Robinson, Hoke	18.00	2,000.00	02-10-56
Best use is pasture and growing timber				
J-1007	Hollaway, Willie Johnson	2.53	525.00	04-05-56
Best adapted to road frontage building lots				
J-1008-1-2	Ivey, Carl	29.79	2,200.00	02-10-56
Best use is grazing and cropland				
J-1008-E-1 & E-2	Ivey, Carl	1.59	67.50	02-10-56
Adaptable to garden and truck crops				
J-1009	Robinson, Nevie Simpson; H. C.	86.10	6,500.00	02-10-56
Best use is pastureland and timber growing				
J-1010	Wages, Dewey C.	36.00	4,750.00	12-28-55
Medium to steeply rolling cropland and woodland				
J-1011	Shuler, A. B.	29.50	3,450.00	12-31-55
Wooded land				
J-1012	Wallace, B. M.	8.95	525.00	01-24-56
Agricultural				
J-1013	Looper, Henry C.; D. B.	46.10	9,375.00	12-27-55
Highest and best use is agriculture				
J-1013-E	Looper, Henry C.; D. B.	1.00	9,875.00	12-27-55
Bottom pasture				
J-1014	Martin, H. C.	25.00	15,475.00	12-29-55
Highest and best uses would be for homesites and some patch farming				
J-1015	Stowers, Anne Ruth Martin	4.00	7,225.00	12-16-55
Topography is gently to medium rolling				
J-1016	Kanady, Homer	9.00	4,125.00	12-29-55
Topography is gently rolling to medium rolling				
J-1017	Ivey, Ralph	1.75	2,450.00	01-14-56
Gently to medium rolling				
J-1018	Hughes, W. N.	17.50	4,900.00	02-16-56
Pasture and grazing land				
J-1019	Caudell, Hoyt	2.00	3,375.00	01-03-56
Best adapted to homesites				

Appendix III - Land Acquisitions Information

J-1020   Garner, Thomas N.   .86   3,375.00   12-30-55
Adapted best for homesite

J-1021   Estes, Mrs. Charles L.   90.00   16,015.00   04-27-56
Best use is agricultural

Fig. A-III-117 J-1021 and J-1022 (Courtesy U.S. Army Corps of Engineers, Mobile District, Official U.S. Army Photograph)

Fig. A-III-118 J-1021 and J-1022 (Courtesy U.S. Army Corps of Engineers, Mobile District, Official U.S. Army Photograph)

J-1022   Fouts, Paul   49.00   20,073.00   07-26-55
Fine Sandy Loam, sodded in Kudzu

J-1023   Byrd Cemetery   .25
Cemetery

J-1024   Holcomb, J. Hubert   27.30   6,950.00   04-27-55
The highest and best use of this tract is for homesite and pasture

J-1025   White, Ford   8.05   650.00   02-03-56
Residential and agricultural

J-1026   White, H. F.   40.47   9,975.00   04-27-55
Topography grading from river bottom cropland to mountainous woodland and cropland

J-1026-E-1   White, H. F.   12.70   650.00   04-27-55
Topography grading from river bottom cropland to mountainous woodland and cropland

J-1027   Stephens, Olen   25.00   4,500.00   01-25-55
Best use for growing timber

J-1028   Whelchel, Claude A.   55.10   15,320.00   12-02-55
Best suited for farm unit

J-1029-1-2   Aycock, C. L.   5.87   5,275.00   02-17-56
Woodland and homesite

J-1030   Duvall Jr., Harley   1.00   2,075.00   02-18-55
Best use is homesite and garden

J-1031   Fletcher, Hulan Jack   3.11   3,200.00   11-15-55
Suitable for homesite, for range and grazing

J-1032   Oliver, H. T.   7.64   5,400.00   12-31-55
Best use homesite and subsistence farming

Fig. A-III-119 J-1032 (Courtesy U.S. Army Corps of Engineers, Mobile District, Official U.S. Army Photograph)

Fig. A-III-120 J-1032 (Courtesy U.S. Army Corps of Engineers, Mobile District, Official U.S. Army Photograph)

J-1033   Light, Norma Rae   3.95   5,675.00   07-23-55
                      Hunt
Best use is homesite and subsistence farming

J-1034   Whelchel, E. M.   2.76   1,500.00   12-29-55
Adaptability is best for building site

J-1035   Whitmire, Fred L.   1.95   1,000.00   02-29-56
Best uses building sites

J-1036   Bruce, Robert   .79   425.00   04-21-56
Best adapted to building site

J-1037-E   McNeal, W. H.   .36   300.00   12-28-56
Highway frontage

J-1038   Quillian, Roxie A.   10.50   4,075.00   09-03-55
Best suited for housesites

J-1039   Maxwell, L. D.   3.23   1,200.00   11-29-55
Best suited for residential purposes

J-1040   Gregory, H. A.; Jones   .82   500.00   06-24-55
                      G. R.
Small building site and tract breaks sharply to a branch

J-1041   Martin, James N.;   2.50   7,900.00   04-14-55
                      Blondean Ladd
Best adapted to site for dwelling or building purposes only

J-1042   Ladd, Pearl F.   63.00   5,000.00   06-30-55
Woodland

J-1042-E-1 & E-2   Ladd, Pearl F.   .90   25.00   06-30-55
Idle and brush

J-1043-E   Ladd, Walter J.   .10   10.00   05-26-55
The part affected lies along a branch and covered with vines and brush and is about 150 feet back from the dwelling and will affect the tract but little

J-1044	Little, Carlton	4.48	250.00	12-05-55

Best use is forestry

J-1044-E	Little, Carlton	.23	10.00	12-05-55

Residential is best use

J-1045	Grindle, R. H.	42.50	8,570.00	03-03-55

Gently rolling to mountainous

J-1046	Coffee, Isabelle M.	4.00	3,100.00	11-15-55

Homesite and road side apple cider stand best use

Fig. A-III-121 J-1046 (Courtesy U.S. Army Corps of Engineers, Mobile District, Official U.S. Army Photograph)

Fig. A-III-122 J-1046 (Courtesy U.S. Army Corps of Engineers, Mobile District, Official U.S. Army Photograph)

J-1047	White, M. J.	36.00	5,900.00	02-28-55

Satisfactory to chicken raising and small grazing project

J-1048	Martin, H. C.; Dan	3.00	3,000.00	04-28-55

Best adapted for poultry raising

J-1049	Robinson, Mrs. A. L.	7.00	2,950.00	06-03-55

The highest and best use are building sites and forestry

J-1050	Shirley, Emeline B.	25.00	8,000.00	04-26-55

Topography is sharp and irregular

J-1051	Conner, Henry Eston	8.00	8,435.00	05-12-55

It is used for raising poultry and small herd of livestock

J-1052	White, Howard William	35.00	11,775.00	12-05-55

Topography is gently to medium rolling

J-1053	Lenderman, Huel B.; F. Ode Parks	102.25	17,000.00	06-13-55

Well adapted to livestock raising

J-1054	Smith Cemetery	.25	20.00	01-17-56

Burial site

J-1055	Thomas, D. O.; Naomi B.	17.28	6,950.00	05-19-55

Best use is for building sites and growing of timber on the remaining

J-1056	Mangum, Guy	10.00	8,135.00	07-08-55

The highest and best use of the property, except that part along the road is believed to be forestry with slight enhancement due to location

J-1057	Cantrell, Charlie J.	2.00	10,300.00	06-03-55

Very desirable for building site

J-1058-E	Duvall, Ethel	.29	116.00	05-13-55

A small strip of land bordering existing highway

J-1059-E	Hyde, Joe	.55	680.00	05-20-55

All of this land is highway frontage

J-1061	Elliott, Ivan	5.10	11,100.00	02-10-56

Adapted to present use of filling station

Fig. A-III-123 J-1061 (Courtesy U.S. Army Corps of Engineers, Mobile District, Official U.S. Army Photograph)

Fig. A-III-124 J-1061 (Courtesy U.S. Army Corps of Engineers, Mobile District, Official U.S. Army Photograph)

J-1062	Looper Jr., D.B.	2.30	6,450.00	10-17-55

Best suited for home, garden and pasture

J-1063	Looper, H.C. (Henry)	1.75	12,680.00	11-05-55

Best use is homesite and garden

J-1064	Looper, D.B.	5.28	15,000.00	12-02-55

Desirable homesite and subsistence unit

J-1065	Browning, G. W.	1.90	3,460.00	03-18-55

Best use for homesite and subsistence farming

J-1066	Clark, J.N.	1.84	3,350.00	02-18-55

Undulating to gently rolling

J-1067	White, Ford	9.40	13,780.00	05-04-55

The highest and best use is for homesites and for pasture

J-1068	Eberhardt, Louie	20.00	11,790.00	12-23-54

Topography is from gently to mostly medium rolling

J-1069	Cape, Coley Grant	5.00	6,250.00	05-26-55

Best use is building sites and pasturage

J-1070	Bennett, Joe M.	2.30	3,990.00	01-25-55

The topography in the bottom is level, rising sharply to the house level

Appendix III - Land Acquisitions Information

J-1071　　　　　　Quillian, Roxie A.　　　　　　1.50　　　　750.00　　　07-23-56
Best use would be commericial since it is bordered on all sides by highways or public roads

J-1072　　　　　　Allison, J. T.　　　　　　　　3.20　　　4,090.00　　02-28-55
Best use for home purposes and small poultry unit

J-1073　　　　　　Martin Jr., James Bailey　　　2.38　　　3,950.00　　01-25-55
Homesite only

J-1074　　　　　　Cross, Gaynelle Martin;　　　　1.00　　　4,450.00　　05-14-55
　　　　　　　　　Martin, J. L.; J.G.
Highest and best use is building lot and residence

J-1075　　　　　　Decking, T.D.;　　　　　　　　1.93　　　5,045.00　　03-07-55
　　　　　　　　　Mrs. Elizabeth
Best use as homesite

J-1076　　　　　　Nalley, J. B.　　　　　　　　　7.00　　　4,700.00　　03-18-55
Best use is homesites and subsistence farming

J-1077　　　　　　Kenney, B. H.　　　　　　　　　4.00　　　3,450.00　　09-22-55
Homesite and timber

J-1078　　　　　　Dale, E. H.　　　　　　　　　　3.21　　　6,680.00　　12-02-55
Best use is residential with space for vegatables

J-1079　　　　　　Cape, Coley Grant　　　　　　　2.96　　　　900.00　　05-26-55
Best use is building lots

J-1080　　　　　　Evans, Leon　　　　　　　　　　3.14　　　　　　　　　02-01-55
Undulating to medium rolling

J-1082　　　　　　Gregory, Henry;　　　　　　　　4.15　　　7,225.00　　04-04-55
　　　　　　　　　Annie Irine
Topography is mostly gently rolling

J-1083　　　　　　Elliott Jr., T. L.　　　　　　8.53　　　8,810.00　　03-08-55
Topography is from undulating to mostly gently rolling to steeply rolling

J-1084　　　　　　McNeal, N. A.　　　　　　　　　9.18　　　13,525.00　04-29-55
Running branch water is available to the pasture, pasture is in a highly improved state, homesite has been improved on this tract

J-1085　　　　　　Jones, T. Q.　　　　　　　　　11.20　　　10,750.00　03-29-55
Best use is for homesite and subdivision property

J-1086　　　　　　Elliott, Edwin　　　　　　　　14.01　　　10,705.00　10-28-55
Best use is for homesite and subsistence farming

J-1087　　　　　　Elliott, T. L.　　　　　　　　5.58　　　2,225.00　　11-29-55
Best use is building lot and subsistence farming

J-1088　　　　　　Pirkle, Claud　　　　　　　　　3.00　　　3,600.00　　08-11-55
Highest and best use is homesite and building lots

J-1089	Mason, Mrs. J. G.	3.90	1,875.00	12-02-55

Best use is building lot

J-1090	Ivey, Lina Bell	2.64	4,735.00	04-13-55

Gently rolling for a small portion which drops sharply over a bluff

J-1091	Reed, Cora Bell	2.80	5,010.00	07-22-55

Best use for homesite and subsistence farming

Fig. A-III-125 J-1091 (Courtesy U.S. Army Corps of Engineers, Mobile District, Official U.S. Army Photograph)

Fig. A-III-126 J-1091 (Courtesy U.S. Army Corps of Engineers, Mobile District, Official U.S. Army Photograph)

Fig. A-III-127 J-1092 (Courtesy U.S. Army Corps of Engineers, Mobile District, Official U.S. Army Photograph)

Fig. A-III-128 J-1092 (Courtesy U.S. Army Corps of Engineers, Mobile District, Official U.S. Army Photograph)

J-1092	Tanner, Mrs. Marelle B.; Ellis	10.33	7,725.00	12-31-55

Best use is business and homesite and subsistence farming

J-1093	Byrd, C. W.	8.73	5,000.00	03-30-55

Best use is for a homesite and subsistence farming

J-1094	Rundles, W. D.	2.45	5,700.00	04-28-55

Gently rolling

J-1095	Mason, J. G.	7.46	3,000.00	09-22-55

Highest and best use is building sites

J-1096	Stephens, Blanche Ethel	32.25	11,350.00	04-26-55

Best use if forestry

J-1096-E-1-2	Stephens, Blanche Ethel	8.49	310.00	04-26-55

Best use is forestry

J-1097	Brookshire, J. J.	6.30	500.00	12-28-55

Best use is agricultural

Appendix III - Land Acquisitions Information

ID	Name	Acres	Price	Date
J-1098	Cagle, G. H.	1.38	125.00	12-27-55
Best suited for small scale farming and homesite				
J-1099	Campbell, Knox; Rosa Lee	20.70	1,525.00	12-27-55
Highest and best use is agricultural				
K-1102	Elliott, Eston	16.75	4,700.00	12-17-55
Best use is agricultural				
K-1102-E	Elliott, Eston	.60	10.00	12-17-55
Woodland				
K-1103	Rundles, W. D.	11.48	1,550.00	02-23-56
Well suited for agriculture and forestry				
K-1104	Spain, E. C.	1.50	4,580.00	12-23-55
Best suited for a homesite and a vegetable garden				
K-1105	Rundles, W. D.	.25	250.00	07-22-55
Best use is for homesite				
K-1106	Reed, Ralph	.52	550.00	12-09-55
Desirable homesite				
K-1107	Rundles, W. D.	.53	5,050.00	07-23-55
Best use is homesite				
K-1108	Smith, Clarence	.53	3,300.00	08-19-55
Homesite only				
K-1109	Martin, Mrs. W. Walker	.53	3,550.00	12-09-55
Building lot fronting				
K-1111	Smith, Earl E.	4.65	3,150.00	12-30-55
Highest and best use is for homesites				
K-1112	Martin, Mrs. W. Walker	1.46	4,075.00	12-09-55
Best suited for vegetable gardens or pasture				
K-1113	Richards, Francis F.	1.46	1,250.00	11-29-55
Building site				
K-1114	Rainey, Edwin	4.06	11,250.00	02-15-56
Highest and best use is residential and subsistence farming				
K-1115	Barnes, Mrs. Don T.	6.38	27,410.00	03-26-56
Best suited for residential purposes				
K-1116	Skinner, Beulah	3.43	950.00	12-23-55
One acre open and the rest in pines				
K-1116-E	Skinner, Beulah	.57	20.00	12-23-55
Wooded				

K-1117   Terrell, Harold A.   18.37   16,400.00   05-17-56
Residential and pasture land

Fig. A-III-129 K-1117 (Courtesy U.S. Army Corps of Engineers, Mobile District, Official U.S. Army Photograph)

Fig. A-III-130 K-1117 (Courtesy U.S. Army Corps of Engineers, Mobile District, Official U.S. Army Photograph)

K-1117-E   Terrell, Harold A.   10.10   4,450.00   05-17-56
Residential and pasture land

K-1118   Walker, Ernest   .69   100.00   12-02-55
Highest and best use is residential and subsistence farming

K-1121   Hall County Board   5.27
                   of Education
No description

K-1121-E-1-2   Hall County Board   1.34
                   of Education
Perpetual flowing easement

K-1122   Land (Ladd), L. G.   5.35   4,390.00   12-30-55
Highest and best use is residential

K-1123-E   Allison, Herschel   8.27   1,200.00   12-16-57
Topography is undulating. The best use is for part of a subsistence farm unit or subdivision

K-1125   Hatcher, Frank   60.60   11,735.00   04-09-56
Best for livestock and poultry unit

K-1125-E-1-2   Hatcher, Frank   1.10   910.00   04-09-56
Pastureland

K-1126   Brackett, Stewart   7.34   1,050.00   07-23-56
Medium rolling land (agricultural)

K-1126-E   Brackett, Stewart   2.76   265.00   07-23-56
Medium rolling land (agricultural)

K-1127   Miller, Dr. John N.   36.74   10,710.00   12-30-55
Best use is agricultural

K-1128   Roark, Fred; Mrs. A. W.;   7.35   800.00   06-08-56
                   Eula; Margaret; Martin;
                   Bell, R; Hulsey, Mary R.
Medium rolling woodland and best adapted to timber growing and subsistence farming

K-1129　　　　　　　　Hulsey, J. D.　　　　　　　　1.03　　　　100.00　　　　07-23-56
Best suited for timber

K-1129-E　　　　　　　Hulsey, J. D.　　　　　　　　.60　　　　　100.00　　　　07-23-56
Best suited for timber

K-1130　　　　　　　　Ladd, Mrs. V. S.　　　　　　16.00　　　　1,500.00　　　11-19-55
Eight idle acres and eight wooded acres

K-1131-E　　　　　　　Elliott Jr., T. L.　　　　　　　.17　　　　　10.00　　　　08-22-55
Wooded

K-1132　　　　　　　　Ladd, Clarence　　　　　　　3.86　　　　4,300.00　　　10-22-55
Best suited for homesite

K-1133-E　　　　　　　Ladd, Mrs. V. S.　　　　　　.80　　　　　40.00　　　　05-12-55
Woodland tract with mixed hardwoods

K-1134-E　　　　　　　Rundles, Annie　　　　　　　1.44　　　　800.00　　　　10-12-55
Gently rolling

K-1136-E-1　　　　　　Cash, G. S.　　　　　　　　　6.63　　　　2,100.00　　　05-26-55
Topography is medium to steeply rolling

K-1136-E-2　　　　　　Cash, G. S.　　　　　　　　　.04　　　　　10.00　　　　05-26-55
Woodland

K-1137-E　　　　　　　Dunagen, Ray; G. C.　　　　5.00　　　　1,900.00　　　12-16-55
Cultivable medium rolling land and unimproved pasture

Fig. A-III-131 K-1137-E (Courtesy U.S. Army Corps of Engineers, Mobile District, Official U.S. Army Photograph)

Fig. A-III-132 K-1137-E (Courtesy U.S. Army Corps of Engineers, Mobile District, Official U.S. Army Photograph)

K-1139-E-1-2　　　　　Dunagan, G. C.　　　　　　　3.26　　　　490.00　　　　05-12-55
Gently to medium rolling

K-1141-E　　　　　　　Robb, Leroy　　　　　　　　.29　　　　　58.00　　　　05-31-55
Topography is gently rolling

K-1142-E　　　　　　　Rundles, W. D.　　　　　　　2.00　　　　200.00　　　　05-12-55
Partially improved pasture, other being partially a gully

K-1143-E　　　　　　　Cleghorn, Ora;　　　　　　　2.29　　　　98.76　　　　　05-17-55
　　　　　　　　　　　　Bill
Gently to medium rolling

K-1145-E   Conner, Hugh E.   .73   50.00   05-13-55
This small tract was formerly set out as a building site, no development was ever made

K-1146-E   Conner, Charles C.   1.34   73.00   05-13-55
Topography is gently rolling

K-1147-E   Glass, Ruby   2.02   115.00   05-26-55
Topography is gently rolling

K-1148-E   Waldrip, Lee   4.88   640.00   06-06-55
Woodland

K-1149-1-2   Roark, Fred; Mrs. A. W.;   72.59   9,050.00   06-02-56
                 Eula; Margaret; Martin;
                 Bell, P.; Hulsey, Mary R.
The best use of the tract is believed to be forestry and small scale farming

K-1151   Roark, Fred   4.33   5,325.00   03-14-56
Road frontage and cropland

Fig. A-III-133 K-1151 (Courtesy U.S. Army Corps of Engineers, Mobile District, Official U.S. Army Photograph)

Fig. A-III-134 K-1151 (Courtesy U.S. Army Corps of Engineers, Mobile District, Official U.S. Army Photograph)

K-1152   Martin, Lloyd (deceased)   42.94   14,000.00   06-23-56
Adapted to agricultural uses

K-1153   Martin, Hubert J.   21.10   11,000.00   03-14-56
Gently to medium rolling and best suited for farming and building purposes

K-1154-1-2   Roark, Fred   53.03   18,975.00   03-14-56
The highest and best use of the tract is believed to be agricultural

K-1154-E-1-2   Roark, Fred   4.82   250.00   03-14-56
Medium rolling with about 40 percent open pastureland

K-1155-1-2   Adderholdt, H.H.; W.D.   345.49   97,630.00   02-28-56
Partly wooded and improved pastureland

K-1155-E   Adderholdt, H.H.; W.D.   .53   25.00   02-28-56
Medium rolling land suited for building lots

K-1156-E   Conner, Mrs. R.L.   11.06   725.00   05-19-55
Topography is gently to medium rolling

K-1157-E   Sanders, Mrs. L.B.   3.08   1,090.00   05-04-55
Suitable only for fuel uses

Appendix III - Land Acquisitions Information

K-1158   Owens Jr., John Henley   10.73   500.00   07-23-56
Wooded and bushed bottom land

K-1158-E   Owens Jr., John Henley   1.84   15.00   07-23-56
Wooded and bushed bottom land

K-1159-E   Guinn, Thomas L.   .09
Perpetual flowing easement

K-1160-E   Elrod, Marvin E.   .06
No description

K-1161   Johnson, J. O.   193.00   8,230.00   08-29-55
Cultivation for bottom lands with timber growing for uplands

K-1162   Unknown Cemetery
No description

K-1163   The Bowden Company   149.00   3,400.00   06-06-55
Topography is level to undulating for bottom land and medium rolling to rough for upland

K-1163-E   The Bowden Company   9.14   340.00   06-06-55
Cut over woodland and medium to steeply rolling topography

K-1164   Robertson Jr., T. H.   97.50   3,390.00   09-03-55
Topography is level for bottom land and medium to rough and broken for upland

K-1164-E-1   Robertson Jr., T. H.   9.26   450.00   09-03-55
Gently to medium rolling

K-1164-E-2   Robertson Jr., T. H.   .10   10.00   09-03-55
Woodland

K-1165-1-2   Carter, J.F.   79.25   12,200.00   03-02-56
Best use is agricultural

K-1168   Harper, H.A.   2.68   1,920.00   12-09-55
Agricultural and home site

Fig. A-III-135 K-1168 (Courtesy U.S. Army Corps of Engineers, Mobile District, Official U.S. Army Photograph)

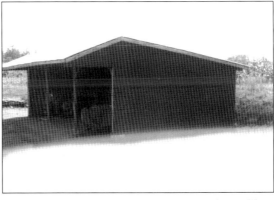

Fig. A-III-136 K-1168 (Courtesy U.S. Army Corps of Engineers, Mobile District, Official U.S. Army Photograph)

K-1169   Waldrip, G.E.   37.00   11,335.00   12-14-55
Growing crops and agricultural purposes

Tract	Owner	Acres	Amount	Date
K-1170	Gober, Cleo J.	199.00	12,500.00	04-05-56
Cropland and woodland				
K-1171	Evans, Clay	1.00	2,885.00	11-30-55
Best use is residential				
K-1172	Martin, U.M.	68.90	17,375.00	12-29-55
Best use for agricultural				
K-1173	Hill, Mrs. J. Foster; Martin, H. Lester	36.30	1,375.00	07-23-56
Idle cropland, reverting and steep hardwood land				
K-1174	Lawson, U.A.	12.40	975.00	03-15-56
Forestry and small scale farming				
K-1175	Gordon, Lawrence	.19		
No description				
K-1175-E-1-2	Gordon, Lawrence	.35		
Perpetual flowing easement				
K-1177-1-2	Christian, Ann	34.44	4,000.00	12-29-56
Highest and best use is agricultural and forestry				
K-1178	Burns, Dr. John K.	48.70	18,820.00	12-31-55
Gently to medium rolling land and the greater part is highly improved grazing land				
K-1179	Smith, Glenn	44.30	10,925.00	04-14-56
Medium to steeply rolling				
K-1181	Whelchel, Zane	19.52	1,150.00	12-16-55
Best use is agricultural and forestry				
K-1181-E	Whelchel, Zane	.69	10.00	12-16-55
Forestry				
K-1182	Baughcum, Thomas H.	22.04	4,650.00	02-17-56
Best for grazing unit				
K-1185	Highsmith, N. L.	2.07	700.00	12-19-55
Highest and best use for livestock and poultry raising				
K-1186	Martin, Wade H.	2.53	1,875.00	12-30-55
Well suited for residential and subsistence farming				
K-1188	Skinner, Ford	.82	1,746.00	05-05-56
The highest and best use of the property is residential and business				
K-1188-E	Skinner, Ford	.26	15.00	05-05-56
Best suited for building lots				
K-1191	Gober, Ford	4.70	1,225.00	12-30-55
Best suited for homesite				

K-1192	Spainhour, Ben R.	19.02	32,775.00	08-03-56

The land lies gently to medium rolling and is about 45 percent open land

K-1193	Smith, David V.	5.36	9,120.00	12-27-55

Highest and best use is residential

K-1194	Martin, V. S.	65.00	13,500.00	12-30-55

Highest and best use is agricultural

K-1195	Martin, W. A.	64.46	19,400.00	04-05-56

Cropland and pastureland

Fig. A-III-137 K-1195 (Courtesy U.S. Army Corps of Engineers, Mobile District, Official U.S. Army Photograph)

Fig. A-III-138 K-1195 (Courtesy U.S. Army Corps of Engineers, Mobile District, Official U.S. Army Photograph)

K-1196-1-2-3-4	Gober, Cleo J.	132.32	15,150.00	04-05-56

Cropland and pasture

K-1197	Martin, Evelyn B.	1.22	12,250.00	12-28-56

Homesite

K-1198-1-2	Harben Jr., Grover S.	65.20	4,100.00	07-07-56

Gently to steeply rolling and only a small part is cleared

M-1360-1-2	Georgia Power Company	159.76	6,425.00	04-05-56

Adapted to general crops

M-1360-E	Georgia Power Company	.30	10.00	04-05-56

Timber production is best use

M-1369	Brackett, Lewis G.	31.90	1,675.00	12-28-56

The highest and best use of the land is believed to be forestry

M-1370	Brackett, Harold G.	26.40	1,300.00	12-28-56

Highest and best use of property is timber production

M-1371-1-2	Brackett, Eugene	37.88	1,850.00	12-28-56

Best adapted to growing timber

M-1372-1-2	Robinson, J. T.; W. R.	62.41	3,075.00	12-28-56

The best use of the property is small scale farming and forestry

M-1373	Nix, Pearl Grace	60.00	2,800.00	06-22-56

Steeply rolling and best adapted to timber production

M-1375　　　　　　　　Grant, Jerd　　　　　　　　　　95.00　　　　　5,500.00　　　　04-05-56
Highest and best use is agricultural or forestry

M-1376　　　　　　　　Brice, R. A.　　　　　　　　　　4.52　　　　　　215.00　　　　03-23-56
Medium rolling land without improvements of any kind

M-1377　　　　　　　　Dill, Curtis; Herbert　　　　　　2.69　　　　　　140.00　　　　07-28-56
Medium rolling wooded land, with a small amount of merchantable timber

M-1382　　　　　　　　Smith, A. R.　　　　　　　　　　4.59　　　　　　450.00　　　　12-03-56
Agricultural and forestry purposes

M-1382-E　　　　　　　Smith, A. R.　　　　　　　　　　1.45　　　　　　20.00　　　　12-03-56
Open pastureland

M-1383　　　　　　　　Grant, Guy A.　　　　　　　　　6.20　　　　　　475.00　　　　04-26-56
Medium rolling land of which about 40 percent is cleared

M-1384　　　　　　　　Robinson, C. O.　　　　　　　　58.00　　　　　5,600.00　　　　12-04-56
Agricultural and forestry

M-1385　　　　　　　　Martin, Vossie S.　　　　　　　12.40　　　　　　725.00　　　　09-14-56
Medium rolling wooded land with some pine sufficient for saw timber and pumpwood

M-1386　　　　　　　　Georgia Power Company　　　　5.00　　　　　　500.00　　　　05-07-56
Best use for cabin site and forestry

M-1387　　　　　　　　West Lumber Company, Inc.　　112.00　　　　　7,200.00　　　　06-22-56
The land is generally of a rugged, rocky nature and is best suited to forestry

M-1387-E-1-2　　　　　West Lumber Company, Inc.　　1.22　　　　　　10.00　　　　　06-22-56
Steep wooded area best suited for forestry

N-1401　　　　　　　　Mundy, J. B.　　　　　　　　　132.00　　　　　20,250.00　　　04-26-55
Tract well located, general and dairy farm, with added value for home development purposes

N-1401-E　　　　　　　Herman, E.F.　　　　　　　　　2.19　　　　　　　　　　　　　06-18-58
Perpetual road easement

N-1402-1-2-3-4　　　　Chattahoochee Country Club,　288.36　　　　　66,800.00　　　02-10-56
　　　　　　　　　　　Inc.
Suited for cultivation, pasture and building sites

Fig. A-III-139 N-1402-1-2-3-4 (Courtesy U.S. Army Corps of Engineers, Mobile District, Official U.S. Army Photograph)

Fig. A-III-140 N-1402-1-2-3-4 (Courtesy U.S. Army Corps of Engineers, Mobile District, Official U.S. Army Photograph)

N-1402-E-1	Chattahoochee Country Club, Inc.	.34	100.00	02-10-56
Best use is for home development purposes				
N-1402-E-2 thru 18	Chattahoochee Country Club, Inc.	14.67	15.00	02-10-56
Roadway and woodland				
N-1403	Holcombe, J. Hubert	78.00	8,450.00	02-29-56
Forestry and agriculture is best use				
N-1403-E	Holcombe, J. Hubert	.62	10.00	02-29-56
Suited for forestry				
N-1404	Smith, Monroe C.	16.00	2,115.00	02-17-56
Gently to steeply rolling and best use is for pasture				
N-1405-E	McIntyre, Hershell A.	1.90	15.00	02-26-57
Reverting creek bottoms				
N-1406-E	Souther, O. J.	.92	10.00	03-23-57
Reverting creek bottoms				
N-1407	Hooper, O. M.	5.58	660.00	02-23-56
Best suited for grazing				
N-1407-E	Hooper, O. M.	1.77	20.00	02-23-56
Best suited for grazing				
N-1408	Sargent, G.F.	.31		
No description				
N-1410	Fuller, Minnie Dunlap	45.20	4,750.00	07-23-56
Gently to medium rolling				
N-1410-E	Fuller, Minnie Dunlap	.01		06-27-58
Perpetual road easement				
N-1411	Mundy, J. B.	14.92	2,176.00	04-05-56
Best use is farming and chicken raising				
N-1413	Thompson Graveyard	1.00	1.00	01-17-57
The topography is from gently to medium rolling				
N-1414	Dunlap Jr., Edgar B.	77.40	8,000.00	07-23-56
Highest and best use is believed to be forestry				

N-1415-1-2-3   Dunlap, James Gayle   52.64   5,850.00   07-23-56
HIghest and best use would be timber growing

Fig. A-III-141 N-1415-1-2-3 (Courtesy U.S. Army Corps of Engineers, Mobile District, Official U.S. Army Photograph)

Fig. A-III-142 N-1415-1-2-3 (Courtesy U.S. Army Corps of Engineers, Mobile District, Official U.S. Army Photograph)

N-1416   Dunlap Jr., Edgar B..   62.80   14,175.00   04-27-56
General farming

N-1417   Hardy, Ann Dunlap   7.42   465.00   12-28-56
Topography steep and rugged and best suited for forestry

N-1418-1-2   Dunlap, James A.   31.57   2,900.00   07-23-56
Believed to be best suited for agriculture purposes

N-1424   Hamilton, Edward C.;   .46   180.00   06-01-56
          Mrs. Edward C.
The highest and best use of the tract is believed to be agricultural

N-1425   Wingo, E. C.   23.60   3,650.00   02-15-56
Level to steeply rolling and adapted to general crops, pasture and woodland

N-1425-E-1-2-3   Wingo, E. C.   1.98   120.00   02-15-56
Level to steeply rolling and adapted to crops, pasture and woodland

N-1426-1-2   McFalls, Velton   11.71   550.00   05-07-56
Consists of some good young pine but largely a mixed variety of hardwood

N-1427   Wilson, Jack   2.18   186.00   03-02-56
Best use is for homesite and timber growing

N-1427-E   Wilson, Jack   .23   10.00   03-02-56
Best suited for growing timber

N-1428   Martin, W. G.   52.70   3,550.00   02-16-56
The highest and best use of the tract is forestry

N-1428-E   Martin, W. G.   .92   10.00   02-16-56
The highest and best use of the tract is forestry

N-1429   McIntyre, Dillie   62.00   4,010.00   03-01-56
Best use is agricultural

N-1429-E   McIntyre, Dillie   .23   10.00   03-01-56
Best use is agricultural

Appendix III - Land Acquisitions Information

N-1430   Wingo, E. C.   8.95   775.00   07-23-56
Highest and best use is for timber production

N-1431   Loggins Sr., W. K.   .91   200.00   05-10-57
The topography is medium rolling and is adapted to timber growing which is the highest and best use

N-1434   Gaddy, W.H.   84.00   10,475.00   02-10-56
Best use is agricultural

N-1435-1-2   Chapman, Joe T.   87.73   8,175.00   04-05-56
Pasture and cropland

N-1436   Johnson, Claude   141.00   17,325.00   02-24-56
Best suited for agricultural purposes

Fig. A-III-143 N-1436 (Courtesy U.S. Army Corps of Engineers, Mobile District, Official U.S. Army Photograph)

Fig. A-III-144 N-1436 (Courtesy U.S. Army Corps of Engineers, Mobile District, Official U.S. Army Photograph)

N-1437   Smith, James M.   132.00   13,480.00   02-16-56
Highest and best use is agricultural and forestry

N-1438   Reynolds, Theron C.;   93.80   13,550.00   12-23-55
                             Mrs. Theron C.
Best suited for dairy farming, pasture and woodland

N-1439   Stephens, Mrs. W. O.   139.21   13,000.00   04-05-56
Cultivated bottoms with reverting uplands

N-1440   Dunlap Jr., Edgar B.   119.00   9,600.00   07-23-56
Best suited for agricultural uses

N-1441-1-2   Parker, Claude W.   36.51   1,850.00   03-01-56
Best suited to growing timber

N-1442　　　　　　　　Haynes, Pierce N.　　　　　　589.80　　　　　　　　12-29-55
No description

Fig. A-III-145
N-1442
(Courtesy
U.S. Army
Corps of
Engineers,
Mobile
District,
Official U.S.
Army
Photograph)

Fig. A-III-146
N-1442
(Courtesy
U.S. Army
Corps of
Engineers,
Mobile
District,
Official U.S.
Army
Photograph)

Fig. A-III-147
N-1442
(Courtesy
U.S. Army
Corps of
Engineers,
Mobile
District,
Official U.S.
Army
Photograph)

Fig. A-III-148
N-1442
(Courtesy
U.S. Army
Corps of
Engineers,
Mobile
District,
Official U.S.
Army
Photograph)

N-1442-E-1-2-3-4-5　　Haynes, Pierce N.　　　　　　13.04　　　　　　　　　　12-29-55
Perpetual road easement

N-1443　　　　　　　　Couch, Mrs. W. T.　　　　　　2.30　　　　500.00　　　04-13-56
Topography is gently rolling and part of the area is an idle old field and part woodland

N-1443-E-1　　　　　　Couch, Mrs. W. T..　　　　　　.23　　　　　950.00　　　04-13-56
Topography is gently rolling

N-1443-E-2　　　　　　Couch, Mrs. W. T.　　　　　　.23　　　　　10.00　　　　04-13-56
Best uses would be woodland and growing timber

N-1447　　　　　　　　Green, Minnie　　　　　　　　154.00　　　11,300.00　　04-05-56
Best suited for agriculture

N-1448　　　　　　　　Couch, Sallie B.　　　　　　　65.10　　　　4,500.00　　12-29-55
Best adapted to general farming

N-1448-E　　　　　　　Couch, Sallie B.　　　　　　　4.55　　　　300.00　　　12-29-55
Unimproved pasture

N-1449-E-1-2　　　　　Fuller, Ernest　　　　　　　　2.47　　　　250.00　　　03-23-56
Wooded

N-1451-E　　　　　　　Pittman, William　　　　　　　.46　　　　　25.00　　　07-26-57
Best suited for building lot

APPENDIX III - LAND ACQUISITIONS INFORMATION

N-1455-E Buffington, Irene G.; R. D. .02 10.00 02-25-56
This very small piece of land is a traingular shaped body along old road

N-1456-E Satterfield, Maxie G. .33 140.00 10-19-55
Yard and garden

N-1459 Robertson, T. H. .23 1,720.00 07-10-57
Used as nursery

N-1460-E Green, Idell 1.26 150.00 12-31-55
Wooded , suited for building lots

N-1461-E Couch, Charlie B. .23 60.00 08-16-57
Woodland

N-1462 Couch, W. T. 1.68 1,100.00 05-19-56
Medium rolling land adapted to residential and subsistence farming

N-1462-E Couch, W. T. .34 85.00 05-19-56
Medium rolling land adapted to resident and small scale farming uses

Fig. A-III-149 N-1442 and N-1463 (Courtesy U.S. Army Corps of Engineers, Mobile District, Official U.S. Army Photograph)

Fig. A-III-150 N-1442 and N-1463 (Courtesy U.S. Army Corps of Engineers, Mobile District, Official U.S. Army Photograph)

N-1463 Anderson, Boyd .75 7,800.00 03-22-56
Building site

N-1464 Martin, Cora 9.25 6,100.00 08-03-56
Gently to medium rolling and highest and best use of the subject tract is for subdivision

N-1466 Minor, Mrs. Hugh 1.15 500.00 07-23-56
Highest and best use is for residential purposes

N-1467 Little, L. L. 1.15 1,000.00 12-29-55
Best use is agriculture

N-1467-E Little, L. L. .23 250.00 12-29-55
Best use is agricultural

N-1469-E Haynes, D. T. 1.29 6,700.00 04-11-56
Homesite and wooded area

N-1471 Thomas, Franklin 3.75 9,150.00 05-07-56
Subdivision

Tract	Owner	Acres	Price	Date
N-1472-E Building lot	Elrod, Mrs. Wynell C.	.13	50.00	06-08-57
N-1473-E-1 Residential	Pinson, Clyde; Cordell	.32	2,200.00	08-31-56
N-1473-E-2 Residential	Pinson, Clyde; Cordell	.69	50.00	08-31-56
N-1474 Perpetual flowing easement	Whelchel Estate, E.H.	.46		12-06-57
N-1476 Best use part time farming	Whelchel, S. B.	36.70	6,450.00	04-26-56
N-1480 Topography is gently to medium rolling	Allison, B. N.	1.75	4,835.00	04-11-56
N-1481 Best suited to row crop farming and lies from level to gently rolling	Whelchel, Mrs. D. C.	48.90	8,000.00	04-05-56
N-1481-E Road frontage	Whelchel, Mrs. D. C.	.32	160.00	04-05-56
N-1482 Topography is gently rolling and best adapted to building site	Hulsey, K. G.; Mrs. K. G.	3.00	20,125.00	03-08-56

Fig. A-III-151 N-1482 (Courtesy U.S. Army Corps of Engineers, Mobile District, Official U.S. Army Photograph)

Fig. A-III-152 N-1482 (Courtesy U.S. Army Corps of Engineers, Mobile District, Official U.S. Army Photograph)

Tract	Owner	Acres	Price	Date
N-1486 Topography is gently rolling and best adapted to pasturing	Patterson, Paxton K.	4.13	6,350.00	04-27-56
N-1487 Small corn or grazing patch	Patterson, Octavia Smith	3.04	12,425.00	03-02-56
O-1502-E Consists of part of a tract which is a very desirable building site	Sailors, Horace	.17	3,000.00	07-23-56
O-1503-E Made land borrowed from surrounding area	Davis, J. B.	.26	9,500.00	12-29-55
O-1504-E Highway frontage	Davis, Mattie J.	.42	125.00	12-29-55

Appendix III - Land Acquisitions Information

O-1505-E   Smith, J. M.   1.01   4,300.00   12-29-55
Housesite

O-1506-E-1   Moon, Mrs. S. C.   .34   675.00   12-31-55
Gently rolling

O-1506-E-2   Moon, Mrs. S. C.   .15   45.00   01-27-56
Gently rolling

O-1508-E   Telford, Joe K.   .49   900.00   02-15-56
Acreage here just large enough for house and small garden or yard

O-1509-E-1   Kanaday, Ruth; Wilma   .53   325.00   12-27-55
Medium rolling wooded and brush land, well suited for homesite

O-1509-E-2   Kanaday, Ruth; Wilma   .69   4,400.00   12-27-55
Highest and best use is residential

O-1510-E-1   O'Kelley, N. E.   .02   500.00   06-22-56
Building lot

O-1510-E-2   O'Kelley, N. E.   .03   25.00   06-22-56
Building lot

O-1513   Lawson, G. A.   2.98   13,425.00   12-15-55
Best suited for homesites and subsistence farming

Fig. A-III-153 O-1513 (Courtesy U.S. Army Corps of Engineers, Mobile District, Official U.S. Army Photograph)

Fig. A-III-154 O-1514 (Courtesy U.S. Army Corps of Engineers, Mobile District, Official U.S. Army Photograph)

O-1514   Peck, Frank   .29   6,050.00   07-23-56
Topography is gently rolling and adaptable for homesite

O-1515   Griffin, Mood   .34   3,900.00   03-27-56
Topography is gently rolling

O-1516   Oliver, R. A.   2.98   11,915.00   02-09-56
The highest and best uses being residential and subsistence farming

O-1517   Oliver, Robert Rogers   .91   6,750.00   02-17-56
Topography is not very good but is a very desirable homesite

O-1518   White, Bennie H.   .62   7,700.00   04-12-56
Topography is level to medium rolling

O-1519	Nagle Sr., Clyde W.	12.25	24,000.00	12-10-55

Adaptable to residence and small operation of truck, etc., or just a homesite and residence

O-1520	Whelchel, William P.	17.49	7,000.00	11-15-55

Woodland and highway frontage

Fig. A-III-155 O-1520 (Courtesy U.S. Army Corps of Engineers, Mobile District, Official U.S. Army Photograph)

Fig. A-III-156 O-1520 (Courtesy U.S. Army Corps of Engineers, Mobile District, Official U.S. Army Photograph)

O-1521	Grizzle, Raymond; Ora	.70	2,450.00	03-08-56

Suitable for housesite and supporting buildings

O-1523	Dale, E. C.	12.47	8,890.00	12-09-55

Bottom and woodland

O-1524-1-2-3	Merritt, W. V.	8.22	850.00	12-29-55

Best suited to wooded growth and timberland

O-1524-E	Merritt, W. V.	1.60	375.00	12-29-55

Wooded area

O-1525	Wilkerson, Maude	16.30	1,300.00	04-19-56

Adapted to growing timber and grazing

O-1526	Wiley, Leonard	7.81	2,335.00	12-31-55

Topography steeply to medium rolling

O-1526-E	Wiley, Leonard	.04	25.00	12-31-55

Topography is medium to steeply rolling

O-1527-E	Wiley, Mrs. L. M.	.10	3,350.00	12-30-55

Highway frontage

O-1528-1-2	Lawson, I. L.	27.78	1,800.00	05-17-56

Best adapted to growing of timber and woodland

O-1529	Baker, Willie W.	16.53	1,000.00	05-07-56

Best adaptable to timberlands

O-1530	Waters, Virginia Love	9.18	575.00	03-26-56

Best suited to woodland

O-1539	Gaines, Virgil Rufus	6.34	

No description

Appendix III - Land Acquisitions Information

O-1540 Clarke, Pierce L. 23.00 1,600.00 05-07-56
Best use timber growing

O-1543 Pittman, L. E. 9.18 775.00 06-02-56
Adapted to woodland and growing of timber

O-1544-1-2 Griffin, Mood 12.83 800.00 08-25-56
Topography is gently to medium rolling, best suited to growing timber

O-1545 Coker, J. F. 9.41 770.00 03-26-56
Topography varies from gently to steeply rolling and adapted to timber production

O-1546 Truelove, Ralph 2.07 125.00 07-23-56
Topography is steeply rolling and its best and highest uses would be growing timber

O-1547 Holcomb, Claud 7.65 775.00 07-23-56
Topography is medium to steeply rolling and is best adapted to woodland and pasture

O-1547-E Holcomb, Claud .45 07-23-56
Perpetual flowing easement

O-1548 Moon, S. C.; McConnell, 6.20 800.00 07-23-56
Robert G.
Best suited for growing timber

O-1549 Chaney, Fannie R. 16.76 1,650.00 05-07-56
Best adapted to woodland and timber growth

O-1550 Holcomb, Claud 2.53 150.00 08-16-56
Topography medium rolling. Best adapted to growing timber

O-1551 Whelchel, S. B. 1.61 100.00 07-23-56
Area is best adapted to wooded growth or that of a building site

O-1552 Lawson, G. A. 2.25 125.00 07-23-56
Topography is gently to medium rolling and highest and best uses would be in timberland

O-1553 Whelchel, E. H. 12.85 870.00 05-07-56
Patch farming

O-1554 Haynes, D. T. 71.40 11,975.00 10-10-56
Row crops and grazing

Fig. A-III-157 O-1554 (Courtesy U.S. Army Corps of Engineers, Mobile District, Official U.S. Army Photograph)

Fig. A-III-158 O-1554 (Courtesy U.S. Army Corps of Engineers, Mobile District, Official U.S. Army Photograph)

O-1556	Stancil, Hubert	61.00	6,000.00	05-07-56
Best suited to growing timber				
O-1557	Grier, H. B.	76.90	11,650.00	08-16-56
Building site				
O-1558	Waters, Clyde	61.00	11,000.00	08-17-56
Cropland				
O-1559	Wofford, B. D.	6.30	700.00	08-17-56
Lands are best adaptable for building sites at present time				
O-1560	Little, L. L.	66.60	7,600.00	08-16-56
Bottomland and woodland				
O-1561	Wiley, Mrs. King G.	15.00	1,500.00	12-29-56
Crops and woodland				
O-1562	Pittman, L. E.	8.04	1,150.00	08-03-56
Lands best adapted to crops and also growing of timber				
O-1563	Wilson, A. H.; White E. B.	.63	50.00	12-29-56
Timber growth				
O-1564	Cagle, Mrs. E. G.	19.20	5,500.00	08-03-56
Gently to medium rolling and best suited to corn or grain crops				
O-1565	Harrison, L. C.	51.20	9,400.00	08-03-56
Topography of the land is gently to medium rolling				
O-1566-1-2-3	Norrell, Howard	61.95	7,000.00	12-28-56
The terrain is gently to medium sloping and best adapted to present use				
O-1566-E	Norrell, Howard	2.07	35.00	12-28-56
The soil in Congaree and is adapted to its present use				
O-1567	Pittman, L. E.	48.20	3,500.00	08-03-56
Highest and best use is timber growing				
O-1568	Autry, C. O.	5.19	340.00	08-03-56
Hilly and rough, its highest and best use is considered to be growing of timber				
O-1568-E	Autry, C. O.	.37	10.00	08-03-56
The terrain is hilly and it is best adapted to its present use				
O-1569	Harrison, Blanche C.	3.90	2,500.00	08-03-56
Tract is adaptable only to a dwelling and garden				

O-1575	Buffington, Christine Simpson	89.00	9,000.00	08-17-56

Topography of lands range from gently rolling to steeply rolling

Fig. A-III-159 O-1575 (Courtesy U.S. Army Corps of Engineers, Mobile District, Official U.S. Army Photograph)

Fig. A-III-160 O-1575 (Courtesy U.S. Army Corps of Engineers, Mobile District, Official U.S. Army Photograph)

O-1577	Coley, H. J.	6.20	600.00	09-10-56

Wooded tract

O-1578	Fowler, Mae	58.40	3,800.00	09-13-57

The highest and best use is believed to be agriculture and forestry

O-1580	Harrington, Mrs. John C.	103.00	12,500.00	05-07-56

Suitable for cropland or grazing

P-1600	Wilkerson, George	17.90	1,500.00	02-16-56

Level to medium rolling and adapted to pasture and woodland

P-1601	Smith, D. C.	6.84	600.00	03-01-56

Best suited for pasture and timber production

P-1602	Ridgway, B. G.	1.84	100.00	03-12-56

Topography is steeply rolling and the soil is of the Cecil-Madison series

P-1603	Shope Jr., J. B.	34.10	1,900.00	05-04-56

Level to medium rolling adapted to general crops, pasture and/or meadow and woodland

P-1605	Shope Jr., J. B.	19.05	1,100.00	02-23-56

Level to steeply sloping and best adapted to timber production

P-1606	Green, H. D.	5.11	475.00	03-16-56

Adapted to general and truck crops, pasture and/or meadow and timber

P-1607	Loggins, Charlie N.	8.26	500.00	04-14-56

Adapted to general and truck crops, pasture and/or meadow and timber production

P-1608	Puckett, Carl L.	17.45	1,500.00	08-30-56

Cropland, pasture and woodland

P-1608-E-1-2	Puckett, Carl L.	3.18	95.00	08-30-56

Cropland, pasture and woodland

P-1610-E	Harrington, Y.J.	42.36		12-06-57

Perpetual flowing easement

P-1615	Peck, Mrs. T. A.	5.35	600.00	05-07-56

General truck crops

P-1615-E	Whiten, Ethel P.	4.51		07-23-56

Perpetual flowing easement

P-1617-1-2	Lawson, I. L.	139.14	16,250.00	05-07-56

Best adapted to woodland

Fig. A-III-161 P-1617-1-2 (Courtesy U.S. Army Corps of Engineers, Mobile District, Official U.S. Army Photograph)

Fig. A-III-162 P-1617-1-2 (Courtesy U.S. Army Corps of Engineers, Mobile District, Official U.S. Army Photograph)

P-1617-E	Lawson, I.L.	.38		07-23-56

Perpetual flowing easement

P-1618	Rogers, R. L.	5.62	575.00	05-07-56

Highest and best use is for pasture and timber production

P-1620-1-2	Shirley, S. L.; Blalock, Dr. John C.	117.56	21,750.00	05-08-56

Level to steeply rolling and adapted to crops, pasture and/or meadow and timber production

P-1620-E-1-2-3	Shirley, S. L.; Blalock, Dr. John C.	.90	30.00	05-08-56

Level to steeply rolling and adapted to timber production

P-1621	Addis, John	.54	140.00	02-16-56

Adapted to truck and general crops and woodland

P-1622	Lawson, G. A.	66.00	11,900.00	05-07-56

Pasture and mixed woodland

P-1623	Lawson, I. L.	67.00	33,750.00	05-07-56

Best adapted for residential purposes

P-1624	Thomas, Amion	73.30	8,500.00	05-02-56

Adapted to general and truck crops, pasture, meadow and timber

Appendix III - Land Acquisitions Information

P-1625   Flynt Jr., John J.   142.00   15,200.00   05-07-56
Cropland and pasture

Fig. A-III-163 P-1625 (Courtesy U.S. Army Corps of Engineers, Mobile District, Official U.S. Army Photograph)

Fig. A-III-164 P-1625 (Courtesy U.S. Army Corps of Engineers, Mobile District, Official U.S. Army Photograph)

P-1626   Smith, Cecil   23.20   2,750.00   05-22-56
Topography is level to medium rolling and the highest and best use is timber and homesites

P-1627   Stephens, Claud   83.56   10,000.00   05-07-56
Adapted to general and truck crops

P-1628   Martin, G. T.   20.00   2,750.00   07-18-56
Level to medium rolling and adapted to general crops, pasture and/or meadow and timber

P-1629-1-2   Whelchel, Harold; Claude   45.22
No description

P-1629-E   Whelchel, Harold; Claude   .90   15.00   06-08-56
Medium rolling and adapted to crops, pasture, meadow and timber production

P-1630   Raven, Grover   22.57   3,000.00   04-12-56
Level to medium rolling and adapted to general crops, pasture, meadow and timber

P-1631-1-2   Miller, W. H.   218.40   28,900.00   02-03-56
Level to steeply rolling and adapted to their present use

P-1632   McDonald, John Wesley   6.51   1,025.00   05-07-56
Adapted to general crops

P-1632-E   McDonald, John Wesley   1.53   75.00   05-07-56
Cropland

P-1633-E   Fraser, G.C.   .54   01-29-59
Perpetual flowing easement

P-1634   Whelchel Cemetery   .08   1.00   01-17-57
Best use is that of a cemetery

P-1636   Parks, C. W.   14.92   3,400.00   05-07-56
Adapted to general crops

P-1636-E   Parks, C. W.   4.05   200.00   05-07-56
Cropland

P-1637-1-2   McCrary Jr., R. W.   33.59   4,150.00   05-07-56
Adapted to general and truck crops

P-1637-E-1-2   McCrary Jr., R. W.   2.98   120.00   05-07-56
Woodland and cropland

P-1638   DeVane, Felton A.   60.00   4,900.00   10-27-56
Level to medium rolling and adapted to pasture and general crops

P-1638-E-1-2   DeVane, Felton A.   1.00   20.00   10-27-56
Level to medium rolling

P-1639   Loggins, H. K.   52.80   4,800.00   05-07-56
Adapted to general and truck crops

P-1640   Cochran, J. B.   18.82   3,000.00   05-07-56
Adapted to general and truck crops

P-1641   Martin, Cora Bryan   4.13   475.00   03-31-56
Adapted to general or truck crops, pasture, meadow and timber production

P-1642   Cochran, R. C.   6.03   750.00   05-07-56
Adapted to general and truck crops

P-1642-E   Cochran, Cecil   9.57   07-23-56
Perpetual flowing easement

P-1644   Saxon, Clarence   3.74   450.00   03-30-56
Adapted to truck crops and/or timber production

P-1645   Lawson, Bessie Kemp   .52   5,335.00   04-06-56
Residential

P-1646   Lawson, William Joseph   .34   14,300.00   03-31-56
Residential

Fig. A-III-165 P-1646 (Courtesy U.S. Army Corps of Engineers, Mobile District, Official U.S. Army Photograph)

Fig. A-III-166 P-1646 (Courtesy U.S. Army Corps of Engineers, Mobile District, Official U.S. Army Photograph)

P-1648   Stepp, A. N.   27.50   2,250.00   04-14-56
Level to medium rolling and adapted to crops, pasture and timber

P-1648-E   Stepp, A. N.   4.59   50.00   04-14-56
Topography is gently to medium rolling and is open to semi-wooded pasture

Appendix III - Land Acquisitions Information

| P-1649 | Whitehead, Mrs. C. W. | 63.52 | 3,125.00 | 05-07-56 |

Adaptable to improved pasture grasses

| P-1649-E | Whitehead, Mrs. C. W. | 7.27 | 40.00 | 05-07-56 |

Woodland

| P-1650 | Stepp, R. N. | 2.00 | 125.00 | 03-29-56 |

Woodland

| P-1651 | Stepp, R. N. | 6.21 | 400.00 | 03-29-56 |

Woodland

| P-1652 | Elrod, Robert A.; Melvin F.; Lloyd D. | 24.56 | 3,350.00 | 04-27-56 |

Level to medium rolling and adapted to cattle grazing

| P-1653 | Smith, J. Alvin | 35.10 | 3,375.00 | 08-15-56 |

This is a fairly well improved farm best suited for farming and cattle raising

| P-1654 | Strickland, Will | 28.90 | 1,425.00 | 03-31-56 |

Level to medium rolling and adapted to timber production

| P-1655 | Barrett, Samuel D. | 5.75 | 1,025.00 | 05-07-56 |

Pasture and mixed woodland

| P-1655-E | Barrett, Samuel D. | 15.15 | 300.00 | 05-07-56 |

Pasture, cropland and woodland

| P-1656 | Howser, Dora A. | 44.00 | 17,400.00 | 05-23-56 |

Major portion woodland

Fig. A-III-167 P-1656 (Courtesy U.S. Army Corps of Engineers, Mobile District, Official U.S. Army Photograph)

Fig. A-III-168 P-1656 (Courtesy U.S. Army Corps of Engineers, Mobile District, Official U.S. Army Photograph)

| P-1656-E-1-2 | Howser, Dora A. | 2.92 | 50.00 | 05-23-56 |

Major portion woodland

| Q-1720 | Logan, Sarah A. | 178.00 | 12,850.00 | 08-02-55 |

Best use is forestry

| Q-1720-E | Logan, Sarah A. | 6.26 | 500.00 | 08-02-55 |

Wooded

| Q-1721-1-2 | Couch, Texie Lee; Carnes, Mary Couch; Garrett, Juanita | 8.87 | 575.00 | 12-28-55 |

Pine woodland

Q-1721-E	Couch, Texie Lee; Carnes, Mary Couch; Garrett, Juanita	2.41	500.00	12-28-55

Open cropland

Q-1723	Thomas, O. H.	17.20	2,600.00	09-18-56

Level to medium rolling and adapted to general crops

Q-1723-E-1-2	Thomas, O. H.	1.72	15.00	09-18-56

Level to gently rolling

Q-1727	Robinson, Henry L.	35.60	5,000.00	06-05-56

Level to medium rolling and adapted to general crops, pasture and/or meadow

Q-1728	Robinson, L. E.	24.70	3,400.00	10-25-56

Level to medium rolling and adapted to general crops

Q-1728-E	Robinson, L. E.	7.35	130.00	10-25-56

Narrow strip of open pasture and cropland

Q-1731	Liveright, Addie E.	190.00	8,900.00	09-24-56

Gently to steeply rolling land with 60 acres of bottom land which is growing up with brush

Q-1732	Whelchel Jr., R. A.	264.00	20,000.00	09-18-56

Level to steeply rolling

Q-1732-E	Whelchel Jr., R. A.	1.84	10.00	09-18-56

Area is Mixed woodland, medium rolling, highest and best use is for timber production

Q-1740	Garmon, E.L.	100.00	

No description

Q-1743-1-2-3-4	O'Kane, Jessie Kate	46.86	3,150.00	09-24-56

Level to medium rolling and adapted to general crops, pasture and timber

Q-1744	Smith, Cleveland	59.20	7,600.00	12-28-56

Residential

Q-1745	Smith, Florence	5.28	400.00	12-15-56

Open land, bushed up bottoms and pine woodland

Fig. A-III-169 Q-1745 (Courtesy U.S. Army Corps of Engineers, Mobile District, Official U.S. Army Photograph)

Fig. A-III-170 Q-1745 (Courtesy U.S. Army Corps of Engineers, Mobile District, Official U.S. Army Photograph)

Q-1745-E	Smith, Florence	3.21	100.00	12-15-56

Open pasture

Appendix III - Land Acquisitions Information

ID	Name	Acres	Price	Date
Q-1746	Smith, H. L.	27.60	2,250.00	06-23-56
	Open land formerly cultivated but now in pasture			
Q-1746-E	Smith, H. L.	.17	10.00	06-23-56
	Gently rolling and adapted to pasture and timber			
Q-1747	Underwood, J. T.	50.20	6,700.00	10-25-56
	Level to medium rolling and adapted to general crops, pasture and timber			
Q-1747-E-1-2-3	Underwood, J. T.	2.41	30.00	10-25-56
	Medium rolling and adapted to pasture			
Q-1748	Abercrombie, H. M.	103.91	8,224.00	08-11-56
	Level to steeply rolling and adapted to crops, pasture, meadow and timber			
Q-1749	Burkholder, Roy	9.80	1,300.00	12-26-56
	Creek bottom land, wooded upland, 1 acre highly improved pasture			
Q-1749-E	Burkholder, Roy	.63	15.00	12-26-56
	Improved pastureland			
Q-1753-1-2	Hightower, Sallie	31.32	6,450.00	01-29-57
	Bottom and upland cropland, pastureland and woodland			
Q-1753-E	Hightower, Sallie	2.07	45.00	01-29-57
	Cropland and woodland			
Q-1755-E	Whelchel, Blanche E.	9.64		08-30-58
	No description			
Q-1756-E	Underwood, J. A.	3.90	145.00	09-13-57
	The highest and best use is believed to be agriculture			
Q-1758	Keith, William David	3.60	5,000.00	09-24-56
	Level to medium rolling and adapted to general crops, pasture and/or meadow			
Q-1759	Truelove, Curtis T.	23.00	2,500.00	02-26-57
	General crops, pasture and/or meadow and timber			
Q-1760-E	Blalock, B. B.	5.97	515.00	06-14-57
	Forest products			
Q-1761-E	Etris, Mrs. A. W.	.68	25.00	08-16-57
	Road frontage			
S-1902	Bell Jr., A. W.; Bell Sr., Mrs. A.W.	184.00	9,200.00	03-30-57
	The highest and best use is for timber growing and some farming on the bottoms			
S-1905	Cagle, Dallas	3.14	250.00	08-03-56
	It is probably best suited for growing timber and subsistence farming			
S-1906	Cagle, E. J.	3.44	175.00	08-03-56
	Best suited for forestry purposes			

S-1907	Cagle, Marion J.	8.27	260.00	09-20-56

The highest and best use of the tract is believed to be agriculture and forestry

S-1908	Martin, Claudie S.	38.10	2,950.00	08-03-56

Cultivated land

S-1909	Grier, Carrie	21.35	1,400.00	03-29-57

Best use is agricultural and forestry

S-1909-E	Grier, Carrie	.23	10.00	03-29-57

Homesite and forestry

S-1910	Martin, Roy J.	67.30	2,300.00	08-03-56

The highest and best use of the property is believed to be forestry

S-1910-E	Martin, Roy J.	.30	10.00	08-03-56

The highest and best use of the property is believed to be forestry

S-1911	Rome Kraft Company	31.70	1,450.00	02-13-57

Cropland and wooded area

S-1911-E	Rome Kraft Company	.46	10.00	02-13-57

Wooded land

S-1915	Smith, John Carl	10.56	775.00	07-13-56

Gently to medium rolling with part cropland

S-1916	Savage, Homer	6.43	300.00	12-28-56

Highest and best use is forestry

S-1916-E	Savage, Homer	6.50	75.00	12-28-56

Highest and best use is forestry

S-1917	Pittman, James Allen	46.60	2,525.00	08-03-56

The highest and best use is forestry

T-2001	Perry, Ivylyn O.	23.90	1,800.00	06-22-56

Best adaptable to pasturing

T-2002	Tate, G. O.	8.70	800.00	07-13-56

Best use of subject tract is row cropping on the bottom land and timber on the upland

T-2003	Wilbanks, Guy L.; Clarence; Albert F.; Wilbanks Jr., James H.; White, Violet Wilbanks	10.56	900.00	12-08-56

Best use would be timberland

T-2004	Collins, Joseph G.	9.64	1,800.00	08-03-56

Level to undulating and adapted to general crops or as a meadow for hay production

T-2005	Wilbanks, Clyde M.	11.00	600.00	12-08-56

Timberland

Appendix III - Land Acquisitions Information

T-2008	Savage, Lillie	53.65	3,000.00	12-28-56

Best suited to pasturing with some row cropping

T-2008-E	Savage, Lillie	.46	10.00	12-28-56

Best suited for timber growing

T-2009	Wiley, Rex; Guy; Farmer, Hattie Wiley	17.00	1,400.00	06-29-56

Topography is gently to medium rolling, best adapted to cropland and pasturing

T-2010	Savage, Fred	7.86	725.00	12-28-56

Lands best suited to cropland and pasture

T-2011	Lomax, Winnie	37.93	1,850.00	12-28-56

Gently to medium rolling and best adapted to pasture

T-2014	Rome Kraft Company	98.00	4,950.00	02-13-57

Forestry

T-2014-E	Rome Kraft Company	34.44	325.00	02-13-57

Wooded

T-2015-E	Gordon, Katherine B.	8.50		07-24-58

Perpetual flowing easement

U-2101	Pittman, Mrs. H. W.	129.00	7,400.00	08-03-56

Level to steeply rolling

U-2102	Robinson, Irene Pittman	13.55	3,925.00	08-30-56

Woodland and bottom land

Fig. A-III-171 U-2102 (Courtesy U.S. Army Corps of Engineers, Mobile District, Official U.S. Army Photograph)

Fig. A-III-172 U-2102 (Courtesy U.S. Army Corps of Engineers, Mobile District, Official U.S. Army Photograph)

U-2103	Browning, J. C.	17.90	1,200.00	10-29-56

Medium rolling and best adapted to timber growing

U-2104-1-2-3-4-5-6   Mose Gordon Lumber Co.   478.93   83,000.00   08-03-56
7-8-9
Cropland and timberland

Fig. A-III-173 U-2104-1/9 (Courtesy U.S. Army Corps of Engineers, Mobile District, Official U.S. Army Photograph)

Fig. A-III-174 U-2104-1/9 (Courtesy U.S. Army Corps of Engineers, Mobile District, Official U.S. Army Photograph)

Fig. A-III-175 U-2104-1/9 (Courtesy U.S. Army Corps of Engineers, Mobile District, Official U.S. Army Photograph)

Fig. A-III-176 U-2104-1/9 (Courtesy U.S. Army Corps of Engineers, Mobile District, Official U.S. Army Photograph)

U-2104-E-1-2-3-4-5   Mose Gordon Lumber Co.   42.88   620.00   08-03-56
6-7-8-9
Level to medium rolling and adapted to pasture and timber production

U-2107   White, Luke   71.00   4,900.00   08-03-56
Level to steeply rolling and best adapted to pasture

U-2108   Gowder, Harry F.   117.00   7,250.00   07-07-56
Level to steeply rolling and adapted to general crops, pasture and timber

U-2108-E   Gowder, Harry F.   2.98   15.00   07-07-56
Medium rolling and adapted to timber

U-2109   Pittman, Bee; J. J.   23.65   2,225.00   12-14-56
Woodland

U-2109-E   Pittman, Bee; J. J.   .70   10.00   12-14-56
Adapted to timber production

V-2201   Grier, W. J.   222.00   18,750.00   08-03-56
Lands are adaptable to row cropping and timber growth

V-2202-1-2   Ferguson, Bob   14.70   775.00   08-16-57
Reverting - Highest and best uses woodland and timber growing

Appendix III - Land Acquisitions Information

V-2203   Dalton, Thomas   11.48   500.00   12-28-56
Topography is gently to medium rolling and best adapted to timberland

V-2208   Myers, Flora   22.30   2,300.00   08-03-56
Gently to medium rolling and has some very good timber on tract

V-2209-1-2   Rome Kraft Company   45.94   2,075.00   02-13-57
Wooded tract

V-2210   Grier, W. J.   12.00   1,150.00   08-03-56
Topography is gently rolling and adapted to row crops and woodland

V-2214   Wiley, Buford   14.70   1,925.00   08-13-57
Adapted best to general crops, pasture and/or meadow and the upland to timber production

V-2215-1-2   Oliver, T. D.   12.16   2,000.00   07-13-56
Medium to steeply rolling and adapted to row crops and pasture

V-2216   Faulkner, C. R.   9.36   800.00   12-28-56
Land adaptable to row crops and woodland

V-2217   Luthi, Cora Faulkner;   9.40   475.00   08-20-56
                 Jordan, Stella Faulkner
Topography is gently to medium rolling and best adapted to timber growing

Lumpkin County

Tract	Property Owner	Acres	Price	Date

Q-1735   Sosebee, Minnie   36.70   2,500.00   09-18-56
Gently to steeply rolling land

Q-1736   Reeves, Albert   6.12   600.00   12-14-56
Agriculture and forestry

Q-1741-1-2   Kimbrough Jr., Mrs. E. E.   15.84   750.00   06-18-57
HIghest and best use is believed to be agricultural

Q-1741-E   Kimbrough Jr., Mrs. E. E.   5.74   70.00   06-18-57
Level to gently rolling with idle cropland and remainder in alder bushes and small pines

Q-1742   Jones, Robert   11.71   550.00   09-24-56
Steeply rolling and it is best adapted to its present use

Q-1743-1-2-3-4   O'Kane, Jessie Kate   46.86   3,150.00   09-24-56
Level to medium rolling and adapted to general crops, pasture and timber

Q-1744 Residential	Smith, Cleveland	59.20	7,600.00	12-28-56

Fig. A-III-177 Q-1744 (Courtesy U.S. Army Corps of Engineers, Mobile District, Official U.S. Army Photograph)

Fig. A-III-178 Q-1744 (Courtesy U.S. Army Corps of Engineers, Mobile District, Official U.S. Army Photograph)

R-1801-1-2-3 The highest and best use is farming and timber growing	Jones, Robert	39.25	4,600.00	03-25-57
R-1801-E Highest and best use is for farming	Jones, Robert	4.66	100.00	03-25-57
R-1802 Best use is timber growing	Reeves, H. W.; Mrs. Missouri	10.02	675.00	12-27-56
R-1803 The tract is best adapted to agricultural and timber growing	Tucker, Roscoe	40.60	4,000.00	07-26-57
R-1804 Highest and best use is for timber growing	Poore, G. A.	15.45	850.00	12-28-56
R-1805 The land is level to gently rolling	Whelchel, Johnnie	18.40	5,000.00	08-23-57
R-1808 No description	Tate, Hubert O.	11.70		
R-1814 Best use for agriculture and stock raising	Smith, Vernon H.	43.60	8,200.00	03-22-57
R-1815 Highest and best use is for raising cattle	Head, Carrie; Martin, Mrs. Nancy H.	2.07	360.00	09-17-56
R-1816 Pastureland	Head, Floyd	7.58	600.00	09-17-57
R-1817 The best use is for timber growing	Hollis, Eugene	2.52	135.00	07-27-57
R-1818 The highest and best use is for agriculture and timber growing	Adams Sr., D. B.	21.34	2,000.00	03-27-57
R-1819 The highest and best use of this tract is for timber growing	Georgia Power Company	63.60	5,000.00	09-18-56

Appendix III - Land Acquisitions Information

*Fig. A-III-179
R-1819
(Courtesy
U.S. Army
Corps of
Engineers,
Mobile
District,
Official U.S.
Army
Photograph)*

*Fig. A-III-180
R-1819
(Courtesy
U.S. Army
Corps of
Engineers,
Mobile
District,
Official U.S.
Army
Photograph)*

NOTES

1. Promissory deed records and segment map information provided by the United States Army Corps of Engineers, Mobile District.

Appendix IV. Pertinent Statistical Data

Stream Flow

Drainage area at dam site-square miles	1,040
Estimated minimum discharge (8-25-25)-cfs	119
Minimum mean monthly flow (9-25)-cfs	263
Average annual flow (1,903 - 1,959)-cfs	202
Discharge at bankfull stage-cfs	10,000
Maximum mean monthly flow (12-32)-cfs	8,590
Maximum recorded discharge (1-8-46)-cfs	55,000

Spillway - Design Flood

National Weather Service 72 - hour storm at Long. 85 47' Lat. 35 34'	
Total rainfall - inches	30.67
Initial loss - inches	0.00
Average infiltration rate - inches per year	0.04
Total storm runoff - inches	28.52
Total volume of storm runoff -acre feet	1,581,600
Peak rates of flow	
Inflow to full reservoir - cfs	581,300
Total reservoir outflow -cfs	40,400
Spillway discharge -cfs	28,400
Duration of flood - days	5

Reservoir

Pool Elevations - feet msl	
Maximum pool, spillway design flood	1,100
Top of flood control pool	1,085
Top of conservation pool	1,071
Minimum conservation pool	1,035
Stream bed (Bottom of Flood Control Sluice)	919
Storage volumes -acre feet	
Maximum pool, spillway design flood	3,332,000
Total storage - elev. 1,085	2,554,000
Flood control storage, elev. 1,085 to 1,070 (11.48")	637,000
Conservation storage, elev. 1,070 to 1,035 (18.91")	1,049,000
Dead storage, below elev. 1,035	867,600
Reservoir areas - acres	
Maximum pool, spillway design flood	62,900
Top of flood control pool, elev. 1,085	47,182
Top of conservation pool, elev. 1,070	38,024
Top of dead storage, elev. 1,035	22,442
Area within taking line - acres	
Purchased in fee simple	56,155
Right to inundate acquired by easement	719
River bed	58,007
Total	58,007
Length of shoreline - miles	
Top of flood control pool, elev. 1,085	760
Top of conservation pool, elev. 1,070	540
Length of reservoir at elevation 1,070 - river miles	

Chattahoochee River	44
Chestatee River	19

Dam

Type	Roll - fill earth
Length along crest of main dam - feet	1,630
Top width - feet	40
Base width - feet	1,000
Height of main dam above river bed - feet	192
Total length of saddle dikes - feet	6,600
Elevation, top of dam and saddle dikes - feet msl	1,106

Spillway

Type	Uncontrolled chute
Width of chute - feet	100
Crest elevation - feet msl	1,085

Flood Control Sluice

Number of sluices	1
Diameter - feet	13.25
Discharge capacity at elev. 1,085 - cfs	11,590
Discharge capacity at elev. 1,070 - cfs	11,030
Discharge capacity at elev. 1,035 - cfs	10,080
Discharge capacity at elev. 919 (Invert) - cfs	0

Powerhouse

Size of building		
Length - feet		205
Width - feet		94.5
Type - Indoor, reinforced concrete and structural steel const.		
Elevation - feet msl		
Bottom of substructure		885
Low point of draft tube		888
Centerline of distrubuter, 40,000 kw units		927
Centerline of distrubuter, 6,000 kw units		922.5
Generating units - kw	6000	40,000
Number of units	1	2
Speed of 1 6,000 and 2 40,000 kw units, rpm	277	100
Spacing between 2 40,000 kw units centers, feet		62
Turbines		
Type - Francis		
Rotation	counterclock	clock
Guaranteed capacity - best gate,		
136 - foot net head - hp	8,400	55,000
Generators		
Rated capacity, continuous,		
60 C rise - kva	6,667	44,444
Guaranteed capacity, continuous,		
80 C rise - kva	7,667	51,111

Power factor	0.90	0.90
Voltage	13,800	13,800
Date of Initial Service	7/26/57	10/10/57
		6/19/57

Power Data

Drawdown for storage - feet	35
Volume in power storage (elev. 1,035 - 1,070) - acre feet	1,049,400
Rated net head, feet	136
Tailwater elevations, feet msl	
Maximum, all units at full gate - outflow 12,000 cfs	927
Flood Control Sluice - outflow 10,650 cfs	926
Normal, 3 units operating - outflow 8,200 cfs	924
Normal, 2 large units operating - outflow 8,000 cfs	923
Normal, 1 large unit operating - outflow 3,800 cfs	920
Minimum - no flow	914
Plant output	
Dependable capacity - kw	73,000

INDEX

access road, 72, 73, 83, 89, 121, 179, 264
access tunnel, 100, 101, 120, 121, 127
acquiring land, see Land Acquisitions-Chapter Four
advanced monies, see Appropriations-Chapter Three
advanced planning, see Appropriations-Chapter Three
Aiken, South Carolina, 264
Alabama, State of, 3, 6, 17, 18, 23, 33, 220, 238
Albany, Georgia, 3
Albrecht, Frank, 242, 246, 247
Allatoona Dam, 256
Allatoona Project, 76
Allen, Stanley, 38, 42, 43, 311
Alta Vista Cemetery, 256, 257
alternating current generators, 261
American Bridge Division, U.S. Steel Corporation, 264
Anderson, Mary Jane, see Contribution of a Georgia Poet-Chapter Eleven
Anderson, South Carolina, 256
Andrews, George W., 5, 8
annual flood damage cost, see Why Build a Dam?
Appalachian Regional Development Program, see Phil Landrum
Apalachicola, Chattahoochee, Flint River System, 1, 2, 4, 5, 6, 13, 20, 70, 74, Introduction
Apalachicola Basin, 17, 25, 33, 34, 170
Apalachicola River, 3, 4, 6, 7
appraisal section, v
appraisers, 63, 64, 65
Appropriations, 4, 37, 38, 39, 40, 41, 42, 47, 48, 49, 50, 51, 52, 53, 54, 55, 56, 251, 252, 256, 257, 258, 261, 265
arch dam, 140
Archer, Weldon, 38, 42, 43, 54, 71
Arlington Cemetery, Sandy Springs, Georgia, 252
Arlington National Cemetery, 254
Armstrong and Hand Incorporated, 262
A Song of Love, see Contribution of a Georgia Poet
A Song of the Future, see Contribution of a Georgia Poet
Asheville, North Carolina, 222, 223
Atlanta as a port city, see Why Build a Dam?
Atlanta Chamber of Commerce, 37, 38, 42, 43, 54, 226
Atlanta Freight Bureau, 25, 37, 38, 42, 43, 53, 54, 72, 76, 226
Atlanta, Georgia, 5, 17, 180, 218, 224, 249, 251, 255, 259, 262, 264
Atlanta Regional Commission, 23
Baggett, Jess, 38, 42, 43, 44, 215, 224, 257
Bagwell, Art, v, vi
Bainbridge, Georgia, 6, 7
Ballenger Paving Company, 176, 201, 202, 263, 264
Baltimore, Maryland, 75, 221, 222, 223
Barter, Edward J., 63
Bartletts Ferry Dam, 10, 11
Bell's Mill Bridge, 176, 186, 203, 204, 205, 206, 209, 235, 263, 264
Bellville, New Jersey, 262
belly dump trucks, 160
Birmingham, Alabama, 264
Bisbort, Harold E., 226, 242, 246
Board of Geographic Names, 218
boatcade, 241
Bolling Bridge, 173, 175, 197, 198, 200, 210, 263
borrow area, 92, 141, 142, 147, 153
bottom dump earth movers, 141, 147
Bradley, Omar, 253
Brasstown Bald, 20

bridge and highway relocation, see Bridge and Highway Relocation and Construction
Bristol Steel and Iron Works Incorporated, 182, 188, 262, 263
Bristol, Virginia, 182, 188, 262, 263
Brown's Bridge, 21, 182, 183, 185, 186, 188, 197, 228, 262, 264
Budget Bureau, 49, 53, 54
budget reductions, see Appropriations
Buford Dam, iii, v, 1, 2, 5, 7, 12, 13, 17, 18, 20, 21, 22, 23, 24, 25, 26, 27, 31, 33, 34, 35, 37, 38, 39, 42, 43, 48, 49, 51, 54, 59, 62, 71, 76, 82, 83, 118, 129, 142, 170, 172, 173, 178, 179, 214, 215, 216, 217, 218, 219, 227, 226, 239, 240, 244, 253, 256, 258, 261, 269,
Buford Dam Project, 12, 22, 34, 35, 36, 38, 40, 41, 42, 44, 45, 50, 53, 55, 56, 60, 70, 75, 76, 121, 227, 250
Buford Dam Road, 70, 73, 89, 152, 177, 178, 179, 241
Buford, Georgia, ii, 13, 33, 34, 74, 77, 80, 148
Bull Sluice Project, 12
butterfly valve, 131
buttress dam, 140
calyx hole, 14, 15, 16
Cannon and Jefferies, 13
Cannon, Clarence, 41, 42
Capital Construction Company 180, 262
carbon dioxide fire extinguishing equipment, 262
cemeteries, 223, 228, 249, 251, 252, 253, 254, 256, 257, 264, 280, 282, 286, 296, 302, 309, 310, 311, 314, 315, 316, 324, 329, 330, 336, 340, 342, 344, 352, 368
Centennial Exposition, 222
Central Georgia, 24
ceremonial plaques, 226
cfs, 26, 380, 381, 382
Chancellorsville, 220
Charles Scribner's Sons, 222
Charlotte, North Carolina, 92, 262
Chattahoochee National Forest, 21
Chattahoochee River, 2, 3, 6, 7, 8, 9, 12, 13, 17, 18, 20, 21, 23, 24, 25, 26, 27, 33, 34, 37, 38, 39, 66, 70, 74, 83, 87, 96, 109, 111, 118, 119, 121, 123, 141, 142, 143, 144, 145, 146, 150, 159, 170, 174, 179, 181, 182, 188, 192, 206, 215, 216, 217, 218, 219, 226, 229, 230, 235, 236, 238, 242, 264, 381
Chattahoochee River Valley, 13
Cheeley, Joe, 43
Cherokee Indians, 215, 224, 230
Chester, South Carolina, 264
Chief of Army Engineers, 71, 72, 121, 217, 243
Chipola River, 3
Chorpening, General, 18, 33, 34
City Mills Dam, 9
Civil Service Committee, 251
Civil War, 3, 9, 62, 219, 220
Clark, A.L., 43
Clark, English, 43
Clark's Bridge, 173, 237, 264
Cleveland, Georgia, 258
Coca Cola, 244, 245
cofferdam, 126, 128, 132, 136, 137,
cold war, iii, 7
Columbia River, 254
Columbus Construction Company, 203, 209, 264
Columbus, Georgia, 3, 4, 6, 9, 11, 24, 25, 74, 192, 203, 209, 262, 264
commercial growth, 21, 22, 24, 25, 26
Committee on Agriculture and Forestry, 253
Committee on Agriculture, Nutrition, and Forestry, 253
Committee on Appropriations, 38, 40, 41, 50, 54, 251, 268

Committee on Armed Services, 251
Committee on Finance, 253
Committee on Foreign Relations, 253
Committee on Immigration, 251
Committee on Manufactures, 251
Committee on Privileges and Elections, 253
Committee on Rivers and Harbors, 4, 6, 17, 18, 224
commodities, 7, 24
Commodores, honorary, 245
Compton, California, 13
Communications Zone across France, 254
concrete batching and mixing plant, 111, 128
condemnation procedures, 65
conference committee, 40, 41, 51, 244
concerned citizens over proposed dam, see Land Acquisitions
congressional appropriations, see Appropriations
contracts, 27, 53, 261
Cooper, John M., 38, 42, 43, 226
core trench, 111, 153, 156
Corn, poem, 222
Creek Indians, 20
Crow, Sorghum, 21
Cudahy, Wisconsin, 262
Culpepper, C.B., 43, 54
Cumming, Georgia, 71, 84, 258
Cushman, Charlotte, 222
Cyclops Iron Works, 264
C.Y. Thomason Company, 175, 182, 192, 262
damaged property, 55, 65
Davis, James C., 14, 33, 37, 39, 40, 71, 73, 75, 76, 89, 117, 139, 226, 243, 247, 251
Dawson County, iii, 44, 173, 176, 201, 202, 269
Day, Charles, 220
DBA Williamette Iron and Steel Company, 262
Decatur, Georgia, 161, 186, 262, 264
DDT, 233
dedication, 42, 74, 239, 240, 241, 242, 244, 245, 247, 253
defense role of river, see Apalachicola, Chattahoochee, Flint River System-Introduction
DeKalb County, 37, 43, 44
DeKalb Federal Savings and Loan, 251
Department of the Army, ii, 23, 33, 50, 255
Deputy Chief of Engineers, 72, 77, 254
destroyed property, 62
Director of the Joint Construction Agency in France, 254
District of Columbia Committee, 39, 251
Dodd, Bobby, 214
Douglasville, Georgia, 203, 206, 263
Dover, Paul, 42, 43
draft tubes, 121, 128, 129, 130, 131, 132, 136, 137, 264, 381
Drake, Lionel, 43
dredging, 3, 4, 24, 189
Drewry's Bluffs, 220
drilling penstocks, 52, 83, 97, 98, 99, 100, 101, 102, 103, 107, 108, 109, 112, 118, 121, 122, 123, 124, 126, 127, 128, 130, 131, 132, 133, 145
Duluth, Georgia, 21, 24, 37
dumptor, 98, 99
dump trucks, 160
Dunlap Dam, 232
East Bank Park, 142, 179
East Pittsburgh, Pennsylvania, 261
Eagle-Phenix Dam, 9
E day, 234
Ed Smith and Sons, 264
Eisenhower, Dwight, 53, 54, 219, 253
electric lines, 263
Elks Lodge, 256
Emergency Relief Appropriations Act, 4
Eminent Domain, 62

Engineer Commissioner for District of Columbia, 254
Engels, Albert J., 42
estimated cost of planning, see Appropriations
Europe,, 215, 219
Ewing, L.D., 42, 43, 44, 71, 256, 257
extension of navigation channel, see Why Build a Dam?
Extension Service, 63
families relocated, see Land Acquisitions
Faye, Spofford, and Thordike, 253
Federal Pacific Electric Company, 263
Felton, Rebecca Latimer, 253
Fifty (50) Year Flood, 23
final appraisal, 64
first reservoir tract purchased, see Land Acquistions
fiscal year appropriations, see Appropriations
Flint River, 1, 2, 3, 4, 5, 6, 7, 13, 20, 21, 22, 24, 26, 70, 243
flood control, 2, 4, 5, 7, 12, 20, 21, 22, 24, 27, 36, 38, 48, 50, 237, 380, 381, 382
flood plain information study, 23, 24, 33
flood storage, 5, 22, 23, 217
Florida, 3, 4, 6, 33, 221, 222, 327
Flowery Branch, Georgia, 37, 175, 228, 229, 236, 319
Ford Foundation, 250
Ford, Gerald R., 34
forebay, 51, 52, 53, 83,, 86, 91, 92, 93, 94, 95, 96, 97, 98, 99, 100, 101, 103, 104, 107, 108, 109, 110, 111, 113, 114, 118, 119, 120, 122, 123, 126, 144, 145, 154, 159, 177, 181, 228, 261,
Forrester, E.L., 43
Forsyth County, ii, v, vi, 15, 21, 42, 51, 58, 63, 64, 66, 67, 93, 139, 154, 156, 157, 159, 183, 184, 186, 198, 199, 228, 236, 258, 259, 264, 279
Franklin, North Carolina, 175, 262
Frederick R. Harris Organization, 37
Fulton County, 25, 37, 42, 44
funding, see Appropriations
Furcron, A.S., 215
Gainesville Auto Wrecking Company, 264
Gainesville, Georgia, v, vi, 31, 37, 38, 40, 42, 43, 45, 49, 54, 57, 59, 63, 68, 71, 72, 76, 78, 173, 175, 176, 188, 189, 191, 192, 194, 203, 204, 206, 229, 256, 257, 263, 264, 268, 334, 337
Galloway, T.O., 43, 54
gantry crane, 264
Gardner, Weldon, ii, 14, 42, 43, 44, 54, 71, 72, 74, 76, 77, 80, 225, 226, 227, 241, 245, 256, 257
gate closing ceremony, see Lake Sidney Lanier
Gates and Fox, Incorporated, 97
General Electric Company, 263
generators, 27, 131, 133, 135, 234, 261, 381
George, Walter F., 9, 25, 40, 41, 71, 75, 243, 252, 253
George W. Andrews Lock and Dam, 5, 8
Georgia Pacific Plywood Company, 255
Georgia Power Company, ii, 9, 10, 11, 12, 18, 27, 38, 216, 230, 276, 314, 324, 329, 337, 354, 355, 377
Georgia Public Health Service, 233
Georgia State Route no.11, 263
Georgia State Route no.53, 262
Georgia State Route no.115, 263
Georgia State Route no.136, 263
Georgia Supreme Court, 254
Glenwood Cemetery, 254
Goat Rock Dam, 10
Goat Rock Lake, 10
government facilities, see Why Build a Dam?
government leased areas, see Why Build a Dam?
Grants Pass, Oregon, 97
grassing main earth dam, see Main Earth Dam Construction
gravity dam, 13, 49, 140, 141
Great Depression, 216
Great Georgian Award, 250

Greenville, South Carolina, 175, 176, 182, 192, 201, 202, 263, 264
Greenwood, South Carolina, 262
Griffin, Marvin, 243, 246, 247
ground breaking, 51, 69, 70, 71, 72, 73, 74, 75, 77, 78, 80, 178, 226, 227, 241, 242, 243, 244, 252, 254, 255, 256, 257
ground breaking luncheon, 77
Groves, Lundin, and Cox Incorporated, 83, 92, 97, 177, 261
Guy F. Atkinson Company, 262
Gulf of Mexico, 7, 13, 21, 22, 24, 25, 37, 250
Gwinnett County, iii, 16, 26, 37, 42, 44, 70, 72, 73, 118, 139, 141, 144, 154, 156, 159, 257, 258, 306
Gwinnett County Chamber of Commerce, 42, 71, 77, 256, 258
Gwinnett County Industrial Development Authority, 257
Gwinnett Federal Savings and Loan Association, 258
Gwinnett Hospital Authority, 257
Gwinnett Memorial Gardens, 258
Gwinnett Park, 83, 87
Habersham County, 44, 223
Hall County, iii, 20, 26, 37, 40, 42, 43, 44, 57, 59, 63, 66, 72, 171, 173, 174, 175, 182, 183, 184, 185, 188, 192, 196, 197, 198, 199, 201, 202, 203, 204, 211, 223, 229, 230, 231, 232, 235, 238, 256, 264, 308, 349
Hamilton, Drew, 43
Hampton, Georgia, 253, 263
Hancock County, Mississippi, 256
Harnischfeger Corporation, 263
Harris, Arthur L., 43, 54
Hart, Eugene, 42, 43, 72
Hartsfield, William B., 25, 35, 36, 37, 38, 39, 42, 53, 70, 71, 74, 76, 77, 78, 80, 102, 117, 214, 224, 226, 227, 241, 242, 244, 245, 247, 249, 250, 256, 257, 258
Hartwell Dam, 76, 256
head gates, see Forebay Excavation and Intake Construction
Highway 53, 174, 175, 176, 188, 190, 197
Highway 60, 177, 192, 231
Highway 129, 203, 206, 235
Highway 136, 177, 201, 202, 203, 231
Highway 141, 24, 175, 183, 228, 262, 264
Highway 306, 175
Highway 369, 175, 182, 186
Highway 400, 175
Highway 996, 175
Henry Newton Company, 186, 262
Hill, J.E., 161, 264
H.M. Rodgers and Son, 87, 261
Hoeffner, H., 226, 227, 242
hoist car, 262
Holder, Robert M., 43, 54
Holle, General, 53, 117
Hosch, Lester W., 38, 42, 43, 44, 57, 63, 255, 256
House of Representatives, U.S., 4, 6, 17, 18, 33, 34, 37, 39, 40, 41, 43, 46, 51, 53, 54, 217, 219, 224, 251, 252,
Houser's Mill Bridge, 264
Houston, Texas, 262
H.R. 308, 4, 17
H.R. 6407, 6, 7
humidity controlled building, 161
hydraulic turbine, 261
hydro power, 2, 27
Hyms of the Marshes, poem, 222
impounding reservoir, 231
impoundment delay, see Lake Sidney Lanier-Chapter Twelve
industrial growth, 20, 22, 25, 36
Inland Bridge Company Incorporated, 201, 202, 264
intake structure, 14, 54, 55, 92, 93, 100, 101, 107, 108, 109, 110, 111, 112, 113, 114, 132, 141, 149, 159, 164, 185, 199, 200, 202, 219, 226, 228, 230, 240, 241, 262

Intermediate Regional Flood, 23
Interstate 985, 175
intracoastal waterway, 5, 7, 250
Ivey Brothers Construction Company, Incorporated, 262
Jackson, Charles, 36, 42, 51, 76, 117, 121, 150, 256
J.A. Jones Construction Company, 92, 262
James Leffer and Company, 261
Jared, Edmond F., 43
Jasper, Georgia, 252
Jaycees, 256
J.E. Hill, 161, 264
Jenkins, Ed, 252
Jerry D. Jackson Bridge, 188
Jewett, Colonel, 72, 77, 90
Jim Woodruff Lock and Dam, 7, 8, 9, 11, 12, 243
John Hopkins University, 222
John J. Harte Company, 255
Joint Committee on Internal Revenue Taxation, 253
Joint Construction Agency in France, 254
Jones Private Argument, poem, 222
Jones, Seaborn, 9
Johnston, James R., 114
Julius A. Schwerin Jr., 264
J.W. Moorman and Son, 141, 262
Keith's Bridge, 66, 171, 174, 228
Kennedy, John, 243, 251, 255
Kenton, Ohio, 262
kilowatt production, 8, 9, 10, 11, 12, 27
King Arthur series of books, 222
Kiwanis Club, 71, 77, 258
Kleckley, J. Larry, 42, 43, 44, 71, 76, 256
KSL, ii, 28, 29, 30
Lake George W. Andrews, 8
Lake Harding, 11
Lake Lanier Islands Authority, 29, 257
Lake Oliver, 10
Lake Seminole, 7, 8, 243
Lake Sidney Lanier, ii, iii, 12, 13, 17, 18, 22, 31, 33, 34, 60, 170, 216, 217, 218, 219, 226, 238, 259, 266
Lake Warner, 232
land acquisitions, 60, 62, 63, see chapter 4
land acquisition concerns, see Land Acquisitions
land acquisition talks, see Land Acquisitions
Langdale Dam, 11
Landrum-Griffin Act , 252
Landrum, Phil, 61, 117, 217, 243, 246, 252
Lanier Bridge, 176, 188, 189, 190, 191, 192, 230, 262, 263
Lanier, Clifford, 219, 220, 222, 228
Lanier, Mary Jane, 219
Lanier, Park, 83, 87
Lanier Park Hospital, 256
Lanier Project Management Office, 178
Lanier, Robert Sampson, 219
Lanier, Sidney Clopton, iii, 214, 218, 219
L.A. Tvedt Contractors, 261
Lawrenceville, Georgia, 37, 38, 42, 43, 224, 257, 258
lawsuits, see Land Acquisitions-Chapter Four
Lazer Creek Lake Dam, 26
legal challenges, see Land Acquisitions
Leather's Ford, 172, 232
Lee's Slough, 3
levee, 4, 24
Library Services Act, 252
Lights Bridge, 228
Little-Davenport Funeral Home Incorporated, 264
Lippincott's Magazine, 222
Lions Club, 258
lobbying, 40, 52, 54, 257
Lockheed C-130 Transport, 241
locks, 2, 3, 5, 12, 25
Londonderry, New Hampshire, 254
Longstreet Bridge, 172, 176, 203, 206, 207, 208, 209, 210, 211, 230, 235, 263, 264
Los Angeles, California, 263
Lower Auchumphee Creek Lake Dam, 26

Lower Chipola River, 3
Lower MeKong River Basin, 254
LUCY, blockade runner, 220
Lumpkin County, iii, 44, 172, 173, 376
Lumpkin County Commissioner of Roads and Revenue, 172, 212
Lynch, R.S., 43, 54
Lynn, North Carolina, 222, 223
Macon Construction Company, 175, 262
Macon Volunteers of the Second Georgia Battalion, 219
main earth dam, see also chapter nine, 50, 54, 55, 57, 82, 83, 84, 92, 109, 118, 119, 123, 126, 127, 128, 139, 141, 142, 143, 144, 146, 147, 150, 153, 156, 157, 158, 160, 161, 165, 177, 179, 180, 182, 226, 231, 237, 241, 259, 261, 262
Malvern Hill, 220
management study, 26
Manchester, Missouri, 254
marinas, v, 28, 30, 31, 174
Maryland, 220, 221, 223
Mattingly, Mack, 253
McGurdy, Julius, 43
Medlock Bridge, 23, 24
Memorial Park, Gainesville, Georgia, 256
Memphis, Tennessee, 87, 261
Metropolitan Atlanta Waters Resources, 26
Meyer, Sylvan, 43, 54, 71
Midway, Georgia, 219
military use of Chattahoochee River, see Apalachicola, Chattahoochee, Flint River System-Introduction
Milwaukee Crane and Service Company, 262
Milwaukee, Wisconsin, 263
Minneapolis, Minnesota, 83, 92, 177, 261
Mobile, Alabama, 17, 18, 23, 33, 238, 255, 259, 263
Mobile District Chief, 7, 65, 71, 72, 75, 77, 121, 242, 243
modified reservoir clearing, 64
monolith no.1, 104, 105, 107, 109, 110, 112
monolith no.2, 105, 107, 108, 109
monolith no.3, 106, 107
Montezuma, Georgia, 3
Montgomery, Alabama, 220
Moore, Fred, 43, 54
Moore, Wiley, 43
Morgan Falls, 12
mosquitoes, v, 233
motorcade, 72, 73, 241
motor pool, 180, 181
Mountain Home, Arkansas, 263
Mountain View Park, 182
Mountain Willie, 256
mucking operation, 98, 99, 100
Muskogee, Oklahoma, 262
NASA testing facilities, 256
NATO, 253
Nashville, Tennessee, 188, 230, 262
National Vocational Education Act, 252
navigation on the Chattahoochee River, see Why Build a Dam?-Chapter One
Navy bombers, 241
negotiators, see Land Acquisitions
New Bridge, 172, 173, 196, 232, 236
Newport News Shipbuilding and Dry Dock, Company, 261
Newport News, Virginia, 254, 261
New York, 220, 221, 222, 224, 259
Nine from Eight, poem, 222
Nix Bridge, 173, 212, 232
Nixon, Richard M., 218, 253
Norcross, Georgia, ii, 37, 42, 44, 256, 257
Norfolk, Virginia, 220
normal pool for first time, see Lake Sidney Lanier-Chapter Twelve
North Carolina, iii, iv, v, 3, 7, 13, 22, 25, 31, 36, 37, 41, 44, 70, 72, 74, 109, 230, 242, 256
North Highlands Dam, 10
Oak Hill Cemetery, 251
Ochlocknee River, 7

Oglethorpe College, 219
oil circuit breakers, 263
old river bed, 148, 149, 150
Oliver Dam, 10
Oliver, James M., 10
Oman Construction Company, 188, 262
operations building, 15, 178, 180, 262
original design of dam, see Main Earth Dam Construction, see also Apalachicola, Chatthaoochee, Flint River System
origin and destination survey, 172, 173
Otwell, Roy P., 38, 42, 43, 44, 67, 71, 72, 76, 226, 258, 279, 281, 282, 287
overhead trolley crane, 26
Patterson, Cecil, v, 18, 33, 90, 116, 212
Paules, Colonel, 34
Paul Harris Fellow, 256
Peabody Symphony, 221,222
Peachtree Memorial Cemetery, 257
Pearl River, 7, 256
Pelton Water Wheel Company Incorporated, 263
Pennsylvania, 221, 222, 261
penstocks, 52, 83, 97, 98, 99, 100, 101, 102, 103, 107, 108, 109, 112, 118, 121, 122, 123, 124, 126,127, 128, 131, 132, 133, 145
penstock no.1, 99, 101, 102, 122, 124, 1300
penstock no.2, 97, 99, 100, 101, 102, 103, 108, 118, 122, 124, 128, 130, 131
penstock no.3, 103, 118, 122, 124
Petersburg, 220
Phillips and Davies Incorporated, 262
Picher, J.L., 43
Pick, Lewis, 71, 254, 255
Pick-Sloan Plan, 255
Pickens General Hospital, 252
pit liner, 133, 134
policies governing land sales, see Land Acquisitions
Polk County, North Carolina, 222
pollution abatement, 20, 36
post lake map, see Bridge and Highway Relocation and Construction-Chapter Ten
Post Office Committee, 39, 251
powerhouse, 10, 11, 27, 33, 35, 47, 50, 54, 55, 100, 103, 105, 118, 120, 122, 126, 127, 128, 129, 131, 132, 133, 134, 135, 136, 137, 138, 156, 161, 228, 234, 262, 381
powerhouse road, 119, 144, 155, 178, 179, 180
power production, 2, 5, 7, 9, 12, 13, 20, 24, 27, 36, 38, 49, 137, 237
Prattville, Alabama, 220
pre-lake map, see Bridge and Highway Relocation and Construction-Chapter Ten
presidential bid, see Early Proponents, Richard B. Russell,-Chapter Two
president pro tempore, 251, 253
property owners, tracts of land purchased for the reservoir:
    Abercrombie, H.M., 372
    Abercrombie, Robert M., 323, 329
    Adams, D.B., 377
    Adderholdt, H.H., 351
    Adderholdt, W.D., 351
    Addis, John, 367
    Aiken, Mrs. Dewey, 381
    Allen Inc., Bona, 286, 308
    Allen Jr., Bona, 287
    Allen, Mrs. Ann Wallis, 293
    Allen, Mrs. L.C., 293
    Allen, Mrs. Willie, 294
    Allen, Stanley, 311
    Allison, B.N., 361
    Allison, Herschel, 349
    Allison, J.A., 336
    Allison, J.T., 346
    Almond, Henry, 328
    Anderson, Boyd, 360
    Anderson, Charles, 297
    Anderson, C.C., 270, 304, 305
    Anderson, Irma, 269, 305
    Anderson, Zephyr, 335

Anderson, Zephyr Rine, 335
Arthur Pugh Construction Company Incorporated, 277
Ashcraft, Gus, 310
Autry, C. O., 365
Aycock, C.L., 342
Babb Jr., G.B., 281
Bagby, F.F., 292, 296
Bagby, W.E., 315
Bagheri, M.T., 274
Bagwell, A.D., 326
Bagwell, Billy, 301
Bagwell, C.A., 300, 301
Bagwell Farms Incorporated, 326
Bagwell, J.W., 326
Bagwell, Mrs. Rosa Lou Bowman, 306, 312
Bagwell, Myrtle Brown, 326
Bagby, T.E., 307
Bailey, G.W., 320
Baker, Willie W., 363
Banks Jr., R., 322, 328, 330
Barker, Floyd, 274
Barker, Mrs. J.R., 273
Barnes, Mrs. Don. T., 348
Barnes, J. Alvin, 332
Barnes, Joe, 328
Barrett, Mrs. E.M., 297
Barrett, Mrs. Eula Mae, 281
Barrett, J.G., 270
Barrett, R.H., 322
Barrett, Samual D., 370
Barron, Mrs. Emily, 301
Barron, H.F., 301
Barron, L.T., 302
Bartlett, Mildred Irene, 309
Baughcum, Thomas H., 353
Beard, Mrs. Parilee, 316
Bell Jr., A.W., 372
Bell Sr., Mrs. A.W., 372
Bell, Cecil C., 320
Bell, G.C., 320
Bennett, Addie, 294
Bennett, Brice, 295
Bennett, Estil, 303
Bennett, Gladys, 274
Bennett, Hubert J., 291
Bennett, Jackson, 328
Bennett, Jim, 294
Bennett, Joe M., 345
Bennett, Lannie, 274
Bennett, Mrs. Laura, 303
Bennett, Lyman, 272
Bennett, Mrs. Lyman, 272
Bennett, Ralph, 294, 295
Bennett, R.R., 291
Bennett, Viola, 295
Bethel Baptist Church, 297
Bettis, R.T., 273
Beyers, X.T., 299
Black, C.M., 320
Black, W.A., 320
Blalock, B.B., 372
Blalock, Dr. John C., 367
Blondean, Ladd, 343
Blue Ridge Broadcasting Company, 339, 340
Bowden Company, The, 352
Bowen, Cecil E., 290
Bowman, Lucian, 307
Boyd, James F., 292, 293
Brackett, Eugene, 354
Brackett, Harold, G., 354
Brackett, Lewis, G., 354
Brackett, Stewart, 349
Brady, William, 320
Bragg, G.W., 287
Bragg, Jewell, 282
Brice, R.A., 355
Brogdon, E.D., 298
Brogdon, Frank, 286, 309, 310, 313
Brogdon, Martha, 298

Brogdon, Row W., 313
Brookshire, J.J., 347
Brown, Alberta, 310
Brown, Mrs. Annie T., 311
Brown, Eva Ruby, 325
Brown, Hannah B., 321
Brown, J.A., 314
Brown, Jack, 313
Brown, Mrs. Mertice, 301
Brown, Rosa, 312
Browning, G.W., 345
Browning, J.C., 374
Bruce, E.C., 330
Bruce, Ralph, 275
Bruce, Robert, 343
Bryant, Mrs. Annie Mae, 299
Bryant, Cemetery, 311, 330
Bryant, Willie, 330
Bryson, Howard Luther, 274
Buffington, Mrs. Christine Simpson, 366
Buffington, Mrs. Irene G., 260
Buffington, R.D., 260
Buford, City of, 317
Buice, Kate, 312
Buice, R.A., 331
Bunnel, Mrs. Florida, 327
Burdett, J.C., 271, 303
Burkholder, Roy, 372
Burns, Dr. John K., 334, 358
Burruss, George E., 284
Burruss, Ralph W., 285
Burtz, Mrs. Flora, 303
Burtz, W.N., 303
Butler White Cemetery, 311
Byers, Aaron L., 297
Byers, Sanford, 327
Bryant, Rufus, 301
Byrd, C.W., 347
Cagle, Dallas, 372
Cagle, Mrs. E.G., 365
Cagle, E.J., 372
Cagle, G.H., 348
Cagle, L.H., 293
Cagle, Marion J., 373
Cagle, N.R., 288
Cagle, Mrs. T.S., 328, 329
Cain, O.D., 330
Cain, S.H., 291
Cain, W.M., 295
Camp, C.C., 313
Campbell, Knox, 348
Campbell, Rosa Lee, 348
Cantrell, Charlie J., 345
Cape, Coley Grant, 345, 346
Cape, Grover C., 316
Cape, Reba, 316
Carlisle Cemetery, 316
Carlisle, Grover, 310
Carnes, Mary Couch, 370, 371
Carter, J.F., 352
Carter, L.B., 321
Carter, Linton C., 334, 335
Cash, G.S., 350
Castleberry, James T., 292
Castleberry, Mrs. James T., 292
Caudell, Hoyt, 341
Cauthon, M., 318
Chadwick, Mrs. Pauline, 288
Chambers, Bob, 324
Chambers, Edgar, 310, 317
Chaney, Mrs. Fannie R., 364
Chapman, Harry R., 333
Chapman, Joe T., 358
Chastain, Mrs. C.A., 298
Chattahoochee Baptist Cemetery, 315
Chattahoochee Church, 315
Chattahoochee Country Club Incorporated, 355, 356
Christian, Mrs. Ann, 353
Clark, A.C., 316
Clark, Carl N., 320

Clark, C.C., 328
Clark, Don, 319
Clark, H.E., 319
Clark, J.N., 345
Clark, R.J., 317
Clarke, Ima, 269
Clarke, Pierce L., 364
Cleghorn, Bill, 350
Cleghorn, Mrs. Ora, 350
Cline, Mrs. P.M., 318
Cochran, Cecil, 369
Cochran, J.B., 369
Cochran, R.C., 369
Coffee, Isabelle M., 344
Coker, J.F., 364
Coley, G.F., 323
Coley, H.J., 366
Coley, Vernie B., 323
Collins, E.J., 273
Collins, Joseph G., 373
Collins, Troy B., 297
Collins, Troy E., 289
Compton, H.E., 308
Compton, Hubert, 320
Conner, Charles C., 351
Conner, Clifton H., 340
Conner, Henry Eston, 344
Conner, Hugh E., 351
Conner, Mrs. R.L., 351
Cook, J.A., 336
Cook, Robert Lee., 330
Coons, Forrest H., 304
Coons, Marie A., 304
Couch, C.A., 322
Couch, Charlie B., 360
Couch, Glen, 277
Couch, Mrs. Sallie B., 359
Couch, Mrs. Texie Lee, 370, 371
Couch, Mrs. W.T., 359
Couch, W.T., 360
Cox, Hubert, 314
Cox, Mrs. Vada, 271
Crain, Roy M., 307, 309, 313
Crane, B.B., 310
Cross, Gaynelle Martin, 346
Crow, Bessie B., 296
Crow, Emory, 295
Crow, G.C., 328
Crow, Guy, 293
Crow, Nora, 293
Crow, Missy Lee, 296
Dale, E.C., 363
Dale, E.H., 346
Dalton, Thomas, 376
Darracott, T.A., 299
Davies, G.L., 337, 338
Davies, M.C., 285
Davis, C.E., 283
Davis, J.B., 361
Davis, Mrs. Mattie J., 361
Davis, T.J., 282, 283
Day, Alvious, 302
Day, A.M., 304
Day, Cynthia, 304
Day, Thurston, 280
Day, Winified, 304
Decking, Mrs. Elizabeth, 346
Decking, T.D., 346
DeFoor Properties Inc., 322
DeVane, Felton A., 369
Dill, Herbert, 355
Dill, Curtis, 355
Dockery, Homer, 271
Dollar, Vera M., 310
Dolvin, Lane, 327
Dorsey, J.D., 317
Doss, S.E., 331
Doolittle, Edna, 324
Dunagan Cemetary, 336
Dunagan, G.C., 350
Dunagen, Ray, 350
Duncan, Elizabeth, 276

Duncan, Emma E., 276
Duncan, Lee, 275
Duncan, R.F., 312
Duncan, Robert L., 275
Duncan, Silvie, 276
Duncan, Thomas P., 275
Duncan, T.P., 276
Duncan, W.D., 335
Duncan, Mrs. Wilma, 275
Dunlap Jr., Edgar B., 356, 357, 358
Dunlap, James A., 357
Dunlap, James Gayle, 357
Dunnaville, Bessie, 335
Duran, G.L., 296
Duran, J.H., 295
Durand, Egbert L., 297
Durand, John W., 293
Duvall, Ethel, 345
Duvall, H.A., 335
Duvall Jr., Harley, 336, 342
Driskell, G.D., 287
Driskell, J.B., 288
Driskell, John C., 288
Eades, Eston, 324
Eberhardt, Louie, 345
Egbert, Keith, 298
Elliott, A.W., 273
Elliott, Edwin, 346
Elliott, Eston, 348
Elliott, Ivan, 345
Elliott, Ruby Hughes, 274
Elliott, Rufus, 323
Elliott, T.L., 346
Elliott Jr., T.L., 346, 350
Ellis, Mrs. Francis Puett, 340
Ellis, James H., 339
Ellis, L.B., 340
Ellis, Mrs. L.B., 340
Ellis, L.J., 282, 283
Elrod, Lloyd, D., 370
Elrod, Marvin E., 352
Elrod, Melvin F., 370
Elrod, Robert A., 370
Elrod, Mrs. Wynell C., 361
Erwin, J.B., 314
Estes, Artrue H., 318
Estes, Mrs. Charles L., 342
Estes, R.C., 314
Etris, Mrs. A.W., 372
Eugene, Henry Ford, 318
Evans, Clay, 353
Evans, F.W., 278
Evans, John T., 303, 304
Evans, Leon, 346
Fannie, Gaines T., 303, 304
Faulkner, C.R., 346
Ferguson, Bob, 375
Fletcher, Hulan Jack, 342
Flowery Branch, Town of, 319
Floyd, W.L., 290, 291
Flynt Jr., John J., 368
Fouts, Claud, 291
Fouts, J.Claud, 293
Fouts, Paul, 342
Fouts, Taft, 271
Fowler, Alam K., 279
Fowler, Mae, 366
Fraser, Aurora G., 316
Fraser, Gaines Felton, 316
Fraser, G.C., 368
Fraser, G.G., 321
Fraser, J.C., 286, 321
Fraser, T.L., 321
Fraser, Virginia G., 316
Freeland, C.D., 300
Freeland, W.H., 300
Freeman, Mrs. Nellie, 300
Frix, Mrs. Anna, 332
Fulford, Bert, 335
Fuller, Ernest, 359
Fuller, Mrs. Minnie Dunlap, 356
Gaddy, W.H., 358

Gaines, Ellie, 316
Gaines, I.P., 315
Gaines, Virgil Rufus, 363
Gainesville, City of, 334, 337
Garmon, C.L., 278
Garmon, E.L., 371
Garner, Inez, 331
Garner, Lee W., 331
Garner, Thomas N., 342
Garrett, Hiram R., 277
Garrett, J.E., 271
Garrett, Juanita, 370, 371
Garrett, Leonard, 309
Garrett, Mae, 309
Gazaway, Mrs. George, 269
Gee, A.J., 292
Georgia Power Company, 276, 314, 324, 329, 337, 354, 355, 377
Georgia Railway and Power Company, 308
Georgia Shoe Manufacturing, 321
General Capital Corporation, 316
Ghegan, Drury W., 289
Gilleland, Irene R., 327
Glass, Mrs. Ruby, 351
Gober, Cleo J., 353, 354
Gober, Ford, 353
Godfrey, A.J., 275
Golden Jr., Mrs. D.E., 329
Good, Jack, 286
Gordon, Mrs. Katherine B., 374
Gordon, Lawrence, 353
Gould, Jay S., 333
Gowder, Harry F., 375
Grant, Guy A., 355
Grant, Jerd, 355
Grant, V.M., 277, 278
Green, H.D., 366
Green, H.G., 306, 309
Green, Mrs. Idell, 360
Green, Mrs. Minnie, 359
Greer, Ernest, 299
Greer, Pat, 315
Gregory, Annie Irine, 346
Gregory, H.A., 343
Gregory, Henry, 346
Grier, Mrs. Carrie, 373
Grier, H.B., 365
Grier, W.H., 299
Grier, W.J., 375, 376
Griffin, M., 334
Griffin, Mood, 310, 362, 364
Grindle, H.E., 337
Grindle, R.H., 344
Grizzle, Mrs. Ora, 363
Grizzle, Raymond, 363
Grogan, W.D., 308
Guinn, Thomas L., 352
Guy, D., 296
Hall, Charles H., 337
Hall County Board of Education, 349
Hall, Mamie, 327
Hamby, Mattie Effie, 271
Hamilton, Alma Mae, 306
Hamilton, Edward C., 357
Hamilton, Mrs. Edward C., 271
Hamilton, J. Paul, 307
Hammond, Daniel C., 283
Hammond, L.O., 283
Hamner, A.E., 315
Hamner, J.C., 286, 287, 308, 310, 314, 315, 322
Hamner Lumber Company, 279, 286
Hamner, W.B., 288
Harben Jr., Grover S., 354
Hardeman, R.A., 298
Hardy, Mrs. Ann Dunlap, 357
Harper, H. A., 352
Harrington, W.A., 310
Harrington, Y.J., 338, 366
Harris, J. Homer, estate, 300
Harrison, Blanche C., 365

Harrison, Mrs. John C., 366
Harrison, L.C., 365
Hatcher, Frank, 349
Hathcock, W.C., 297
Hayes, M.R., 298
Haynes, D.T., 360, 364
Haynes, Hollis, 328
Haynes, Pierce N., 359
Head, Miss Carrie, 377
Head, Floyd, 377
Heard, Annie Odell, 288
Heard, Clarence, 285
Heard, Hoyt, 285, 288
Heard, Luther, 288
Heard, Nettie, 285
Helton, Mrs. J.W., 278
Helton, R.C., 277
Hemphill, Minnie C., 294
Henderson, A.B., 283
Henderson Jr., A.B., 288
Henderson, Cleburne, 283
Henderson, Gladstone, 284
Henderson, Mary V., 302
Henderson, T.W., 283
Hendrick Cemetery, 280
Hendrix Cemetery, 314
Hendrix, Harold M., 274
Herman, E.F., 355
Higgins, S.T., 336
Highsmith, N.L., 353
Hightower, Mrs. Sallie, 372
Hill, Mrs. J. Foster, 353
Hinson, Mrs.F.B., 300
Holcomb, Claud, 364
Holcomb, J. Hubert, 342
Holcombe, J. Hubert, 356
Holland, A.H., 317
Holland, Howard M., 284
Holland, Mrs. Lizzie, 324
Holland, Mrs. Lou Dell, 326
Hollifield, Monroe J., 339
Hollis, Eugene, 377
Holloway, Willie Johnson, 341
Holman, Lester, 316
Holtzclaw, J.G., 281
Holtzclaw, J.J., 283
Hood, W.E., 323
Hooper, O.M., 356
Horne, Jr., T.L., 270
Houser, E.F., 336
Howser, Dora A., 370
Hudgins, Mrs. Avie, 339
Hudgins, Raymond, 339
Hudgins, Otto, 304, 318, 324
Hughes, Alton I., 307
Hughes, Clifford D., 307
Hughes, Felton C., 307
Hughes, H.G., 272, 273
Hughes, J.C., 277
Hughes, T.F., 272
Hughes, Vernon, 318
Hughes, W.N., 341
Hulsey, D.C., 332
Hulsey, Mrs. Frankline, 323
Hulsey, J.D., 350
Hulsey, K.G., 361
Hulsey, Mrs. K.G., 361
Hulsey, Mary R., 349, 351
Humphrey, J.C., 317
Humphrey, Minnie Sims, 318
Hunt, Lewis K., 314
Hutchin, Barry, burial site, 315
Hyde, Joe, 345
Ivey, Balus, 332
Ivey, Carl, 341
Ivey, C.E., 299
Ivey, G.E., 301
Ivey, Linda Bell, 347
Ivey, Ralph, 341
Ivey, R.F., 301
Jackson Cemetery, 340
Jackson, Corine Bertha, 327

Jackson, Charlie, 327
Jay, Theo, 337
Jett, A.H., 331
Jenkins, Roy E., 274
Jewell, Mrs. Edith Lilly, 305
Jewell, J.D., 334
Johnson & Johnson Incorporated, 322
Johnson, Bernard C., 316
Johnson, Claude, 358
Johnson, Cleo, 296
Johnson, Ella, 311
Johnson, Fletcher M., 321
Johnson Jr., Hammond W., 334
Johnson, Hershiel, estate, 308
Johnson, Hebert M.,320
Johnson, J.O., 352
Jones, Amanda, 301
Jones, Burl R., 332
Jones, C.E., 305
Jones, Clark T.,319
Jones, Edwin L., 305
Jones, G.R., 343
Jones, Hoyt M., 305
Jones, Mrs. Katie Lou Cagle, 328, 329
Jones, Lester C., 301
Jones, Ora, 305
Jones, Robert, 376, 377
Jones, Ruby Flossie, 305
Jones, T.Q., 346
Jones, Thurman V., 300
Jordan, C.G., 296
Jordan, Stella Faulkner, 376
Kanady, Homer, 341
Kanady, Ruth, 362
Kanady, Wilma, 362
Keith, William David, 372
Kellogg, W.T., 291
Kelley, Mrs. F.W., 290
Kemp Cemetery, 280
Kemp, Cordie, 349
Kennedy, Eloise, 306
Kennedy, Idus, 306
Kenney, B.H., 346
Kilgore, T.R., 318
Kimbrell, Mrs. Agnes, 317
Kimbrough Jr., Mrs. E.E., 376
King, James.P., 273
Kingloff, Mildred L., 309
Kitchens, Mrs. Myrtle, 339
Kocurek, Ernest, 282
Ladd, Clarence, 350
Ladd, L.G, 349
Ladd, Mrs. Pearl F., 343
Ladd, Mrs.V.S., 350
Ladd, Walter J., 343
Lake, G.V., 320
Lawson, Mrs. Bessie Kemp, 369
Lawson, Clyde W., 291
Lawson, G.A., 362, 364, 367
Lawson, I.L., 363, 367
Lawson, U.A., 353
Lawson, William Joseph, 369
Ledford, A.S., 291
Ledford, J.A., 291
Lee, Booker C., 320
Lee, T.J., 319
Lenderman, F. Ode Parks, 344
Lenderman, H.B., 336
Lenderman, Huel B., 344
Light, Francis J., 297
Light, Mrs. Frances J., 287
Light, Mrs. Norma Rae Hunt, 343
Liles, J.B., 292
Little, Carlton, 344
Little, L.L., 360, 365
Little, M.H., 326
Liveright, Addie E., 278
Logan, Sarah A., 370
Loggins, Charlie N., 366
Loggins, H.K., 369
Loggins Sr., W.K., 358
Lomax, Mrs. Winnie, 374

Long, Ferrell, 290
Long, Luna I., 332
Long, William B., 332
Looper, D.B., 341, 345
Looper, Henry C., 341, 345
Luthi, Cora Faulkner, 376
Mangum, S.A., 289
Mangum, Walter, 289
Mann, E.V., 316
Manston, C.A., 289, 297
Mabry, A.J., 340
Martin, B.E., 303
Martin, Bell P., 351
Martin, Bell R., 349
Martin, Charlie I., 270, 304
Martin, Claudie S., 373
Martin, Clifton, 299
Martin, Cora, 360
Martin, Mrs. Cora Bryan, 369
Martin, Dan, 344
Martin, Eallar, 272
Martin, Mrs. E.G., 317
Martin, Evelyn B., 354
Martin, G.T., 368
Martin, H.C., 341, 344
Martin, Henry Herbert, 319
Martin, H. Lester, 353
Martin, Hubert J., 351
Martin, H.V., 299
Martin Jr., H.V., 299
Martin, Ida Bell, 299
Martin Jr., James Bailey, 346
Martin, James N., 343
Martin, Jay, 341
Martin, J.G., 346
Martin, J.L., 346
Martin, Lee, 306, 312
Martin, Lloyd, 351
Martin, M.M., 300
Martin, Mrs. Mignon, 298
Martin, Mrs. Nancy H., 377
Martin, Roy J., 373
Martin, R.T., 340, 341
Martin, U.M., 353
Martin, V.S., 354
Martin, Vossie S., 355
Martin, W.A., 354
Martin, W.E., 302
Martin, Wade H., 353
Martin, W.G., 357
Martin, Mrs. W. Walker, 348
Mashburn, James, 285
Mashburn, Dr. Marcus, 280, 284
Mashburn Jr., Marcus, 285
Mashburn Sr., Marcus, 279, 285
Mashburn, Maynard, 290
Mason, J.G., 347
Mason, Mrs. J.G., 347
Mathis, Carl, 331
Mathis, Claudie, 296
Mathis, Dewey, 293
Mathis, Glenn, 294
Mathis, Mrs. Mary Jane, 292
Maxwell, L.D., 343
McCleskey Cemetery, 329
McClure, J.C., 271, 276
McClyde, J.A., 304
McConnell, Jonathan E., 299
McConnell, R.G., 322, 324
McConnell, Robert G., 364
McCarver, W.C., 337
McCrary Jr., R.W., 369
McDonald, H.S., 308
McDonald, John Wesley, 368
McFalls, Velton, 357
McGee, James H., 281
McIntyre, Dillie, 357
McIntyre, Hershell A., 356
McKinney, Mrs. Leila, 276
McKinzey, G.M., 328
McNeal, Lillie Brown, 326
McNeal, N.A., 346

McNeal, W.H., 333, 343
McNeal, Mrs. Willie Bell, 299
McNeal, W.W., 298
Mead, Howard N., 330
Meaders, Barney R., 314
Meaders, Polly Stargel, 314
Meredith, Malcolm J., 302
Merritt, E.J., 325
Merritt, George L., 282
Merritt, James F., 282
Merritt, J. Ray, 313
Merritt, Velma, 325
Merritt, W.V., 363
Milam, Walter G., 313
Miller, Dr. John N., 349
Miller, W.H., 368
Millwood, Beulah, 290
Millwood, C.E., 290
Millwood, Virgil C., 290
Minor, H.M., 336
Minor, Toy, 336
Minor, Mrs. Hugh, 360
Mitchell, Mrs. Etta, 299
Moon, S.C., 334, 364
Moon, Mrs. S.C., 362
Mooney, George R., 327
Mooney, J.E., 300
Moore, Ernest, 340
Moore, Travis, 326
Morgan, Jessie, 288
Morgan, Leon B., 288
Morgan, W.E., 290
Morris, E.C., 326
Morris, Fay Mathis, 300
Morris, Maxie, 300
Morrow, Flora Carlisle, 318
Morrow, Jewell T., 318, 319
Mose Gordon Lumber Company, 375
Moss, Emmett D., 277, 278
Moss, K.C., 277, 278
Mullinax, W.A., 279
Mullins, J.R., 287
Mundy, E.C., 326
Mundy Cemetery, 311
Mundy, J.B., 355, 356
Myers, Flora, 376
Nagle Sr., Clyde W., 363
Nalley, J.B., 346
Nix, Arthur E., 304
Nix, Pearl Grace, 275, 276, 334, 354
Noblin, Edna A., 278
Norrell, Howard, 365
Nuckolls, A.B., 318
Nuckolls, E.D., 287
Nuckolls, Nila, 287
Nuckolls, T.L., 280,
Odell Jr., U.S. 326, 327
O'Kane, Jessie Kate, 371, 376
O'Kelley, Mrs. Frankie Lord, 325
O'Kelley, N.E., 362
Old Beaver Ruin Cemetery, 282
Oliver, H.T., 343
Oliver, R.A., 362
Oliver, T.D., 376
Oliver, Robert Rogers, 362
Orr, C.F.,289, 297
Orr, Clarence, 295, 303
Orr, H.W., 287
Orr, Kenneth, 296
Orr, Mrs. L.C., 296
Orr, Mrs. Maude S., 287
Orr, Mrs. W.F., 296
Orr, William E., 319
Orr, W.L., 324
Orschel, J.E., 335
Orschel, Mrs. J.E., 335
Otwell, Edwin, 285, 289
Otwell, Roy P., 279, 281, 282, 287
Owens, Alma, 274
Owens Jr., John Henley, 352
Pair, J. Ronald, 274
Paralee, Edwin, 318

Parker, Claude W., 358
Parks, A.P., 332
Parks, C.W., 368
Parks, F. Ode, 344
Parks, Hoke, 298
Parks, Hoke S., 298
Parks, Perry E., 330, 333
Parsons Jr., Calvin M., 321
Pass, Bruce B., 307, 312
Pass, Elizabeth, 313
Pass, Daisy Mae, 307, 312
Pass, R.V., 312
Patterson, Howard, 313
Patterson, Octavia Smith, 361
Patterson, Paxton K., 361
Patterson, Zack, 308
Peck, Frank, 362
Peck, Mrs. T.A., 367
Peppers, Eston, 309
Perry, Ivylyn O., 373
Pethel Jr., D.T., 277, 329
Pethel, Mrs. Lessie Crain, 323
Phagan, Mrs. Evie L., 318
Phagan, Homer T., 328
Phillips Cemetery, 286
Phillips, H.R., 280
Phillips, L.J., 307
Phillips, R.H., 289
Phillips, W.J., 323, 324
Pierce, A.D., 298, 302, 304
Pinson, Clyde, 361
Pinson, Mrs. Cordell, 361
Pinson, Floy, 293
Pinson, J.H., 336
Pinson, Vista M., 337
Pinson, W.A., 300
Pinson, Wilburn, 293
Pirkle, Claud, 346
Pirkle, Frank, 324
Pirkle, Glen E., 271
Pirkle, Thomas P., 273
Pirkle, Willie J., 281
Pittard, Francis W., 303
Pittard, Joel C., 303
Pittman, Bee, 375
Pittman, Mrs. H.W., 374
Pittman, James Allen, 373
Pittman, J.J., 375
Pittman, L.E., 364, 365
Pittman, William, 359
Plaginos, Paul C., 334
Poore, G.A., 377
Porter, F.M., 295
Porter, Starling, 299
Porter, Mrs. S.W., 299
Powell, Eldridge C., 332
Presnell, Alma, 302
Propers, B.H., 323
Propes, Lawton B., 326
Propes, W.W., 322
Pruett, Mrs. Azalee L., 322
Pruitt, G.L., 280
Pruitt, Ora, 298
Pruitt, P.W., 317
Puckett, Carl L., 334, 366
Puckett, Crawford, 307
Puckett, Henry A., 317
Pugh, Agnes M., 306, 312
Pugh, Freda B., 308
Pugh, George S., 269
Pugh, Martin, Burial Ground, 315
Pugh, Ora L., 306
Pugh, W.H., 315
Pugh, W.R., 308
Quillian, Roxie, 335
Quillian, Roxie A., 343, 346
Raines, Morris T., 291
Rainey, Edwin, 348
Raven, Grover, 368
Red Hen Farms, 333
Reed, Mrs. Belle Luther, 327
Reed, Coleman T., 327

Reed, Mrs. Cora Bell, 347
Reed Jr., James M., 332
Reed, John R., 324
Reed, Lloyd H., 327
Reed, L.O., 323
Reed, Luther A., 327
Reed, Moniam, 327
Reed, Ralph, 348
Reed, R.H., 325
Reed, U.S., 327
Reeves, Albert, 279, 376
Reeves, Mrs. Eugene, 275
Reeves, H.W., 377
Reeves, Laura Belle, 278
Reeves, Mrs. Missouri, 377
Reinero, Mrs. Clara Allen, 286
Reynolds, P.B., 293
Reynolds, Theron C., 358
Reynolds, Mrs. Theron C., 358
Richards, Evelyn I., 277
Richards, Francis F., 348
Richards, Gordon R., 309
Ridgeway, B.G., 366
Rieves, A.B., 291, 292, 295
Riverside Military Academy, Incorporated, 337
Roark, Mrs. A.W., 349, 351
Roark, Eula, 349, 351
Roark, Fred, 349, 351
Roark, Margaret, 349, 351
Robb, Leroy, 350
Robbs Jr., J.L., 285, 288
Robbs, W.V., 295
Robertson, T.H., 360
Robertson Jr., T.H., 352
Robertson, C.O., 355
Robertson, Wilbert, 274, 275
Robinson, Mrs. A.L., 344
Robinson, Ben H., 330
Robinson Cemetery, 329
Robinson, C.O., 355
Robinson, E.E., 306, 310, 313, 314
Robinson, Frank, 308
Robinson, H.C., 340, 341
Robinson, Henry L., 371
Robinson, Hoke, 341
Robinson, Mrs. John, 331
Robinson, Irene Pittman, 374
Robinson, J.T., 354
Robinson, L.B., 324
Robinson, L.E., 351
Robinson, Nevie Simpson, 341
Robinson, Ralph, 308
Robinson, Tom Ed, 308
Robinson, W.R., 354
Rogers, R.L., 367
Romberg, C.J., 321, 322
Rome Kraft Company, 269, 272, 373, 374, 376
Roper, C.E., 329
Roper, Parks, 329
Roper, W.A., 336, 337
Rowe, Fred O., 309
Rowe, W., 313
Rowe, Winfield, 313
Rundles, Mrs. Annie, 350
Rundles, W.D., 347, 348, 350
Sailors, Horace, 361
Samples, George L., 282
Sams Jr., Hansford, 287, 289
Sams, L.R., 272
Sanders, Mrs. L.B., 351
Sargent, G.F., 356
Satterfield, Mrs. Maxie G., 360
Savage, Fred, 374
Savage, Homer, 373
Savage, Mrs. Lillie, 374
Saxon, Clarence, 369
Scales, E.W., 279
Scales, Mrs. E.W., 279
Schultz, A.C., 322
Schultz, Mannie E., 322

Scott Jr., G.B., 270
Sears, Berthel P., 313, 314
Shadburn, H.E., 279
Shadburn, J.E., 281, 282
Shadburn, M.E., 279, 284
Shiretzki, Mrs. D.S., 329
Shirley, Emeline B., 344
Shirley, S.L., 367
Shoal Creek Baptist Church, 314
Shoal Creek Baptist Church and Cemetery, 309
Shockley, Sherman, 339
Shoemake, J.W., 291
Shope, Jr. J.B., 366
Shuler, A.B., 341
Sibley, William Hart, 320
Simpon, W.H., 331
Simpson, Mrs. Will Ella, 331
Skinner, Beulah, 348
Skinner, Ford, 353
Skinner, Mrs. Grace, 301
Skinner, L.C., 305
Skinner, Mrs. Maude Dobbs, 270
Skinner, Olin H., 324
Smith, Mrs. Annie, 281
Smith, A.R., 355
Smith, Arnold, 325
Smith, Bill, 285
Smith, Calvin Floyd, 338
Smith, Cecil, 368
Smith, Cecil M., 321
Smith Cemetery, 344
Smith, Charles W., 271
Smith, Clarence, 348
Smith, Clay, 273
Smith, Cleveland, 371, 377
Smith, Clyde, 325
Smith, Cora, 306
Smith, David V., 354
Smith, D.C., 366
Smith, Dessie, 273
Smith, E.A., 297
Smith, Earl E., 348
Smith, Eli, 282
Smith, Mrs. Elsie Mae, 332
Smith, Mrs. Florence, 371
Smith, Glenn, 353
Smith, Glen E., 272
Smith, G.W., 314
Smith, Henrietta, 332
Smith, Herschell T., 301
Smith, H.L., 292, 372
Smith, Ida Doris, 318
Smith, J. Alvin, 370
Smith, James M., 358
Smith, Mrs. Jamie, 303
Smith, Jason, 281
Smith, J.M., 362
Smith, John Carl, 373
Smith, Lillie Gertrude, 331
Smith, Monroe C., 330, 356
Smith, O.J., 301
Smith, R.G., 270
Smith, Rufus G., 275
Smith, Tate, 303
Smith, Vernon H., 377
Smith, W.T., 299
Smithgall, Charles, 337
Snellings, H.F., 321
Sosebee, Minnie, 279
Souther, O.J., 356
Spain, E.C., 348
Spainhour, Ben R., 354
Sparrow, Frances A., 273
Spencer Hill Baptist Church and Cemetery, Trustees, 310
Spier, Wesley, 274
Spinner, Hazel Quillian, 335
Stancil, Hubert, 365
Stanford, Lewis C., 284
Stephens, Claud, 368
Stepp, A.N., 369

Stepp, R.N., 370
Stephens, Blanche Ethel, 347
Stephens, J. Fred, 338
Stephens, Olen, 342
Stephens, Mrs. W.O., 358
Stewart, C.D., 304
Stewart, Leon, 304
Stewart, Peggy M., 315
Stone, John E., 317
Stovall, Mabel E., 331
Stowers, Ann Ruth Martin, 341
Strayhorn, J.L., 289
Strayhorn, Mrs. M.N., 319
Strickland, Devada, 335
Strickland, Will, 370
Strickland, Winnie Nell, 318
Stringer, Charles, 333
Stringer, Fred, 333
Stringer, Glenn G., 333
Stringer, Mrs. Idell, 316
Summerour, H.W., 292
Tanner, Ellis, 347
Tanner, M., 318
Tanner, Mrs. Marelle B., 347
Tanner, Mrs. Rosie Lee, 332
Tate, G.O., 373
Tate, Guy, 283
Tate, Hubert O., 377
Tatum, E.E., 300
Tatum, Mrs. Elizabeth, 275, 276
Taylor, J. Henry, 269, 271, 304
Taylor, Mrs. Loma, 324
Taylor, Mark, 324
Telford, Joe K. 362
Terrell, Harold A., 349
Thomas, Amion, 367
Thomas, D.O., 344
Thomas, Franklin, 360
Thomas, O.H., 371
Thompson, Mrs. Annie, 297
Thompson Graveyard, 356
Thompson, Ralph C., 296
Thornton Cemetery, 311
Thornton, J.J., 311
Tiner, George, 284
Tiner, Ralph, 283
Toney, Mrs. Emma, 306
Townley, H.C., 274
Townsend, George R., 271
Townsend, Mrs. George R., 271
Townsend, W.L., 297
Travis, L. Edd, 333
Treadway Jr., T. Foley, 287
Trubey, Jessie F., 331
Truelove, Curtis T., 372
Truelove, Ralph, 364
Tucker, Roscoe, 377
Tuggle, Quillian, 307
Tuggle, Homer H., 312
Turner, W.M., 285, 286, 290
Umprey, John W., 327
Unamed Cemetery, 311
University Yacht Club, Inc., 317
Unknown and unnamed cemetery, 311, 316, 324
Unknown Cemetery, 372
Underwood, J.A., 372
Underwood, J.T., 372
Vance, W.A., 287
Vickers, Hershel, 328
Wages, Dewey C., 341
Walding, Mrs. Ella W., 328
Wadrep, R.M., 340
Walden, Mrs. Euzelia, 322
Waldrip, Anna B., 327
Waldrip, C.F., 296, 325
Waldrip, Clyde, 295
Waldrip, E.C., 295, 296
Waldrip, G.E., 352
Waldrip, Lee, 351
Waldrip, Ray V., 293, 329, 331, 332
Walker, Ernest, 349

Wallace, B.M., 341
Wallace, Hazel E., 274
Waters, A.L., 340
Waters, Albert L., 338
Waters, Clyde, 365
Waters, Clyde F., 339
Waters, P.D., 339
Waters, Virginia Love, 363
Wayne, Frances M., 319
Wayne, Mrs. Lena M., 319
Weatherford, E.B., 324
Weatherford, Jr. Lewis M., 324
Weatherford, Paul, 326
Wehunt, Mrs. Butha, 276
Wehunt, Butha Sosebee, 277
Welch, W.F., 294
Westbrook, Cynthy C., 303
Westbrook, H.M., 302
Westbrook, M.H., 302
Westbrook, W.P., 303
West, James W., 333
West Lumber Company, Incorporated, 355
Westmoreland Jr., Charles C., 338
Whelchel, Blanche E., 372
Whelchel Cemetery, 368
Whelchel, Claude, 368
Whelchel, Claude A., 342
Whelchel, Mrs. D.C., 361
Whelchel, E.H., 364
Whelchel, E.H., Estate, 361
Whelchel, E.M., 335, 343
Whelchel, Harold, 368
Whelchel, Johnnie, 377
Whelchel, Julia Bell, 335
Whelchel Jr., R.A., 371
Whelchel , Mrs. Rilla, 277
Whelchel, S.B., 361, 364
Whelchel, William P., 363
Whelchel, Zane, 353
Whidby, Mrs. H.L., 317
Whidby, Mrs. Newton, 313
Whitaker, Dan S., 314
White, Bennie H., 362
White, E.B., 365
White, Ford, 342, 345
White, H.F., 342
White, Howard William, 344
White, Luke, 375
White, M.J., 344
White, Violet Wilbanks, 373
Whitehead, Mrs. C.W., 370
Whiten, Mrs. Ethel P., 367
Whiting, J.G., 318
Whiting, John H., 325, 326
Whitlow, Clifford A., 298
Whitlow, W.S., 298, 299
Whitmire, Fred L., 343
Whitmire, G.T., 270, 271
Whitmire, J.T., 273
Whimire, R.A., 325
Whitmire, Ralph, 323, 324
Wilbanks, Albert F., 373
Wilbanks, Clarence, 373
Wilbanks, Clyde M., 373
Wilbanks, Guy L., 373
Wilbanks Jr., James H., 373
Wiley, Buford, 376
Wiley, Farmer Hattie Wiley, 374
Wiley, Guy, 374
Wiley, Harold, 339
Wiley, Mrs. King G., 365
Wiley, Leonard, 363
Wiley, Mrs. L.M., 363
Wiley, Rex, 374
Wiley, Robert L., 340
Wilkerson, George, 366
Wilkerson, Maude, 363
Williams, Arnold280, 281
Williams, H.A., 280
Williams, H.C., 281
Williams, John R., 287
Williams, Marcus, 331
Williams, Mercer, 280
Willliams, Ralph I., 281
Williams, Richard R., 280
Wingo, E.C., 357, 358
Wingo, R.L., 332
Wison, A.H., 365
Wilson, Jack, 357
Wilson, J.C., 270, 304
Wilson, Marinel Reed, 327
Wilson, Odell, 269, 271, 305
Winn Cemetery, 324
Wofford, B.D., 365
Wofford, Mrs. Dorothy Wall, 334
Wofford, George W., 334
Woodliff, M.B., 292
Woodliff, T.J., 270, 286, 291, 292, 294
Woody, Van J., 269, 305
Woody, Mrs. Van J., 269, 305
Woolfolk, W.W., 302, 304, 305
Wrights Ice Cream Company, 329
Youngblood, Herbert, 289
Youngblood, Herschell, 286
proposed reservoir sites, see Apalachicola, Chattahoochee, Flint River System-Introduction
Pslam of the West, poem, 222
Public Law 99-662, 26, 27
Public Law 525, 6
Public Law 56-457, 219
Public Works on Rivers and Harbors, 6
pusher cats, 160
Quito, Ecuador, 255
Rayburn, Sam, 219
Real Estate Project Office, v, vi, 63, 65, 230
recreation, 2, 7, 20, 24, 25, 27, 28, 29, 36, 173, 233, 234
reforestation, 7, 280
replacing damaged or destroyed property, see Land Acquisitions reregulation dam, 26, 27
reserve property, 64
reserve property auction, see Land Acquisitions-Chapter Four
reserve propety removal, see Land Acquisitions-Chapter Four
reservoir clearing, 64, 165, 166, 263, 267
reservoir filling, see Lake Sidney Lanier
reservoir flooding statistics, see Appendix I
reservoir naming, see Contribution of a Georgia Poet-Chapter Eleven
Resident Engineer's Office, 74, 148, 180
residential growth, see Why Build a Dam?-Chapter One
Resource Manager, v
Resource Manager's Office, 15, 74, 148, 178, 180
retaining wall, 103, 125
R.G. Foster and Company, 197, 263
Richmond Hill, 223
River and Harbor Act of 1874, 3
River and Harbor Act of 1902, 3
River and Harbor Act of 1925, 4
River and Harbor Act of 1934, 4
River and Harbor Act of 1945, 5, 6, 48
River and Harbor Act of 1946, 7, 48
River and Harbors Flood Control Appropriations Bill 1950, 48, 50
Riverview Dam, 11
road relocations, see Bridge and Highway Relocation and Construction-Chapter Ten
Robinson, Bernard Linn, Colonel, 49, 71, 72, 75, 76, 77, 254
rockershovel, 98, 99
Rodgers, H.N., 76
Rogers, Will, 214, 215, 224
Roswell, Georgia, 4, 5, 13
Rotary Club, 256
Rowe, Winfield, 43, 313
Ruhr Valley, 7
Russell, Richard B. Jr., ii, 40, 41, 42, 56, 71, 75, 173, 212, 214, 215, 224, 244, 246, 247, 251, 259
saddle dikes, Chapter 6, 51, 52, 74, 82, 83, 90, 92, 141, 143, 381
saddle dike no.1, 51, 82, 83, 261
saddle dike no.2-A, 51, 82, 83, 8 4, 85, 261
saddle dike no.2-B, 82, 83, 86, 112, 261
saddle dike no.3, 50, 52, 74, 76, 82, 83, 84, 87, 88, 142, 261
Salem Campground, 251
San Antonio, Texas, 221
San Francisco, California, 263, 264
San Luis Obispo, California, 186
Sawnee Campground, 82, 84
Sawnee Electric Membership, 263
Sawnee, Georgia, 263
Sawnee Mountain, 150
Sawnee View Gardens, 258
SCORE, 256
Scottish Rite Free Mason, 256
scrapers, 160
scrolls, 132, 133, 136
seasonal fluctuations of water elevation, 237
Secretary of the Army, 63, 218
seeding, 141, 161, 220
Select Committee on Case Influence, 253
Special Committee on Foreign Assistance, 253
SEPA, 27
service gate, 262
Seven Days Battle, 220
Seven Pines Battle, 220
severance damage, 65
sewerage treatment plant, 24, 263
Shaw, Frank, 14, 42, 43, 53, 226
Sherman, William T., 38
Singleton, Charlie, v
Six Flags, 23, 24
Sloan, Boyd, 62
sluice, 52, 83, 97, 98, 99, 101, 103, 104, 105, 106, 107, 108, 109, 112, 113, 114, 118, 122, 124, 125, 126, 127, 132, 145, 261, 262, 380, 381, 382
sluice block, 125, 126, 128
sluice conduit, 105, 262
sluice gates, 105, 262
Smith, S. Morgan, 12
soil conservation, 7
Sommer, Harry, 42
Sons of Confederate Veterans, John B. Gordon Camp no.46, 215, 216
South Atlantic Division, 5, 13, 17, 18, 226, 254
South Atlantic Division Chief, 13, 14, 18, 49, 51, 71, 75, 76, 242, 253, 255
Southern Bell Telephone and Telegraph Company, 264
Southern Industries Corporation, 255
Southern Georgia, 24
Southern States Equipment Company, 263
speculation, 63
spillway, Chapter 6, 5, 11, 27, 50, 51, 74, 76, 81, 82, 83, 84, 87, 88, 89, 141, 142, 261, 380, 381
Sprewrell Bluff Lake Dam, 26
Springfield, Ohio, 261
Squirrel Creek Road, 263
Standard Project Flood, 23, 24
State Highway Department, 172, 212
stay rings, 132, 133, 135, 136
steam boats, 22
steel liners, 121, 122, 124, 125
steel reinforcing, 102, 104, 105, 140
Stephens County, 44
Stevens, Robert T., 62
stilling basin, 27, 53, 125, 126, 128, 130
St. Josephs Hospital, 251
stockpile no.1, 92, 143, 144
stockpile no.2, 92, 143, 144
stockpiling precious resources, see Apalachicola, Chattahoochee, Flint River System-Introduction
Stone Mountain, 14, 39
stop gap allocation, 51
stop logs, see Forebay Excavation and Intake Construction
stopping impoundment, 231, 233, 234, 266, 267

Styx River, 4
Sub-Committee of the Committee of Appropriations, U.S. House, 38, 46
Sub-Committee of the Committee of Appropriations, U.S. Senate, 40, 41, 46
Suez Canal, 254
Sunnyside, Georgia, 222
Sunrise, poem, 222, 223
switch yard, 135, 262
Symphony, poem, 222
tailrace, Chapter 8, 51, 52, 53, 92, 101, 103, 107, 117, 118, 119, 120, 121, 122, 123, 124, 127, 128, 135, 136, 137, 138, 151, 161, 162, 177, 261, 264
take possession cases, 62
Talmadge, Eugene, 75
Talmadge, Herman, 71, 72, 74, 75, 76, 80, 243, 244, 246, 247, 253
Tampa, Florida, 222
Task Force 200, 255
Taylor, Baynard, 222
tax benefits, see Why Build a Dam?
telephone lines, 264
temporary cofferdam, 126, 132
test borings, 13, 50
Thar's More in the Man Than Thar is in the Land, poem, 222
Theatrical Hall of Fame, 222
The Marshes of Glynn, poem, 222
The Revenge of Hamish, poem, 222
The Song of the Chattahoochee, poem, 222, 223
Thompson Creek Park, 175
Thompson's Bridge, 172, 177, 190, 192, 193, 194, 196, 230, 231, 262, 266
Tidwell Construction Company, 203, 206, 263
Tiger Lilies, poem, 220
topping trees, 231
Toto Creek Bridge, 201, 202, 263
trash guides, 108, 112
trash rake, 108, 262
trestles, 122, 125
Truett-McConnell College, 258

Truman, Harry S., 6, 40, 50, 51
tuberculosis, 222
turbine, 108, 261, 263, 381
turbine runner, 133, 135, 136
turbine runner vanes, 131, 135, 136
Turner, H. Jack, 38, 42, 43, 77
Tuttle, Elbert, 42
TVA, 62
Twitty, Colonel Joseph J., 7
Two-Mile Creek Bridge, 186, 262
types of dams, see Main Earth Dam Construction-Chapter Nine
White County, 44
UCDA, 43, 44, 45, 227, 241, 243, 256, 257, 258
uncontrolled drainage, 23
Underwood, Bob, 43
Upper Columbia Lock and Dam Project, 5, 8
Upper Overlook, 15, 74, 235
U.S. Army Corps of Engineers, ii, iii, v, 4, 13, 14, 17, 18, 22, 24, 25, 27, 28, 33, 34, 36, 37, 39, 40, 48, 49, 52, 53, 57, 59, 62, 63, 75, 80, 90, 116, 142, 170, 172, 212, 227, 228, 230, 238, 240, 242, 243, 256, 259, 261, 268, 269, 379
U.S. Military Academy Planning Board, 255
Vanns Tavern, 66, 229, 230
Vickers, Jimmy, 43
Victory Wrecking Company, 264
Vienna Cemetery, 253
Vienna, Georgia, 253
Virginia, ii, 182, 220, 254, 259, 261, 262, 263
Virginia Supply and Well Company, 262
Wade Lahar Construction Company, 263
Wadley, Georgia, 197, 263
Wahoo Creek road relocation, 264
Walter F. George Lake, 9
Walter F. George Lock and Dam, 9, 25
Walter Kidde and Company Incorporated, 262
Walter Reed Army Medical Center, 251, 254
War Department, 5, 17
War Hill campground, 174
Warren Commission, 251
Watergate, 253

water regulation, 2, 12, 36
Water Resources Act of 1986, 26
water supply, 24, 25, 26, 27, 37, 38, 39
water tower, 157, 181
Watson, Thomas E., 253
Ways and Means Committee, 252
Weir, Paul, 14, 42, 43, 226
wells, 64, 262
West Bank Park, 82, 83, 84, 86, 228
West Bank Overlook, 15, 82, 85
West Chester, Pennsylvania, 222
Westinghouse, Church, Kerr & Company, 12
Westinghouse Electric Company, 261, 263
West Point, Georgia, 4, 22, 25, 216, 217
West Point Lake, 11, 12
West Point Lake Dam, 11, 217
West Point Manufacturing Company, 11
West Point Reservoir, 22
Wewahitchka, 3
Wheeler, Raymond Albert, 49, 254
White County, 44
Whitesburg, Georgia, 24, 33
wicket gates, 135, 136
wildlife, 7, 25, 230
Wilkie Bridge, 172, 173, 186, 201, 202, 234, 263
Wilson, Walter K., 50, 71, 72, 75, 77, 121, 242, 245, 246, 247, 255, 259
wing walls, 110, 111, 112
Wood, Douglas, 43
Wood, John S., 37, 40, 71, 75, 78, 243, 252
wood framing, 86, 102, 129
Woodruff, Jim Jr., 243
Woodruff, Jim Sr., 7, 243, 246, 247
work slow down, see Appropriations
World Bank, 254
World Bank Technical Advisior, 254
World War II, iii, 5, 7, 250
Wright Contracting Company, 192, 262
Youngblood, Jonnie R., 129
Young, Mason J., 13, 14, 18, 36, 253